A CRITIQUE OF THE ONTOLOGY
OF INTELLECTUAL PROPERTY LAW

Intellectual property (IP) law operates with the ontological assumption that immaterial goods such as works, inventions, and designs exist, and that these abstract types can be owned like a piece of land. Alexander Peukert provides a comprehensive critique of this paradigm, showing that the abstract IP object is a speech-based construct, which first crystalised in the eighteenth century. He highlights the theoretical flaws of metaphysical object ontology and introduces John Searle's social ontology as a more plausible approach to the subject matter of IP. On this basis, he proposes an IP theory under which IP rights provide their holders with an exclusive privilege to use reproducible 'Master Artefacts.' Such a legal-realist IP theory, Peukert argues, is both descriptively and prescriptively superior to the prevailing paradigm of the abstract IP object. This work was originally published in German and was translated by Gill Mertens.

ALEXANDER PEUKERT is Professor of civil law, intellectual property, and competition law at Goethe University, Frankfurt am Main/Germany. He has published five books and more than seventy articles in these fields, with a focus on the theoretical foundations of intellectual property law.

CAMBRIDGE INTELLECTUAL PROPERTY AND INFORMATION LAW

As its economic potential has rapidly expanded, intellectual property has become a subject of front-rank legal importance. *Cambridge Intellectual Property and Information Law* is a series of monograph studies of major current issues in intellectual property. Each volume contains a mix of international, European, comparative and national law, making this a highly significant series for practitioners, judges and academic researchers in many countries.

Series Editors

Lionel Bently
Herchel Smith Professor of Intellectual Property Law, University of Cambridge
Graeme Dinwoodie
Global Professor of Intellectual Property Law, Chicago-Kent College of Law, Illinois Institute of Technology.

Advisory Editors

William R. Cornish, *Emeritus Herchel Smith Professor of Intellectual Property Law, University of Cambridge*
François Dessemontet, *Professor of Law, University of Lausanne*
Jane C. Ginsburg, *Morton L. Janklow Professor of Literary and Artistic Property Law, Columbia Law School*
Paul Goldstein, *Professor of Law, Stanford University*
The Rt Hon. Sir Robin Jacob, *Hugh Laddie Professor of Intellectual Property, University College London*
Ansgar Ohly, *Professor of Intellectual Property Law, Ludwig-Maximilian University of Munich*

A list of books in the series can be found at the end of this volume.

A Critique of the Ontology of Intellectual Property Law

ALEXANDER PEUKERT

Goethe University (Frankfurt)

Translated by
GILL MERTENS

CAMBRIDGE
UNIVERSITY PRESS

University Printing House, Cambridge CB2 8BS, United Kingdom

One Liberty Plaza, 20th Floor, New York, NY 10006, USA

477 Williamstown Road, Port Melbourne, VIC 3207, Australia

314–321, 3rd Floor, Plot 3, Splendor Forum, Jasola District Centre, New Delhi – 110025, India

79 Anson Road, #06–04/06, Singapore 079906

Cambridge University Press is part of the University of Cambridge.

It furthers the University's mission by disseminating knowledge in the pursuit of education, learning, and research at the highest international levels of excellence.

www.cambridge.org
Information on this title: www.cambridge.org/9781108498326
DOI: 10.1017/9781108653329

This publication is in copyright. Subject to statutory exception and to the provisions of relevant collective licensing agreements, no reproduction of any part may take place without the written permission of Cambridge University Press.

First published in English by Cambridge University Press 2021 as *A Critique of the Ontology of Intellectual Property Law* by Alexander Peukert

English translation © Gill Mertens 2021

Originally published in German as *Kritik der Ontologie des Immaterialgüterrechts* by Alexander Peukert and © 2018 Mohr Siebeck Tübingen. www.mohr.de

A catalogue record for this publication is available from the British Library.

Library of Congress Cataloging-in-Publication Data
NAMES: Peukert, Alexander, 1973- author.
TITLE: A critique of the ontology of intellectual property law / Alexander eukert, Goethe University (Frankfurt).
DESCRIPTION: Cambridge, United Kingdom ; New York, NY : Cambridge University Press, [2021] | Series: Cambridge intellectual property and information law | Includes bibliographical references and index.
IDENTIFIERS: LCCN 2020054774 (print) | LCCN 2020054775 (ebook) | ISBN 9781108498326 (hardback) | ISBN 9781108735728 (paperback) | ISBN 9781108653329 (epub)
SUBJECTS: LCSH: Intellectual property–Germany.
CLASSIFICATION: LCC KK2636 .P48 2021 (print) | LCC KK2636 (ebook) | DDC 46.4304/8–dc23
LC record available at https://lccn.loc.gov/2020054774
LC ebook record available at https://lccn.loc.gov/2020054775

ISBN 978-1-108-49832-6 Hardback

Cambridge University Press has no responsibility for the persistence or accuracy of URLs for external or third-party internet websites referred to in this publication and does not guarantee that any content on such websites is, or will remain, accurate or appropriate.

Contents

Acknowledgements *page* xi

1 Introduction   1

1.1 The Paradigm of the Abstract IP Object   1
1.2 Irritations: Differences between Real and Intellectual Property Law   4
1.3 Reactions   7
1.4 Objectives and Plan of the Study   15
1.5 Terminology and Preconceptions   20

2 Two Ontologies   24

2.1 The Ontology of Abstract Objects   24
   2.1.1 Characteristics and Application to Intellectual Property   24
   2.1.2 Metaphysics: An Obsolete Anachronism?   26
   2.1.3 The Implausibility of the Abstract IP Object   28
2.2 Social Ontology   34
   2.2.1 Fundamentals of John Searle's Social Ontology   35
   2.2.2 Application to IP Objects   42

3 Two Abstractions   50

3.1 Abstraction 1: General Terms for Similar Artefacts   50
   3.1.1 A New Artefact   51
   3.1.2 The Master Artefact   52
   3.1.3 Secondary Artefacts   57
3.2 Abstraction 2: The Idea of the Abstract IP Object   61
   3.2.1 The Historicity of Conditions for Abstraction 2   63
      3.2.1.1 New Technologies   64
      3.2.1.2 From Nameless Imitation to the Ingenious Work   69

	3.2.1.3 From Dirigiste Regulation of Economic Activity to the Market Economy	74
	3.2.1.3.1 Economic Regulation through Privileges	74
	3.2.1.3.2 The Formation of Markets and the Commodification of All Inputs and Outputs	79
	3.2.2 The Emergence of the Abstract IP Object	85
	3.2.2.1 A History of Terms: Work, Invention, Design	85
	3.2.2.2 The Abstract IP Object in Legal Texts of the Eighteenth and Nineteenth Centuries	89
	3.2.2.2.1 France	90
	3.2.2.2.2 The United Kingdom and the United States of America	92
	3.2.2.2.3 Germany	97
4	**Interim Summary: An Implausible Paradigm**	101
5	**The Legal Explanatory Power of the Two Ontologies**	104
	5.1 The Structure and Practice of Current IP Law	104
	5.1.1 Scope of Application of the Prevailing Paradigm	104
	5.1.1.1 Trademark Law	105
	5.1.1.2 Rights in Innovation, in Particular Rights Related to Copyright and Plant Variety Rights	107
	5.1.2 An Action- and Artefact-Based Reconstruction of IP Rights	110
	5.1.2.1 The Master Artefact as the Reference Point of IP Rights	110
	5.1.2.2 Secondary Artefacts	117
	5.1.2.3 Regulation of Behaviour in Relation to Secondary Artefacts	121
	5.2 Structural Differences between Real Property and IP Rights	126
	5.3 Particularities of the Justification of IP Rights	128
	5.3.1 Effect and Justification of IP Rights	129
	5.3.2 Economic Analysis of IP Rights	131
	5.4 The Normativity of the Abstract IP Object	132
	5.4.1 The Raison d'Être of the Abstract IP Object Is Its Normativity	132
	5.4.2 Proof: The Reach of Physical and Idealistic IP Regimes	135
	5.4.3 The Instability of the Distinction between Law and Reality	140
6	**Normative Critique of the Abstract IP Object**	143
	6.1 Radical Critique without Extreme Consequences	143
	6.1.1 In Support of a New Understanding of Reality	143

	6.1.2 In Support of the Form of Exclusive Rights	145
	6.1.3 Alternative Terminology	147
6.2	Change of Perspective: From Immaterial Objects to Actors, Actions and Artefacts	150
	6.2.1 Actors and Actions	151
	6.2.1.1 Innovators and Investors	151
	6.2.1.2 Manufacture and Use of Secondary Artefacts by Third Parties	154
	6.2.2 Master Artefacts, Secondary Artefacts and Similarity	158

Summary in Theses   161
Bibliography   171
Index   201

Acknowledgements

The translation of this work was funded by Geisteswissenschaften International – Translation Funding for Work in the Humanities and Social Sciences from Germany, a joint initiative of the Fritz Thyssen Foundation, the German Federal Foreign Office, the collecting society VG WORT and the Börsenverein des Deutschen Buchhandels (German Publishers and Booksellers Association).

1

Introduction

1.1 THE PARADIGM OF THE ABSTRACT IP OBJECT

Intellectual property (IP) law is based on a specific notion of reality. According to this understanding, there exist immaterial objects which are exclusively assigned to a rights holder.[1] Unlike corporeal objects ('things'),[2] these immaterial objects cannot be touched, nor can their physical existence be measured as with intangible, yet still physical data or software.[3] They are also not identical with specific exemplars of a copyrightable work (e.g. a book or a digital file), with products, mechanical or other technical processes, with product signs on packaging or advertising material etc. Instead the objects protected by IP law are merely accidentally embodied in these manifestations. The work, the invention, the design, the distinctive sign etc. exist strictly separated from their instantiations as immaterial ('intellectual'), abstract objects (in the following: abstract IP objects).[4] Thus, three types of objects can be

---

[1] Kohler, Autorrecht, 1–2; Klippel, 6 ZGE 443, 453–54 (2014); Art. L-111-1, 111-3 CPI ('propriété incorporelle'); Merges, *in* Dreyfuss & Pila (eds.) *The Oxford Handbook of Intellectual Property Law*, forthcoming ('assets').

[2] *Cf.* Section 90 of the German Civil Code (*Bürgerliches Gesetzbuch*, BGB), available in English at www.gesetze-im-internet.de/englisch_bgb/ ('Concept of the thing – Only corporeal objects are things as defined by law').

[3] 'Other objects' according to Section 453(1) alt. 2 of the German Civil Code (BGB) ('The provisions on the purchase of things apply with the necessary modifications to the purchase of rights and other objects').

[4] Inventions: Sections 1, 9 German Patent Act (PatG); Godenhielm, 45 GRUR Int. 327, 328 (1996); Zech, 119 GRUR 475 (2017). Copyrightable works: Art. 2(1) Mari, Section 44 German Copyright Act (UrhG), 17 USC § 101 ('embodied'); BGH 27 February 1962 Case no. I ZR 118/60, GRUR 1962, 470, 472; BGH 15 November 2006 Case no. XII ZR 120/04, NJW 2007, 2394 paras. 16–17; BGH 10 July 2015 Case no. V ZR 206/14, NJW 2016, 317 para. 20 with further references; Microsoft Corp. v. AT & T Corp., 550 US 437, 447–48 (2007) ('Software, the 'set of instructions, known as code, that directs a computer to perform specified functions or operations', can be conceptualised in (at least) two ways. One can speak of software in the abstract: the instructions themselves detached from any medium. (An analogy: The notes of Beethoven's

distinguished under German private law: the movable or immovable tangible thing (Section 90 of the Civil Code); other intangible yet physically measurable, material objects such as electric energy, a digital file or a computer program embodied on a data carrier (Section 453(1) alt. 2 of the Civil Code); and the immaterial, abstract IP object.[5]

The idea that immaterial objects exist separately is the prerequisite for considering them capable of being owned according to the model of real property ownership.[6] Private property regulates who may do what with regard to a certain object.[7] This applies to both real property (*Sacheigentum*) and intellectual property (*geistiges Eigentum*), which therefore have the same legal structure.[8] These are exclusive rights that negatively exclude all unauthorised persons from certain uses of a physical thing or an immaterial object, and at the same time positively place these uses at the discretion of the rights holder. Interference in the scope of protection of such a primary exclusive right is, in principle, unlawful, and entails secondary remedies. The exclusive rights are transferable at least to a limited extent by legal disposition. Their constitutional basis is also the same – namely the fundamental right to property according to Article 14 of the Basic Law (*Grundgesetz*, GG), and Article 17 of the Charter of Fundamental Rights of the EU (CFR).

The philosophical justifications of real property and intellectual property law also run largely in parallel. The focus is on the recognition of, and incentive for, personal work and performance. This activity-related justification goes hand in hand with analogies between processed things (in particular cultivated land) and immaterial

---

Ninth Symphony.) One can alternatively envision a tangible 'copy' of software, the instructions encoded on a medium such as a CD-ROM. (Sheet music for Beethoven's Ninth)'); Ulmer, *Urheber- und Verlagsrecht* 11–12; Madison, 19 J. Intell. Prop. L. 325, 333 (2012) ('The work subject to copyright is solely and purely an intangible thing'); König, 46 NJW 3121, 3122 (1993). Design: Sections 1 no. 1, 2 and Section 38 German Design Act (DesignG); Art. 1 EU Design Protection Dir.; Art. 1 EU Design Protection Reg.; Art. 26(1) TRIPS. Signs protectable as trademarks: Sections 3, 14 German Trademark Act (MarkenG); Art. 3, 10 EU Trademark Dir.; Art. 4, 9 EU Trademark Reg.; Art. 15, 16 TRIPS. Topographies of semiconductor products: Art. 36 TRIPS and Art. 1(b) EU Topographies Dir. Trade secrets: Art. 2 no. 1, 2 and 4 EU Trade Secrets Dir. *See also* International Accounting Standard 38, Intangible Assets, Section 8 ('identifiable non-monetary asset without physical substance').

[5] *See* Peukert, *Gemeinfreiheit* 49–50; Peukert, *in* Leible et. al. (eds.) *Unkörperliche Güter* 95–122. In the Anglo-American legal tradition, this concerns the distinction between corporeal, intangible and intellectual property; *cf.* People v. Aleynikov, NYS WL 4110801, 16, 22 (2015). *See also* International Accounting Standard 38, Intangible Assets, Section 4 ('Some intangible assets may be contained in or on a physical substance such as a compact disc (in the case of computer software), legal documentation (in the case of a licence or patent) or film'.).

[6] Rognstad, *Property Aspects of Intellectual Property* 43–46; Pottage & Sherman, *Figures of Invention* 4.

[7] Rognstad, *Property Aspects of Intellectual Property* 42–67; Zech, *Information als Schutzgegenstand* 91 et seq.; *see also* Peukert, *Güterzuordnung* 50 et seq.

[8] Kohler, *Autorrecht* 2; Peukert, *Güterzuordnung* 56 et seq., 660 et seq.; Jänich, *Geistiges Eigentum* 185; Rognstad, *Property Aspects of Intellectual Property* 42–67; Merges, *in* Dreyfuss & Pila (eds.), *The Oxford Handbook of Intellectual Property Law*, forthcoming.

products of labour.[9] Conceptual loans of this kind also dominate the economic analysis and justification of IP rights. Orthodox property rights theorists simply attribute the same economic effects to IP rights as to real property rights. All these property rights are intended to ensure an efficient allocation of the resources concerned.[10] Other economists emphasise the contrast between corporeal things as private goods and immaterial IP objects – the use of which, unlike corporeal objects, is non-exclusive and non-rivalrous. However, this theorising also assumes that there are assignable IP objects for which, in addition, regular use is made of examples taken from physical reality, such as lighthouses and public roads.[11]

Even attentive observers such as Jefferson, Kant and, more recently, Drahos, Lemley and Drassinower are unable to escape the impact of the dominant thinking in terms of abstract IP objects that can be owned. They refer to the peculiar dynamic properties of IP and its inseparable connection with speech and other communication acts. Ultimately, however, their analyses also revolve around the question of the correct regulation of the handling of a good as an object capable of being owned in principle.[12] In the meantime, the object-oriented approach even prevails in trademark law, which up to the end of the twentieth century was still predominantly seen as a part of unfair competition law.[13]

---

[9] For example, Le Chapelier's report (1791), *in* Bently & Kretschmer (eds.) *Primary Sources on Copyright* www.copyrighthistory.org; Hegel, *Elements of the Philosophy of Right* § 69; Shiffrin, *in* Goodin et al (eds.) *A Companion to Contemporary Political Philosophy* 653 et seq.; Merges, *Justifying Intellectual Property*. See also Peukert, *in* Drahos et al. (eds.) *Kritika* 1 114, 116 et seq.; Nazari-Khanachayi, *Rechtfertigungsnarrative des Urheberrechts* 27 et seq.

[10] Demsetz, 12 Journal of Law and Economics 1 (1969); Kitch, 20 Journal of Law and Economics 265 (1977); Landes & Posner, *Economic Structure of IP* 11; Posner, 19 Journal of Economic Perspectives 57, 59 (2005) ('Whereas the "pure" economist (...) is likely to approach the question of optimal regulation of intellectual property from the standpoint of the economics of innovation, public goods and marginal-cost pricing, the economic analyst of law is more likely to begin with the parallels between intellectual and tangible property'.); Epstein, 62 Stanford L. Rev. 455, 461 (2010) ('The basic principles of property law are alive and well, and they are capable of reasonable extension to all forms of intellectual property'.).

[11] Coase, 17 Journal of Law and Economics 375 (1974); Landes & Posner, *Economic Structure of IP* 14.

[12] *Cf.* Jefferson, *in* Kurland & Lerner (eds.) 3 *The Founders' Constitution* ('That ideas should freely spread from one to another over the globe, for the moral and mutual instruction of man, and improvement of his condition, seems to have been peculiarly and benevolently designed by nature, when she made them, like fire, expansible over all space, without lessening their density in any point, and like the air in which we breathe, move, and have our physical being, incapable of confinement or exclusive appropriation'); Drahos, *Philosophy of IP* 156 et seq., 212; Scotchmer, *Innovation and Incentives* 32 ('For information goods, the template is the information itself, for example music ...'); Lemley, 90 N.Y.U. L. Rev. 90 460, 468 (2015) ('In effect, the point of IP laws is to take a public good that is naturally nonrivalrous and make it artificially scarce, allowing the owner to control how many copies of the good can be made and at what price'.); Pottage & Sherman, *Figures of Invention* 4. On the concepts of the public domain and the commons *see* Peukert, *Gemeinfreiheit* 8 et seq., 44–46 with further references; critical also Barron, *in* Bently et al. (eds.) *Copyright and Piracy* 93 et seq.

[13] See Sections 1.5, 3.2.1.3.2, 5.1.1.1.

1.2 IRRITATIONS: DIFFERENCES BETWEEN REAL AND INTELLECTUAL PROPERTY LAW

As self-evident and internationally codified as ownership and object-oriented thinking may be in IP law, Le Chapelier's assessment that patent and copyright law are not only the 'most sacred' example of ownership, but at the same time 'une propriété d'un genre tout différent des autres propriétés' proves to be stubbornly true.[14]

The dominant perspective is able to justify the more numerous – and also in substance more extensive – limitations to and exceptions from IP rights by reference to the more intensive social embeddedness of the 'public' goods concerned, without having to relinquish the uniform ownership doctrine.[15] Other conspicuous features, however, can no longer be made plausible on the basis of the prevailing doctrine. Only IP rights are subject to a maximum term of protection or – in trademark law – tied to a use requirement;[16] conversely, the *numerus clausus* of admissible dispositions only governs the law of real property;[17] the calculation of damages with a view to restoring the position that would exist if the IP infringement had not occurred, which is codified as the normal case in Section 249(1) of the Civil Code (BGB), is of no practical relevance in IP law.[18] The fact that these are not marginal details, but rather characteristics of IP rights, is confirmed by US constitutional law, which provides for separate federal competence norms for patents and copyrights on the one hand and for trademark law on the other.[19] The fundamental rights status of real property and intellectual property rights in Europe, which at first glance appears homogeneous, also shows considerable differences on closer inspection. In particular, in the case of IP rights there are systemic conflicts with fundamental rights of third parties, which wear away the apparently sharp boundaries of the exclusive rights in the course of a permanent balancing of interests.[20] Only ownership of real

---

[14] Le Chapelier's report (1791), in Bently & Kretschmer (eds.) *Primary Sources on Copyright* www.copyrighthistory.org.

[15] Penner, Idea of Property 120; *but see* Breakey, in Howe & Griffiths (eds.) *Concepts of Property* 137, 152–53.

[16] Renouard, Traité des droits d'auteur 438 et seq. Regarding the use requirement in trademark law, *see* Art. 15(3), 19 TRIPS; Art. 16 EU Trademark Dir.

[17] Jänich, *Geistiges Eigentum* 234 et seq., 357; Peukert, in Grundmann & Möslein (eds.) *Vertragsrecht und Innovation*, 69 et seq.

[18] *See* Art. 13 EU Enforcement Dir.; Wimmers, in Schricker & Loewenheim (eds.) *Urheberrecht* Section 97 German Copyright Act (UrhG) paras. 265–66; Raue, *Dreifache Schadensberechnung* 340 et seq.

[19] *See* on the one hand Article I, Section 8, Clause 8 US Constitution ('Congress shall have power ... To promote the Progress of Science and useful Arts, by securing for limited Times to Authors and Inventors the exclusive Right to their respective Writings and Discoveries'.) and on the other hand Article I, Section 8, Clause 3 US Constitution ('Congress shall have power ... To regulate Commerce with foreign Nations, and among the several States, and with the Indian Tribes'.) as well as In re Trade-Mark Cases, 100 US 82 (1879).

[20] Peukert, *in* Geiger (ed.) *Handbook on Human Rights and IP* 132 et seq. with further references; Waldron, 68 Chicago-Kent L. Rev. 841 et seq. (1993).

property has the purpose and hard kernel to guarantee the owner the expectation of undisturbed enjoyment of his or her movable things and land, which in and of itself does not necessarily affect the fundamental rights of third parties – think about, for example, the ability to read a book at the desired time.[21] All these differences are an expression of diverging fundamentals on which the law of real property on the one hand and intellectual property on the other are based. The absence of possession and ownership of tangible objects is conceived of as a temporary exception. Anyone can acquire an ownerless chattel by taking possession of it and then owning it as their property; in the case of real estate, the right of appropriation is vested in the state.[22] In contrast, immaterial objects are and remain in the public domain, unless they are allocated to a person by means of IP rights limited in terms of time, territory and subject matter. Therefore, the starting points of real property and intellectual property law differ. Whereas all chattels and real estate are owned or can be reappropriated, abstract IP objects belong to no one.[23]

At second glance, the legal-philosophical parallels between the two areas also prove to be fragile.[24] In this context, ontological differences between ownership of real property and intellectual property also come into play.[25] This is because the justification of real property ownership is predominantly based on the protection of a de facto possession which was legitimately acquired by first acquisition or by labour and which is then to be protected in its existence by exclusive ownership. The reference to the legitimate possession of an object may suffice to justify the protection of trade secrets and unpublished writings – but not to explain IP rights such as patents, copyrights and trademark rights, which arise in the first place (or at least become practically relevant) when the invention, work or sign in question has reached the public and is thus in fact beyond the control of the inventor, author or entrepreneur. Accordingly, the two most influential philosophers of modern times – John Locke and Immanuel Kant – did not apply their general property doctrines to works and inventions, but formulated special justifications for them.[26]

---

[21] Schmidt, 52 DZPhil 755, 762 (2004).
[22] Sections 928(2), 958, 872 German Civil Code (BGB); Geulen, in Gephart (ed.) *Rechtsanalyse als Kulturforschung* 309, 317.
[23] Cf. Peukert, *Gemeinfreiheit* 49–50, 66 et seq.; Diamond v. Chakrabarty, 447 US 303, 309 (1980); Funk Bros. Seed Co. v. Kalo Inoculant Co., 333 US 127, 130 (1948); Bilski v. Kappos, 130 S. Ct. 3218, 3225 (2010) (non-patentable discoveries 'free to all men and reserved exclusively to none'); Ochoa, 28 U. Dayton L. Rev. 215, 256 et seq. (2002).
[24] Drahos, *Philosophy of IP* 212 ('The analogy between intellectual property rights and other kinds of property rights is only superficial'); Wilson, 93 The Monist 450, 451 et seq. (2010); Sherman & Bently, *The Making of Modern Intellectual Property Law* 20 et seq.
[25] Therefore against the term 'intellectual property' (*geistiges Eigentum*) Kohler, *Handbuch des deutschen Patentrechts* 57, 70 et seq.; Kohler, *Urheberrecht an Schriftwerken und Verlagsrecht* 26–27; see also Jänich, *Geistiges Eigentum* 218 (significant differences).
[26] Cf. Kant (1785), in Bently & Kretschmer (eds.) *Primary Sources on Copyright* www.copyrighthistory.org. On Kant, see Schefczyk, 52 DZPhil 739, 745 et seq. (2004); Wilson, 93 The Monist 450, 452–53 (2010); *but see* Jacob, *Ausschließlichkeitsrechte an immateriellen*

Kant was rewarded with sharp rejection from leading IP law academics for his pertinent work on the illegality of reprinting books.[27] In the middle of the nineteenth century, Bluntschli said that Kant gave an 'immature' portrayal of the topic.[28] And the doyen of German IP law, Josef Kohler, who was not otherwise embarrassed by clear words, defamed Kant as a 'formalistic cozy schematist' whose text on the unlawfulness of reprinting books was an 'adventurous spawn of a non-juristic mind'.[29] Kant's exclusion from the circle of relevant IP theorists – which was unusually vehement even by Kohler's standards and had a long-lasting effect in the German-speaking world – becomes understandable when one realises that Kant does not base the prohibition of reprinting books on the protection of the work (*opus*) in an object- and property-oriented manner, but as a condition of a functional, enlightening discourse in which authors use the services of publishers for the mediation of their autonomous speech (*opera*), whereas publishers require a certain, purely instrumental legal protection in order to amortise their investments.[30]

The economic analysis of real property ownership on the one hand and IP rights on the other also ultimately reveals more differences than similarities. While the former is primarily considered from the point of view of the sustainable efficient use of *existing* resources, intellectual property rights are generally considered to serve the coming into being of goods that *do not yet exist*.[31] In other respects, too, publicly accessible IP is almost the counter-example to tangible property. It is de facto non-exclusive and non-rivalrous; its use does not generate negative but positive externalities (e.g. learning progress among pupils), which is why its public availability does not lead to a tragedy of the commons. And, finally, the concept of scarcity can only be applied in a modified form to IP, since these immaterial objects can potentially be reproduced indefinitely and are therefore not scarce once they have been produced.[32] Mark Lemley, one of the leading IP scholars, even predicts the end of the very scarcity that patents, copyrights and other IP rights are considered to remedy. In his view, under conditions of current technologies such as the

---

Gütern, passim. On Locke see Oberndörfer, *Die philosophische Grundlage des Urheberrechts*; Shiffrin, in Munzer (ed.) *New Essays in the Legal and Political Theory of Property* 138; Lemley, 62 UCLA L. Rev. 1328, 1338 et seq. (2015). For a justification of IPRs from the perspective of speech act theory see Stallberg, *Urheberrecht und moralische Rechtfertigung* 300 et seq.

[27] See Hubmann, 106 UFITA 145, 151, 154 (1987); Gieseke, *Vom Privileg zum Urheberrecht* 170; Bosse, *Autorschaft als Werkherrschaft* 119–20; Stallberg, *Urheberrecht und moralische Rechtfertigung* 154 et seq.

[28] Bluntschli, *Deutsches Privatrecht I* 189.

[29] Translated from the original German. Kohler, 123 UFITA 99, 127 (1993).

[30] Barron, 31 Law and Philosophy 1 et seq. (2012); Drassinower, *What's Wrong with Copying?* 8 referring to Kant (1785), in Bently & Kretschmer (eds.) *Primary Sources on Copyright* www.copyrighthistory.org.

[31] J. Cohen, 52 Houston L. Rev. 691, 693 (2014).

[32] *Cf.* Landes & Posner, *Economic Structure of IP* 18; Lemley, 83 Texas L. Rev. 1031 (2005); Benkler, *Networks* 36 et seq.; Wilson, 93 The Monist 450, 453 (2010); Pottage & Sherman, *Figures of Invention* 4; Steinvorth, 52 DZPhil 708, 728 (2004).

Internet, 3D printing and robotics, an abundance of innovative products can be expected precisely when the artificial scarcity caused by IP rights will be eliminated.[33]

The list of differences between real and intellectual property rights could be continued. Only three striking observations shall be mentioned here. First, IP rights in their present form are a much younger phenomenon than real property ownership – hardly more than 250 years old.[34] Secondly, although they are now practically recognised worldwide, IP rights are at the same time politically much more controversial than the ownership of movable and immovable things.[35] Thirdly, it is noticeable that the relationship between 'is' and 'ought' is particularly unstable in IP law. Historians argue about whether the concept of the abstract IP object was only discovered by the law, or whether this idea was actually brought about by the law.[36] And quite a few theorists believe that in IP law it is ultimately impossible to distinguish between reality and the rules of law, since the protected objects are defined in the course of the application of the relevant laws and thus constituted at the same time as elements of legal reality.[37] Paradigmatic for these difficulties is the current state of patent law, which generates its object from itself – namely from highly formalised patent documents.[38]

1.3 REACTIONS

According to the prevailing view, all these divergences are merely the expression of gradual differences resulting in different scopes of protection, but do not change the fundamental characterisation of both real and IP rights as exclusive property titles that assign an object to an owner.[39] The pertinent legal theory revolves around the purely legal question of whether copyrights and industrial property rights are to be understood as property rights or as the regulation of competitive behaviour.[40] Even

---

[33] Lemley, 90 N.Y.U. L. Rev. 460 (2015).
[34] See Section 3.2.
[35] Peukert, 81 RabelsZ 158 et seq. (2017).
[36] Sherman & Bently, *The Making of Modern Intellectual Property Law* 57; George, *Constructing Intellectual Property* 112.
[37] Madison, 56 Case Western Reserve L. Rev. 381, 465 (2005) ('"factual" and "legal" things are identical; once rules governing protection and infringement are applied, the legal right is coextensive with what the right owner in fact created, invented, or made distinctive'); van Dijk, *Grounds of the Immaterial* 30 ('insurmountable problem of correspondence between these concepts and supposed extra-legal things').
[38] For more details *see* Section 5.4.3.
[39] BVerfG 29 June 2000 Case no. 1 BvR 825/98, NJW 2001, 598; J. Cohen, 94 Texas L. Rev. 1, 32 et seq. (2015); Merges, in Dreyfuss & Pila (eds.), *The Oxford Handbook of Intellectual Property Law*, forthcoming; unclear Drahos, *Philosophy of IP* 210–13.
[40] *Cf.* Hirsch, 36 UFITA 19, 47 et seq. (1962) ('Werkherrschaft'); Jänich, *Geistiges Eigentum* 185 et seq.; Peukert, *in* Basedow et al. (eds.) I *Handwörterbuch Europäisches Privatrecht* 648 et seq.; Ohly, 58 JZ 545 et seq. (2003); Renouard, *Traité des droits d'auteur* 441 et seq.; Pfister, 205 RIDA

authors who – like Felix Cohen and Alf Ross – belong to the legal realist camp and are therefore sceptical in principle about abstract concepts, aim their criticism at legal concepts such as the subjective right or the fairness of competition and the effects of these legal ways of speaking and thinking about the regulation of reality.[41]

But this inner-juridical criticism falls principally short of the mark. The differences between the legal characteristics of real property ownership and IP rights cannot be explained by precisely these legal characteristics.[42] Anyone doing so goes round in legal circles and tends to take legal concepts ('the' property, 'the' subjective right etc.) in the tradition of conceptual jurisprudence from meanings that they themselves have given them. The worldwide discussion about whether patents, copyrights etc. may or may not be regarded as *Eigentum*/property/*propriété*, which is completely out of proportion to the result, bears eloquent testimony to this.

The hypothesis presented here is, instead, that the differences between real property ownership and IP rights are the expression of a categorically different way of existence of the legal objects concerned. This shifts the interest in understanding from the law to the reality of the law. The reality of current IP law seems to be the abstract IP object: the invention, the work, the design, the logo etc. as assigned to the rights holder. If the peculiar character of IP rights cannot be fully explained on the basis of the prevailing paradigm of the abstract IP object, then this ontology must be critically examined.[43]

Attempts in this direction have been surprisingly rare.[44] The overwhelming majority even of theoretically ambitious writings on IP proceed without further doubt from the existence of abstract IP objects capable of being owned, without further questioning this assumption.[45] Those who, like Alexander Elster, Heinrich Hubmann, Alois Troller and Nicolas Druey, comment on the ontological status of

---

117 et seq. (2005); Helena R. Howe & Jonathan Griffiths (eds.) *Concepts of Property*; Merges, in Dreyfuss & Pila (eds.) *The Oxford Handbook of Intellectual Property Law*, forthcoming.

[41] Cohen, 35 Columbia L. Rev. 809 et seq. (1935); Ross, 58 Tidsskrift for Rettsvitenskap 321, 350–51 (1945); Ross, *On Law and Justice* 172–73, 178. See also Jhering, Scherz und Ernst 245 et seq.

[42] van Dijk, *Grounds of the Immaterial* 9–10; *but see* Gray, 50 Cambridge L.J. 252, 299 (1991).

[43] Pottage & Sherman, *Figures of Invention* 4; van Dijk, *Grounds of the Immaterial* 2–3.

[44] Pottage & Sherman, *Figures of Invention* 4 ('... normative and political debates ... have effectively eclipsed the question of what kinds of things ideas are in the first place'); Wreen, 93 The Monist 433, 435 (2010) ('Both the law and philosophy are virtually silent on the matter.'); Hick, 51 British Journal of Aesthetics 185 (2011) ('And unfortunately, while copyright law assumes some metaphysical basis to its objects, this basis tends to go largely uninvestigated'.); Chin, 74 University of Pittsburgh L. Rev. 263, 268 (2012); van Dijk, *Grounds of the Immaterial* 2; Wadle, in Wadle (ed.) *Beiträge zur Geschichte des Urheberrechts* 11, 15.

[45] Zech, Information als Schutzgegenstand 36; Pottage & Sherman, *Figures of Invention* 4 ('too obvious to require any explanation'); Tamura, Nordic Journal of Commercial Law 1 (2012); Teilmann-Lock, *The Object of Copyright* 143; George, *Constructing Intellectual Property* 97 ('The intellectual property object is, in effect, a legal delineation of the part of the ideational object over which intellectual property law provides a monopoly'.); critical Alexander-Katz, in *Festgabe Wilke* 3, 6.

immaterial objects or information do so by briefly reconstructing the prevailing understanding that these abstract objects exist as something 'intellectual', independent from their instantiation in books, digital files, industrial products etc.[46] In 1955, Alois Troller wrote that

> [a]ll jurists ... agree that the work of literature and art is not a physical, but an intellectual thing, that it is his work of the mind, an intellectual work. This is an ontological statement: the work is recognised as having independent existence. Its essence is determined as intellectual. Furthermore, no one doubts, and cannot do, that the work has arisen from the mind of the author (through his intellectual achievement); likewise it is certain that the work, as soon as it has been made physically perceptible, is separated from the author and has its own existence. It is independent, objective mind.[47]

By and large, this assessment still accurately reflects the current state of the *jurisprudential* debate. The only difference is that works and other IP objects are no longer described as *objektivierter Geist* (objectified mind), as they were during the idealistic renaissance of natural law in post-war Germany, but are referred to as types, which are manifested in various tokens.[48]

At the same time, there is ample evidence that the notion of the abstract IP object has remained unclear and obscure. The reprint debates of the eighteenth century in the United Kingdom and Germany focused to a large extent on the subject matter of the new rights or prohibitions.[49] And even after the abstract IP object had established itself as the dominant paradigm, the fundamental uncertainty about the ontological basis of the entire body of law occasionally surfaced. According to an oft-quoted saying of the influential justice at the US Supreme Court Joseph Story, patent and copyright cases concern the 'metaphysics of the law'.[50] His equally famous successor Oliver Wendell Holmes Jr. said about copyright that '[t]he right to exclude is not directed to an object in possession or owned, but is *in vacuo*, so to speak'.[51] This observation in turn strongly resembles a statement made by his contemporary Josef Kohler, who assumed that the immaterial object 'floats' above the earth's surface

---

[46] Elster, 6 RabelsZ 903, 913 (1932); Hubmann, *Das Recht des schöpferischen Geistes* 46–48. Regarding similarities between Hartmann's general ontology and Ingarden's ontology of artworks see Bertolini, in Petersen & Poli (eds.) *Philosophy of Nicolai Hartmann* 171 et seq. See also Troller, 1 *Immaterialgüterrecht* 55 et seq.; Merkl, *Der Begriff des Immaterialgüterrechts* 72 et seq.; Druey, *Information als Gegenstand des Rechts* 3–4.

[47] Translated from the original German. Troller, 50 UFITA 385, 389 (1967); Troller, 1 *Immaterialgüterrecht* 55 with note 11.

[48] Shiffrin, in Goodin et al. (eds.) *A Companion to Contemporary Political Philosophy* 653, 654; Chin, 74 University of Pittsburgh L. Rev. 263, 275 (2012). See also Section 2.1.1.

[49] See *infra* Section 3.2.2.2 and Hubmann, 106 UFITA 145 (1987).

[50] Folsom v. Marsh, 9. F.Cas. 342, 344 (C.C.D. Mass. 1841) (Story, J.); Hogg v. Emerson, 47 US 437, 485–86 (1848); Chin, 74 University of Pittsburgh L. Rev. 263, 268 (2012) with further references.

[51] White-Smith Music Pub. Co. v. Apollo Co., 209 US 1, 19 (1908, Holmes, J., concurring).

without, of course, 'growing together' with it,[52] which prompted one critic to make the derisive remark that 'the abstract work [is] in a sense the astral body of the work, if I use this image from the concepts used by spiritualists'.[53] More recently, there has been talk of a 'somewhat airy' object,[54] a *corpus mysticus*,[55] and a 'spooky entity'.[56] In one of the rare cases in which the ontological status of IP was considered to be relevant, the US Supreme Court ruled in 2007 that a distinction had to be made between abstract software and its embodiment on data carriers, whereby abstract software was more comparable with 'notes of music in the head of a composer' than with a 'roller that causes a player piano to produce sound'.[57]

Some writings with albeit very different theoretical backgrounds and normative approaches tend to regard IP law less as an allocation of static objects than as a regulation of behaviour with regard to dynamic objects. Thus, Immanuel Kant's philosophy of enlightenment does not regard written statements as a finished work (*opus*), but primarily as an activity – namely as the author's speech to the audience (*opera*) within the framework of an enlightening discourse.[58] Thomas Jefferson also understood ideas and inventions as 'the action of the thinking power', which by their nature cannot be the 'property' of a person.[59] Post-structuralist literary studies decompose the idea of the work as a fixed object with an unambiguous meaning and clearly defined boundaries – replacing it with the authorless, fluid 'text', which is only constituted in discourse through the act of reception and its possibly transformative further use, and which only exists as an element of a large inter- and hypertextual context.[60] Another social science-inspired theory considers works,

---

[52] Translated from the original German. Kohler, *Handbuch des deutschen Patentrechts* 72.
[53] Translated from the original German. Alexander-Katz, in *Festgabe Wilke* 3, 9 with note 1.
[54] Strömholm, GRUR Int. 433, 437 (1963).
[55] Spoor, 105 Weekblad voor Privaatrecht 165 (1974); Ricolfi, in Drahos et al. (eds.) *Kritika* 1 134, 143–44.
[56] Drahos, *Philosophy of IP* 17.
[57] Microsoft Corp. v. AT & T Corp., 550 US 437, 451 (2007).
[58] Kant (1785), in Bently & Kretschmer (eds.) *Primary Sources on Copyright* www.copyrighthistory.org; Drassinower, *What's Wrong with Copying?* 95. Ferner Milton, *Areopagitica* ('Truth and understanding are not such wares as to be monopoliz'd and traded in by tickets and statutes, and standards. We must not think to make a staple commodity of all the knowledge in the Land, to mark and licence it like our broad cloath, and our wooll packs'.)
[59] Jefferson, in Kurland & Lerner (eds.) 3 *The Founders' Constitution* ('It would be curious then, if an idea, the fugitive fermentation of an individual brain, could, of natural right, be claimed in exclusive and stable property. If nature has made any one thing less susceptible than all others of exclusive property, it is the action of the thinking power called an idea, which an individual may exclusively possess as long as he keeps it to himself; but the moment it is divulged, it forces itself into the possession of every one, and the receiver cannot dispossess himself of it. . . . Inventions then cannot, in nature, be a subject of property'.). On Jefferson's influence on US IP theory, *see* Mossoff, 92 Cornell L. Rev. 953 (2007); Opderbeck, 49 Jurimetrics Journal 203 (2009).
[60] *See* Barthes, in Barthes (ed.) *Image Music Text* 155, 157 ('the work can be held in the hand, the text is held in language, only exists in the movement of a discourse'), 160 ('The author is reputed the father and the owner of his work'), 161 ('As for the Text, it reads without the

inventions and other IP objects as 'quasi-objects' or 'boundary objects' that enable communication across different social fields – for example, when lawyers talk to technicians or artists about inventions and works. This view does not regard IP objects as a given, static subject matter of discourse, but as an inherently active component of communication (actants). Accordingly, a trademark, for example, is not only a passive vehicle that the trademark proprietor uses to convey information, but it also communicates something that the trademark proprietor cannot completely control.[61] Finally, a primarily economic argument sees IP rights as a regulation of market behaviour. The legislature grants a person the right to exercise a certain degree of control over competition either by prohibiting other market participants from engaging in certain market conduct or by making the necessary consent subject to the payment of a royalty.[62]

All these theories are characterised by the fact that they dynamise and liquefy the abstract IP object to a certain extent. Instead of a purely object-oriented property theory, there is an understanding of IP law in which the regulated communicative and other actions come to the fore. However, such approaches ultimately remain a half-hearted approach. For they by no means disband the thinking in terms of an abstract-immaterial object that exists separately from concrete embodiments, but merely theorise the still distinct, yet dynamic object in a different way – namely as 'the' speech of the author, 'the' text, 'the' quasi-object and 'the' public good.[63]

---

inscription of the Father ... the metaphor of the Text is that of the network ... the restitution of the inter-text paradoxically abolishing any legacy'); Rotstein, 68 Chicago-Kent L. Rev. 725, 727 (1993) ('The central thesis of this Article is that current copyright dogma does not recognize that so-called "works of authorship" are ... unstable and dependent on context'.). *See also* Aoki, 68 Chicago-Kent L. Rev. 805 (1993). Contra Reicher, *in* Borkowski et al. (eds.) *Literatur interpretieren* 191, 202.

[61] *Cf.* Pottage & Sherman, *Figures of Invention* 4; Sherman, 12 Theoretical Inquiries in Law 99, 120 (2011) ('Instead of thinking of the work as being either tangible or intangible, the copyright work is better seen as a quasi-object or hybrid that is both tangible and intangible at the same time', with reference to Latour's social theory; van Dijk, *Grounds of the Immaterial* 25, 42. On 'boundary objects' see Susan Leigh Star & James R. Griesemer, 19 Social Science Studies 387 (1989); Star, 35 Science, Technology, & Human Values 601 (2010); Burk, 69 Vanderbilt L. Rev. 1603 (2016). *See also* Madison, 19 J. Intell. Prop. L. 1, 27 (2012) ('A work qua work is communicative, not simply functional; a work communicates the fact that humans produced it').

[62] Lemley, 92 Tex. L. Rev. 107–8 (2014); Lemley, 62 UCLA L. Rev. 1328, 1330–31 (2015). Contra Merges, *in* Rochelle C. Dreyfuss & Justine Pila (eds.), *The Oxford Handbook of Intellectual Property Law*, forthcoming.

[63] On Jefferson *see* Opderbeck, 49 Jurimetrics Journal 203 et seq. (2009); Drassinower, *What's Wrong with Copying?* 95, 178 with note 68; Susan Leigh Star & James R. Griesemer, 19 Social Science Studies 387, 393 (1989) ('These boundary object may be abstract or concrete'.); Burk, *in* Lai & Maget Dominicé (eds.) *Intellectual Property and Access to Im/material Goods* 44, 58 ('The new materialist approach would likely be to instead traverse ideal/material dualism, treating the instantiation of creative goods as a unified whole rather than a conceptual division'.); Lemley, 90 N.Y.U. L. Rev. 460, 468 (2015) ('In effect, the point of IP laws is to take a public good that is naturally nonrivalrous and make it artificially scarce, allowing the owner to control how many copies of the good can be made and at what price'.); equally ambivalent

The step of radically questioning this object-based ontological basis of IP law is only taken in very isolated cases, at least by lawyers.[64] Occasionally one encounters an unexplored statement that IP law deals with a 'fiction'.[65] The view that 'the' work etc. represents a historically contingent construct is – not surprisingly – already more widespread among historians and can even be considered settled among those who explicitly address this question.[66] One looks, however, in vain for a critique of the dominant ontology and for an alternative understanding of the reality of IP law. As far as can be seen, such an attempt has only been seriously undertaken three times, at long intervals and from different theoretical perspectives.

The first attempt in this direction is the *Kritik Der Grundbegriffe Vom Geistigen Eigenthum* (A Critique of Fundamental Concepts of Intellectual Property) by Max Lange, published in 1858, which should not only be mentioned and quoted in detail from a chronological point of view. Although Josef Kohler regarded this crossover between academia and practice as 'far more meaningful' than 'conceptual attempts' by other authors, it quickly fell into oblivion, which was not changed by a reprint in 1991.[67] Lange wrote:

> Of course, neither the manuscript of a work nor a single printed copy, which both represent the author's intellectual product externally or physically, but this physical representation itself was regarded collectivistically and in abstract thought as an object of the new genre of property. [...] Thus the well-known legal principle that the creator of a physical thing acquires ownership of it is extended in an analogous sense to the production of intellectual products, but the difference between a physical thing and an intellectual activity or a result of such activity is overlooked. This highly unfortunate confusion had the most momentous effect on the later perception. [...] In this way, one created a possession of thoughts or at least of their

---

Shavell, *Foundations* 137 ('For convenience, I will sometimes write of information in the abstract, but other times I will refer to embodiments of information in goods and services...').

[64] See the remarks in Peukert, *Güterzuordnung* 39; Peukert, in *Geiger Criminal Enforcement of Intellectual Property* 151, 164 et seq. Carvalko, 2 ABA SciTech Lawyer 7–9 (2005) does not address the abstract IP object but only the ontological status of corporeal artefacts. See also van Dijk, *Grounds of the Immaterial* (sociology); Pettersson, *The Idea of a Text* (linguistics).

[65] Foucault, in Rabinow & Rose, *The Essential Foucault* 377, 382 ('fiction of the work'); Penner, *Idea of Property* 118–19 ('idiotic fiction that intellectual property constitutes property in ideas (patents) or expressions'; 'in general it does no harm to speak of rights in ideas, or in manuscripts, or in marks, any more than it does to refer to one's rights in one's labour'); Drahos, *Philosophy of IP* 111, 151–56, 211; Breakey, in Howe & Griffiths (eds.) *Concepts of Property* 137, 152–53; Rotstein, 68 Chicago-Kent L. Rev. 725 (1993); König, 46 NJW 3121, 3122 (1993); Tamura, Nordic Journal of Commercial Law 1, 2 (2012).

[66] See Chapter 3 note 54 and Sherman & Bently, *The Making of Modern Intellectual Property Law* 28; Pottage & Sherman, *Figures of Invention* 4, 7 ('Intangibility is a figment'.); Höffner, *Geschichte und Wesen des Urheberrechts* II 323 (abstract IP object a fantasy); Biagioli, in Gaudillière et al. (ed.) *Living Properties* 241, 250.

[67] Translated from the original German. Lange, *Kritik der Grundbegriffe vom geistigen Eigentum* (1858), reprinted in 117 UFITA 169 (1991); on Lange see Kohler, *Urheberrecht an Schriftwerken und Verlagsrecht* 85; Jänich, *Geistiges Eigentum* 86 et seq.

external form, but did not consider that *having* thoughts means nothing more than *thinking*, that having thoughts in a certain form means nothing more than *combining and expressing* thoughts, in short that the object had to be thought of as an activity, and that an intellectual product receives its fair value only through production and reception. [...] From this one can clearly see how activity relationships always form the basis and how the right in question is directed only towards the prohibition of a free activity of others. But with this we enter into the field of obligations and recognise how property theory has judged itself. [...] The above remarks have shown how the author's right guaranteed by legislation cannot consist in the power over a thing, but only in the legal power to restrict others in their free activity.[68]

This extract already contains essential elements of the view to be developed throughout this book, according to which IP rights have no other effect than regulating the production and use of brute, measurable mental and physical artefacts.[69] However, Lange did not elaborate his observations – possibly inspired by Kant – into a comprehensive critique of abstract object thinking. Kohler's praise signals that Lange, too, was ultimately not able to break free of this paradigm. And indeed, in his commentary on the Prussian Copyright Law of 1837, Lange rejects the term *Geistiges Eigentum* – which Kohler also reviled – but (like Kohler) argues quite naturally with the concept of the literary work as a *Geistesprodukt* (intellectual product).[70]

It took almost a hundred years until the abstract IP object was once again examined more closely, this time in Scandinavia. The trigger was again the discussion about the concept of ownership, which the Danish jurist Vinding Kruse had debated in a multi-volume work at the end of the 1920s and applied to immaterial goods such as the copyrightable work.[71] This proliferation of the concept of ownership was opposed by the legal theorist (and later judge at the European Court of Human Rights) Alf Ross, who also came from Denmark, in a review essay published in 1945. Like Max Lange's study, Ross' essay addressed 'basic concepts' of copyright.[72] In the course of reviewing Vinding Kruse's book, Ross formulated en passant a brilliant critique of the idea of the abstract work as an object of copyright

---

[68] Translated from the original German. Lange, *Kritik der Grundbegriffe vom geistigen Eigentum* (1858), *reprinted in* 117 UFITA 169, 173–74, 179 (1991).

[69] See also Göpel, *Über Begriff und Wesen des Urheberrechts* 22 (exclusive rights to exploit works); Hauptmann, *in Festgabe der Juristischen Fakultät der Universität Freiburg (Schweiz)* 50, 56; Höffner, *Geschichte und Wesen des Urheberrechts* I 377; Höffner, *Geschichte und Wesen des Urheberrechts* II, 327 (possibilities to act as the subject matter of IPRs); Schmidt, 52 DZPhil 755, 759–60 (2004); *also* Breakey, *in* Helena R. Howe & Jonathan Griffiths (eds.) *Concepts of Property* 137, 159–60; Balganesh, *in* Howe & Griffiths (eds.) *Concepts of Property* 161, 180.

[70] Lange, *Kritik der Grundbegriffe vom geistigen Eigentum* (1858), *reprinted in* 117 UFITA 169, 173, 226, 248 (1991).

[71] See Kruse, 1 *Das Eigentumsrecht*.

[72] Ross, 58 Tidsskrift for Rettsvitenskap 321, in particular 340–52 (1945).

law. According to Ross, this concept draws upon a false and misleading analogy to real property ownership, a 'romantic fantasy', a 'fiction', an 'abstraction' without corresponding reality. Only the first materialisations (the original), copies and personal performances exist in the real world.[73] Their production, use or implementation is regulated by copyright law in such a way that the author is granted a veto right. The author is thus in a position to permit or prohibit the said conduct of third parties (in return for payment). These actual effects of copyright would be more concealed than explained by the predominant object- and property-centred approach.[74] Ross' legal realist provocation triggered an intense discussion that continues to this day, but which remained confined to Scandinavia and ultimately surrendered to the fact that Scandinavian law is also based on the idea of the abstract IP object. Ross' ontological criticism bounced off positive law.[75]

Fifty years later, and without recourse to the legal-theoretical contributions of Lange and Ross, the economists Michele Boldrin and David Levine finally formulated a theory of the efficient allocation of innovations in which they renounce the abstract IP object on a very similar ontological basis:

> Central to understanding the market for ideas and the incentives for the adoption of new ideas is discovering how ideas might be different from other goods. The starting point of the economic analysis of innovation is to recognize that the economically relevant unit is a copy of an idea. That is, typically, many copies of an idea exist in physical form, such as a book, a computer file or a piece of equipment, or in the form of knowledge embodied in people who know and understand the idea. When embodied in humans, copies of ideas are labeled with a variety of different names, which often obscure their common nature: skills, knowledge, human capital, norms, and so on. Careful inspection shows, though, that each and everyone of these apparently different entities is, at the end, nothing but the embodied copy of an idea, and that the latter was either discovered first by the person in whom it is currently embodied, or costly acquired (possibly via observation and imitation) from other humans, in whom it had been previously and similarly embodied. Economically valuable copies of ideas do not fall from the heavens, like manna, but are the product of intentional and costly human efforts. Only these copies matter, first, in the sense that if they were all to be erased, the idea would no longer have any economic value, and, second, in the sense that the copies are relatively good substitutes for each other: whether a copy of an idea is the original copy or the hundredth copy, it is equally economically useful. From the perspective of the functioning of markets, then, property rights in copies of ideas is assured by

---

[73] Rudner, 10 Philosophy and Phenomenological Research 380, 384 (1950) ('The problematic locutions are simply recognized as convenient shorthand'.). On Rudner see Pettersson, *The Idea of a Text* 26 et seq. with further references.
[74] Ross, 58 Tidsskrift for Rettsvitenskap 321, 343–46, 350 (1945).
[75] See Strömholm, GRUR Int. 433, 439–40 (1963); Godenhielm, 45 GRUR Int. 327 (1996); Rognstad, *Property Aspects of Intellectual Property* 47–51 with further references; Drassinower, *What's Wrong with Copying?* 174–75.

the ordinary laws against theft – what is ordinarily referred to as 'intellectual property' protects not the ownership of copies of ideas, but rather a monopoly over how other people make use of their copies of an idea.[76]

According to Boldrin and Levine, it is wrong to ask abstract questions about the promotion of abstract innovations. Economics should instead be concerned with the real conditions for the production of innovations and their implementation and further dissemination. In other words, Boldrin and Levine are no longer concerned about the efficient allocation of abstract IP objects, but about the efficient allocation of scarce innovation and imitation skills among human beings and other scarce prerequisites for new technologies.[77]

1.4 OBJECTIVES AND PLAN OF THE STUDY

In the following chapters, these unconnected approaches will be developed into a comprehensive critique of the prevailing ontology of IP law. The primary purpose of the exercise is to formulate a theory of IP law on the basis of an ontological analysis, which is capable of explaining the differences between real property ownership on the one hand and IP rights on the other, and which thus makes the latter legal field with its peculiarities better understandable.

This is a descriptive project in two respects. First, the reality regulated by IP rights must be described as precisely as possible. In the following, two different ontologies will be discussed: firstly, an object ontology that philosophically reconstructs the dominant paradigm, but which is entangled in continuous contradictions (see Section 2.1), and secondly, a social ontology as elaborated by John R. Searle, according to which the abstract IP object is to be understood as a language-based social fact (see Section 2.2).

The latter thesis is examined in the third section from a diachronic perspective. The hypothesis in this respect is that the abstract IP object should be able to be historicised if it does not form a given external reality that is subject to law as if it were a plot of land or a movable thing. Indeed, it can be shown that the concept of

---

[76] Boldrin & Levine, 2 Review of Economic Research on Copyright Issues 45, 66 (2005).
[77] Boldrin & Levine, 2 Review of Economic Research on Copyright Issues 45, 48 (2005); Boldrin & Levine, *Against intellectual monopoly* 128; similar Gruner, 13 Colum. Sci. & Tech. L. Rev. 1, 5–6 (2012) ('In short, patents influence choices that are highly rivalrous in that patents mediate how decisions about the use of scarce innovation resources (including the time of inventors) are made'.); on different theoretical grounds Burk, in Lai & Maget Dominicé (eds.) *Intellectual Property and Access to Im/material Goods* 44, 53 ('Just as public-goods analysis indulges in a category mistake by equating my molecules of air with another's molecules of air, or my patch of the park with another's patch of the park, so public-goods analysis of copyright mistakes two artefacts with similar qualities for the same artefact. It is the concept of the work that enables this sleight, conflating my music file with another's music file because they have in some way the same intangible essence. The mistake is the same whether the material affordances of the artefact are analogue or digital').

the abstract IP object is based on a two-fold, language-based process of abstraction. The first abstraction concerns the designation of several physical and mental artefacts (such as books, machines, performances etc.), which are similar to each other but exist independently of each other, with a general term (such as a work title, a designation of an invention or a design, or a sign of origin). This language practice is not placed in a concrete historical context, but reconstructed in its general logic (see Section 3.1). Since it can be considered certain that the exercise of giving similar artefacts a uniform designation is *much* older than modern IP law, the broader question arises as to whether the discourse and idea of abstract-immaterial goods has a history of its own.

That this is indeed the case is explained in Section 3.2 under evaluation of legal-historical research and in consideration of primary sources. These sources show that a second process of abstraction took place in the eighteenth century. Since then, a work title such as Goethe's *Faust* no longer designates a plurality of concretely existing copies and otherwise similar artefacts, but it represents the abstract work, which is only accidentally embodied in all the copies and theatrical performances. This firstly represents a change of terminology. Words such as 'work', 'invention' and 'design' are given a new meaning. They no longer refer to the external reality of physical and mental artefacts, but to an idealised abstraction. Secondly, there is a change in the perception of individual items, such as books, machines and other corporeal products. They no longer stand for themselves, but from now on count as mere embodiments of an immaterial work, an immaterial invention etc., whose abstract existence is independent of all these individual tokens – an amazing, even eccentric idea!

The results of the ontological and historical discussions are summarised in Chapter 4. This summary shows that the reality regulated by IP rights can be conceived of in two ways. Either one talks and regulates as if abstract IP objects really exist, and not only in our socially shared imagination. On this basis, property-like exclusive rights – 'intellectual property' rights – can be constructed. Or one relates the legal regulations only and directly to physical and mental artefacts such as books, machines, products, goods bearing signs or personal live performances, whose production and other use is regulated. The finding of an infringement then depends on a comparison between 'Secondary Artefacts' challenged as infringing, and a 'Master Artefact' (the original, the entry in the register etc.). Such an action- and artefact-based approach was once dominant. It was the ontology of the early modern privilege – an exclusive right to perform certain actions.

Chapter 5 tests the legal explanatory power of these two competing understandings of reality. Thus, the purpose and level of analysis change. In contrast to Chapters 2 and 3, the issue in question is no longer the subject matter of IP laws but IP law itself. At the same time, the analysis remains descriptive. For I do not question how the law should be structured in order to do justice to the reality it regulates, but I look for a description of the law that accurately describes its structures and real-world effects. In this respect, it is noticeable that the dominant paradigm of the abstract IP object as the subject matter of IP laws/rights is not applied across the board. The subject matter of trademark law, of the rights related to copyright and of plant variety rights are not conceived as immaterial objects in the relevant codifications and legal practice. Rather, there dominates (still) an action- and artefact-based understanding in these areas of law according to which the entitled parties are granted exclusive rights to use marks, cultural products such as phonograms and propagating material of plants (see Section 5.1.1).

Otherwise, however, there is no doubt that current copyright and industrial property laws are based on the concept of the abstract IP object. Therefore, many observers consider a critique of the ontology of IP law to be superfluous and even misleading.[78] In addition, an alternative ontology runs the risk of itself committing a naturalistic fallacy by inferring a different legal regime from a reality understood in a different way.[79] The importance of these concerns is demonstrated by the history of the Scandinavian discussion following Alf Ross. His criticism of the concept of the abstract copyrightable work has indeed triggered an intensive and theoretically rich debate. However, in view of current positive law, this debate has now largely died away without consequences. For also under Scandinavian laws it is the author who holds exclusive rights in his abstract work. And this legal status quo is, it is claimed, missed by those who deconstruct the work into acts and exemplars.[80]

But such resignation is premature. An understanding based on actions and artefacts can provide a better explanation of current IP law even in areas where the paradigm of the abstract IP object appears to have been fully implemented – namely in copyright, patent and design law. First, the structure and effects of these rights can be fully reconstructed on the basis of an action- and artefact-based understanding. The rights always relate back to a Master Artefact that is claimed by the rights holder who has to submit either an exemplar or a copy of the registration. Whether the Master Artefact meets the statutory protection requirements is assessed by comparing it with other pre-existing artefacts that make up the state of the art. In a further comparison, it is determined whether the artefacts used by the defendant are infringing the claimed rights because they display sufficient relevant similarities and – in copyright law – they have been derived from the Master Artefact. In this case, the defendant is prohibited from producing and otherwise using the Secondary Artefacts (see Section 5.1.2). Secondly, a neo-realist critique of the abstract IP object can explain the fundamental structural and legal-philosophical

---

[78] *Cf.* Pudelek, *in* Barck et al. (eds.) *Ästhetische Grundbegriffe* VI 526; Carrier, 54 Duke L.J., 1 (2004); Madison, 19 J. Intell. Prop. L. 1, 31 (2012) ('for practical reasons the work cannot be deleted entirely'); *but see* Thierse, 36 Weimarer Beiträge 240, 261 (1990).
[79] *Cf.* Strömholm, GRUR Int. 481 (1963).
[80] *See* Strömholm, GRUR Int. 481, 488 (1963); Godenhielm, 45 GRUR Int. 327, 330 (1996) (one should give up on this question). *But see* Rognstad, *Property Aspects of Intellectual Property* 47–51.

differences between IP rights on the one hand and real property ownership on the other (see Sections 5.2 and 5.3). It is this legal explanatory power that makes the project undertaken herein appear meaningful. The goal is the elaboration of a superior legal theory.

In addition, only a critique of the ontology of IP law makes possible the idea that the object of IP rights may not be a simple aspect of external reality but that thinking, speaking and regulating in terms of the abstract IP object ('the' work, 'the' invention etc.) is already inherently normative. In other words, an ontological critique can explain that and why the ruling paradigm is not simply an innocent depiction of reality, but a fundamental normative choice. In view of the linguistic-social mode of existence, the genealogy and the legal function of the abstract IP object, the thesis put forward here is that the whole meaning and purpose of this notion consists in faking a distinct object capable of being owned. The purpose of the abstract IP object is its normativity (see Section 5.4.1). This possibly surprising claim, which is ultimately inconceivable on the basis of the prevailing paradigm, can even be proven from a legal-historical and legal comparative point of view. This is because legal systems, such as Anglo-American copyright (i.e. the right to copy, or the right to the copy), which are based on actions and artefacts, grant rights holders less protection than more idealised legal systems, such as French and German copyright laws. It can be shown that in general, the more abstract the legal object, the more extensive the legal protection (see Section 5.4.2). Finally, recognising the inherent normativity of the work, the invention etc. also provides an explanation for why the distinction between 'is' and 'ought' in IP law is systemically unclear and unstable (see Section 5.4.3). For unlike in real property law, not only IP *law* is a normative-institutional fact, but already its idealised reality – the abstract IP object.

Consequently, it does not constitute a categorical error to criticise the prevailing concept of reality from a normative point of view.[81] This normative critique is laid out in the concluding Chapter 6. The question is: Should we talk and think as if there is an abstract IP object that is exclusively assigned to a proprietor like a piece of land? In view of the fictionality of these assumptions and the growing doubts as to whether the ever-expanding field of IP law fulfils the purposes attributed to it, I propose to answer this question in the negative. Instead of believing in the existence of abstract IP objects and in the effectiveness and justice of the exclusive rights 'in' these idealised objects, the actors concerned, their actions and the artefacts of their actions should come to the fore. The legal realist proposition is this: The closer the law comes to brute reality, the greater the probability that it is effective and achieves its goals. Conversely, the greater the distance between real-world actions and things on the one hand and the law on the other, the more likely it is that undesirable side effects and misuses will occur. Such dysfunctionalities are favoured by an intermediate linguistic instance such as the abstract IP object. This is

---

[81] *Cf.* Madison, 56 Case Western Reserve L. Rev. 381 et seq. (2005).

because it acts as an additional level between the law and the brute facts of human behaviour and physical resources.

If one tries, along these lines, to reduce the distance between IP law and reality, the focus shifts to the conditions of creative, innovative, investment and otherwise entrepreneurial activities (see Section 6.2). It then becomes clear what the really relevant questions are, namely: Under what conditions are artistic works created, technical inventions, designs and other innovations brought about and developed into marketable products? Does this require exclusive rights in the respective work product or are there other incentive mechanisms and ways of appropriating innovation returns? Or, in trademark law, what market communication rules are necessary to ensure dynamic, functioning competition that allows consumers non-deceptive access to high-quality and diversified products? It is true that such questions are being posed in the current IP debates, but only via the unnecessary detour of the abstract IP object, which cannot satisfy human needs under any circumstances, since it is supposed to be independent of concrete artefacts and actions.

A consistent, direct focus on the innovative and imitative actions and the artefacts produced or used in their course, which are all subject to the classical economic laws of scarcity, exclusivity and rivalry, is helpful in distinguishing real from purely hypothetical regulatory problems and protection demands. Demands for new or expanded rights can be exposed from this point of view as in fact anti-competitive calls for the protection of a market position or market opportunity.[82] At the same time, competition-based incentive and distribution mechanisms come to the fore. Overall, an approach focusing on actions and artefacts favours an instrumental understanding of IP law. Protection is earned only by those who are innovative or who invest, and would not have done so without a special preferential right.[83] At the same time, incremental improvements of already existing achievements should be exempted from the scope of exclusive IP rights to a greater extent than is currently the case. For they are based on the use of the resources of an independent third actor, who makes his or her own contribution to increasing the pool of artefacts.

These moderate consequences already show that rejecting the concept of the abstract IP object does not lead to a rejection of the idea of exclusive rights. Rather, this legal form should also be retained for the area of law of interest here, since it forms the basis of a decentralised market and social structure (see Section 6.1). Consequently, this book supports exclusive rights to perform certain acts – to produce and use Secondary Artefacts. On the one hand, the fact that exclusive

---

[82] Rotstein, 68 Chicago-Kent L. Rev. 725, 795 (1993) ('By contrast, the interests at stake may seem far different if a copyright infringement case is viewed as a resolution of the competing right of speakers to engage in acts of speech – a more realistic view in light of contemporary literary thought'.).

[83] BGH 19 November 2015 Case no. I ZR 149/14, GRUR 2016, 725 para. 28; Peukert, *Güterzuordnung* 812 et seq.

rights to act have always been judged sceptically in modern, liberal legal orders fits well with the instrumental understanding of IP law advocated herein. On the other hand, the French Revolution has in principle cleared up such privileges and monopoly rights and replaced them by property rights in idealised, abstract objects.[84] In the absence of other models, the concept defended here therefore amounts to a renaissance of the early modern privilege – albeit not in the sense of the historical privilege system that was embedded in an absolutist-hierarchical social order, but in the sense of a statutory-based, fungible, temporally, territorially and objectively limited privilege to exploit a Master Artefact.

1.5 TERMINOLOGY AND PRECONCEPTIONS

This right will not be referred to in Josef Kohler's terms as an *Immaterialgüterrecht* (right in immaterial goods) because the notion of an immaterial, abstract good/object will prove to be an ontologically misleading and normatively problematic fiction. There is, however, a lack of appropriate terminology to articulate the actual effects of the rights addressed here. In the absence of better alternatives, exclusive rights to exploit reproducible artefacts are hereinafter referred to as 'IP rights'. This way of speaking has the advantage that it follows on from current language practice and makes what is being referred to immediately understandable. Even in German-speaking countries, *Immaterialgüter* (immaterial goods) and rights in these immaterial goods are increasingly referred to as 'IP' (intellectual property) or IP law. It is true that this terminology is also infected by the dominant paradigm of the abstract IP object. Nevertheless, the term 'intellectual property' and even more its abbreviation 'IP' are so in need of elaboration that, at least in the German-speaking world, it can be understood as an action- and artefact-based understanding. However, the author is aware that this is a potentially misleading crutch that is only used where the textual flow requires it.

Accordingly, for the purposes of the following investigation, IP rights are defined as transferable exclusive rights to produce and otherwise use reproducible Master Artefacts. I use the terms 'work', 'invention', 'design', 'sign' etc. in the sense of a general signifier for sufficiently similar artefacts (abstraction level 1), but not in the sense of an abstract IP object as a further abstraction (level 2). Secondary Artefacts are copies and other independently produced artefacts that are sufficiently similar to a Master Artefact for which a claimant is seeking legal protection.

This terminology and the theses outlined in Section 1.4 are valid for all rights which are subsumed internationally in the TRIPS Agreement and in the EU under the term 'intellectual property', i.e. copyrights, rights related to copyright, patents, utility models, plant variety rights, design rights, rights in layout-designs (topographies) of integrated circuits, trademark rights and their respective subject matter, i.e.

---

[84] Section 3.2.2.2.

works, cultural products of all sorts such as phonograms, inventions, plant varieties, designs, topographies, as well as signs signifying products and persons.[85] To the extent necessary, I also take account of adjacent areas of law such as the protection of trade secrets and unpublished personal information. Such a programme can only be realised at a high level of abstraction. As a rule, only the subject matter of the three main areas of IP law – namely literary, scientific and artistic works (copyright law), inventions (patent law), and product signs ('trademarks', trademark law) – is dealt with in greater detail. At first glance, this approach contradicts the project's legal realist approach, which is characterised by scepticism towards abstractions from reality. Yet my comprehensive programme is the inevitable downside of the equally comprehensive claim of the ruling paradigm, which understands all the objects of protection mentioned as abstract IP objects and regulates them in a proprietary manner. The fact that necessary differentiations are lost in this process can only become an issue if an equally holistic approach is adopted.

Trademark law deserves particular scrutiny. This area of law is interesting because it is generally omitted from ontological and historical studies of the subject matter of IP rights.[86] In addition, trademark rights play a special role in comparison to all other IP rights in several respects, which can be explained in the context of the theory presented here. Firstly, they do not concern a technical-creative innovation. Unlike rights in innovations, trademark law does not have the purpose of increasing the number of distinctive signs. Rather, the aim is to ensure undistorted competition, free from misleading and unfair aggression, which promises a diversified, high-quality range of products.[87] Secondly, it is unclear and controversial what the subject matter of trademark law actually is: the sign in its classical and specific function as a guarantee of identity of origin;[88] the reputation or goodwill which the sign evokes in the mind of the relevant public;[89] or the investment in the

---

[85] See Art. 1(2) TRIPS; Statement by the European Commission of 13 April 2005 (2005/295/EC), 2005 O.J. (L 94/37); Peukert, in Jürgen Basedow et al. (eds.) *I Handwörterbuch Europäisches Privatrecht* 648 et seq. with further references.

[86] Biron, in Goldhammer et al. (eds.) *Geistiges Eigentum im Verfassungsstaat* 127, 132.

[87] CJEU Case C-265/09 OHIM v. BORCO-Marken-Import, ECLI:EU:C:2010:508 with further references; CJEU Case C-51/10 OHIM v. Technopol, ECLI:EU:C:2011:139; CJEU Case C-48/09 OHIM v. Lego, ECLI:EU:C:2010:516; In re Trade-Mark Cases, 100 US 82, 94 (1879); Ty Inc. v. Ruth Perryman, 7th Cir. (2002); Dogan & Lemley, 97 The Trademark Reporter 1223 et seq. (2007).

[88] *Cf.* Art. 15(4) TRIPS; In re Trade-Mark Cases, 100 US 82, 95 (1879) ('The argument is that the use of a trade-mark – that which alone gives it any value – is to identify a particular class or quality of goods as the manufacture, produce, or property of the person who puts them in the general market for sale'); CJEU Case C-689/15 W. F. Gözze v. Verein Bremer Baumwollbörse, ECLI:EU:C:2017:434.

[89] *Cf.* Bone, 86 Boston University L. Rev. 547, 567–68 (2006). ('goodwill was the property and the mark merely a device to reap its benefits'); Beebe, *in* Dinwoodie & Janis (eds.) *Trademark Law and Theory* 42, 47.

brand?[90] The view taken here promises to contribute to a better understanding of the hybrid status of trademark law between IP and unfair competition law, i.e. a non-proprietary, activity-based body of law.[91] At the same time, trademark law offers excellent illustrative material for testing the explanatory power of an action- and artefact-based approach.

Before this program is carried out, the following preconception must be disclosed. I understand this project as an exercise in realism in a double sense. Firstly, the analysis of the law should be realistic. This means that the mode of operation and evolution of law can only be understood if its possibly imagined subject matter is fully understood, whereas a purely internal, legal point of view tends to ascend to heights of abstraction far removed from non-legal reality, from which conceptual-legal nonsense is proclaimed.[92] Therefore, like other legal realist currents, I rely on insights of other sciences about law's reality.[93] These are primarily philosophy (ontology) and history. In this respect, a second realism takes its place. For I rely on analyses that assume that there is an observer-independent physical reality about which epistemically objective statements can be formulated. This is true in particular for the social ontology of John R. Searle, who starts from the existence of only one world consisting entirely of physical particles and defends this realism also and especially with regard to the institutional reality generated by human beings through language.[94] Realistic in the sense understood here is a preconception that does *not* proceed from the existence of immaterial, abstract objects.[95]

In contrast, this study is not intended as a contribution to critical legal studies. I am assuming that law has its own status, which can be distinguished from its non-legal subject matter. Only the distinction between law and non-law makes it possible to look at the reality regulated by the law and to identify normativity which may be inherent in that non-legal reality, and which remains a non-legal normativity. In this way, a much more differentiated picture of the legal and non-legal reality can be

---

[90] CJEU Case C-487/07 L'Oréal v. Bellure, ECLI:EU:C:2009:378; CJEU Case C-323/09 Interflora v. Marks & Spencer, ECLI:EU:C:2011:604; Fezer, *Markenrecht Introduction C* paras 8–10, Introduction D, Section 14 German Trademark Act (MarkenG) para. 144.

[91] See Beebe, in Dinwoodie & Janis (eds.) *Trademark Law and Theory* 42 et seq.; Bently, in Dinwoodie & Janis (eds.) *Trademark Law and Theory* 118 et seq.; Peukert, *Festschrift Fezer* 405 et seq.

[92] Critical Ross, 58 Tidsskrift for Rettsvitenskap 321, 340, 352 (1945); Cohen, 35 Columbia L. Rev. 809, 815 (1935). German locus classicus: Jhering, Scherz und Ernst 245 et seq.

[93] *Cf.* Eller, 97 KritV 191, 197 (2014) with further references. On differences between the American and the Scandinavian legal realism Ross, *On Law and Justice* 68–69.

[94] Searle, *The Construction of Social Reality* 6; Searle, *Making the Social World* 6, 43; contra Berger & Luckmann, *The Social Construction of Reality* 49–50 ('Social order, needless to add, is also not given in man's natural environment, though particular features of this may be factors in determining certain featurers of a social order').

[95] Proponents of classical object ontology use the term 'realism' in the exact opposite sense. According to this view, a realist theory assumes that abstract objects (types) do exist beyond human cognition and communication. See Reicher, 61 DZPhil 219, 226–27 (2013); Marinkovic, *Sprache – Geltung – Recht* 89.

drawn than under the assumption that everything is politics.[96] Furthermore, not everything that exists is constructed. Searle's social ontology teaches us that alongside linguistic-social constructions such as money, property and – as we shall see – the abstract IP object, there is a reality of raw, observer-independent facts whose existence and properties cannot be eliminated by even the most elaborate (de)constructions.

Regarding my understanding of purely legal aspects of property and especially of IP rights, I refer the reader to earlier writings. In those writings, I have explained in particular that the content and the limits of exclusive property rights do not derive from the 'nature' or 'essence' of the allocated object, but rather from the statutes.[97] These statutes can only achieve their aims if there is an accurate, realistic idea of the reality they address. This, however, is precisely not the case in IP law.

---

[96] On this characteristic of critical theory, see Eller, 3 KritV 191, 196 et seq. (2014) with further references.
[97] Art. 14(1) sentence 2 German Basic Law (GG) and Peukert, *Güterzuordnung* 37 et seq., 891 et seq.

2

Two Ontologies

In order to substantiate this scepticism, two different understandings of reality will be presented and critically analysed in the following. One tries to make the subject matter of IP rights (IPRs) understandable as abstract objects (see Section 2.1); the other recognises only brute and social facts as existing (see Section 2.2).

2.1 THE ONTOLOGY OF ABSTRACT OBJECTS

2.1.1 *Characteristics and Application to Intellectual Property*

While the ontological status of the abstract IP object is only rarely – and then rather casually – discussed among lawyers, there is a comprehensive philosophical literature that deals with the ontology of the work of art in particular.[1] Its reception in copyright and IP law literature is already overdue because its proponents explicitly refer to the law and its understanding of the work of art.[2]

Within philosophy, this literary genre belongs to ontology, i.e. to the teaching of that which exists, its possibility and classification.[3] This philosophical discipline, still called 'general metaphysics' today, continues in a certain way – albeit often with new terms – the thousand-year-old dispute between Platonists/universalists and nominalists.[4] However, language now plays a central role in this debate. For it is agreed that reality cannot be recognised immediately and, moreover, can only be

---

[1] See Livingston, *in* Zalta (ed.) *The Stanford Encyclopedia of Philosophy*; *see also* Pettersson, *The Idea of a Text* 159 et seq.
[2] Ortland & Schmücker, 12 German L.J. 1762, 1767 (2005); Hick, 51 British Journal of Aesthetics 185, 188 (2011); Bahr, 61 DZPhil 283, 285 (2013).
[3] Meixner, *Einführung in die Ontologie* 9; Reicher, *in* Schmücker (ed.) *Identität und Existenz. Studien zur Ontologie der Kunst* 180 et seq.
[4] *Cf.* Künne, *Abstrakte Gegenstände* 100 et seq.; Meixner, *Einführung in die Ontologie* 86 et seq.; Wreen, 93 The Monist 433, 441–42 (2010); Pottage & Sherman, *Figures of Invention* 4–5.

communicated using the vehicle of language. In view of these epistemological difficulties, today's descriptive ontology does not claim to grasp and articulate the immediate being. Rather, it is a matter of explaining which entities are presumed to exist in our language practice.[5] The proponents of this relatively weak variant of metaphysics are well aware that signifiers are only uncertain indicators of the existence of the signified.[6] Nevertheless, they assume that each everyday, general term prima facie represents an existing object.[7] In other words, they operate with a presumption of the existence of the signified, which is apparently based on the supposition that an established language practice is unlikely to be based on an error.

These assumptions also underlie the ontological studies of 'the' work of art. These aim to explicate what is implied in the speech practice and everyday common sense concept of 'the' work prevailing since the eighteenth century.[8] Accordingly, ontological studies of art confirm and explain the often only implicit understanding of lawyers that the object of protection of copyright and other IP rights is not a concrete corporeal object, but an immaterial good.[9] In this respect, recent literature, especially Anglo-Saxon literature, often distinguishes between types and tokens.[10] A token (also called manifestation or instantiation) is an event with corporeal properties that occurs at a certain point in time at a certain location.[11] In the case of the copyrighted work, these are physical entities such as books, digital files, code, personal performances on stage etc., as well as mental states or occurrences of thought among authors and recipients who acutely perceive or remember those physical artefacts or performances.[12] It is important to stress that the latter mental states are also perceived as corporeally existent, measurable entities in the human brain.[13] Under no circumstances do tokens have a non-corporeal, 'intellectual' existence.

---

[5] On the difference between descriptive and revisionist ontology, see Wilson, 93 The Monist 450, 451 (2010).

[6] Meixner, Einführung in die Ontologie 32.

[7] Meixner, Einführung in die Ontologie 33; Künne, Abstrakte Gegenstände 310; critical Rudner, 10 Philosophy and Phenomenological Research 380, 386 (1950).

[8] See Pudelek, in Barck et al. (eds.) Ästhetische Grundbegriffe VI 563–64; Schmücker, Was ist Kunst? 267; Reicher, in Schmücker (ed.) Identität und Existenz. Studien zur Ontologie der Kunst 180, 182; Reicher, 61 DZPhil 219, 227–28 (2013). Regerding patentable inventions see Chin, 74 University of Pittsburgh L. Rev. 263 (2012).

[9] Pettersson, The Idea of a Text 2, 164.

[10] Shiffrin, in Goodin et al. (eds.) A Companion to Contemporary Political Philosophy 653, 654.

[11] Schmücker, Was ist Kunst? 171, 206; Reicher, in Schmücker (ed.) Identität und Existenz. Studien zur Ontologie der Kunst 180; Reicher, 61 DZPhil 219, 226 (2013).

[12] Schmücker, Was ist Kunst? 206 et seq., 235; Reicher, in Schmücker (ed.) Identität und Existenz. Studien zur Ontologie der Kunst 180, 181; Reicher, 61 DZPhil 219, 226 (2013); Reicher, in Malcher et al. (eds.) Fragmentarität als Problem der Kultur- und Textwissenschaften 211, 222.

[13] BGH 27 March 1969 Case no. X ZB 15/67, GRUR 1969, 672–73; Zech, Information als Schutzgegenstand 31.

This abstract level is only reached with 'types'. This philosophical technical term is used to describe predicative and non-predicative universals such as the type 'motor vehicle' in contrast to a specific embodiment of a motor vehicle (token), the type 'Goethe's *Faust*' in contrast to a printed exemplar and, even more generally, the concept of a work under copyright in contrast to a specific work and its 'manifestations'.[14] According to an idealistic-Platonic understanding, abstract types exist neither materially/corporeally nor mentally in space and time. Consequently, they are not physically perceptible.[15] These non-corporeal types, decoupled from space and time, also include works and other IP objects.[16] Accordingly, IP is considered 'ownership of a type, not of a specific thing'.[17] This type is realised/manifested/embodied in corporeal and mental tokens, but not identical with them. Types exist as abstract objects independent of whether and how they are realised.[18] Or by recourse to economic analysis: '[IP] objects are ideas in the Platonic sense, since they are imperishable. They are not worn out by their use and can be used by an infinite number of users. As economists say, they are not rival goods'.[19]

2.1.2 *Metaphysics: An Obsolete Anachronism?*

Such an ontology faces serious fundamental objections. First, the traditional philosophical dispute between universalists and nominalists has long found itself in an argumentative dead-end. While universalists must allow themselves to be accused – and, in part, openly admit – that their ontological preconception amounts to a non-falsifiable belief in the existence of objects that cannot be physically perceived,[20]

---

[14] *See generally* Meixner, Einführung in die Ontologie 85; Hick, 51 British Journal of Aesthetics 185, 188 (2011).
[15] Reicher, 61 DZPhil 219, 226–27 (2013), Reicher, *in* Schmücker (ed.) *Identität und Existenz. Studien zur Ontologie der Kunst* 180; Schmücker, *Was ist Kunst?* 237.
[16] Reicher, *in* Schmücker (ed.) *Identität und Existenz. Studien zur Ontologie der Kunst* 180, 182; Reicher, 61 DZPhil 219, 227–28 (2013); Reicher, *in* Malcher et al. (eds.) *Fragmentarität als Problem der Kultur- und Textwissenschaften* 211, 219 (ontological commitment); Ortland & Schmücker, 12 German L.J. 1762, 1767 (2005); Merkl, *Der Begriff des Immaterialgüterrechts* 72–73; Biron, 93 The Monist 382, 384 (2010); Biron, *in* Goldhammer et al. (eds.) *Geistiges Eigentum im Verfassungsstaat* 127, 133 et seq.; Hick, 51 British Journal of Aesthetics 185, 188 (2011).
[17] Reicher, 61 DZPhil, 219, 227–28 (2013).
[18] Carnap, *The Logical Structure of the World* no. 24; Patzig, *in* Schmücker (ed.) *Identität und Existenz. Studien zur Ontologie der Kunst* 107, 112; Reicher, 61 DZPhil 219, 227 (2013) with further references; Reicher, *in* Schmücker (ed.) *Identität und Existenz. Studien zur Ontologie der Kunst* 180; Bahr, 61 DZPhil 283, 285 (2013); Levinson, 77 The Journal of Philosophy 5–6 (1980) ('widespread consensus that a musical work is in fact a variety of abstract object . . ., a structural type or kind').
[19] Translated from the original German. Steinvorth, 52 DZPhil 708, 728 (2004); *cf. also* Madison, 19 J. Intell. Prop. L. 1, 16 (2012).
[20] Patzig, *in* Schmücker (ed.) *Identität und Existenz. Studien zur Ontologie der Kunst* 107, 117 (dogmatism); Reicher, *in* Klauk & Köppe (eds.) *Fiktionalität* 159, 176; Dilworth, 66 Journal of Aesthetics and Art Criticism 341, 349 (2008) (opposing view 'metaphysically impossible');

nominalists are exposed to the equally fatal accusation of an infinite regress if they want to establish and explain similarities between tokens.[21] It seems that the circularity of the arguments of both camps can ultimately be attributed to the fact that the classical metaphysical discussion of the existing ignores the irreversible blind spot of the speaker, and thus the paradox that a reality is described to which the observer belongs and can therefore never completely grasp.[22] Furthermore, classical metaphysics argues ahistorically, although its proponents admit that the problem of universals was discussed differently at different times.[23] In this way, classical object ontology ignores the fact that social facts – such as a certain language practice or a common sense understanding, from which ontological analysis proceeds – cannot be understood without the historical process in which they arose.[24] The same applies to the cultural context in which individual words and language exercises are embedded and from which they must be analysed.[25]

Because of these difficulties, general metaphysics has long since moved to the margins of contemporary philosophy. It is even claimed that it operates with a form of knowledge that has become incomprehensible. For Niklas Luhmann, classical ontology is the philosophy of the hierarchically stratified ancient and medieval society, whose static mode of being was explained. But since this form of society has been replaced by a completely differently structured, functionally differentiated society, general metaphysics is an anachronism for which Luhmann has nothing but ridicule.[26] Foucault's epistemology comes to the same result. The proponents of object ontology either practice a 'traditional' form of knowledge based on things – according to which a complete correspondence between language and things is assumed – or they attribute to language the 'classical' idea of being able to really represent things. According to Foucault, both epistemes have become incomprehensible or are insufficient. In particular, the language-based, social world cannot be explained without consideration of its genesis.[27]

However, it would be wrong simply to ignore the findings of the ontology of art.[28] For in current copyright law at least, and probably also in art theory and practice,

---

Drahos, *Philosophy of IP* 153 ('A belief in the existence of abstract objects may simply turn out to be false'.)

[21] See Wreen, 93 The Monist 433, 447–48 (2010); Bahr, 61 DZPhil 283, 285 (2013) with note 10.
[22] *John & Rückert-John & Esposito*, in John et al. (eds.) *Ontologien der Moderne* 7–8; on the interpretation of texts see Barthes, in Barthes (ed.) *Image Music Text* 155, 164.
[23] Meixner, *Einführung in die Ontologie* 199 et seq.
[24] Berger & Luckmann, *The Social Construction of Reality* 52, 90.
[25] Hess-Lüttich & Rellstab, in Barck et al. (eds.) *Ästhetische Grundbegriffe* VI 247, 261.
[26] Luhmann, *Gesellschaft der Gesellschaft* 893–912.
[27] See Foucault, *The Order of Things* 29, 74, 101; sceptical already Rudner, 10 Philosophy and Phenomenological Research 380 et seq. (1950).
[28] George, 7(1) W.I.P.O.J. 16 (2015) ('Without mindfulness of its metaphysics, the law risks incoherence and internal inconsistencies'.); O'Connor, 27 George Mason Law Review 205, 261 (2019) (wider appreciation for the different kinds of property at play in the field of IP needed).

one indeed speaks and thinks as if the work of art exists independently of its manifestations in physical exemplars, performances and individual memories. This common sense is a social reality that is analysed and explained by proponents of the ontology of art. Niklas Luhmann's contradictory definition of the artwork also confirms that there is a need for this. On the one hand, Luhmann describes the artwork as 'the last unit of the art system that cannot be further decomposed', which is 'nothing but an object'.[29] On the other hand, the artwork is supposed to be a 'compact communication', which Luhmann defines not as an 'object', but as an 'event'.[30] The inadequate theorisation of the artwork is further demonstrated by the fact that Luhmann pays little attention to the relationship between the artistic system and the economic system. The abstract work of art unfolds its meaning precisely at this neuralgic point: as an object of IPRs that in turn institutionalise the transactions of the economic system.[31]

If one seeks to understand this legal-economic function of the abstract IP object, one must not shy away from ontological questions. In other words, the ontological project remains meaningful as long as the idea of the abstract IP object is effective. With their categorical rejection of metaphysical questions, proponents of contemporary social theories run the risk of ignoring important social facts only because they are based on 'traditional', 'classical' or 'modern' ideas, and can only be understood as such. If anything has become obsolete in the context here, then it is not the ontology of art, but its object of investigation: the abstract 'work', forming a closed unit.

2.1.3 *The Implausibility of the Abstract IP Object*

A closer examination of the literature on art ontology reveals, however, that it cannot hold out its thesis that the copyrightable work exists as an abstract type without contradiction. Works and other abstract IP objects do not have the characteristics that define types/universals according to general metaphysics. But then, for reasons of internal theoretical consistency, they cannot be considered as abstract objects.

First, according to classical metaphysical assumptions, universals such as Pythagoras' theorem are characterised by double acausality. They are neither the consequence of other events, nor do they have any effect. Only on the basis of this assumption can they exist independently of real life occurrences and various manifestations (tokens).[32] Works, inventions, product names and other objects of protection under IP law do not, however, exhibit such acausality. They are the result of

---

[29] Translated from the original German. Luhmann, in Gumbrecht & Pfeiffer (eds.) *Stil* 620, 627; Luhmann, *Kunst der Gesellschaft* 61–62.
[30] Luhmann, in Gumbrecht & Pfeiffer (eds.) *Stil* 620, 627; Luhmann, *Kunst der Gesellschaft* 63.
[31] On the function of property in the economic system Luhmann, *Wirtschaft der Gesellschaft* 188 et seq.
[32] See Chapter 2 note 15.

human action and in this respect artefacts.[33] It is the very purpose of IP law to reward and incentivise innovation and investment in products. In contrast, the discovery of natural correlations, scientific theories, mathematical methods 'as such' always remain in the public domain.[34] Because, one could say from an ontological point of view, they do not change the world, but only describe it.[35] The mere discovery or explanation of the world does not justify an IP right, because even the one who decodes it does not create a new reality. Only those who, through their actions, create a new and sensually perceptible reality that is subject to the laws of causality – an artefact[36] – has prospects of legal protection. Consequently, Frege's problematic assumption that the truth of the Pythagorean theorem, for example, indicates its eternal existence[37] independent of human actualisation and other manifestation, does not support the assumption that IPRs also protect abstract objects. In any case, 'truth' is not a prerequisite for IP protection and therefore not a feature of current IP rights. Ultimately, innovations and trademarks are not only brought about, but in turn unfold effects. They are perceived, (mis)understood, used, further developed, discussed etc.

Secondly, the existence of works and other IP subject matter is limited in time. Also in this respect they differ fundamentally from traditional universals such as Plato's Ideas and Frege's Thoughts, which have 'always' been there and, according to Platonists, will exist forever, completely independent of human activities.[38] However, this does not apply to the objects of copyright and industrial property

---

[33] Margolis, 36 The Journal of Aesthetics and Art Criticism 45, 49 (1977) ('artworks are culturally emergent entities'); Schmücker, *Was ist Kunst?* 251, 254–55; Livingston, in Zalta (ed.) *The Stanford Encyclopedia of Philosophy* no. 3.1; Hick, 51 British Journal of Aesthetics 185, 186 (2011); Biron, 93 The Monist 382, 385 (2010).

[34] See Sections 1(3) no. 1, no. 3 German Patent Act (PatG); Section 1(2) German Utility Model Act (GebrMG); Art. 52(2) EPC in conjunction with Art. II Section 6(1) no. 1 German International Patent Law Act (IntPatÜbkG); Art. 9(2) TRIPS, Art. 2 WCT; Alice Corp. v. CLS Bank International, 134 S.Ct. 2347, 2350 (2014); Peukert, *Gemeinfreiheit* 20 et seq.; Kevles, 23 Perspectives on Science 13 et seq. (2015).

[35] Biron, 93 The Monist 382, 384 (2010); Feist Publications, Inc. v. Rural Telephone Service Co., 499 US 340, 347 (1991) ('Facts do not owe their origin to an act of authorship. The distinction is one between creation and discovery: The first person to find and report a particular fact has not created the fact; he or she has merely discovered its existence'); Hughes, 83 Notre Dame L. Rev. 43 et seq. (2007). On the exclusion of patentability for 'presentations of information' according to Section 1(3) no. 4 German Patent Act (PatG) – see BGH 27 September 2016 Case no. X ZR 124/15, GRUR 2017, 261 para. 17.

[36] On the concept of artefacts see Reicher, in Malcher et al. (eds.) *Fragmentarität als Problem der Kultur- und Textwissenschaften* 211, 215 (intentionally produced things); Reicher, 61 DZPhil 219, 220 (2013) (artificially created); Bahr, 61 DZPhil 283, 284 (2013); Zahrádka, 65 Filosofický časopis 739, 743 (2017). Breedings and genetically engineered organisms are also new artefacts in this broad sense.

[37] Frege, *Logical Investigations* 7, 25–30; Schmücker, *Was ist Kunst?* 255. Frege's extrapolation from truth to abstract existence is problematic because the assumption of a definately verified truth is problematic.

[38] Reicher, 61 DZPhil 219, 228 (2013).

rights.[39] These are created by authors and inventors and used by companies as trademarks at a certain point in time, even if the precise point in time may no longer be ascertainable. Without a first artefact, it makes no sense to say that a work, a soundtrack, a model, a fantasy mark or a consumer image of the origin or quality of a product exists.[40] The existence of a work and other IP objects can also come to an end – as confirmed by countless historical examples of lost writings, of which only the title has survived, and which is illustrated by a small thought experiment. Let us assume that someone writes a poem of which he does not make a copy and whose wording he forgets. Due to unfortunate circumstances, the manuscript is burned before the poem reaches the public performance or printing stage, so there is no one who knows the wording. Could one say that the poem still exists?[41] 'No' is the realistic answer of most art ontologists. Works and other IP objects exist only 'as long as there is at least one physical object in which they ... manifest themselves'.[42] This applies not only to artworks. Technologies, designs, signs, even spoken words and – as history shows – entire languages can also be lost.[43] Only the probability that this event will occur diverges. The more known an artefact is, and the more copies there are of it, the smaller is the probability that the last physical or mental exemplar will be lost.

Third, the temporary nature of works and other subject matter of IP rights demonstrates that they are generally linked to the existence of their 'embodiments'. In other words, there is no type without a corresponding token. Thus, the context of existence does not run from the abstract IP object to its 'manifestations', but – in a way that will have to be explained in more detail – conversely from the brute physical and mental facts to the work, the invention etc.[44] Or, in the words of

---

[39] Schmücker, *Was ist Kunst?* 251 (historicity of artworks); Reicher, 61 DZPhil 219, 228 (2013).
[40] Section 3.1.1, Section 5.1.2 and Schmücker, *Was ist Kunst?* 255; Reicher, *in* Malcher et al. (eds.) *Fragmentarität als Problem der Kultur- und Textwissenschaften* 211, 221; Zahrádka, 65 Filosofický časopis 739, 740 (2017).
[41] Schmücker, *Was ist Kunst?* 257; for a similar thought experiment *see* Peukert, *Güterzuordnung* 39.
[42] Translated from the original German. Schmücker, *Was ist Kunst?* 258; Patzig, *in* Schmücker (ed.) *Identität und Existenz. Studien zur Ontologie der Kunst* 107, 111; Zahrádka, 65 Filosofický časopis 739, 749 (2017); *see also* v. Wächter, *Das Urheberrecht an Werken der bildenden Künste, Photographien und gewerblichen Mustern* 151 (copyright lapses with the destruction of all exemplars of a work); Höffner, *Geschichte und Wesen des Urheberrechts II* 321; Zech, *Information als Schutzgegenstand* 38, 40; *contra* Reicher, *in* Malcher et al. (eds.) *Fragmentarität als Problem der Kultur- und Textwissenschaften* 211, 225 (abstract artefacts cannot be destroyed); *see also* Merkl, *Der Begriff des Immaterialgüterrechts* 79 (abstract IP objects as platonic ideas).
[43] On words and languages *see* Hilpinen, 93 Proceedings of the Aristotelian Society 155, 173 et seq. (1993); Patzig, *in* Schmücker (ed.) *Identität und Existenz. Studien zur Ontologie der Kunst* 107, 108; Schmücker, *Was ist Kunst?* 267 et seq.
[44] Hartmann, *Das Problem des geistigen Seins* 411 (there is no art without physical things); Hubmann, *Das Recht des schöpferischen Geistes* 46–48 (intellectual and material layer of artworks); Zech, *Information als Schutzgegenstand* 45; Reicher, *in* Schmücker (ed.) *Identität und Existenz. Studien zur Ontologie der Kunst* 180, 181; Kölbel, 10 Text. Kritische Beiträge 27,

economists Boldrin and Levine: '[N]ew valuable ideas are always embodied in either people or things'.[45] This observation is also mandatory from a legal point of view. For IP rights legitimately only regulate human behaviour that is perceptible and otherwise possible.[46] The prevailing opinion, however, postulates an object that is completely independent of human states of consciousness and fixations in books, products etc. It is not clear how right holders and third parties should control such an abstract object and make it the object of their legally regulated behaviour, if not mediated by a concrete action or a physical artefact with spatial-temporal existence.[47] And indeed, all IP rights – both with regard to the protected subject matter and with regard to the infringing acts – are linked without exception to such brute facts which are subject to human will.[48] Most IP cases concern tangible or corporeal, but in any case physically measurable things, such as analogue or digital writings, drawings and other representations, pictures, computer programs, products such as machines and consumer goods, as well as signs affixed thereto, on packaging, business letters etc.[49] In other cases, human states of consciousness,

---

32 (2005); Koepsell, *The Ontology of Cyberspace* 95 ('Ultimately, intellectual property is composed of the same stuff as ordinary property. Expressions exist in the world of physical objects'); Drahos, *Philosophy of IP* 21 (condition of materiality); Ross, 58 Tidsskrift for Rettsvitenskap 321, 340, 346 (1945); Redeker, 10 CR 634, 639 (2011); Steinvorth, 52 DZPhil 708, 728 (2004); Merkl, *Der Begriff des Immaterialgüterrechts* 75; Troller, 1 *Immaterialgüterrecht* 55 with note 11; Bergström, 7–8 GRUR Ausl. 364, 365 (1962); Pfister, *Das technische Geheimnis 'Know How' als Vermögensrecht* 11–13; Strömholm, GRUR Int. 481, 489 (1963); van Dijk, *Grounds of the Immaterial* 36; *cf. also* Burk, in Lai & Maget Dominicé (eds.) *Intellectual Property and Access to Im/material Goods* 44 et seq.

[45] Boldrin & Levine, 2 Review of Economic Research on Copyright Issues 45, 49 (2005).

[46] Ulmer, Urheber- und Verlagsrecht 13; BGH 27 March 1969 Case no. X ZB 15/67, GRUR 1969, 67, 673; BGH 30 June 2015 Case no. X ZB 1/15, GRUR 2015, 983 para. 27 (definition of technology).

[47] *Cf.* Merkl, *Der Begriff des Immaterialgüterrechts* 77; People v. Aleynikov, N.Y.S. WL 4110801, 18 (2015) ('Any "reproduction" or "representation" is associated with some physical medium. Whether information is conveyed visually, orally or through some other sense, it must be associated with something in the physical world. The only possible exception would be some kind of extra-sensory communication. But extra-sensory communications, assuming they exist, are certainly not legally cognizable').

[48] See Section 5.1.2.

[49] Regarding copyrightable works *cf.* Microsoft Corp. v. AT & T Corp., 550 US 437, 451 (2007) ('What retailers sell, and consumers buy, are copies of software. Likewise, before software can be contained in and continuously performed by a computer, before it can be updated or deleted, an actual, physical copy of the software must be delivered by CD-ROM or some other means capable of interfacing with the computer'.); Bartsch, 9 CR 2010 553, 554 (2010); Schmücker, Was ist Kunst? 186 et seq. with further references, 199 (distinguishing between transitory (dance), allographic (writings), and autographic (paintings) art.
Regarding patentable products and processes *cf.* BGH 21 August 2012 Case no. X ZR 33/10, GRUR 2012, 1230 para. 23; BGH 27 September 2016 Case no. X ZR 124/15, GRUR 2017, 261 para. 21; Godenhielm, 45 GRUR Int. 327 (1996); Koepsell, *The Ontology of Cyberspace* 93; Carvalko, 2 ABA SciTech Lawyer 7–9 (2005); Lai, in Lai & Dominicé (eds.) *Intellectual Property and Access to Im/material Goods* 94, 95; Houkes & Vermaas, *Technical Functions* 1 et seq.

statements and other concrete actions are of direct relevance for the application of IP law. These actions include spontaneous improvisations of works, happenings and performances in copyright law, oral disclosures of a technology that are prejudicial to patent novelty, as well as the frequently undocumented but ex post reconstructed understandings of the relevant public in trademark law.[50] Also the transmission of copyrighted expressions, technical teachings, product signs and information in general requires the use of measurable energy and physical energy carriers such as sound waves, digital transmission signals, paper, servers etc.[51] According to the prevailing paradigm, all these measurable, brute facts are regarded as merely accidental embodiments of primarily authoritative abstract objects, but which – due to their abstractness – cannot be the subject of legitimate commands or prohibitions.

The aforementioned differences between artworks and traditional universals are recognised by proponents of contemporary art ontology.[52] Nevertheless, they stand by the existence of abstract IP objects. Their more or less understandably formulated reply consists in declaring the work to be an immaterial type of its own kind.[53] This, of course, is nothing but a rhetorical trick that, by creating a new category, wipes out all previously extensively discussed characteristics of abstract objects in order to save the project of a classical metaphysical art ontology.[54]

Just as immune against critique as the assertion of an abstract object *sui generis* is the widespread (albeit often only implicitly expressed) view among twentieth-century copyright lawyers that mental states of consciousness – such as a poem learned by heart, or a book just read – belong to the immaterial world of the 'mind',

---

[50] On the significance of mental states in the creation of IP cf. Zech, Information als Schutzgegenstand 36–37; Schmücker, Was ist Kunst? 206 et seq.; Reicher, in Malcher et al. (eds.) Fragmentarität als Problem der Kultur- und Textwissenschaften 211, 221; Reicher, 61 DZPhil 219, 229 (2013); Patzig, in Schmücker (ed.) Identität und Existenz. Studien zur Ontologie der Kunst 107, 114 –15; Strömholm, GRUR Int. 481, 489 (1963); Kawohl, Urheberrecht der Musik in Preussen 109. On expressions as physical occurances Pettersson, The Idea of a Text 31 et seq. On trademark law cf. Beebe, 51 UCLA L. Rev., 621 (2004) (trademark law).

[51] Wiener, Human Use of Human Beings 24–25; Sterne, The Audible Past 22; Troller, 50 UFITA 385, 401 (1967). Regarding musical works see Ortland, in Polth et al. (eds.) Klang – Struktur – Metapher 3, 17. On digital information storage and transmission cf. BGH 17 February 2004 Case no. X ZB 9/03, GRUR 2004, 495, 497; BGH 21 August 2012 Case no. X ZR 33/10, GRUR 2012, 1230 para. 20; BGH 27 September 2016 Case no. X ZR 124/15, GRUR 2017, 261 para. 21; Sega Enterprises Ltd & Anor v. Galaxy Electronics Pty Ltd & Anor, FCA 761, 69 FCR 268 (1996); Public Relations Consultants Association Ltd v. The Newspaper Licensing Agency Ltd & Ors, UKSC 18 (2013); Ricolfi, in Drahos et al. (eds.), Kritika 1 134, 144.

[52] Reicher, in Malcher et al. (eds.) Fragmentarität als Problem der Kultur- und Textwissenschaften 211, 220 (artefact-types as contingent and temporary matter); Künne, Abstrakte Gegenstände 94; Schmücker, Was ist Kunst? 264–65.

[53] Schmücker, Was ist Kunst? 262; cf. also Troller, 1 Immaterialgüterrecht 55 with note 11; Jänich, Geistiges Eigentum 226–27; Zech, Information als Schutzgegenstand 37.

[54] Pettersson, The Idea of a Text 14 ('clearly illogical'), 166 ('But what sort of thing is a half-abstract and half-concrete entity?').

which as such is the object of 'intellectual' property.[55] However, this 'spiritual science', influenced in particular by Nicolai Hartmann's ontology, is confronted with the naturalistic objection that consciousness is a biological phenomenon that is localised in a human body at a given point in time.[56] Moreover, the concern – which is possibly behind this view – for the maintenance of the fundamental distinction between the legal subject and the legal object, between the person and the thing, has precisely the opposite effect. For by stylising human cognition into an immaterial 'mind' capable of being owned, consciousness/thinking become commodities. In contrast, a physicalist-mentalist approach opens up a perspective on IP rights as the regulation of human thought and action. The physicalist, seemingly objectifying understanding of the 'mind' recognises the person taking action.

Finally, an idealistic-Platonic reconstruction of the abstract IP object proves to be unsustainable even where this approach should actually have its particular strengths – namely in explaining the 'identity' of the work etc. as an independently existing object. If the theory of the abstract IP object would make its being understandable, then the boundaries of this type would also have to become clear. But this is not the case. Proponents of art ontology do not offer a comprehensible definition of 'the' artwork, but on the contrary note its notorious indeterminacy in aesthetic and legal debates. That indeterminacy belongs – so it is succinctly said – simply 'to the essence of types', which only defines 'some, but not all, properties of their realisations'.[57] This is as unproductive an explanation as the reference to unspecified similarities between different exemplars and performances.[58] At the same time, 'the' work, like any other abstract IP object, moves ever closer to Blumenberg's 'absolute metaphor', which – such as 'the state' or 'history' – cannot be illustrated by any exemplar, but which nevertheless (or precisely because of this) unfolds a life of its own and generates and dominates human ideas about the illustrated object.[59]

---

[55] Bluntschli, *Deutsches Privatrecht I* 188 (spoken word as the genuine example of intellectual works); Elster, 6 RabelsZ 903, 914 (1932); Troller, 1 *Immaterialgüterrecht* 55 with note 11; Troller, 50 UFITA 385, 406 (1967); Hubmann, *Das Recht des schöpferischen Geistes* 46–48 (the spirit of the author); Druey, *Information als Gegenstand des Rechts* 102.

[56] On the mind/body problem *see* Searle, *Mind, Language and Society* 39–65; Jefferson, *in* Kurland & Lerner (eds.) 3 *The Founders' Constitution* (the invention as a 'fugitive fermentation of an individual brain'; 'action of the thinking power called an idea, which an individual may exclusively possess as long as he keeps it to himself').

[57] Translated from the original German. Reicher, 61 DZPhil 219, 229 (2013); *see also* George, 7(1) W.I.P.O.J. 16 (2015) ('a metaphysical characteristic of intellectual property objects is that they are intrinsically difficult to survey and their full scope is always to be determined').

[58] Patzig, *in* Schmücker (ed.) *Identität und Existenz. Studien zur Ontologie der Kunst* 107, 115 (what two text interpretations have in common); Schmücker, *Was ist Kunst?* 245 (parodies and imperfect translations no manifestation of a particular work); Zahrádka, 65 Filosofický časopis 739, 753 (2017); Barron, 52 New Formations 58, 69 et seq. (2004).

[59] Translated from the original German. Blumenberg, 6 Archiv für Begriffsgeschichte 7 et seq. (1960).

Whether eleven words count as a copyrightable work,[60] whether a serial novel[61] or a carnival costume intended to evoke associations with a novel character,[62] can be regarded as partial reproductions of the respective originals – the answers to these and other questions on the subject matter and scope of protection of copyright and other IP rights do not follow from an ontological definition of the claimant's work etc., but from a legal evaluation of and comparison between specific artefacts.[63]

2.2 SOCIAL ONTOLOGY

For IP law, the contradictoriness and unproductiveness of the metaphysical ontology of the abstract IP object has potentially far-reaching implications, since its object threatens to become lost. On the one hand we speak, think and regulate as if there were an abstract IP object, and on the other hand the existence of such an object cannot be made plausible.[64] However, this statement means a contradiction only for those who, like the proponents of classical metaphysical object ontology, assume that in case of doubt every common term represents an entity that actually exists. Alternatively, this contradiction dissolves if one assumes that humans can create a reality – such as the reality of the idea of the abstract IP object – that is to some extent decoupled from physical, perceptible facts. Regarding the abstract IP object, this implies that we are dealing with an object that exists only in our language and imagination. A static abstract object that simply exists without a history then becomes an entity that is the result of cultural negotiation processes that take place according to certain norms, including legal norms.[65] An elaborate ontology for such an understanding is provided by US philosopher John R. Searle, who divides being into two classes: An observer-*independent*, 'brute' reality of physically measurable facts on the one hand, and an observer-*dependent*, language-based and constructed, social-institutional reality on the other hand.[66]

---

[60] CJEU Case C-5/08 Infopaq International A/S v. Danske Dagblades Forening, ECLI:EU:C:2009:465.
[61] BGH 29 April 1999 Case no. I ZR 65/96, GRUR 1999, 1984.
[62] BGH 19 November 2015 Case no. I ZR 149/14, GRUR 2016, 725.
[63] Section 5.1.2.2.
[64] See Biron, 93 The Monist 382, 386 (2010) ('Getting rid of types leaves us with an ontological gap for a property object; keeping hold of types seems impossible in light of the fact that we want to say that types cannot be created, but objects of intellectual property can be created. Something has to give'.).
[65] Kulenkampff, *in* Schmücker (ed.) *Identität und Existenz. Studien zur Ontologie der Kunst* 121, 139 (there is no ontological problem of the artwork, just confusing talk about exemplars and performances); Margolis, 36 The Journal of Aesthetics and Art Criticism 45, 49 (1977) ('artworks are culturally emergent entities'); Thomasson, 68 The Journal of Aesthetics and Art Criticism 119–20 (2010) ('the ontological status of artworks is, at bottom, fixed by human intentions and practices').
[66] For an introduction into Searle's oeuvre Kober & Michel, John Searle.

2.2.1 Fundamentals of John Searle's Social Ontology

Searle elaborated his theory mainly in two monographs, published in 1995 and 2010: *The Construction of Social Reality* and *Making the Social World: The Structure of Human Civilization*. Like Searle's earlier works on the philosophy of language[67] or artificial intelligence,[68] these writings have been widely received and have become influential beyond the boundaries of philosophy. The philosophical and social science literature on Searle's ontology is already vast.[69] But in jurisprudence Searle's theses have so far only been taken up sporadically, although Searle emphatically points to the normative dimensions of his analyses.[70] In view of this state of research, the main features of Searle's social ontology will be briefly summarised (Section 2.2.1). This also provides the conceptual framework for the subsequent application of Searle's theory to the phenomenon of abstract IP objects. Neither Searle himself nor – as far as can be seen – the secondary literature on his social ontology have so far closely addressed the status of works, inventions and other IP objects.[71] This omission will be rectified in Section 2.2.2.

With his social ontology, Searle pursues the same research question as proponents of classical metaphysical object ontology. He also seeks to fathom the being of the world and in particular of social facts such as marriage, ownership and money.[72] However, he chooses a different starting point than Platonists and other idealists. According to Searle, there are not two or even three worlds that coexist in a kind of dualism of mind and matter, but only one world that ultimately consists entirely of organic and inorganic matter.[73] This matter has an observable, scientifically measurable existence. According to Searle, a philosophical ontology must keep up with the state of the art in physics, chemistry and biology – in particular with physical

---

[67] Searle, Speech acts.
[68] Searle, 3 Behavioral and Brain Sciences 417 et seq. (1980); with reference to Searle Spindler, 12 CR 766, 767 (2015) with footnote 16 (strong artificial intelligence still a vision for the future).
[69] Miller, in Zalta (ed.) *The Stanford Encyclopedia of Philosphy*; Grewendorf & Meggle, *Speech Acts, Mind, and Social Reality* 245 et seq.; Gross, 6 Anthropological Theory 45 et seq. (2006); Tsohatzidis, *Intentional Acts and Institutional Facts*; Tuomela, Philosophy of Sociality 182 et seq.; Schützeichel, 38 Soziologische Revue 503 et seq. (2015); Gephart & Suntrup (eds.), *Normative Structure of Human Civilization*; Jansen, *Ontologie des Sozialen*; see also Pettersson, *The Idea of a Text* 24–25.
[70] See Searle, in Gephart & Suntrup, *Normative Structure of Human Civilization* 21 et seq.; Gärtner, *Ist das Sollen ableitbar aus dem Sein?* 122 et seq.; *but see* George, *Constructing Intellectual Property* 90–137.
[71] *But see* Hughes, 83 Notre Dame L. Rev. 43, 60–62 (2007); Madison, 56 Case Western Reserve L. Rev. 381 (2005), in particular note 153; without reference to the abstract IP object also Carvalko, 2 ABA SciTech Lawyer 7–9 (2005). George, *Constructing Intellectual Property* 15, 90 et seq., primarily discusses IP *laws/rights* as institutional facts ('How is "intellectual property" constructed within the legal system?').
[72] Searle, *The Construction of Social Reality* 5–6.
[73] Searle, *Making the Social World* 3–4; Tuomela, *Philosophy of Sociality* 210; Ross, *On Law and Justice* 67 ('There is only one world and one cognition'.).

knowledge about the smallest particles and with evolutionary theory.[74] Theories which, like classical metaphysics, proceed from an intangible and thus from the outset epistemically inaccessible world of abstract ideas, thoughts and objects do not fulfil this fundamental requirement, and are therefore ruled out as serious ontological proposals. Likewise, Searle rejects subjective relativism according to which no true statements about reality can be formulated, since in any case everything exists only as a construct in our imagination.[75] Searle therefore assumes that there is a reality about which epistemically objective, true statements can be made that are not dependent on subjective thinking and observation. In this sense, Searle takes a realist perspective.[76]

On this epistemological basis, Searle distinguishes two qualitatively different, but in each case epistemically objective (i.e. not subjectively dependent) categories of facts – namely 'brute' (or 'rude') facts on the one hand, and social or institutional facts on the other. The first category of facts exists regardless of whether people observe, understand and articulate them.[77] This category firstly includes inorganic matter, whether separately tangible things or intangible yet physically measurable, material objects one cannot touch such as electrical energy, sound waves and data or computer programs fixed on a storage medium.[78] Secondly, living systems such as plants, animals and humans also exist independently of observers. While knowledge about this 'brute' reality can be gathered objectively, verifiable phenomena like thoughts, pains, feelings and consciousness take a special role according to widespread opinion, which often evokes an idealistic conception of the 'intellect'.[79] This dualism between the intellect and the physical is also rejected by Searle. According to the findings of natural science, consciousness, for example, is a biological and therefore physical property of certain higher-order organic systems. The mental states mentioned can often only be perceived by the affected living being. According to Searle, however, this ontological subjectivity is no reason for the assumption that an objective, secure knowledge cannot be gained about consciousness, thoughts etc., which proves and explains the brute existence of these facts, just as it can be gained about inorganic matter. Advances in neurological research that have made brain processes visible and locatable speak for Searle's physical understanding of the mind.[80]

In addition to all these brute facts, there is a second category of facts among humans, namely the facts that Searle calls 'institutional'.[81] They also have an

---

[74] Searle, *The Construction of Social Reality* 6; Searle, *Making the Social World* 42, 43.
[75] Searle, *Making the Social World* 4; Giddens, 53 Social Research 529, 534 (1986).
[76] Searle, *The Construction of Social Reality* 34–35, 190–94.
[77] Searle, *The Construction of Social Reality* 15.
[78] Peukert, *in* Leible et al. (eds.) *Unkörperliche Güter im Zivilrecht* 95 et seq.
[79] See Chapter 2 notes 44–45.
[80] Searle, *in* Gephart & Suntrup (eds.) *Normative Structure of Human Civilization* 21, 22.
[81] Searle, *Making the Social World* 17; Tuomela, *Philosophy of Sociality* 182 et seq.

epistemic objective existence. They exist, and not only in the opinion of individuals.[82] In contrast to brute facts such as a piece of paper, however, these facts are observer-dependent. This means that they only exist because people speak, think and act as if these facts existed. Searle's preferred example of such an institutional fact is money.[83] A ten-euro note, for example, is initially only a piece of paper. Due to various declarations and social practices, however, this piece of brute reality is regarded as a means of payment in certain places and under certain conditions. This function does not add anything to brute reality, to organic or inorganic matter. The piece of paper is and remains a piece of paper. But, in an act of collective intentionality, people assign this paper a specific function that is not immanent to the piece of paper, i.e. does not follow from its scientifically measurable properties.[84] And indeed, the possibility of using a piece of paper as a means of payment depends solely on people recognising it as such – as money. This social fact cannot be explained by hard science. So money and other institutional facts such as ownership (property in the legal sense), marriage, police etc. must have a different ontological status than brute, experimentally measurable facts.

Searle's key to understanding such social facts is language.[85] For Searle, language is the condition of possibility of civilisation. It is language that distinguishes humans from animals, and allows them to develop complex conventions and other institutions such as money. As soon as there is a common language, there is already (so to speak) a social contract – because in large parts what one can say and how one says it is fixed. Communication, in turn, is the specific characteristic of society,[86] which occurs in utterances – be they ephemeral or fixed in written documents, analogue or digital images and sounds – as well as in other representations such as clothing or jewellery (e.g. a wedding ring).[87]

Up to this point one might think that Searle's social ontology offers nothing but old sociological wine in new, language-analytical bottles. And in fact it is one of the basic tenets of sociology that religious and other beliefs are of the highest importance for society, that they actually constitute social reality and thus

---

[82] Berger & Luckmann, *The Social Construction of Reality* 57–58; Luhmann, *Gesellschaft der Gesellschaft* 34–35.
[83] On money see also Blumenberg, *Theorie der Unbegrifflichkeit* 54; Tuomela, *Philosophy of Sociality* 182 et seq.
[84] See also Tuomela, *Philosophy of Sociality* 204.
[85] Searle, *The Construction of Social Reality* 59–78; Searle, *Making the Social World* 62–63; Searle, in Gephart & Suntrup (eds.), *Normative Structure of Human Civilization* 21, 29; Miller, in Zalta (ed.) *The Stanford Encyclopedia of Philosphy*; Giddens, 53 Social Research 529, 534 (1986); Wiener, *Human Use of Human Beings* 85 et seq.; Luhmann, *Gesellschaft der Gesellschaft* 205 et seq.
[86] Luhmann, *Gesellschaft der Gesellschaft* 80; Baecker, in Barck et al. (eds.) *Ästhetische Grundbegriffe III* 384, 404 (communication as construction of the social).
[87] Ong, *Orality and Literacy* 66–67.

separate it from external reality.[88] Of course, society cannot be explained by the laws of nature.

But this criticism underestimates the explanatory power of Searle's language-analytical approach. Searle is not a sociologist, but a proponent of the analytical philosophy of language. It is therefore no coincidence that for him the key to understanding social reality lies not in actions, conventions, ideas or functions, but in language. This starting point is supported by his unchallenged, true observation that there are language communities that do not know certain social facts (such as paper money) but that, conversely, there is no society that has paper money but not a common language.[89] And to understand this basal societal level, it requires an elaborate language analysis, which Searle can offer, in contrast to sociological theories from Durkheim to Berger and Luckmann and beyond.

According to Searle's theory of language, one has to distinguish several types of speech acts, each of which relates differently to brute, extra-linguistic reality and which therefore has a special significance in the construction of social reality. Through an 'assertive' speech act, a speaker communicates that something is the case. Like, 'snow is white' or 'this is a copy of Goethe's *Faust*'. According to Searle, such speech acts have a word-to-world orientation. The words should fit to external reality, represent it in language. Assertive speech acts are epistemically objective, they can be true or false. The situation is different if a speaker tells the listener what to do or not to do (directive speech act), or if someone commits themselves to future behaviour (commissive speech act, such as a promise). According to Searle, such speech acts express a reversed, namely world-to-word intentionality. The world should fit with the word. Therefore, at the moment of their utterance, such messages cannot be true or false. Rather, one can only observe whether they are complied with or ignored.[90] From a legal point of view, the distinction mentioned corresponds roughly to the dichotomy of 'is' and 'ought'.

But precisely this fundamental distinction is notoriously fragile in IP law, unlike in the law of real property. Is the statement that something *is* a work of art or an invention an assertive statement of fact, or already a normative statement from which it follows that this object enjoys IP protection? And what about the statement: 'This *is my* work'?

Utterances like these, which are on the one hand descriptive, but on the other hand evidently not speech acts to be classified as true or false without further ado,

---

[88] Gross, 6 Anthropological Theory 45 et seq. (2006) (unreconstructed Durkheimianism); *further* Schützeichel, 38 Soziologische Revue 503 et seq. (2015). On constructivism in general *see* Pörksen, *Schlüsselwerke des Konstruktivismus* 11; Hay, 21 New Political Economy 520 (2016).

[89] Searle, *The Construction of Social Reality* 37–43; Luhmann, *Gesellschaft der Gesellschaft* 205–6; Tuomela, *Philosophy of Sociality* 193; Berger & Luckmann, *The Social Construction of Reality* 60–61 ('Language provides the fundamental superimposition of logic on the objectivated social world').

[90] Searle, *in* Gephart & Suntrup (eds.) *Normative Structure of Human Civilization* 21, 26.

stand at the centre of Searle's social ontology and at the same time in the centre of interest here. They are called *declarative* utterances in speech act theory. A declaration does not describe, report or claim anything in relation to external brute reality. Rather, with a declaration, a speaker announces that something specific is the case, such as: 'I pronounce you to be man and wife' or: 'This is a/ my work of art!' Under suitable conditions, such a declaration alone brings about a new social reality – for example, a marriage, a work of art or a claim to possession.[91] Declarations have neither the descriptive word-to-world nor the reversed, openly normative world-to-word fit, but they change the social world by presenting it as already changed.[92]

This surprising effect is achieved by a declarative speech act assigning to a brute fact a function that does not (completely) follow from its natural properties. Searle articulates the process of creating such a status function with the now famous formula: X counts as Y in context C. 'We make it the case by declaration that object X now has the status function Y in C'.[93] Applied to the example of the work of art, one can thus state that Marcel Duchamp once declared that a certain urinal counts as a work of art. Through Duchamp's unilateral declaration and its collective recognition,[94] the urinal becomes a work of art. The brute fact urinal (X) has acquired a new social meaning without changing its brute existence. Searle calls this social reality an 'institutional fact'.[95] It only exists because and insofar as people regard the urinal as a work of art, speak, think and act in this sense.[96] At the same time, X and Y are physically the same thing. The only difference is that the X fact has been assigned a new social status by a declaration. This process is language-dependent because 'there is nothing there prelinguistically that one can perceive or otherwise attend to in addition to the X element, and there is nothing there prelinguistically to be the target of desire or inclination in addition to the X element'.[97] The 'status indicators', which turn the X into a Y, are also based on linguistic or equivalent representative (e.g. pictorial) messages – for example, a name sign on the urinal.[98]

As will be shown in more detail the following Section 2.2.2, the abstract IP object is also based on a declarative speech act and its social recognition. Physical and mental artefacts (X) such as books, machines or personal performances are no longer

---

[91] On marriage *see also* Ross, *On Law and Justice* 173–74; Marinkovic, *Sprache – Geltung – Recht* 100 et seq.
[92] *Cf. also* Bendel-Larcher, *in* John et al (eds.), *Ontologien der Moderne* 55, 67; Blumenberg, *Theorie der Unbegrifflichkeit* 40.
[93] Searle, *Making the Social World* 99.
[94] Tuomela, *Philosophy of Sociality* 182 et seq.
[95] Searle, *The Construction of Social Reality* 115–16; Searle, *Making the Social World* 11–15.
[96] Searle, *The Construction of Social Reality* 43–51; Searle, *Making the Social World* 7; Tuomela, *Philosophy of Sociality* 186.
[97] Searle, *The Construction of Social Reality* 68.
[98] Searle, *The Construction of Social Reality* 85, 119–20.

perceived and signified as such but in certain contexts C they count as merely accidental embodiments of an abstract work, an abstract invention etc. (Y). The immaterial ('intellectual') IP object is created by assigning to human actions, tangible things and other physical matter (e.g. digital data stored on a chip) a secondary status as mere 'embodiments' of a supposedly immaterial object. The IP object therefore only exists in our language practices and beliefs that, however, always remain related to concrete exemplars (tokens) such as books, machines etc.

According to Searle, these brute facts generally have a logical precedence over observer-dependent institutional facts.[99] This follows not only from Searle's basic conviction that there is only one world. It also follows from the fact that the basic institution of language, in turn, must be expressed, understood, written down and otherwise communicated by humans in order to exist. Language communities and thus societies are inconceivable without things and people – be it a piece of paper, an electronic file, a sound wave or the thought in the head. Whole languages can perish if they are no longer spoken and not documented.[100] If, however, the entire institution of language depends on brute physical facts, then so do individual institutional facts, which in turn are language-based and expressed in concrete, embodied status indicators. Moreover, all speech acts are more or less closely related to extra-linguistic reality.[101] This reference is most direct in assertive speech acts, which describe a brute fact. Directive and commissive speech acts concern a time interval. They express the expectation that external reality will correspond to the utterance in the future. Declarative speech acts also play a special role in this respect, which will have to be addressed later. Although declarations refer to a brute fact X (e.g. a urinal), they assign to it a status function Y (e.g. the status of an artwork) that is not immanent to it – thus introducing a linguistic level of abstraction that lies, so to speak, 'above' the brute reality. There, in this linguistic-semantic realm, 'exist' money, art, artworks, inventions and other immaterial goods.

However, this existence is not an object-like static existence. First, institutional facts do not acquire social reality by being presented as existing by any individual. Rather, a context C is required for X to count as Y. In the case of Michel Duchamp's declaration that a urinal is a work of art, this context was obviously given. His declaration was collectively recognised by a sufficient number of third parties and thereby acquired the status of a social fact.[102] As we will see, in the case of the notion of the abstract IP object, it also took a very specific historical, socio-economic

---

[99] Searle, *The Construction of Social Reality* 34–35; Schützeichel, 38 Soziologische Revue 503, 509 (2015). For a different constructivist approach *see* Berger & Luckmann, *The Social Construction of Reality* 49–50.

[100] Ong, *Orality and Literacy* 7; contra Pettersson, *The Idea of a Text* 137 (language as acausal, abstract object).

[101] Searle, *in* Gephart & Suntrup (eds.) *Normative Structure* 21, 26.

[102] Searle, *The Construction of Social Reality* 117; Searle, *Making the Social World* 8; Tuomela, *Philosophy of Sociality* 187 et seq.; Berger & Luckmann, *The Social Construction of Reality* 58 ('Society is a human product'.).

context for this initially eccentric and still astonishing institutional fact to gain social recognition.[103]

Second, declarations (speech *acts*) and their recognition by third parties are *actions*.[104] Their result, the collective intentionality that an X is considered a Y, is based solely on human language and other actions. Just as the meaning of a word lies in its use in the language,[105] so a banknote is nothing more than 'a standing possibility of paying for something'.[106] In spite of the parlance of institutional *facts*, social reality can ultimately only be understood from an action perspective. This will also be confirmed with regard to the abstract IP object.

Institutional facts such as money and artworks differ from the brute, extra-linguistic reality in another fundamental point. For according to Searle, 'the whole point of the creation of institutional reality is not to invest objects or people with some special status valuable in itself but to *create and regulate power relationships between people*'.[107] Institutional facts such as money, art, property, marriage and – as will be shown – the abstract IP object, are, in other words, there to make people think or do something they would not have thought or might have done without these institutional facts.[108] This power does not unfold through commandments, prohibitions and promises, but through simple declaration: This is money, this is art, you are married, this is mine etc. The normative force (power) of these institutional facts is based to a large extent on the fact that they are articulated precisely as an 'is' and not as an 'ought'.[109] Their normativity lies in the status function, according to which a brute fact X counts as a Y.[110] The status of the Y is a deontological one. It follows not from the natural qualities of the brute fact X, but from the function assigned qua language, which the brute fact X is to fulfil. As far as the functionality of a brute fact is not determined by natural causes, it is normative.

The power condensed in institutional facts is deontic/symbolic because it is not based on the mastery of natural forces, but solely on the mastery of language and

---

[103] *See* Section 3.2.
[104] Searle, *The Construction of Social Reality* 56–57.
[105] Wittgenstein, *Philosophical Investigations* para. 43; Marinkovic, *Sprache – Geltung – Recht* 89 et seq.; Giddens, 53 Social Research 529, 536 et seq. (1986).
[106] Searle, *The Construction of Social Reality* 36.
[107] Searle, *The Construction of Social Reality* 94 ('In general status-functions are matters of power...'); Searle, *Making the Social World* 106; Searle, *in* Margolis & Laurence (eds.) *Creations of the Mind* 3, 16 ('all of this at bottom is about power'); Tuomela, *Philosophy of Sociality* 191.
[108] On the concept of power *see* Searle, *in* Gephart & Suntrup (eds.) *Normative Structure of the Human Civilization* 21, 22.
[109] For example, US dollar notes declare, 'This note is legal tender for all debts, public and private'. In contrast, Euro notes do not contain any declaration. This silence makes their normativity even more incomprehensible and unassailable; *cf.* Berger & Luckmann, *The Social Construction of Reality* 108 ('The more abstract the legitimations are, the less likely they are to be modified in accordance with changing pragmatic exigencies').
[110] Searle, *Making the Social World* 8–9.

thought. The individual declaration that a urinal is a work of art is not enough. What is required is that this unilateral declaration be given social recognition. If this is not the case or if the corresponding collective intentionality falls away later, the institutional fact and the power relations that have clotted in it will also perish. Thus a currency can quickly lose its status function as a means of payment and only be worth the paper on which the currency symbols (status indications) are printed. Conversely, the normative force (power) of an institutional fact grows the longer and more generally it is recognised and articulated as existing. 'Unlike shirts and shoes, institutions do not wear out with continued usage. On the contrary, the continued usage of such institutions as marriage, private property, and money reinforces the institutions, but the 'usage' requires talk, and that talk functions to maintain and reinforce both the institution and institutional facts within the institution'.[111] In societies, countless such institutions are effective that, in their interaction, form an extremely powerful 'background'[112] or 'structure of rules'[113] from which the individual is practically unable to escape.[114]

Obviously, these language analyses are of great value for jurisprudence. They reveal the normativity already contained in speech acts that come across as purely descriptive. The normative meaning of a statement such as 'This is a work of art' is less obvious than in explicit commandments or prohibitions. But that is precisely what makes declarations effective. This applies in particular to Searle's 'constitutive' institutional facts, which not only regulate concrete behaviour but also form the basis for further actions and institutional facts based on them. As examples for such fundamental social facts, Searle mentions ownership and legal persons.[115]

2.2.2 Application to IP Objects

Searle's social ontology has striking similarities with Scandinavian legal realism, as expounded by Alf Ross. Both post-metaphysical theories start from a single world in which there is a correlation between brute external reality and constructed social reality, which is explained and investigated. Ultimately, Ross and Searle are concerned with naming the real effects of normative ideas and thus making their deontic power visible and open to criticism.[116] In contrast to Alf Ross, however, Searle does not comment on the ontological status of the abstract work and other IP objects. The question therefore arises as to how these phenomena can be classified in terms of Searle's social ontology.

---

[111] Searle, *Making the Social World* 104.
[112] Searle, *The Construction of Social Reality* 129.
[113] Searle, *The Construction of Social Reality* 146–47.
[114] Berger & Luckmann, *The Social Construction of Reality* 59.
[115] Searle, *in* Gephart & Suntrup (eds.) *Normative Structure of Human Civilization* 21, 30.
[116] *Cf.* Ross, *On Law and Justice* 68, *with* Searle, *in* Margolis & Laurence (eds.) *Creations of the Mind* 3, 16 ('all of this at bottom is about power').

In this respect, it should be emphasised once again that the following is neither concerned with intellectual property *rights*, i.e. copyright in the sense of a subjective right, nor with copyright and other IP *laws*. These exclusive rights and their legal bases are undoubtedly institutional facts, as is ownership in real property to which Searle frequently refers.[117] Statutes and rights are created in a two-stage procedure by a legislature and by courts or authorities qua declaration. First, a general law is enacted, which is then executed in the individual case. In both instances, declarations are made according to the formula 'X counts as Y in context C'. Property ownership assigns a new status Y to a brute fact X – for example, a plot of land or a chattel, which is not immanent to it, i.e. does not follow from its brute properties. The thing is then no longer simply an excerpt of external reality that exists independently of observers and is measurable, but counts from now on as being the property of a person who can use it at will and exclude third parties from its use (Section 903 of the German Civil Code, BGB). For the institutional fact 'ownership' to attain social reality, apart from talking and thinking in terms of my and yours, a whole apparatus of organisations such as parliaments, courts, bailiffs etc. (all of which must also enjoy collective recognition) is required. Searle refers to 'nonlinguistic institutional facts',[118] which is unfortunate, because these institutions, too, achieve their specific social function only through linguistic declarations. A person (X), for example, counts as a judge with the power to decide ownership disputes between private individuals (Y), because the judge has been appointed for this purpose and communicates and maintains this status function through various status indicators.[119] Only the use of brute force to enforce ownership is non-linguistic.[120] Legal norms, on the other hand, are based entirely on language, whether oral or written, or communicated via other representations such as robes, uniforms, red traffic lights etc.

The situation is different with the *object* of real property ownership, to which the relational rights and obligations refer. This is a brute fact that is identified in legal and other communication contexts by numbers (such as the land register page or serial number of a motor vehicle) or other signs. The speech acts in this regard are purely assertive. They name a thing ('This is a car. This is the car with the serial number...'). Only the ownership talk ('This is my car'.) brings normativity into play.

The reality of IP law is much more complex.[121] According to the prevailing opinion, the abstract IP object does not count among the brute facts. Rather, it is characterised by the fact that it can neither be measured nor otherwise scientifically

---

[117] Searle, *The Construction of Social Reality* 5; George, *Constructing Intellectual Property* 90–134.
[118] Searle, *Making the Social World* 93.
[119] Searle, *Making the Social World* 99 ('We make it the case by Declaration that for any x that satisfies a certain set of conditions p, x can create an entity with Y status function by Declaration in C'.).
[120] See Menke, *Recht und Gewalt* passim.
[121] *Cf.* Pettersson, *The Idea of a Text* 2 et seq. (a text as a 'cluster', composed of physical exemplars, signs, and meaning); Ong, *Orality and Literacy* 74–75; contra: Carvalko, 2 ABA SciTech Law. 7–9 (2005).

explained. It is held to be neither identical with individual physical or mental manifestations nor understood as the sum of all these 'embodiments'.[122] Instead, it is said to exist as a immaterial ('intellectual') object in a kind of second world – which in turn is out of the question for Searle from the outset, because no epistemically objective knowledge compatible with the state of scientific knowledge can be gained from such a world.[123]

On the other hand, the physical and mental copies of works, inventions, designs and signs (i.e. books, files, industrial products, packaging etc.) undoubtedly have existence *independent* of observers and languages. According to the dominant paradigm, however, these brute facts do not form the objects of protection of IP rights. Only if this were the case would the structure of IP rights correspond to that of real property ownership. Rights and obligations would then refer to brute facts, the use of which would be regulated and which, in this context, would be given a specific name. Such a legal form has indeed existed. It is the early modern privilege to print a book, to sell it or to use another technology etc.[124]

Two elements of the privilege system can be clearly assigned to the two Searlean categories of facts – namely the legal norm of privilege on the one hand and the printings, machines etc. affected by the privilege on the other. The privilege is an institutional fact; regulated artefacts and acts are brute facts.

Difficulties arise, however, when it comes to classifying typical privilege terms like 'book', 'writing', 'invention' etc., which may not be reprinted, exported or disseminated.[125] In contrast to real property, these objects do not signify a single piece of brute reality (such as a car with a serial number), but a plurality of artefacts and actions that are sufficiently similar to a prototype and can therefore be given the same name, like Goethe's *Faust*. This general term is more open to semantic abstraction and thus social construction than to a precise assertive speech act related to a concrete thing. For it presupposes a comparison of several artefacts which necessarily differ, since they exist as separate tokens of external reality. Even a copy identical in typeface is on a different sheet from the original and printed with a different ink. Consequently, the apparently purely assertive statement that two printed books 'are' or 'contain' one and the same *Faust* contains a quite demanding assertion of truth, which at the same time refers to physical entities, character

---

[122] Schmücker, *Was ist Kunst?* 172 et seq., 206 et seq. For a physicalist understanding *see* Hauptmann, *Festgabe der Juristischen Fakultät der Universität Freiburg (Schweiz)* 50, 65–66. For a mentalist understanding *see* Shiffrin, in Goodin et al. (eds.) *A Companion to Contemporary Political Philosophy* 653, 654. ('IP involves rendering concrete and external the unique contents of a human mind so that they may be made accessible to and usable by others. By contrast, land – quintessential physical property – does not depend for existence on cognition and imagination; neither do minerals, water, air, nor many animals and plants'.).
[123] Section 1.1.
[124] Section 3.2.1.3.1.
[125] Ibid.

sequences and meaning.[126] The greater the difference between the artefacts in question, the greater the declarative element of the statement that two exemplars represent *a* book, *a* writing etc. For the artefacts count as this *one* book/writing only regardless of their otherwise independent existence in external reality, which is linguistically faded out. Such a statement contains all elements of Searle's formula 'X counts as Y in context C': The publication X counts as 'reprint' or other copy of the relevant original and thus as a copy of 'Book Y' according to a similarity comparison C. The status as a copy of the book 'Y' does not follow from properties immanent to the single brute fact X. Rather, it follows from a comparison whose standards are both language-based and inherently normative.[127]

If two sheets of paper with characters match completely in their outward characteristics, their designation with the same signifier points in an assertive way to these similarities. It can be proven whether and to what extent a copy agrees with the original. In such a constellation, a word-to-world semantics dominates, i.e. the language should fit to the external reality. But if the common denomination is maintained even if the artefacts concerned differ in their objectively perceptible, brute qualities, then a world-to-word meaning comes to the fore. The external reality, regardless of its diversity, is to be brought under a general concept and thus correspond to a certain, language-based conception. This is the case, for example, if the translation of a text into another language still bears the title of the original (such as Goethe's *Faust* in Japanese). Although the paper, the ink, the language used and possibly also the meaning of individual words and sentences differ, it is still considered the same text. However, this is not explicitly claimed, but simply declared by the use of the same title.[128] The print with Japanese characters is assigned the status of a *Faust* exemplar. Such a declaration only acquires social reality if it is collectively recognised. Finally, the decision to use the same or a different name for artefacts, as in all cases of declarative status functions, is a matter of power. Which artefacts are to be compared and whether a brute property of an artefact represents a 'relevant' match or deviation does not follow from a scientifically verifiable observation and description of external reality, but from a normative positioning of the speaker. This immanent normativity is also a characteristic of institutional facts.

The meaning of book titles, names of inventions and other general terms for an indefinite number of artefacts, oscillating between an assertive and a declarative speech act, still refers to brute reality. This brute reality concerns *reproducible artefacts* such as books, machines, textiles and written or pictorial product signs. A plurality of such artefacts is described in their entirety. Such a speech act requires

---

[126] Pettersson, *The Idea of a Text* 2 et seq. (cluster concept of a text).
[127] *Cf.* Searle, *The Construction of Social Reality* 60 ('The feature of language essential for the constitution of institutional facts is the existence of symbolic devices, such as words, that by convention mean or represent or symbolize something beyond themselves'.). On writings ('text') *cf.* Pettersson, *The Idea of a Text* 2 et seq.
[128] Pettersson, *The Idea of a Text* 2 et seq.

a higher degree of linguistic abstraction than the designation of concrete individual things prevailing in real property law. The more abstract the way of speaking, thinking and regulating is, the further brute reality moves into the background, while strongly normatively charged declarations take hold. The diachronic analysis that follows in the next section will confirm this assessment. Just as privileges were in some respects the precursors of modern IP rights, titles such as Goethe's *Faust*, names of inventions, designs and product signs represent the precursor of abstract IP objects.[129]

In contrast to general terms for numerous artefacts, the talk of the abstract artwork, abstract invention etc. does not refer to any brute, external reality, but in a somewhat reversed direction further up, to a world of immaterial objects. Since these signifiers are, according to the prevailing paradigm, to be strictly distinguished from their embodiments, they can only be classified as institutional facts in a Searlean sense. Consequently, a brute fact X in context C would have to be assigned a status function Y by declaration, which attains social reality if it enjoys collective recognition. And so it is: a print or file, a live performance, a machine, a commercial product etc. (X) is considered in context C as an embodiment of an abstract work, invention, design etc. (Y).[130]

It has to be emphasised again that a brute fact X is assigned a different status with such a declaration than with the designation of several reproducible artefacts with a common name. In the latter, historically older case, the single artefact X counts as an *example of a class of similar artefacts*. According to the current way of speaking and thinking, however, it counts as the *embodiment of an immaterial entity*. Similarity relations between brute artefacts are replaced by the properties of an idealised object. The process of comparison and classification, directed from the world to the word, coagulates into an abstract object whose imagined properties manifest themselves in concrete brute facts (tokens). Consequently, language no longer represents brute reality, but brute reality represents an ideal world. The statement 'This is Goethe's *Faust*' still has a word-to-world fit. But the words 'Goethe's *Faust*' no longer refer to a specific book copy or a performance in the brute reality, but to an immaterial object in an idealised second world.

This change of meaning takes place in the Y-element of Searle's formula. The statement 'Goethe's *Faust*' is no longer understood as a reference to artefacts and actions with certain, objectively ascertainable properties, but as the designation of an abstract object whose characteristics and limits cannot be deduced from any brute fact. Searle calls such institutional facts 'free-standing' – that is, they attain reality only in language and human imagination.[131] The world they represent is an ideal world that exists only because people talk and think as if it exists.

---

[129] Section 3.1 (abstraction no. 1).

[130] Carvalko, 2 ABA SciTech Law. 7–9 (2005), only deals with the ontological status of exemplars, not with that of the abstract IP object.

[131] Searle, *in* Gephart & Suntrup (eds.) *Normative Structure of Human Civilization* 21, 29 (legal person); Pettersson, *The Idea of a Text* 25 (the unity of the text as a mental construct).

Such a social reality is made possible by 'the infinite generative capacity of natural languages' with the help of which people can produce ever-new words and meanings, including those that move further and further away from brute reality.[132] While in general terms for similar artefacts only the signifier counts as institutional reality and, moreover, emerges from a comparison of brute facts which it represents, in the dominant paradigm the signified also forms a purely language-based, socially constructed reality, an idea: the idea or pejoratively also the fiction of the abstract IP object.

As the following historical section will show, it was not until the eighteenth century that this eccentric notion gained such broad collective recognition that it was able to advance to become law's idealised reality.[133] The semantic process of abstraction was also expressed in a changed language practice. In some cases, old words such as 'work' or 'invention' were only applied to very narrowly defined facts such as the creative work of art and the new technical teaching, while in others neologisms such as 'design' were established.[134]

As with all institutional facts, normativity is inherent in these concepts. Theorists of 'the' true tragedy and 'the' true artwork, from Aristotle to Edward Young and Karl Philipp Moritz, were concerned precisely with formulating an ideal to which the reality of human creation should correspond. According to Aristotle, a good tragedy has a beginning, a middle and an end;[135] a work of art worthy of the name must express, in its entirety, the originality of the genius.[136] The originators of the idea of the abstract IP object thus pursued a decidedly normative agenda, which they inserted into their abstract definitions of 'the' tragedy and 'the' artwork. With the collective recognition of these declarations, the concept of the artwork, for example, attained a world-to-word meaning. Since then, artistic creation has had to meet certain requirements (originality, creativity) in order to be considered a work of art. For inventive, design-related and other work products, equivalent criteria were developed. The relevant specifications are not taken from brute reality, but are language-based and deontological. They ultimately coincide with the characteristics of the respective abstract IP object, which also exists only as a social, inherently normative construct.[137]

The normativity of the abstract IP object as a social-institutional fact has not only a regulating but also a constitutive effect.[138] Artefacts and actions are not designated and ordered in their relationship to each other, but an ideal object is generated

---

[132] Searle, *Making the Social World* 64. On the role of the written form *see* Ong, *Orality and Literacy* 106.
[133] Section 3.2.
[134] Section 3.2.2.1.
[135] Section 3.2.1.1.
[136] Section 3.2.1.2.
[137] On the normativity of aesthetics *see* Möllers, *Möglichkeit von Normen* 238 et seq.
[138] On the normativity of constitutive norms *see* Möllers, *Möglichkeit von Normen* 228–9.

whose idealised reality forms the basis for further actions and legal operations.[139] Above all, the concept of ownership can now come into play. While privileges are linked to incriminated behaviour and specific artefacts – for example, the (re-) printing of books – 'intellectual property' assigns copyrightable works and other abstract objects to a proprietor for exclusive use. The idea of the abstract IP object is the condition of the possibility of IP rights and all analogies to real property ownership. Without it, there are only a number of similar artefacts that are compared with each other and possibly uniformly designated. This general designation does not signify, however, an object capable of being owned.

If, on the other hand, the idea of the abstract IP object has become established, the legal-institutional fact of 'ownership' can easily be added: First, a statute declares an abstract IP object capable of being owned. The legal requirements for protection often coincide with the non-legal criteria formulated in aesthetic, technological and economic discourses with regard to artworks, inventions, designs and product signs. On this statutory basis, courts and patent offices then declare works, inventions etc. to be protected under IP law and their unauthorised use to be illegal. According to the prevailing paradigm, all these legal operations do not refer to the brute external reality, but to immaterial ('intellectual') objects.

However, such a legal construction is already doomed to failure for reasons of principle. Legal prohibitions are only legitimate if they are aimed at human behaviour that is possible for legal subjects. This requirement reflects the logical primacy of brute, external reality over the socially constructed, institutional reality of law. Abstract IP objects cannot, however, be controlled by either the rights holder or third parties in such a way that they can adjust their behaviour accordingly. It is precisely the hallmark of abstract IP objects that they are not equivalent to any 'embodiment'. We are thus faced with a paradox. The abstractness of IP objects qualifies and disqualifies them for the law and especially for ownership.

As will be shown in detail Chapter 5, current IP law solves this difficulty by relying on the idea of the abstract IP object only for constructive purposes. The function of the abstract work, the invention, the design etc. is limited to faking an object of ownership. The actual subject matter of regulation are actions relating to certain physical or mental artefacts. IP laws govern who has the exclusive right to authorise or prohibit the manufacture and other use of certain artefacts and the performance of certain activities.[140]

The more firmly anchored and robust the idea of the abstract IP object is, the less these regulatory effects are expressed in legal language. In copyright and design law, for example, the dominant paradigm is the abstract work or design, which is strictly separated from its 'embodiments'.[141] But in patent law the distinction between

---

[139] On the difference between constitutive and regulative norms *see* Searle, *in* Gephart & Suntrup (eds.) *Normative Structure of Human Civilization* 21, 24–25.
[140] *See* Section 5.1.2.3.
[141] *See* Sections 2, 15, 44 German Copyright Act (UrhG); Section 38(1) no. 1 German Design Act (DesignG).

product and process patents and thus concrete-physical artefacts already comes to the fore.[142] In trademark law, the idea of the abstract IP object is no longer fully implemented. The sign protected as a trademark is not allocated to the rights holder as such.[143] The core of trademark law is rather the prohibition of using identical or similar signs in the course of trade, subject to further conditions.[144] At the same time, there are tendencies to replace this action- and artefact-based approach to reality with the concept of the abstract sign, which is attributed a new status function for this purpose. According to this view, a trademark no longer counts as a distinctive sign of origin for certain goods or services, but stands on its own as a commercial sign without any fixed meaning. Accordingly, trademark owners can no longer only defend themselves against certain forms of use, in particular confusing ones, but are able to comprehensively control the meaning of the sign. Using the example of trademark law, the process of the formation and recognition of an abstract IP object can therefore be observed in real time.[145] Rights related to copyright and plant variety rights, the codification history of which dates back only to the twentieth century, finally manage without the idea of abstract IP objects. Exclusive rights to use, for example, sound and video recordings or plant-propagating material prove that an abstract IP object is not a necessary condition for the form of the exclusive right.[146]

These observations, which are only hinted at here, make it reasonable to examine Searle's social ontology from a diachronic perspective. If it is true that the abstract IP object exists as an institutional fact and thus as a language-based, social construct, then – like every language, every word and every meaning – it should have a history that can be told and even historically proven.

---

[142] Section 9 German Patent Act (PatG).
[143] Art. 9 EU Trademark Reg., Art. 10 EU Trademark Dir. do not specify the subject matter of the exclusive rights ('The registration of an EU trademark shall confer on the proprietor exclusive rights therein'.).
[144] Section 14(2) German Trademark Act (MarkenG) and Section 5.1.1.1.
[145] *See* Sections 3.2.1.1, 3.2.1.3.2, 5.1.1.1.
[146] Section 5.1.1.2.

3

Two Abstractions

In the following, a distinction will be made between two processes of linguistic-semantic abstraction, which were already alluded to in the previous section. The first abstraction concerns the designation of an undefined number of physical and mental artefacts with a general signifier. The possibility of subsuming concrete individual facts under a general term forms a central functional feature of languages. As such, it cannot be precisely historically located, but only reconstructed in its tripartite logic (see Section 3.1). Such a generalising language practice already goes beyond a purely assertive speech act, since the implicit comparison between several artefacts always requires an evaluation. But it still refers to the brute, observer-independent reality.[1] After completing the second abstraction, which primarily concerns the signified and thus the semantic level, people speak and think differently. In this process, the generally designated artefacts are replaced by the abstract IP object. From now on, the statement 'Goethe's *Faust*' no longer refers to one or more publications, performances or mental states, but to a 'work' that is not identical with any of these brute facts. The history of this abstraction from brute reality to a world of immaterial objects is well documented. It took place in the eighteenth century (see Section 3.2).

3.1 ABSTRACTION 1: GENERAL TERMS FOR SIMILAR ARTEFACTS

The much older language practice of using general terms for similar artefacts comprises three steps. The starting point is the change of brute reality by the creation of an artefact that differs from earlier artefacts (see Section 3.1.1). This artefact or one of its representations is then given a proper name by an actor and declared as a 'Master Artefact' under this name (see Section 3.1.2). The last step concerns the application of this name to copies, imitations and other artefacts which

---

[1] *See* Section 2.2.2.

are similar to the Master Artefact and are therefore called 'Secondary Artefacts' in the following (see Section 3.1.3).

3.1.1 A New Artefact

In order for these naming and language practices to take place, however, there must first be something that is named. According to Searle, this signified always exists as part of the brute, external reality, which thus has a logical precedence over language-based social facts.[2] In our context, it is a man-made change of brute reality – a new artefact.[3]

This starting point becomes obvious in the production of a new non-linguistic, physical object – for example, a painting, an audio or video file, a machine, a tool, a chemical compound, a plant breed, a biotechnologically produced organism, a new outer appearance of a product etc. These brute facts exist first of all without a name. At the same time they differ more or less strongly from the previous external reality, so that it is not sufficient to describe them with a non-specific generic term such as 'machine' or 'tool'. To uniquely identify them, a new name or number must be assigned. The generation of new names is thus a consequence of the human ability to actively change external reality, including the innovation to use existing things in a previously unknown way.

If such behaviour is planned, the externally perceptible, novel artefact is preceded by a thought that is subsequently realised.[4] But also this thought has a spatio-temporally bound, brute existence in the brain of the actor. The same applies to unconscious behaviour that is still bound to the body of the actor. In both cases, ontological subjectivity (only the actor perceives that he is thinking something) cannot be interpreted as a lack of epistemic objectivity (the thought can be measured as a neurobiological process).[5]

New, nameless artefacts also include scripts and computer programs.[6] Language fixed on paper, digital and other media is also an objectively perceptible result of human action in the changed brute reality. This physical entity can refer assertively

---

[2] See Section 2.2.1.
[3] See Ross, 58 Tidsskrift for Rettsvitenskap 321, 345 (1945); Schmücker, *Was ist Kunst?* 255 (primary manifestation); Boldrin & Levine, 2 Review of Economic Research on Copyright Issues 45, 48 (2005) (prototype); Boldrin & Levine, *Against Intellectual Monopoly* 124 et seq.; Shiffrin, in Goodin et al. (eds.) *A Companion to Contemporary Political Philosophy* 653, 654 (primary labour); Zech, *Information als Schutzgegenstand* 43; van Dijk, *Grounds of the Immaterial* 36.
[4] Bahr, 61 DZPhil 283, 285 (2013) (design plan).
[5] See Section 2.2.1.
[6] Microsoft Corp. v. AT & T Corp., 550 US 437, 447–48 (2007) ('master disk' of a computer program) *see also id.* 460 ('In a sense, the whole process is akin to an author living prior to the existence of the printing press, who created a story in his mind, wrote a manuscript, and sent it to a scrivener, who in turn copied the story by hand into a blank book'. (Alito, Thomas, Breyer, J., concurring).

to another brute fact, postulate the adaptation of reality to the word in a directive way, or assert a fictitious reality in a declarative way. Regardless of the meaning of the statement, all these speech acts are themselves part of brute reality. As artefacts they are then given a name. This is even true and necessary if the statement just repeats what others have already expressed before. Also in this case, a new designation – a special title or a document or programme name – is required for precise identification of the new artefact. This example demonstrates the principally unlimited productive potential of language. Writings are produced and named, then that title becomes the point of reference of a new statement, which is again designated, and so on.

From the last observation it follows that novel designations of goods, services and persons can also be understood as first artefacts. This applies regardless of whether the signified is new or exists at all. If well-known products are designated in a new way or signs are developed for future, not yet realised products, then at least a new trademark is created. This is also a new artefact that enters external reality in the form of a first mental or physical token and which in turn requires a signifier (e.g. a register number) in order to be uniquely identified.

Finally, human actions, such as the performance of a piece of music on a stage, also have an existence independent of observers. They exist in the language-external, brute reality. They can be measured and documented with scientific methods. In this respect, they also represent brute facts brought about by human beings. Although they may not permanently alter the inorganic reality, they are therefore subsumed under the term 'artefact'. If a human action has a memorable social significance, a special designation is again required that identifies the action and makes it communicable in this way.

3.1.2 *The Master Artefact*

The first artefact is a brute fact of organic (actions, thoughts) or inorganic matter (books, digital files, machines etc.). Speech-based social reality only comes into play when such a brute artefact is first given a name and secondly declared what will be called in the following a Master Artefact. Through these two declarative speech acts, a certain brute artefact X is assigned a special status, not inherent in it, as the authoritative prototype Y, on which the future language practice is oriented with regard to copies and other Secondary Artefacts.

Both the naming practices and the conventions, which count the artefact as the Master Artefact, are multifaceted. With a view to current IP law, a distinction can be drawn between informal and formalised Master Artefact declarations.[7]

Informal declarations of a Master Artefact occur when authors, inventors, designers, investors or entrepreneurs select the first artefact – for example, a manuscript, a

---

[7] *Cf. Fromer*, 76 Chicago L. Rev. 719 et seq. (2009).

drawing, a model, an audio or video document – as worthy of preservation, name it and declare it to be the original, the finished prototype.[8] Such declarations are not subject to any formalities. They are often only implied – for example, by storing a digital file under a certain file name on a computer. If a single person created the first artefact, he or she has the de facto monopoly of naming and sanctioning the relevant characteristics. If several persons are involved in the production of the first artefact, the naming of the artefact already requires collective and socially conditioned agreement. In other constellations, too, the name is not given by the original innovator but by third parties, such as gallery owners, publishers, employers or even the public.[9]

The identification of a Master Artefact can also cause difficulties if several versions exist. In such a case, the manufacturer of the first artefact, the audience and other stakeholders may have different views about which copy counts as the Master Artefact. In the case of movies, for example, it is often unclear and controversial, whether the director's cut authorised by the director or the version finally released should be regarded as the 'original' film.[10]

Irrespective of whether the selection and designation of the Master Artefact are clear or controversial, from an ontological point of view it should be noted that institutional facts are created by these processes. First, one or more persons express declarative speech acts ('This is the original. It bears the title XY'). However, these one-sided utterances only mature into institutional, social facts if they achieve collective recognition.[11]

As will be explained in more detail in Section 5.2.2.1, current IP law is consistently linked to the Master Artefact as identified and claimed by the author, inventor, designer or trademark holder.[12] However, the informal triad of creation of a first

---

[8] Kulenkampff, *in* Schmücker (ed.) *Identität und Existenz. Studien zur Ontologie der Kunst* 121, 137–38 (musical score); Schmücker, *Was ist Kunst?* 181; Ross, 58 Tidsskrift for Rettsvitenskap 321, 340, 347 (1945); Reicher, *in* Malcher et al. (eds.) *Fragmentarität als Problem der Kultur- und Textwissenschaften* 211, 226; Reicher, *in* Schmücker (ed.) *Identität und Existenz. Studien zur Ontologie der Kunst* 180, 188; Giddens, 53 Social Research 529, 544 (1986); Bergström, 7–8 GRUR Ausl. 364, 365 (1962); Thomasson, 68 The Journal of Aesthetics and Art Criticism 119 et seq. (2010); Sherman, 12 Theoretical Inquiries in Law 99, 108 (2011); Möllers, *Möglichkeit von Normen* 254–55. For a detailed case study of the construction of an invention in a patent infringement proceeding *see* van Dijk, *Grounds of the Immaterial* 77 et seq.

[9] *Cf.* Schack, Kunst und Recht 16 et seq.; Vogt, *Untitled* 13 et seq.; Möllers, *Möglichkeit von Normen* 250–51. On the history of titles of patents *see* Sherman & Bently, *The Making of Modern Intellectual Property Law* 187 with note 51. On the nomenclature of plants and micro organisms *see* Pottage & Sherman, *Figures of Invention* 200 et seq. ('type specimen'); Parry, *in* Gaudillière et al. (ed.) *Living Properties* 21 et seq. (fanciful names only became standard in the late eighteenth century).

[10] Hediger, *in* de Valck & Hagener (eds.) *Cinephilia* 133, 147 ('It seems useful to think of the original as a set of practices, a set of practices employed in the production and circulation of films'.).

[11] Reicher, 61 DZPhil 219, 225 (2013) (intentional acts bring about artefacts).

[12] Section 5.1.2.1.

artefact, its naming and the declaration of the Master Artefact – together with the assertion that this artefact is new in a relevant way or otherwise enjoys priority – triggers different legal consequences.

In copyright law, the full exclusive right arises automatically with the act of creation, which, however, must have 'entered the external world of appearance' in such a way that it 'can be used by third parties by reproduction independently of the intention of its creator'.[13] The same applies to the rights related to copyright, except that the original creation is replaced by other reproducible artefacts – namely photographs, certain editions, artistic performances, new sound and video recordings, broadcasting signals, press articles and databases.

In design and trademark law, further requirements for the acquisition of full legal protection have to be met. For an unregistered Community (EU) design, the design in question must have been exhibited, used in trade or otherwise disclosed – for example, by distributing illustrations to relevant dealers – in such a way that the disclosure of the Master Design could have reasonably become known in the normal course of business to the circles specialised in the sector concerned, operating within the EU.[14] An unregistered trademark presupposes that the claimed sign has been used in the course of trade and has acquired public recognition as a trademark within the affected trade circles.[15] These publicity requirements serve to improve the traceability of the exact time at which the Master design or sign was created. In trademark law it must also be established that the claimed sign is – or at least can be so perceived by the relevant public – a sign of product origin attributed to the rights holder. The fact that only trademark law declares the social recognition of the Master Artefact to be a legal requirement is due to the fact that priority in trademark law does not refer to the creation of the Master sign as such, but to its specific meaning as a sign of origin for certain products. The institutional fact that sign X counts as the claimant's sign of origin Y presupposes the use of the sign in commercial communication and the collective recognition of this meaning. In the case of creative artefacts and other innovations, however, the unilateral declaration by the author, inventor or designer that he has produced the artefact is sufficient.

In the case of patents and other registered rights these informal acts and declarations only give rise to a (fungible) right to full exclusivity and a vindication claim against any person who has taken the essential content of the patent 'from the descriptions, drawings, models, implements or equipment of another person or from

---

[13] Translated from the original German. BGH 27 February 1962 Case no. I ZR 118/60, GRUR 1962, 470, 472 – AKI; Loewenheim/Leistner, in Schricker & Loewenheim (eds.) *Urheberrecht* Section 2 German Copyright Act (UrhG) para. 47 with further references (unuttered thoughts not a copyrightable work).

[14] Art. 11(1) GeschmVO and CJEU Case C-479/12 H. Gautzsch Großhandel GmbH & Co. KG v. Münchener Boulevard Möbel Joseph Duna GmbH, ECLI:EU:C:2014:75 paras. 24 et seq.

[15] Section 4 nos. 2 and 3 German Trademark Act (MarkenG).

a process used by this person, without his consent (usurpation)'.[16] However, the full exclusive right cannot be invoked directly by reference to a description, representation, model or other prototype. Rather, the Master Artefact must be claimed in a highly formalised manner in a patent office procedure. Only when this registration process has been completed is the Master Artefact defined, to which the full exclusive design or patent right relates and which in turn comes into existence with the entry in the register or its publication.[17] The scope of protection of a patent application and a granted patent is determined by the patent claims, the interpretation of which is to be based on the description and the drawings;[18] design protection is conferred on those features of appearance of a registered design which are shown visibly in the application;[19] and a trademark application must contain, inter alia, an exact representation of the trademark which is decisive in infringement proceedings.[20]

How the Master Artefact is to be presented for this purpose is again subject to different legal requirements. If biological material is patented or if a plant variety is submitted for plant variety protection, exemplars of the microorganism concerned or the propagating material for the cultivation of the plant variety must be submitted.[21] This requirement is based on the assumption that the organic material is not artificially reworked, but replicates itself through natural reproduction.[22] In the event of a dispute, the deposited organic material is compared with the microorganism or plant variety used by the alleged infringer.[23]

Design and trademark law practice is equally concretistic in that the claimed product appearance or sign is to be applied for and presented in the register 'in a manner which enables the competent authorities and the public to determine the clear and precise subject matter of the protection afforded to its proprietor'.[24] For this purpose, applicants have to submit two-dimensional visual representations, sheets of music or sound recordings according to precisely defined specifications, which reproduce the claimed design or trademark. In contrast, registered word

---

[16] Translated from the original German. Cf. e.g. Sections 15(1) s. 1, 21(1) no. 3 German Patent Act (PatG).
[17] See Sections 58(1) German Patent Act (PatG), 27(1) German Design Act (DesignG), 4 no. 1 German Trademark Act (MarkenG).
[18] Section 14 German Patent Act (PatG).
[19] Section 37 German Design Act (DesignG).
[20] Section 32(2) no. 2 German Trademark Act (MarkenG) and Ingerl & Rohnke, German Trademark Act (MarkenG) Section 32 para. 8.
[21] Cf. Section 34(8) German Patent Act (PatG) and Budapest Treaty on the International Recognition of the Deposit of Microorganisms for the Purposes of Patent Procedure; Section 26(3) German Plant Variety Act (SortSchG).
[22] Pottage & Sherman, *Figures of Invention* 153 et seq., 186 et seq.
[23] OLG Düsseldorf 3 July 2015 Case no. I-15 U 75/14, GRUR-RS 2015, 11859 para. 57 – Summerdaisys Maxima.
[24] Art. 4(b) EU Trademark Reg.

marks, which claim a letter, syllable or word as such, have a lower degree of specification.

Finally, in order to obtain patents with regard to inorganic products and processes, it is not necessary to submit a copy or a model, but the technical teaching realised in a product or process is expressed in written patent claims and the description as well as additionally explained by drawings.[25] This translation of a physical artefact into the medium of language not only causes a notorious legal insecurity.[26] The verbalisation of technology has also decisively contributed to the prevailing understanding that the invention is an abstract IP object. For written language abstracts more from external reality than three-dimensional models and two-dimensional pictorial representations, thereby strengthening the notion that the object described exists as something 'intellectual' or immaterial.[27]

As important as the modes of presentation or construction of the Master Artefact are for the functioning and effects of IP rights,[28] they appear secondary to the prevailing paradigm. For this, the abstract IP object remains ultimately decisive, which is only accidentally 'embodied' in patent office and judicial documents, in concrete copies and models.[29] Instead of determining the object of protection inductively on the basis of the concrete Master Artefact, the prevailing opinion deductively applies the abstract concept of the work, the invention etc. This conceptual-legal approach opens up considerable scope. In particular, the indefinite concept of the work, the invention, the design, the sign can be extended to artefacts that differ more than insignificantly from the Master Artefact.[30]

This prevailing view can be criticised already at this point by reference to the fact that Master Artefacts always exist in the form of brute physical facts such as microorganisms, register entries or originals or copies submitted in a judicial process.[31] These brute facts X attain their special status as Master Artefact Y through declarations by the claimant or applicant and their possibly limiting confirmation by patent offices and courts. Legal practice consistently relies on them to decide disputes about the protectability and scope of IP rights. Their name is applied to copies and other Secondary Artefacts sufficiently similar to the Master Artefact. If

---

[25] Art. 78(1) EPC, Section 34 German Patent Act (PatG).
[26] Section 5.4.3.
[27] Biagioli, 73 Social Research: An International Quarterly 1129, 1143 et seq. (2006); Pottage & Sherman, *Figures of Invention* 54 et seq. On copyright registries in the nineteenth century *see* Sherman & Bently, *The Making of Modern Intellectual Property Law* 180 et seq. See also art. 4 French Patent Act 1791, reprinted in Kurz, *Weltgeschichte des Erfindungsschutzes* 243–45.
[28] Fromer, 76 Chicago L. Rev. 719 et seq. (2009).
[29] *See also* International Accounting Standard 38, Intangible Assets, Section 4 ('Some intangible assets may be contained in or on a physical substance such as a compact disc (in the case of computer software), legal documentation (in the case of a licence or patent) or film'.).
[30] Section 3.2.2.
[31] *Cf.* Godenhielm, 45 GRUR Int. 327, 329 (1996).

this nomenclature finds collective recognition, a general term is created for an indefinite number of similar artefacts.

3.1.3 *Secondary Artefacts*

The name of the Master Artefact is thus signifying a single artefact. The naming and sanctioning of a brute artefact as a Master Artefact instead reflects the fact that the organic or inorganic material in question can be *reproduced*, whether by natural reproduction, manual reproduction or machine copying.[32] If this possibility of reproduction is lacking, there is no need to determine a general term for a multitude of similar artefacts and to enforce it socially. Then there are only single things that have a proper name.

The introduction of reproductive technologies thus poses the same naming and classification problem as with regard to the natural environment. Already the order of those things constantly raises the question whether two separately existing brute facts (e.g. two four-legged creatures) should be subsumed under the same general term or whether they are specimens of different animal breeds. If human products and actions can be reproduced, it must also be decided whether an artefact is to be signified with an existing title – thus becoming a Secondary Artefact and entering into a relationship with a Master Artefact – or whether it is to be designated by its own name.

This classification problem is becoming more and more acute as increasing numbers of human products become reproducible and virtually all human thoughts, expressions and actions can be fixed and subsequently copied. In an oral culture, reproducible artefacts are limited to simple tools, expressions and actions that are actively remembered. The latter carry a name, but are perceived as activities or qualities rather than objects because of their purely mental existence. With the invention of writing, especially phonetic transcription, this changes fundamentally. Now ephemeral thoughts, utterances, real and even fictitious events and observations can be captured permanently and copied by transcription. Characters and scripts exist as external, brute facts. If they are reproduced, their name is applied to all copies of the writings whose external appearance coincides in such a way that the same message is communicated. Thus already writing resulted in the two singulars – the designation and the information – which dominate today's thinking about reproducible artefacts, while the multiplicity of the signified and at the same time signifying message carriers recede into the background. This abstraction and displacement effect intensified with each new, more efficient reproduction technology – especially book printing and digitisation.

Progress in reproductive technology is indeed increasing the number of Master and Secondary Artefacts to be named and thus the tendency towards linguistic

[32] Ross, 58 Tidsskrift for Rettsvitenskap 321, 345–46 (1945).

abstraction. As will be shown in the following section, however, the qualitative-semantic leap from the general designation of brute artefacts to the abstract IP object did not occur until the eighteenth century. Until then, one only spoke about external reality in a generalising way. This old language practice remains comprehensible today.[33]

It also corresponds to the typical genesis of a general term for a work, an invention, design etc., as it can be observed anew every day. A clear example is a digital copy of a text file. This even automatically has the same file name as the copy template; the file content including the text heading also remains unchanged. Other copies that correspond in composition, appearance and function and that trace back to the same Master Artefact in the history of their origin are also referred to uniformly.[34] The more perfectly reproduction technologies work, the more natural this language practice becomes. At the same time, the Master Artefact is receding further and further into the background. It remains indispensable, but disappears in a sea of identical copies.

However, as soon as one leaves the field of machine-made, historically linked copies, language practice begins to falter. This also applies to the case in which two texts or technical solutions are identical in all their characteristics, but have arisen completely independently of each other,[35] as well as to the inverse constellation of two historically linked but – in their physical existence and/or functionality – different artefacts. The context of reception, in which an externally identical copy is used, can also play a role.[36] The larger the differences, the less clear is the nomenclature.

All these observations prove that general designations are not images of metaphysical similarities, but are a matter of language convention. They are based on declarations and their collective recognition by third parties, which can be highly controversial.[37] In the dispute over the 'correct' designation practice, power relations are regulated with regard to the status of the artefact, which is compared with the Master Artefact. If this artefact is given the name of the Master Artefact, it automatically counts as a Secondary Artefact that falls under the spell of the 'original'. If it is called differently, it acquires an independent, prima facie more legitimate status. Neither the one nor the other result is a foregone conclusion. This indeterminacy

---

[33] Ross, 58 Tidsskrift for Rettsvitenskap 321, 340, 346 (1945); Boldrin & Levine, 2 Review of Economic Research on Copyright Issues 45, 48, 66 (2005); Shiffrin, in Goodin et al. (eds.) *A Companion to Contemporary Political Philosophy* 653, 654 (ordered collection of words).

[34] On the concept of a copy *cf.* Carrara/Soavi, 93 The Monist 414, 426 (2010); Hick, 51 British Journal of Aesthetics 185, 192–93 (2011).

[35] *See* Hick, 51 British Journal of Aesthetics 185, 195–96 (2011).

[36] *See* Irvin, 63 The Journal of Aesthetics and Art Criticism 315 et seq. (2005); Rotstein, 68 Chicago-Kent L. Rev. 725 (1993).

[37] Bourdieu, *Market of Symbolic Goods* 1, 24 ('collective judgements'); Decock/Douven, 2 Rev. of Phil. and Psychol. 61 et seq. (2011).; Hick, 71 The Journal of Aesthetics and Art Criticism 155 et seq. (2013); Danto, 61 The Journal of Philosophy 571, 581 (1964).

follows from the fact that the disputed term is an arbitrarily set neologism, the meaning of which becomes more open the greater the number of the signified and their spatial-temporal distance to the speaker is.[38] In both cases, the result of social processes is an institutional fact in Searle's sense: a Secondary Artefact called the name of an existing artefact, or a new Master Artefact called a new name.

From the point of view of the prevailing paradigm, the problem presents itself differently. While trademark law still focuses on the question of the identity or similarity of signs and products, copyright, patent and design law do not deal with a bi-polar comparison of books, machines etc., but with the subsumption of an artefact challenged as infringing under the legal concept of the abstract work, invention, design etc. Of course, the decision thus conceived is also based on an artefact comparison. The claimant submits an entry in the register or a copy that he or she claims to be a protected Master Artefact. Whether this artefact meets the requirements for protection is judged on the basis of the known state of the art, which in turn consists of concrete artefacts. Finally, the Master Artefact is compared with the challenged artefact, which has to be clearly identified in the claim. What characterises the work, the invention, the design and whether the allegedly infringing artefact makes use of these abstract features, is only worked out by a detailed comparison.[39]

According to its wording, plant variety protection law even manages without the abstract IP object and instead operates on the basis of the concept of a general term for a multitude of similar artefacts, i.e. on abstraction level 1. It defines a plant variety as a plant grouping.[40] This grouping does not refer to an immaterial object in an abstract World² but to a particular 'genotype' or a particular 'combination of genotypes' which give rise to characteristics of the plants which make them appear as a uniform variety different from other varieties.[41] The necessary determination of similarity is not lost in an infinite recourse. Their last unit is a certain genotype, which can be identified by scientific methods.[42] The general variety denomination selected by the breeder or entitled applicant and then collectively recognised also relates back to this measurable brute fact, which exists independently of observers.[43] The variety denomination represents the correspondence of the external

---

[38] Cf. Blumenberg, *Theorie der Unbegrifflichkeit* 9 et seq.; Ong, *Orality and Literacy* 51 et seq.
[39] Drahos, *Philosophy of IP* 154–55 and Section 5.1.2.2.
[40] Art. 5(2) EU Plant Variety Reg.; Art. 1(vi), 9 UPOV (grouping of plants); Section 2 no. 1a German Plant Variety Act (SortSchG).
[41] Translated from the original German. Section 2 no. 1a German Plant Variety Act (SortSchG); Art. 5(2) EU Plant Variety Reg.; Art. 1(vi) UPOV; Seitz & Kock, GRUR Int. 711, 712 (2012); Würtenberger et al., *EU Plant Variety Protection* para. 3.14; Leßmann/Würtenberger, *Sortenschutzrecht Section 2 para.* 73; contra Sabelleck, in Metzger & Zech (eds.) *Sortenschutzrecht Section 2 German Plant Variety Act (SortSchG) paras.* 11–13 with further references (the genome is 'physical matter and intangible information at the same time').
[42] Sabelleck, in Metzger & Zech (eds.) *Sortenschutzrecht Section 2 Plant Variety Act para.* 17.
[43] Section 7 German Plant Variety Act (SortSchG), Art. 17–18 EU Plant Variety Reg., Art. 20 UPOV.

characteristics and their constant homogeneity in the course of natural reproduction.[44] Finally, an alleged infringement is not decided according to a subsumption under an abstract legal term. Instead, infringement is regularly assessed by comparative cultivation of the plants at issue in order to find out whether the plants attacked as infringing are based on propagating material of the protected variety or are 'essentially derived' from it – which implies, among other things, that the plaintiff's initial variety was predominantly used for the breeding or discovery of the allegedly infringing plants.[45] All these solid, comparative investigations can do without deductions of abstract terms. The reality of plant variety law is therefore a scientific, not a metaphysical-idealistic or institutional-social one.[46] The actors relevant in plant variety protection law (breeders, biologists and other scientists) and the state of scientific knowledge at the time of the establishment of plant variety protection law in the twentieth century may have contributed to the orientation of this legal area towards the world[1] of brute facts.[47]

Further evidence of the social and legal relevance of these designation practices is provided by the protection of trade secrets.[48] Here there is often a lack of a publicly known and therefore socially recognised name, but in any case of an artefact (such as the description of a recipe for a caffeinated drink) that discloses the relevant information. In the absence of a publicly accessible Master Artefact, no generalising language practice regarding Secondary Artefacts develops. Instead, the holder of the secret must present and prove in each individual case that the defendant or a third party has unlawfully acquired, used, or disclosed an artefact (e.g. a file or a memory of a recipe) in violation of trade secrecy rules.[49] Because it is a secret, no common name can be established for a plurality of its copies. Rather, the manifestations of the secret are perceived and named individually. On this fragmented basis, the idea of the abstract IP object cannot gain a foothold. Accordingly, legal protection of trade

---

[44] Cf. BGH 30 April 2004 Case no. Xa ZR 156/04, GRUR 2009, 750 para. 17 – Lemon Symphony; CJEU Case C-625/15 P Schniga, ECLI:EU:C:2017:435 para. 54 ('the assessment of the characteristics of a plant variety necessarily contains a particular uncertainty due to the nature of the object itself to which the technical examination relates, namely a plant variety, as well as the length of time required to conduct such an examination').

[45] Cf. Section 10 German Plant Variety Act (SortSchG), Art. 13 EU Plant Variety Reg., Art. 14 UPOV; BGH 30 April 2004 Case no. Xa ZR 156/04, GRUR 2009, 750 para. 17 – Lemon Symphony; OLG Düsseldorf 3 July 2015 Case no. I-15 U 75/14, GRUR-RS 2015, 11859 paras. 56–57 – Summerdaisys Maxima, with further references; Würtenberger et al., *EU Plant Variety Protection* paras. 6.11 et seq.

[46] CJEU Case C-625/15 P Schniga, ECLI:EU:C:2017:435 para. 46 ('the CPVO's task is characterised by the scientific and technical complexity of the conditions governing the examination of applications for Community plant variety rights').

[47] On the history of plant variety protection *see* Kevles, *in* Biagioli et al. (eds.) *Making and Unmaking IP* 253 et seq.; Metzger, *in* Metzger & Zech (eds.) *Sortenschutzrecht Einf. B para. 1*; Gaudillière et al. (eds.) *Living Properties*.

[48] I thank Niklas Bruun for pointing me to the peculiar status of trade secrets.

[49] Cf. art. 4(1) EU Trade Secrets Dir.

secrets is still perceived by the prevailing opinion as a kind of tort or delict and not as fungible exclusive property right in an abstract object.[50]

3.2 ABSTRACTION 2: THE IDEA OF THE ABSTRACT IP OBJECT

In the following section, this second abstraction – from the general designation of a multitude of raw artefacts [Word↓↑World^1] to the designation of an IP object that exists in an abstract World^2 [Word↓↑World^2] – will be traced. The historicisation of the idea of the abstract IP object provides further evidence for the ontological thesis that this is an institutional fact that does form part of external reality, but only in collective speech and thought. If it is a social fact, then the idea of the abstract work, the abstract invention etc. should have a history.

On the one hand, this question has received relatively little attention, especially among German-speaking legal historians. Rather, the focus is on genuine legal discourses and concepts such as 'intellectual property', privileges etc.[51] In this context, even for the fifteenth and sixteenth centuries there is often unquestioned talk of the 'work' as the object of legal protection, although parallel to this the difference between absolutist reprint privileges and modern copyright laws is worked out.[52] In a similar anachronistic way, ancient and medieval signs on amphorae and other goods are discussed under the topos of contemporary trademark law, although according to the findings of the author concerned they were only used as owner's signs or for other purposes such as customs and taxation.[53]

On the other hand, it is *undisputed* among historians and other social scientists, who do not presuppose the abstract IP object as a timeless reality, but view and study it as something that has become social on a time axis, that the idea of a work capable of being owned, an invention capable of being owned etc., is comparatively recent.[54] According to these studies, even areas of law such as copyright, patent

---

[50] Niebel, in Festschrift Fezer 799 et seq.
[51] Klippel, 7 ZGE/IPJ 49 et seq. (2015); Wadle, in Wadle (ed.) *Geistiges Eigentum I* 99 et seq. with further references; Otto & Klippel (eds.) *Geschichte des deutschen Patentrechts*; Alexander & Gómez-Arostegui (eds.) *History of Copyright Law*.
[52] Schuster, *Das Urheberrecht der Tonkunst* 7; Osterrieth, 131 UFITA 171, 249 (1996) [1895]; Gieseke, *Vom Privileg zum Urheberrecht* 1; Ginsburg, in Alexander & Gómez-Arostegui (eds.) *History of Copyright Law* 237, 245–46 ('works' protected by sixteenth-century Vatican privileges).
[53] See e.g. Di Palma, *History of Marks* 70.
[54] On the work concept *see* Goehr, *Imaginary Museum* 120 et seq.; Jaszi, 40 Duke L.J. 455, 471–80 (1991); Kawohl & Kretschmer, 2 Intellectual Property Quarterly 209, 221 et seq. (2003); Barron, 15 Social & Legal Studies 101 (2006); Bracha, *Owning Ideas*; Bracha, 118 Yale L.J. 186, 238 (2008); Toynbee, 15 Music, Social & Legal Studies 77, 82 (2006); Rose, Authors and Owners 6; Woodmannsee, *The Author, Art and the Market* 39; Edelman, in Edelman & Heinich (eds.) *L'art en conflits* 102, 120–21; Pila, 71 Modern L. Rev. 535, 556 (2008) ('The history of the copyright system has been described as a history of the law's struggle to come to grips with the subject matter it protects'.); Sherman & Bently, *The Making of Modern Intellectual Property Law* 47 ('In its pre-modern form, the intangible (as distinct from the areas of law which granted

and design law, which today operate quite naturally with the idea of abstract IP objects, have only been conceived on this basis since the end of the eighteenth century. Previously, an action- and artefact-based approach dominated, which generally referred to books, scripts, machines etc., and which did not refer to an abstract object, but to a multitude of brute artefacts. The legal counterpart of this understanding of reality was the privilege. The prevailing opinion among legal historians meanwhile classifies the privilege as a qualitatively different legal institution than 'intellectual property'.[55] This latter legal concept can also be traced back no further than the late eighteenth century.[56] And indeed, you cannot have one without having the other. Before the emergence of the idea of the abstract ('intellectual') work and invention, it was quite simply unthinkable to apply the concept of property to anything other than tangible things: no property without an object.[57]

Although it is thus recognised that the abstract IP object is a construct with a history, IP law in general is rarely historicised from the perspective of its imagined reality. As a rule, the focus is on the history of genuine legal concepts. The emergence of the idea of the abstract work or invention is only noted incidentally.[58] The opposite perspective is taken in particular by Pottage and Sherman and Biagioli, who put the historical practices of patenting (models or written descriptions) into context with the emergence of the idea of the abstract invention and the patent as an exclusive IP right.[59] The history of the abstract work concept in music has been

---

property rights in mental labour) was thought of not as a thing but more as something which was done: or, as it was described at the time, a form of action or performance'.); Hesse, 131 Daedalus 26 et seq. (2002); O'Connor, 27 George Mason Law Review 205, 252–53 (2019).

On inventions see Dölemeyer, in Otto & Klippel (eds.) Geschichte des deutschen Patentrechts 13, 17; Pottage & Sherman, Figures of Invention 23; Long, 32 Technology and Culture 846–84 (1991); Prager, 26 Journal of the Patent Office Society 711 et seq. (1944); Phillips, 3 Journal of Legal History 71 et seq. (1982); Kostylo, in Bently & Kretschmer (eds.) Primary Sources on Copyright www.copyrighthistory.org with further references. Contra regarding the Venetian law of 1477 Silberstein, Erfindungsschutz und merkantilistische Gewerbeprivilegien 16 et seq.; Kurz, Weltgeschichte des Erfindungsschutzes 41 et seq. (first patent act of the world).

[55] Cf. Wadle, in Wadle (ed.) Geistiges Eigentum I 119 et seq. with further references; Wadle, in Wadle (ed.) Beiträge zur Geschichte des Urheberrechts 29, 33; Klippel, 7 ZGE/IPJ 49, 55 et seq. (2015) with further references; May, 20 Prometheus 159, 161 (2002); Galvez-Behar, La république des inventeurs 21 et seq.; Renouard, Traité des droits d'auteur 5. On patent law cf. Damme, Der Schutz technischer Erfindungen als Erscheinungsform moderner Volkswirtschaft 59–60; Kurz, Weltgeschichte des Erfindungsschutzes 191 et seq.

[56] Bosse, Autorschaft als Werkherrschaft 7; Gieseke, Vom Privileg zum Urheberrecht 115 et seq.; Pahlow, in Cordes et al. (eds.) Handwörterbuch zur deutschen Rechtsgeschichte 2010 et seq. The German terminology of Urheberrecht (authors rights) and Patentrecht (patent law) only became prevalent in the nineteenth century; cf. Köbler, in Festschrift Wadle 499, 519, 523.

[57] Hesse, 131 Daedalus 26 et seq. (2002) ('The prevailing theories of knowledge and of political legitimacy made such rights inconceivable').

[58] See e.g. Jaszi, 40 Duke L.J. 455 (1991); Sherman & Bently, The Making of Modern Intellectual Property; Bosse, Autorschaft als Werkherrschaft.

[59] Pottage & Sherman, Figures of Invention passim; Biagioli, 73 Social Research: An International Quarterly 1129–72 (2006); Biagioli, 22 Anthropological Forum 285–99 (2012).

presented by the philosopher and musicologist Lydia Goehr, who, however, does not go into the subject of copyright in depth.[60] This thematic focus can be found in essays by Anne Barron, who grounds her arguments, however, more in social theory than in history.[61]

Against this background and on the basis of this state of research, an attempt will be made in the following to reconstruct the history of IP law with a view to the history of its subject matter. Although the focus is on copyright and patent law as the two oldest and best historically researched subjects, design and trademark law are also included in the diachronic investigation.[62] The thesis for all these fields of law is that 'intellectual property' rights only became conceivable after an object capable of ownership had been constructed. Here, as everywhere else, the law presupposes a fact which is regulated. The peculiarity of IP law is that this fact is an institutional-social fact, which only becomes reality when it is declared and collectively recognised.

Such an undertaking can only be carried out at a considerable level of abstraction. In view of the very well-researched primary sources,[63] some of which are available online, the associated risk of historical inaccuracies seems justifiable. Moreover, only a comprehensive look at the history of the abstract IP object conveys an understanding of the power relations that are objectified in it. It is ultimately this normativity of the abstract IP object that is relevant from a legal point of view and that provides the key to explaining the numerous unsolved puzzles of IP theory.[64] With this goal in mind, the technological, epistemic and socio-economic conditions of the possibility of the idea of the abstract IP object are first historicised (see Section 3.2.1) before its formation is traced in the word histories of work, invention and design, as well as in legal discourse (see Section 3.2.2).

3.2.1 The Historicity of Conditions for Abstraction 2

Social facts such as the talk and the idea of the abstract IP object do not occur abruptly. They have prerequisites which in turn have a history. Three of the numerous circumstances, interwoven in a complex way, which contributed to the formation of the eccentric idea of the abstract IP object – qualified as 'wild' by a British judge in 1769[65] – stand out as particularly significant.[66] Firstly, technological

---

[60] Goehr, *Imaginary Museum*, passim.
[61] See Barron, 52 New Formations 58–81 (2004); Barron, 15 Social & Legal Studies 101–27 (2006).
[62] On the history of design law *see* Sherman & Bently, *The Making of Modern Intellectual Property Law* 210–11.
[63] *Cf.* Bently & Kretschmer (eds.), *Primary Sources on Copyright* www.copyrighthistory.org.
[64] Section 5.4 and Chapter 6.
[65] Millar v. Taylor, 4 Burrow 2303, 2357 (1769); Sherman & Bently, *The Making of Modern Intellectual Property Law* 19 et seq.
[66] *Cf.* Goehr, *Imaginary Museum* 107; Pudelek, in Barck et al. (eds.) *Ästhetische Grundbegriffe* VI 545; Bracha, 38 Loyola of L.A. L. Rev. 177, 241 (2004) ('A good contextual story would describe a

progress and in particular the invention of ever-new reproductive technologies (see Section 3.2.1.1); secondly, the fundamental change from the ideal of imitation to ingenious innovation (see Section 3.2.1.2); and thirdly, the replacement of a strictly regulated economy embedded in the feudal-absolutist social order by a market economy in which all kinds of work results must be tradable (see Section 3.2.1.3). It was only when these three developments, which themselves were complexly interrelated, culminated in France and the UK in the eighteenth century that the ground was prepared for the institutional innovation of the 'immaterial good'.

3.2.1.1 New Technologies

The fact that our history begins with a history of technology corresponds to Searle's recognition of the logical primacy of the brute over the social-institutional facts: without external reality there is no need and ultimately no point of reference for speech acts and the social reality generated by them.[67] Even the first abstraction already discussed – the setting and collective recognition of general terms for a multitude of similar artefacts – can only be achieved if man-made artefacts can be reproduced.[68] This requires the use of technologies that change external reality.

The speech of mnemonics or memory techniques proves that already human memory as well as its training belong in this context. With them, people are able to reproduce messages that are generally referred to – for example, with the name of a myth transmitted by word of mouth. However, since reproduction takes place in the human body, these techniques are still primarily perceived as human activity. This alone prevents the emergence of an object idea.[69] At the same time, from a legal point of view there is no need for regulation which, like (intellectual) property, presupposes an object of protection.[70] It is sufficient to regulate who is allowed to know and communicate something.

---

complex web of causation in which all factors, including the legal-institutional ones, were both active and reactive'.); Bracha, *Owning Ideas* 522 ('Some of the shaping forces were technological, some were ideological, others were economic, others still political, and finally some of the forces are best understood as internal to legal discourse'); Barron, 15 Social & Legal Studies 25 et seq. (2006); Plumpe, 23 Archiv für Begriffsgeschichte 175 et seq. (1979); MacLeod, *Inventing the Industrial Revolution* 202; Deazley, *On the Origin of the Right to Copy* 221 et seq.; Feather, in Woodmansee & Jaszi (eds.) *The Construction of Authorship* 191; Barron, 15 Social & Legal Studies 25 (2006); Cornish, 13 The Edinburgh L. Rev. 8, 9–10 (2009); Kristeller, 12 Journal of the History of Ideas 496 et seq. (1951); Kristeller, 13 Journal of the History of Ideas 17 et seq. (1952); Mattick (ed.) *Eighteenth-Century Aesthetics and the Reconstruction of Art*; Wadle, in Wadle (ed.) Geistiges Eigentum I 119 et seq.; Klippel, 7 ZGE/IPJ 49, 55 et seq. (2015); May, 20 Prometheus 159, 161 (2002).

[67] Section 2.2.1.
[68] Section 3.1; Zech, *Information als Schutzgegenstand* 167 et seq.
[69] On oral societies see Ong, *Orality and Literacy* 32, 42–43.
[70] See Rognstad, *Property Aspects of Intellectual Property* 43–46, 124.

The abstract object idea comes closer if this 'something' is written down in characters or lettering and these – like other artefacts – can be copied manually.[71] For then there is not only a general term for a myth or a tool, but several concrete things that need to be named and thus ordered. The quantity of original first artefacts and the quantity of their copies are rapidly increasing due to the storage medium of writing, because not everything depends on the limited memory capacity of individual people. There is then no longer only one myth, but many tragedies and, building on this, a new abstract level – namely the ideal type of tragedy.[72] In Aristotle's poetics, this type already takes on the object-like form of a closed unit with a beginning, middle and end.[73]

At the same time, it is noticeable that ancient and medieval writings generally did not have a title chosen by the author that could have become a signifier for an abstract object.[74] In any case, no copyright or patent laws in the current sense have been handed down from antiquity or the Middle Ages.[75] As will be shown, this is not only due to the fact that there was no idea of innovation nor a market economy during these times.[76] For the development of IP law in its current form, there was already a lack of reproductive technologies that triggered a special need for regulation, which was later responded to with privileges and finally with IP rights. The number of people who could write was relatively small.[77] Both the use of this technique and of other craft techniques could be effectively controlled by regulating access to, or the exercise of, these skills. The sophisticated concept of ownership of the abstract IP object was not required. This also applies to the orderly practice of using product marks on mass-produced objects, such as amphorae, which merely indicated to whom the thing in question belonged, what characteristics it possessed or who produced it.[78]

This situation did not change until the late Middle Ages, when reproducible machines were developed that could replace human labour on a larger scale. From

---

[71] Ong, *Orality and Literacy* 77 et seq.; on the invention of the phonetic alphabet loc. cit., 90 ('The alphabet ... has lost all connection with things as things. It represents sound itself as a thing, tranforming the evanescent world of sound to the quiescent, quasi-permanent world of space'.); McLuhan, *Gutenberg Galaxy* 183 et seq.; Luhmann, *Gesellschaft der Gesellschaft* 249 et seq.; Hartmann, *Das Problem des geistigen Seins* 414–15; Zech, *Information als Schutzgegenstand* 169.

[72] Ong, *Orality and Literacy* 49 with further references.

[73] Aristotle, *Poetics* 13–14; *see also* Thierse, 36 Weimarer Beiträge 240, 245, 247 (1990); Pudelek, *in* Barck et al. (eds.) *Ästhetische Grundbegriffe* VI 530. On the rise of the written score as the primary representation of the musical work *see* Pudelek, *in* Barck et al. (eds.) *Ästhetische Grundbegriffe* VI 557. See also Ong, *Orality and Literacy* 79–80 (Plato's theory of ideas a consequence of literacy).

[74] Rothe, *Der literarische Titel* 34 et seq.; Ong, *Orality and Literacy* 123.

[75] Gieseke, *Vom Privileg zum Urheberrecht* 3; Kurz, *Weltgeschichte des Erfindungsschutzes* 5 et seq.

[76] Section 3.2.1.3.

[77] Houston, *Literacy* 1.

[78] Kohler, *Recht des Markenschutzes* 42 et seq.; Di Palma, *History of Marks* 17 et seq.

this time on, economic policy could not be limited to only controlling the particularly skilled craftsmen. Instead, it had to be regulated who could or should 'make' the 'art' of the drainage of mines in Bohemia[79] or build windmills.[80] The agreements and privileges made for this purpose in the fourteenth century designated the technologies with their special (in relation to other machines) and at the same time general (in relation to individual copies) names. The number of signifiers – which in turn represented a large number of reproducible artefacts – grew. The practice of speaking about a plurality of things in a singular, such as about 'the' windmill, became more common. Thus the question arose as to what the commonality of the numerous things is that are uniformly described. Only in their outer similarity or in an internal plan (such as the plan of a building) that an architect claims to be his intellectual product?[81]

These tendencies received a clear boost with the machine mass production of paper and the invention and spread of woodblock printing, copperplate engraving and, not least, letterpress printing in the fifteenth century.[82] The whole purpose of these technologies was to reproduce artefacts on a massive scale. As a result, the number of general artefact names (abstraction level 1) increased exponentially. In addition to the tools and machines, which could – albeit with some effort – be reproduced themselves, ever larger numbers of different graphics, books and writings were (re)produced at ever-greater speed. All these reproducible artefacts had to be distinguished from each other and signified with special names.[83] These general terms in turn were used in privileges regulating the production and further use of reproduction technologies and their output.[84]

The influence of these technological developments and their linguistic processing on the emergence of the idea of the abstract work and other abstract IP objects can be measured by the temporal relationship between the invention of the reproductive technology in question and the recognition of an immaterial object capable of being owned. Since the fifteenth century, printed writings have been subject to privileges. Writings, in turn, have been the most prominent, and often the first,

---

[79] Silberstein, *Erfindungsschutz und merkantilistische Gewerbeprivilegien* 43–44, 56; Dölemeyer, in Otto & Klippel (eds.) *Geschichte des deutschen Patentrechts* 13, 30 et seq. with further references; Kurz, *Weltgeschichte des Erfindungsschutzes* 28 et seq.
[80] May, 20 Prometheus 159, 174 (2002) (Venetian privilege from 1332 regarding wind mills); O'Connor, 27 George Mason Law Review 205, 252 (2019) ('Much of the value of ingenious devices or machines, and of texts or performative art resides in their replicability').
[81] *Cf.* Kostylo, in Bently & Kretschmer (eds.) *Primary Sources on Copyright* www.copyrighthistory.org.
[82] Eisenstein, *The Printing Revolution*; Johns, *The Nature of the Book*; van Dijk, *Grounds of the Immaterial* 10–11 with further references; Ong, *Orality and Literacy* 116 ('Print suggests that words are things far more than writing ever did'.); McLuhan, *Gutenberg Galaxy* 237 et seq. On improvements of paper production in the late eighteenth century see Bosse, *Autorschaft als Werkherrschaft* 124.
[83] Ong, *Orality and Literacy* 123.
[84] Section 3.2.1.3.1.

application of early copyright law.[85] Even today, literary works rank at the top of the work categories listed in Section 2(1) of the German Copyright Act (UrhG). The 'works of music' mentioned in Section 2(1) no. 2 have only attained this abstract status long after literary works, because even in the eighteenth century music was primarily regarded as an ephemeral event of performing music and listening. This perception only changed in the second half of the eighteenth century under the impression of mass printing of sheet music.[86] What we subsume today under the concept of fine art has always been copied by hand and since the fifteenth century by means of printing technology, which already in the Renaissance raised the question of the status of the original and its creator.[87] However, the mass reproduction of paintings and sculptures true to the original was a long time coming, and even today art theory still distinguishes between autographic and allographic artworks, i.e. those in which every correct copy (such as of a photograph) or only a very specific artefact (such as the original oil painting) is *regarded* as a true exemplar of the work.[88] The fact that in the eighteenth century visual art was not yet the subject of mass mechanical reproduction – unlike the speech of an author or the expression of a thought – may also have led Kant and Fichte to explicitly exclude this sector from their theories justifying prohibitions of reprinting.[89] The dominant, singular status of the original as a brute, physical Master Artefact stood in the way of the application of the concept of the abstract work to the field of fine arts for a long time.[90]

The connection between the invention of technologies for the mass (re)production of practically indistinguishable artefacts on the one hand, and the development of categories of the abstract IP object related to these artefacts on the other, can be shown by many other examples that trickle down to the present day.

The possibility of manufacturing and imitating everyday objects such as fabrics, furniture etc. on a massive scale, which had existed since industrialisation in the nineteenth century, aroused a need for protection on the part of the 'art industry', which was finally satisfied by the legal protection of 'industrial designs'.[91] The

---

[85] Section 3.2.1.3.1; Ong, *Orality and Literacy* 129 ('Typography had made the word into a commodity'.); McLuhan, *Gutenberg Galaxy* 142 et seq.
[86] Bach v. Longman (1777), in Bently & Kretschmer (eds.) *Primary Sources on Copyright* www.copyrighthistory.org; Kawohl & Kretschmer, 2 Intellectual Property Quarterly 209, 214–15 (2003); Barron, 15 Social & Legal Studies 101, 119 (2006); Kawohl & Kretschmer, 15 Social & Legal Studies 25, 39 (2006); Kawohl, in Sanio & Scheib (eds.) *Form – Luxus, Kalkül und Abstinen* 136 et seq.; Schuster, *Das Urheberrecht der Tonkunst* 16, 21–22, 26.
[87] Section 3.2.1.2; Thierse, 36 Weimarer Beiträge 240, 247 (1990).
[88] Schmücker, *Was ist Kunst?* 186 et seq. with further references, 199.
[89] Kant (1785), in Bently & Kretschmer (eds.) *Primary Sources on Copyright* www.copyrighthistory.org 13; Fichte (1793), in Bently & Kretschmer (eds.) *Primary Sources on Copyright* www.copyrighthistory.org 21 et seq.
[90] Teilmann-Lock, *The Object of Copyright* 120–21 (the dominant paradigm of the abstract visual work only became prevalent in the early twentieth century).
[91] Weigert, *Musterschutz* 10 et seq.; Breimesser, *Urheberrecht und Rechtsbegriff* 55 et seq.

possibility, which has existed since the late nineteenth century, to record sounds and images of external reality on audio and video carriers and to copy them has given rise to a whole series of new rights, including abstract objects of protection. In this regard, and in contrast to Anglo-American law, continental European law distinguishes between works protected by copyright on the one hand and 'achievements' protected by rights related to copyright on the other.[92] The first group includes photographic, cinematographic and pantomimic works; the second group, in the order of their mention in the German Copyright Act, includes photographs, performances by performing artists, audio recordings, broadcast signals and video recordings.[93] All these objects of protection found their way into law only after sounds and images had become reproducible artefacts.[94] Digitisation has extended the list of related rights by two new entries – namely databases and, most recently, press publications.[95]

In the field of industrial property law, computerisation and biotechnology have expanded the circle of reproducible artefacts. Towards the end of the twentieth century, this led to topographies of semiconductor products[96] as well as computer-implemented and biotechnological inventions finding their way into IP law.[97]

Improved technologies for the registration of Master Artefacts also contribute to the expansion of the objects of protection. For example, microorganisms can be deposited on a long-term basis[98] and three-dimensional patterns of the layers of which a semiconductor product is composed can be depicted.[99] EU trademark law has recently abandoned the requirement of a graphical representation of the sign and thus opened the door for sounds, which are deposited as audio files.[100]

---

[92] Rehbinder & Peukert, *Urheberrecht* paras 641 et seq.; Cornish, 13 The Edinburgh L. Rev. 8, 19 (2009).

[93] Section 2(1) no. 3, 5 and 6 and Sections 72, 73 et seq., 85–87, 94–95 German Copyright Act (UrhG).

[94] See the contributions in Sherman & Wiseman, *Copyright and the Challenge of the New passim*; on the history of the rights related to copyright Rehbinder & Peukert, *Urheberrecht* para 645; on performances see Sterne, *The Audible Past* 23; on the history fotography Busch & Albers, in Barck et al. (eds.) *Ästhetische Grundbegriffe II* 494 et seq.; Edelman, *Ownership of the Image*; on movies Barron, 67 Modern L. Rev. 177, 181 et seq. (2004); Barron, 52 New Formations, 58, 72 et seq. (2004); on broadcasts BGH 27 February 1962 Case no. I ZR 118/60, GRUR 1962, 470, 475 – AKI.

[95] Art. 15 DSM Directive.

[96] Art. 2(1) Directive 1987/54 on the legal protection of topographies of semiconductor products.

[97] See Lee, 45 IDEA: The Intellectual Property L. Rev. 321 et seq. (2005); Lai, in Lai & Maget Dominicé (eds.) *Intellectual Property and Access to Im/material Goods* 94, 119; Biagioli, 22 Anthropological Forum 285, 289 (2012); Zech, 119 GRUR 475 (2017) (dematerialisation of patent law).

[98] See Chapter 3 footnote 21.

[99] Cf. Art. 1(1)(b) Directive 1987/54 on the legal protection of topographies of semiconductor products.

[100] Art. 3 and recital 13 EU Trademark Dir.; Art. 4 and recital 9 EU Trademark Reg. ('A sign should therefore be permitted to be represented in any appropriate form using generally available technology, and thus not necessarily by graphic means, as long as the representation

The connection between technological progress and the emergence of the idea of the abstract IP object can generally be observed in the context of trademark law, albeit in a modified form. In this case, the abstract IP object is the (well-known) sign as such, which is embodied on packaging, websites etc. and which is protected detached from certain goods or services and irrespective of any risk of confusion. The trigger for the two-fold decoupling of the sign protected by trademark law from concrete embodiments and the designated products and their perception by the public was the industrial mass production of goods in the second half of the nineteenth century, which were no longer sold by local manufacturers but via institutional trade.[101] In order to create customer loyalty for such anonymous, exchangeable products, entrepreneurs such as Karl August Lingner invented imaginative product brands such as 'Odol' in the last decade of the nineteenth century, which – although they said nothing about the origin of the product – were outstandingly suitable for memorable advertising in the mass media.[102] In an affluent society in which machines do most of the work, such product marks become the decisive instrument of sales promotion and distinction. They thus advance to become an abstract object whose creation is rewarded and promoted by contemporary trademark law for its own sake in the same way as an artistic-technological innovation.[103]

3.2.1.2 From Nameless Imitation to the Ingenious Work

The aforementioned examples demonstrate the dynamism triggered by technological progress. With IP rights, legislators are reacting to new reproduction technologies and related regulatory needs. However, this observation does not claim a monocausal relationship. Technologies for the mass production of externally identical or largely similar artefacts are a necessary, but not a sufficient, reason for the emergence of the idea of the abstract IP object. The mere fact that more than 300 years passed between the invention of book printing and the French Revolutionary Copyright Act shows that there must be other causes for the eccentric, long unthinkable idea of the immaterial artwork and other abstract IP objects.[104]

A further, now social-epistemic prerequisite for this development is the view that humans can create something new at all, instead of just carrying out God's plan or imitating nature. For only on the basis of this assumption are new artefacts perceived

---

offers satisfactory guarantees to that effect'. On the history of colour marks in the UK *see* Sherman & Bently, *The Making of Modern Intellectual Property Law* 190.

[101] Isay, GRUR 23, 25 (1929); Hellmann, *Soziologie der Marke* 46 et seq.
[102] Hellmann, *Soziologie der Marke* 51 et seq.; Heydt, 78 GRUR 7, 14–15 (1976); Bently, *in* Dinwoodie & Janis (eds.) *Trademarks and Unfair Competition* 118, 149 with further references.
[103] See Section 5.1.1.1.
[104] *See also* Pohlmann, *Die Frühgeschichte des musikalischen Urheberrechts* 121–22.

as something worth striving for, as an asset to be legally protected by privileges and finally by IP rights.[105]

Such thinking was alien during antiquity. Inventiveness in solving problems or improving war techniques was appreciated. Men with such abilities were called *ingeniosus* (πολύμητις).[106] However, their achievements were not ultimately attributed to the originality or creativity of the actor concerned. All technical-aesthetic achievements always had only a referral meaning, but neither their own meaning nor truth.[107] That applies to ancient Egypt[108] and Ancient Greece, where Aristotle defined tragedy as a whole (see Section 3.2.1.1), but at the same time stated that

> [e]pic poetry and the composition of tragedy, as well as comedy and the arts of dithyrambic poetry and (for the most part) of music for pipe or lyre, are all (taken together) imitations. ... The poet is engaged in imitation, just like a painter or anyone else who produces visual images, and the object of his imitation must in every case be one of three things: either the kind of thing that was or is the case; or the kind of thing that is said or thought to be the case; or the kind of thing that ought to be the case.[109]

In this world, man does not create *ex nihilo*. In him and through him there are other forces at work that cause nature to be imitated, or the truth of the eternal realm of ideas to be expressed.[110] 'The possibility of experiencing something unique is still not thought of in the work of art, the work is not yet a medium of self-knowledge and self-affirmation of man'.[111] It is integrated into a fateful activity of man, into a social order that does not recognise any innovation.

This order of thinking and of things only began to change in the late Middle Ages.[112] In 1421 Filippo Brunelleschi refused to join the Florentine guilds and instead looked for individual patent protection.[113] At the same time, Nikolaus von Kues saw

---

[105] Plumpe, 23 Archiv für Begriffsgeschichte 175 et seq. (1979). On the formation of the idea of the abstract sign in trademark law *see* Section 3.2.1.3.2.

[106] Grimm & Grimm, *Deutsches Wörterbuch III* 800; Pudelek, *in* Barck et al. (eds.) *Ästhetische Grundbegriffe VI* 536; Ortland, *in* Barck et al. (eds.) *Ästhetische Grundbegriffe II* 664.

[107] Blumenberg, *in* Blumenberg (ed.) *Ästhetische und metaphrologische Schriften* 9, 27; Thierse, 36 Weimarer Beiträge 240, 244 (1990).

[108] Pottage & Sherman, *Figures of Invention* 25 with note 24.

[109] Aristotle, *Poetics* 3, 42.

[110] Blumenberg, *in* Blumenberg (ed.) *Ästhetische und metaphrologische Schriften* 9, 22; Hesse, 131 Daedalus 26 et seq. (2002); Ortland, *in* Barck et al. (eds.) *Ästhetische Grundbegriffe II* 665 et seq. with further references; Wetzel, *in* Barck et al. (eds.) *Ästhetische Grundbegriffe I* 480, 502–3; Fontius, *in* Klotz et al. (eds.) *Literatur im Epochenumbruch* 409, 417 et seq. Nowadays, any artefact is ascribed to a human actor; *cf.* OLG Frankfurt/M. 13 May 2014 Case no. 11 U 62/13, GRUR 2014, 863.

[111] Translated from the original German. Blumenberg, *in* Blumenberg (ed.) *Ästhetische und metaphrologische Schriften* 9, 27.

[112] Wetzel, *in* Barck et al. (eds.) *Ästhetische Grundbegriffe I* 480, 504; Gieseke, *Vom Privileg zum Urheberrecht* 10.

[113] Kostylo, *in* Bently & Kretschmer (eds.) *Primary Sources on Copyright* www.copyrighthistory.org.

something new, not predetermined by nature in the rather profane products of a spoonmaker.[114] In the sixteenth century, analogies of God and the artist became more common;[115] artists like Dürer signed their works and demanded that *alieni laboris et ingenii* not be appropriated without authorisation;[116] the talk of the creative 'genius' begins to displace the medieval *ingenium*;[117] and authors received privileges for the scripts they wrote.[118]

Nevertheless, Pohlmann's reading of these events, according to which copyright was a child of the Renaissance, was mostly rejected.[119] This is not only due to the controversial historical findings as to how often author privileges instead of publisher privileges were granted and whether author privileges must not also be read in the context of censorship and absolutist economic control.[120] The decisive factor speaking against Pohlmann's theory of early modern privileges as precursors of authors' rights is rather the realisation that it is not enough just to look at the status of the innovative or creative person. Rather, it must also be asked whether in the sixteenth century the idea of the abstract work and other immaterial goods was also present, which exist as self-explanatory objects for themselves.

But this is not the case. Even in the artist biographies of Giorgio Vasari, divine inspiration is the source of genius.[121] The rebirth (sic!) of ancient thought is also a return of the idea of imitation, against which the concept of the authentically creative human being had to assert itself slowly and laboriously.[122] The *musica poetica* of the sixteenth century, for example, transferred the Aristotelian concept of a closed and imitative tragedy to the field of music.[123] French baroque music of the seventeenth century still followed fixed composition rules.[124]

Only since the complete decomposition of the mimesis idea in the eighteenth century has the work of art not merely imitated or referred to something else, but has

---

[114] Cf. Blumenberg, *in* Blumenberg (ed.) *Ästhetische und metaphrologische Schriften* 9, 13–14.
[115] Blumenberg, *in* Blumenberg (ed.) *Ästhetische und metaphrologische Schriften* 9, 13–14 (Nikolaus von Kues); Pudelek, *in* Barck et al. (eds.) *Ästhetische Grundbegriffe* VI 543; on the significance of printing *see* McLuhan, *Gutenberg Galaxy* 177 et seq.
[116] Gieseke, *Vom Privileg zum Urheberrecht* 28–29; Pudelek, *in* Barck et al. (eds.) *Ästhetische Grundbegriffe* VI 538; Wetzel, *in* Barck et al. (eds.) *Ästhetische Grundbegriffe* I 480.
[117] Ortland, *in* Barck et al. (eds.) *Ästhetische Grundbegriffe* II 664; Pudelek, *in* Barck et al. (eds.) *Ästhetische Grundbegriffe* VI 545.
[118] Pohlmann, *Die Frühgeschichte des musikalischen Urheberrechts* 192–93 (privilege for Hans Neusidler from 1535 *id.* at 263.
[119] *See* Pohlmann, *Die Frühgeschichte des musikalischen Urheberrechts* 19; Silberstein, *Erfindungsschutz und merkantilistische Gewerbeprivilegien* 16 et seq.
[120] Cf. Schuster, *Das Urheberrecht der Tonkunst* 10–11; MacLeod, *Inventing the Industrial Revolution* 221.
[121] Ortland, *in* Barck et al. (eds.) *Ästhetische Grundbegriffe* II 671 et seq.; Wetzel, *in* Barck et al. (eds.) *Ästhetische Grundbegriffe* I 480, 508.
[122] Blumenberg, *in* Blumenberg (ed.) *Ästhetische und metaphrologische Schriften* 9, 16 et seq. with further references.
[123] Thierse, 36 *Weimarer Beiträge* 240, 248 et seq. (1990) (Listenius' 'musica' from 1533).
[124] Wetzel, *in* Barck et al. (eds.) *Ästhetische Grundbegriffe* I 480, 509–10.

become something in its own right and thus finally attained an ontological self-status.[125] This process runs parallel to the emergence of the romantic idea of the author, who creates an original of which he is considered the natural owner.[126] Also in science and technology in the late seventeenth century the Newtonian, sceptical-scientific view of reality and man as inventor and manipulator of nature displaced the ancient world view that had understood man as an agent of God's will.[127] The author is even considered capable of creating fantasy worlds that imitate nothing existing in brute reality.[128] What the genius creates is by definition inimitable, so the work of the genius cannot be imitation.[129] But if divine, natural or otherwise external normative specifications of the artwork are omitted, the meaning of these originals can only be founded in themselves.[130]

In England, it was Edward Young, in particular, who drew this radical consequence and cut off all ties between the artwork and art-external ideals. In his 1728 writing *On Lyric Property*, Young explains that the author has to strive for a perfection 'in' the work, which could only be regarded as the work of a genius if it was 'original'.[131] Despite different political and economic conditions, very similar tones were struck in the culturally leading France of the *age classique*. Around the numerous academies for language, painting and sculpture, music and dance, a discourse established itself in the first half of the eighteenth century on the characteristics of an *ouvrage excellent* that were not brought to the artwork from outside.[132] While in Germany at that time poets still practised rule poetry and tried to please

---

[125] Blumenberg, in Blumenberg (ed.) *Ästhetische und metaphrologische Schriften* 9, 45; Becq, in Mattick Jr. (ed.) *Eighteenth-Century Aesthetics and the Reconstruction of Art* 240 et seq.
[126] Haferkorn, 5 Archiv für Geschichte des Buchwesens 523, 631 et seq. (1964); Rose, *Authors and Owners* 6; Woodmansee, *The Author, Art and the Market* 39; Woodmansee, 17 Eighteenth-Century Stud. 425 (1984); Jaszi, 40 Duke L.J. 455 (1991); Sherman & Bently, *The Making of Modern Intellectual Property Law* 35 et seq.; Bracha, 118 Yale L.J. 186, 192 et seq. (2008); Pudelek, in Barck et al. (eds.) *Ästhetische Grundbegriffe* VI 546; Thierse, 36 Weimarer Beiträge 240, 253 (1990); Ortland, in Barck et al. (eds.) *Ästhetische Grundbegriffe* II 681 et seq.; Wetzel, in Barck et al. (eds.) *Ästhetische Grundbegriffe* I 480, 503; MacLeod, *Inventing the Industrial Revolution* 16; Waldron, 68 Chicago-Kent L. Rev. 841, 878 (1993).
[127] MacLeod, *Inventing the Industrial Revolution* 202, 219–20 with further references; Biagioli, 73 Social Research: An International Quarterly 1129, 1143–44 (2006); Lai, in Lai & Maget Dominicé (eds.) *Intellectual Property and Access to Im/material Goods* 94, 109 with further references; Galvez-Behar, *La république des inventeurs* 21.
[128] Blumenberg, in Blumenberg (ed.) *Ästhetische und metaphrologische Schriften* 9, 42.
[129] Pudelek, in Barck et al. (eds.) *Ästhetische Grundbegriffe* VI 545.
[130] Pudelek, in Barck et al. (eds.) *Ästhetische Grundbegriffe* VI 564; Ortland, 52 DZPhil 773, 783–84 (2005); Rotstein, 68 Chicago-Kent L. Rev. 725, 729 et seq. (1993).
[131] Young, in Young (ed.) *Conjectures on original composition* 56. On Young and his influence on Germany *see* Plumpe, 23 Archiv für Begriffsgeschichte 175, 188 et seq. (1979); Ortland, in Barck et al. (eds.) *Ästhetische Grundbegriffe* II 680.
[132] Kristeller, 12 Journal of the History of Ideas 496, 521 et seq. (1951); Kristeller, 13 Journal of the History of Ideas 17, 18–19 (1952); Ortland, in Barck et al. (eds.) *Ästhetische Grundbegriffe* II 687; Häseler, in Barck et al. (eds.) *Ästhetische Grundbegriffe* VII 638, 640; Höffner, *Geschichte und Wesen des Urheberrechts* I 251 et seq.

their patrons,[133] in 1728 Heinrich Christoph Koch presented the *Versuch einer Anleitung zur Composition* (Attempt of a Guide to Composition), in which he broke with Aristotelian poetics for music and sought musical poetry in the 'inner character', in the 'spirit of tone pieces', which in turn reflected the creative spirit of genius.[134]

Karl Philipp Moritz finally presented a comprehensive theory of these approaches in 1785 with his *Versuch einer Vereinigung aller schönen Künste und Wissenschaften unter dem Begriff des in sich Vollendeten* (Attempt to Unite All Fine Arts and Sciences under the Concept of the Self-Completed).[135] For Moritz, it was already a historical fact that '[m]an ... has rejected the principle of the imitation of nature as the main end purpose of the fine arts and subordinated it to the purpose of pleasure ...'. While the 'useful object' as a result of the 'mechanical' arts does not in itself represent anything whole or perfect, but is always created for a purpose, the situation is different in the 'fine' arts. Their results are to be understood as something 'accomplished in itself, which thus constitutes a whole in itself and grants me pleasure for its own sake'. The beautiful has 'its purpose not without itself' and is 'not because of the perfection of something else, but because of its own inner perfection', its 'inner expediency'. '*The object must be something perfect in itself*'.[136] Or in the words of Friedrich Schlegel: 'A work is educated if it is sharply limited everywhere, but within the limits it is limitless and inexhaustible, if it is completely faithful to itself, equal everywhere, and yet sublime above itself'.[137] The only criteria by which such 'pure' art *may* (!) still be measured are generated in the autonomous art system.[138]

The decoupling of the work of art from all external specifications has far-reaching consequences. In contrast to Aristotelian poetics, it is now the work itself that demands fidelity to itself during public performance and printing. The work sets the standards for its realisation. Potentially incorrect performances, book or sheet music exemplars can never fully represent the work. 'The' work is rather only

---

[133] Haferkorn, 5 Archiv für Geschichte des Buchwesens 523, 651 et seq. (1964); Wetzel, *in* Barck et al. (eds.) *Ästhetische Grundbegriffe* I 480, 515.

[134] Thierse, 36 Weimarer Beiträge 240, 251 (1990). On the formation of the abstract musical work see Goehr, *Imaginary Museum* 120 et seq.; Barron, 15 Social & Legal Studies 25, 40 (2006).

[135] Moritz, *in* Jahn (ed.) *Karl Philipp Moritz: Werke in zwei Bänden* I 202–3; see Pudelek, *in* Barck et al. (eds.) *Ästhetische Grundbegriffe* VI 531; Fontius, *in* Klotz et al. (eds.) *Literatur im Epochenumbruch* 409, 417 et seq.; Thierse, 36 Weimarer Beiträge 240, 252, 254 et seq. (1990).

[136] Translated from the original German. Moritz, *in* Jahn (ed.) *Karl Philipp Moritz: Werke in zwei Bänden* I 203.

[137] Translated from the original German. Cf. Kölbel, 10 *Text. Kritische Beiträge* 27, 38.

[138] Luhmann, *Kunst der Gesellschaft* 268–69, 438–39; Kristeller, 12 Journal of the History of Ideas 496 et seq. (1951); Kristeller, 13 Journal of the History of Ideas 17 et seq. (1952); Becq, *in* Mattick Jr. (ed.) *Eighteenth-Century Aesthetics* 240 et seq.; Pudelek, *in* Barck et al. (eds.) *Ästhetische Grundbegriffe* VI 549 et seq. with further references; Thierse, 36 Weimarer Beiträge 240, 251 et seq. (1990).

accidentally embodied in these copies and exists independently of them.[139] The work crystallises into a structural whole, increasingly provided with a distinctive[140] and at the same time purely ideal, title; it even takes on a kind of life of its own. It is considered to be an 'intellectual child', an objectified expression of the author's personality that, like the author, deserves the protection of the law.[141]

Once again, it is necessary to put this second condition of the possibility of the idea of the abstract IP object into context. This context is formed by technological developments and economic upheavals. The ancient and medieval guidelines for artistic creation were directly interwoven with patronage as the dominant form of financing literary and artistic activity. Instead of the guidelines for a commissioned work formulated by the patron in accordance with social practice, the taste of the anonymous audience that decided on success or failure increasingly took its place – first of all in England. Artists like Young and Moritz, who did not want their work to be measured solely by market success, had to establish new criteria for 'good' art, formulated by themselves and addressed to their peers.[142] The irony is that it was with their romantic-emphatic work concept that they created the conceptual basis for the object capable of being owned and thus marketable in the first place. The romantic rejection of all traditional evaluation criteria of art and literature opened the door to the logic of the market.[143]

3.2.1.3 From Dirigiste Regulation of Economic Activity to the Market Economy

The change of the economic system from centralised control by guilds, the church and feudal rulers to a decentralised anonymous market economy has indeed contributed decisively to the formation of the idea of the abstract IP object. In addition to technological progress and the positive connotation of the new and the original, *the market* represents the third condition of the possibility of this social-institutional innovation.

3.2.1.3.1 ECONOMIC REGULATION THROUGH PRIVILEGES Before the decision on the use of reproduction technologies was delegated to market participants, the idea of central control over communication dominated. Since the early modern era,

---

[139] On music Goehr, *Imaginary Museum* 106–19 and 205–42.
[140] Rothe, *Der literarische Titel* 17, 31 et seq. (distinctive titles common since the eighteenth century); Vogt, Untitled 7 (distinctive titles for visual arts common since around 1850).
[141] *Cf.* Schuster, *Das Urheberrecht der Tonkunst* 79; Elster, 6 RabelsZ 903, 915 (1932); Hirsch, 36 UFITA 19, 40 (1962); Troller, 50 UFITA 385, 409 (1967) ('The aesthetic work has an independent individuality'.); Edelman, *in* Edelman & Heinich (eds.) *L'art en conflicts* 102, 120; Jaszi, 40 Duke L.J. 455, 473 et seq. (1991).
[142] Wetzel, *in* Barck et al. (eds.) *Ästhetische Grundbegriffe* I 480, 510–12; Haferkorn, 5 Archiv für Geschichte des Buchwesens 523, 563; Sherman & Bently, *The Making of Modern Intellectual Property Law* 176–80.
[143] Bourdieu, *Market of Symbolic Goods* 1 et seq.

however, rulers had been confronted with the problem that on the one hand they could not and did not want to permanently do without new technologies – such as in mining, but also book printing – but on the other hand they wanted to retain control over these powerful technologies.[144]

The legal instrument to deal with this problem was the privilege. It allowed the privileged person to use the technique in question and at the same time prohibited all others from doing so. In this way, the privilege allowed feudal rulers to control the economy and society in a targeted manner. An incentive was given to introduce or invent new technologies and to produce reproducible artefacts such as books, but only for the benefit of handpicked persons or corporatist organisations dating from the Middle Ages, to which the enforcement of the exclusive rights associated with the privilege was partly delegated.[145] This dirigiste-instrumental concept also formed the basis of privileges for early capitalist manufacturers[146] and mercantilist industrial monopolies.[147] In the field of book production, the privilege was also directly linked to censorship. The privilege was used to determine which printer or bookseller was allowed to print and market which writings under which conditions. Accordingly, it was mainly these entrepreneurs who were granted privileges, but not the writers and artists.[148]

According to their legal structure, privileges were always related to *behaviour* for the production and further use of *tangible things*.[149] This brute regulatory reality concerned all privileges, because in early modern times no distinction was made between technology and art; all areas of economic activity were under the control of the local ruler via privilegien.[150] And even if one differentiates between technical innovations, writings and other printing products, designs and product signs

---

[144] MacLeod, *Inventing the Industrial Revolution* 12–13; May, 20 Prometheus 159, 166, 174 (2002); Damme, *Der Schutz technischer Erfindungen als Erscheinungsform moderner Volkswirtschaft* 47 et seq.

[145] May, 20 Prometheus 159, 164 (2002).

[146] Habermas, *The Structural Transformation of the Public Sphere* 18–19.

[147] Damme, *Der Schutz technischer Erfindungen als Erscheinungsform moderner Volkswirtschaft* 32 et seq.; Silberstein, *Erfindungsschutz und merkantilistische Gewerbeprivilegien* 110 et seq., 214; Bracha, 38 Loyola of L.A. L. Rev. 177, 191 et seq. (2004).

[148] Gieseke, *Vom Privileg zum Urheberrecht* 39 et seq. with further references. *Cf.* e.g. Privilege of the Elector of Saxony (1534), *in* Bently & Kretschmer (eds.) *Primary Sources on Copyright* www.copyrighthistory.org; Nuremberg Printers' Ordinance (1673), *in* Bently & Kretschmer (eds.) *Primary Sources on Copyright* www.copyrighthistory.org; Regulation of the Electorate of Saxony of 27.2.1686, reprinted in Eisenlohr, *Sammlung der Gesetze* 31 et seq. On the English Star Chamber Regulation 1637 *see* Osterrieth, 131 UFITA 171, 227 et seq. (1996) [1895]. *Cf.* Bosse, *Autorschaft als Werkherrschaft* 7.

[149] Gieseke, *Vom Privileg zum Urheberrecht* 72 et seq.; Pohlmann, *Die Frühgeschichte des musikalischen Urheberrechts* 192; Pottage & Sherman, *Figures of Invention* 46 with further references; Madison, 19 J. Intell. Prop. L. Rev. 325, 334 (2012); Teilmann-Lock, *The Object of Copyright* 27; Biagioli, 73 Social Research: An International Quarterly 1129, 1146 (2006) ('the privilege had no need for the idea of the invention (as a category), nor did it have a conceptual or legal space to represent it even if such an idea were to be found in the inventor's mind').

[150] Kostylo, *in* Bently & Kretschmer (eds.) *Primary Sources on Copyright* www.copyrighthistory.org; May, 20 Prometheus 159, 169 (2002).

according to the structure of today's IP law, privileges consistently prove to be action and artefact based.

The chronologically first privileges in the burgeoning machine age concerned products and machine processes, which today are classified as technology and thus fall under the rubric of patent law. They concerned windmills, water pumps, mirrors, ovens and other 'instruments', as well as various 'arts' such as the 1456 'new arts of burning bricks and lime' or extracting salt.[151] The older practice of granting individual case privileges for such products or arts was already regulated in 1474 by a general decree in Venice, which is often cited as the first patent law or at least as the beginning of the modern patent system.[152] It is true that this decree is inevitably formulated more generally than a specific product or process privilege. However, it does not implement an abstract concept of invention, but refers generally to various imaginative devices (*varii ingegnosi artificii*), which the rightful proprietor may exclusively use and exercise (*usar, et exercitar*), while third parties are prohibited from the unauthorised making of a similar artefact based on the model of the protected one (*far algun altro artificio, ad imagine et similitudine de quello senza consentimento et licentia del auctor, fino ad anni X*).[153]

Privileges in the future world power, England, were formulated in the same way. The privilege practice of the Crown in England had already come under legal pressure in 1599, when a privilege ('letters patent') to import, manufacture and market playing cards was declared null and void for lack of parliamentary

---

[151] See the privileges referenced in Silberstein, *Erfindungsschutz und merkantilistische Gewerbeprivilegien* 20, 36–37, 62, 80; Damme, *Der Schutz technischer Erfindungen als Erscheinungsform moderner Volkswirtschaft* 52; Bracha, 38 Loyola of L.A. L. Rev. 177, 212 (2004).

[152] *Cf.* Kraßer & Ann, Patentrecht 63 et seq.; Kurz, *Weltgeschichte des Erfindungsschutzes* 41 et seq. (first patent act of the world).

[153] Venetian Statute on Industrial Brevets, Venice (1474), *in* Bently & Kretschmer (eds.) *Primary Sources on Copyright* www.copyrighthistory.org ('There are men in this city, and also there come other persons every day from different places by reason of its greatness and goodness, who have most clever minds, capable of devising and inventing all kinds of ingenious contrivances. And should it be legislated that the works and contrivances invented by them could not be copied and made by others so that they are deprived of their honour, men of such kind would exert their minds, invent and make things that would be of no small utility and benefit to our State. Therefore, the decision has been made that, by authority of this Council, any person in this city who makes any new and ingenious contrivances not made heretofore in our Dominion, shall, as soon as it is perfected so that it can be used and exercised, give notice of the same to the office of our Provveditori di Comun, having been forbidden up to ten years to any other person in any territory and place of ours to make a contrivance in the form and resemblance of that one without the consent and license of the author. And if nevertheless someone should make it, the aforesaid author and inventor will have the liberty to cite him before any office of this city, which office will force the aforesaid infringer to pay him the sum of one hundred ducats and immediately destroy the contrivance. But our Government will be free, at its complete discretion, to take and use for its needs any of the said contrivances and instruments, with this condition, however, that no one other than the authors shall operate them'.). *See also* May, 20 Prometheus 159, 161 et seq. (2002).

approval.[154] In 1624, the Statute of Monopolies prohibited all 'monopolies' and 'lettres Patentes' 'for the sole buyinge selling makinge worcking or usinge of anie thing' or 'to doe use or excercise anie thinge', but the Act immediately excluded from this prohibition privileges for 'the sole working or makinge of any manner of new manufacture', which could be granted to the 'first and true inventor or inventors of such manufactures which others at the tyme of the makinge of such letters Patentes and grauntes'. Printing privileges remained unaffected by the law, along with privileges 'for the compounding for digging and making of saltpeter or for the casting or makinge of Iron'.[155] It is clear from this differentiated regulation that privileges or monopoly rights were always related to tangible goods and activities. This also applies to the privileges for the use and production of any type of new manufacture, which were exempted from the abolition of monopolies. Their regulated reality is the same as that of the privileges abolished by the Statute of Monopolies.[156] Despite the vagueness of the term 'manufacture',[157] it follows from the context of the Statute of Monopolies that it refers to machines and materials, but not to abstract technical ideas. Accordingly, later English patents specified exactly which artefact and which activity should be covered.[158] Mario Biagioli summarises that 'Privileges rewarded working machines in specific places, period. ... It was all about locality, materiality, and utility'.[159]

The fact that this observation also applies to letterpress printing already follows for England from the reference in the Statute of Monopolies to the still valid privileges 'for the sole printing of ... Bookes'.[160] The reference to physical artefacts and their production or use can be further derived from the typical formulation of privileges, whereby a privileged person is prohibited from reprinting a particular printed script

---

[154] Edward Darcy Esquire v. Thomas Allin of London Haberdasher, 74 E.R. 1131 (1599).
[155] Statute of Monopolies, Westminster (1624), in Bently & Kretschmer (eds.) *Primary Sources on Copyright* www.copyrighthistory.org; MacLeod, *Inventing the Industrial Revolution* 17 et seq. On a decree of the Massachusetts Body of Liberties 1641 see Bracha, 38 Loyola of L.A. L. Rev. 177, 214 et seq. (2004) ('No monopolies shall be granted or allowed amongst us, but of such new Inventions that are profitable to the Countrie, and that for a short time'.).
[156] MacLeod, *Inventing the Industrial Revolution* 1–2, 15 ('a quirk of history'), 40 et seq.; Bracha, 38 Loyola of L.A. L. Rev. 177, 191 et seq. (2004) ('In fact, while the statute and the common law decisions introduced some important developments, they did not break with the patent-privileges framework and they certainly were not a move in the direction of patent rights'.); Lai, in Lai & Maget Dominicé (eds.) *Intellectual Property and Access to Im/material Goods* 94, 95.
[157] Lai, in Lai & Maget Dominicé (eds.) *Intellectual Property and Access to Im/material Goods* 94, 116–17; High Court of Australia, National Research Development Corporation v. Commissioner of Patents, 102 CLR 252 (1959) ('defining 'manufacture' is bound to fail').
[158] Bracha, 38 Loyola of L.A. L. Rev. 177, 188 (2004).
[159] Biagioli, 73 Social Research: An International Quarterly 1129, 1146 (2006); Lai, in Lai & Maget Dominicé (eds.) *Intellectual Property and Access to Im/material Goods* 94, 108; Kostylo, in Bently & Kretschmer (eds.) *Primary Sources on Copyright* www.copyrighthistory.org.
[160] Statute of Monopolies, Westminster (1624), in Bently & Kretschmer (eds.) *Primary Sources on Copyright* www.copyrighthistory.org.

and from importing and selling reprinted copies.[161] However, reprinting means that a physical model (a book, a manuscript) is used to produce further copies according to this model. This dominant discourse,[162] common until the reprint (sic!) debates of the eighteenth century, remains at abstraction level 1, i.e. it operates with general designations for outwardly identical or sufficiently similar books, maps etc. There are no clues to the idea of abstract, immaterial objects to be found in it. Luther's complaint about the false and therefore misleading reprint confirms that the specific way of speaking and looking at things in the sixteenth century was not only technical legal language, but generally accepted.[163]

In view of the increasing number of new books published, however, the practice of the individual case privilege proved to be too cumbersome. Over the course of time, it was replaced by general privileges for the entire production of a printer[164] and in the printing and bookseller centres such as Basel, Frankfurt am Main and Nuremberg by general ordinances on book printing. Those regulations no longer referred to specific titles, but to all 'books' printed in the territory in which the order was applicable. The 'book' thus advanced to become the dominant concept of the privilege system and the reprint discourse,[165] even if divergent ways of speaking – as in the Nuremberg Book Printing Ordinance of 1673, which refers to the reprint of both privileged and non-privileged 'materials'[166] – signalled a permanent uncertainty about what was meant by 'book'. These observations do not only hold true for Germany, but also for England and France. The ordinances of the London book printers in the sixteenth and seventeenth centuries that joined to form the guild of the Stationers' Company[167] refer throughout to the printing of books and other writings such as cards.[168] Article 1 of the French Book Trade Regulations of 1701 states that 'Qu'aucans Libraires, Imprimeurs ou autres, ne pourront faire imprimer ou reimprimer ... aucun Livre ...'(no bookseller, printer or other person may print or reprint ... any book ...).[169]

---

[161] Gieseke, *Vom Privileg zum Urheberrecht* 39 et seq.; Hesse, 131 Daedalus 26 et seq. (2002); on French privileges see Renouard, *Traité des droits d'auteur* 8 et seq.; privilege for Arnolt Schlick (1512), in Bently & Kretschmer (eds.) *Primary Sources on Copyright* www.copyrighthistory.org; Schuster, *Das Urheberrecht der Tonkunst* 13 (privileges for Albrecht Dürer). Privileges in Latin referred to 'libris', cf. Privileg des Erzbischoffs von Würzburg (1479), in Bently & Kretschmer (eds.) *Primary Sources on Copyright* www.copyrighthistory.org.

[162] See Section 3.2.2.

[163] Luther, *Warnung an die Drucker* (1545), in Bently & Kretschmer (eds.) *Primary Sources on Copyright* www.copyrighthistory.org.

[164] Gieseke, *Vom Privileg zum Urheberrecht* 39, 75 et seq.

[165] Cf. Schupp, Der Bücherdieb. Gewarnet und ermahnet, Hamburg (1658), in Bently & Kretschmer (eds.) *Primary Sources on Copyright* www.copyrighthistory.org.

[166] Nürnberger Druckerordnung (1673), in Bently & Kretschmer (eds.) *Primary Sources on Copyright* www.copyrighthistory.org 6.

[167] Gieseke, *Vom Privileg zum Urheberrecht* 6.

[168] Osterrieth, 131 UFITA 171, 175 et seq. (1996) [1895]; Millar v. Taylor, 4 Burrow 2303, 2314 (1769) with further references.

[169] French Royal letters patent (1701), in Bently & Kretschmer (eds.) *Primary Sources on Copyright* www.copyrighthistory.org art. I ('That no Bookseller, Printer or other person may cause to be

Early modern regulations, which from today's perspective fall into the area of design and trademark law, also operated with an understanding of reality based on actions and artefacts. In the centres of European textile production, for example, there were regulations on the use of fabric samples.[170] In Florence, *opera die drappi* (model drawings) could only be imitated legally according to certain rules and only by members of the silk guild;[171] a Lyon decree of 1711 prohibited the transfer and other unauthorised use of *dessins* entrusted to the maker of textiles.[172] From the thirteenth century onwards, bans on forging seals of origin in the tapestry and ceramics sectors have also been documented; and a Nuremberg decree from 1512 prohibited the fraudulent reprinting of art letters signed by Albrecht Dürer.[173] Neither the idea of an abstract sign nor an IP regulation purpose are expressed in these provisions. Like all privileges and other trade regulations, they were elements of a feudalistic economic order in which the production of goods followed fixed rules.[174]

3.2.1.3.2 THE FORMATION OF MARKETS AND THE COMMODIFICATION OF ALL INPUTS AND OUTPUTS As long as such a dirigiste economic order prevailed, it was sufficient to regulate the production and use of reproducible artefacts. In a market economy, on the other hand, business activity follows completely different rules. There is no central institution that specifies who has to produce or consume what. Instead, market participants themselves decide what they offer and demand. In order for this decentralised transaction mechanism to be operational, all the results of human activity, human labour and any other factor of production must be tradable. This is the only way to satisfy all the needs of the market and generate income in line with the market logic. Consequently, the emergence of the market goes hand in hand with comprehensive objectification ('commodification'). This means that all input and output is transformed into a commodity, a 'good' to which fungible exclusive rights attach.[175]

This process was also effective in the area of interest here, i.e. the use of reproduction technologies.[176] In order to subject this economic sector to the laws of the market, the *activities* of publishers, writers, artists, machine builders, textile

printed or reprinted anywhere in the Kingdom any Book, without having previously obtained permission to do so in Letters bearing the great Seal'.).
[170] Werner, *Die Geschichte des deutschen Geschmacksmusterschutzes* 2; Breimesser, *Urheberrecht und Rechtsbegriff* 41 et seq.
[171] Silberstein, *Erfindungsschutz und merkantilistische Gewerbeprivilegien* 168; cf. May, 20 Prometheus 159, 168 (2002) ('figures or patterns').
[172] Kohler, *Musterrecht* 10 ('... de vendre, preter, remettre, ni de se servir directement ni inderectement des dessins qui leur auront été confiés pour fabriquer...').
[173] Kohler, *Recht des Markenschutzes* 42.
[174] Kohler, *Recht des Markenschutzes* 42 et seq., 54 et seq.; Di Palma, *History of Marks* 344; Fezer, *Markenrecht Einl A para.* 17; McKenna, 82 Notre Dame L. Rev. 1839, 1849 et seq. (2007).
[175] See Polanyi, *The Great Transformation* 68–76; Peukert, 29 Fordham Intell. Prop. Media & Ent. L.J. 1151 (2019).
[176] Peukert, 29 Fordham Intell. Prop. Media & Ent. L.J. 1151, 1161–72 (2019).

manufacturers etc., which had previously been regulated as privileges, had to be transformed into tradable objects ('goods'). The physical end-products of the reproduction technologies (the concrete book, the copperplate engraving, the machine etc.) were increasingly less sufficient as connecting points for this commoditisation. For on this basis, the separate ('sunk') effort for the production of the first pattern, the Master Artefact, would have been lost. The special status of this original input became all the clearer the more efficient the reproduction technologies and the more perfect and inexpensive the copies became.[177] At the same time, the need for new artefacts increased as the modern episteme of innovation became more prevalent.[178] The focus shifted to those who delivered this creative, innovative or entrepreneurial achievement – the author, inventor, designer or original producer.[179] The input of time, money and personal skills provided is not captured by e.g. the manuscript given to the printer or publisher. The genuine contribution of authors and other innovators is only *embodied* in this token. It is objectified into an abstract work, an invention, a design, a distinctive sign etc., which are traded as immaterial goods on innovation markets.[180]

This is not the place to trace in detail the marketisation of economic exchange relations and the associated commodification processes in all the many areas that fall into the ambit of today's IP law. In the following, this complex historical process will be explored in greater depth only for literature and music and thus for the abstract work concept, which was also the first abstract IP object that was theorised and thus became a model for other abstract IP objects such as the abstract invention and the abstract design.[181] Literature and music production also seem interesting because the printing press was the first reproduction machine with which large numbers of copies could be produced at relatively low marginal costs. The effects of technological and economic change can therefore be seen particularly clearly in their example.

Nevertheless, several hundred years passed before the use of the printing press was completely subject to market conditions. Until the eighteenth century, the players involved in this technology were integrated into the hierarchically controlled feudal/mercantilist economy. Printers operated legally on the basis of privileges and

---

[177] Section 3.2.1.1; Pottage & Sherman, *Figures of Invention* 19 et seq.
[178] Section 3.2.1.2; MacLeod, *Inventing the Industrial Revolution* 202.
[179] Kawohl, *Urheberrecht der Musik in Preussen* 41; Bracha, *Owning Ideas* 574 et seq.
[180] Bosse, *Autorschaft als Werkherrschaft* 6–7; Plumpe, 23 Archiv für Begriffsgeschichte 175, 192 (1979); Haferkorn, 5 Archiv für Geschichte des Buchwesens 523, 613 et seq.; Hesse, 131 Daedalus 26 et seq. (2002); Barron, 15 Social & Legal Studies 101, 115 (2006); Jaszi, 40 Duke L.J. 455, 477–78 (1991) ('Practically, rapid change in reproduction and distribution technologies called for an abstract concept of the subject of legal protection'.); Bracha, *Owning Ideas* 531 et seq.; Bracha, 118 Yale L.J. 186, 238 et seq. (2008). On news see Habermas, *The Structural Transformation of the Public Sphere* 20–21.
[181] See Section 3.2.1.2.

conducted their vertically integrated business by selling the books they produced.[182] Writers and composers made their living largely from permanent positions and fees they received from feudal rulers and other patrons. Even if copies of their works were in circulation, they were not dependent on a share of the turnover generated from them.[183] In rare individual cases they were granted personal privileges.[184] It was on this legal basis that publishers, who in the sixteenth century had separated from printers and booksellers in a process based on the division of labour, were able to find their own market-based livelihood.[185]

This economy, embedded in the society of the estates, did not begin to disintegrate until the seventeenth century. Instead of the writer, composer and artist being tied into patronage relationships, freelance authors offered their works to the emerging bourgeois public through publishers and other intermediaries.[186] They operated in the market for certain writings or compositions in competition with other authors and were dependent for their survival as authors on earning an income in line with the laws of the market.[187]

But what do authors have to sell? How can they ensure that they can amortise their sunk costs in writing the manuscript, composition etc. and make profits to finance their later work? Apart from temporary attempts at direct marketing without intermediary publishers,[188] for a long time it was just the specific manuscript, the physical thing that the author had to offer. However, transactions in which a manuscript is exchanged for a one-off payment do not give rise to any idea of an abstract IP object. It is still all about raw artefacts used in one way or another: written, painted, printed, reprinted, sold and so on.

The object of the transaction, and thus also the perception of the author's performance, only changed when a recurring sales fee took the place of the one-off manuscript fee. For then the publisher's payment was no longer made for the acquisition of ownership of a physical object, but for the recurring use of another

---

[182] Kiesel & Münch, *Gesellschaft und Literatur im 18. Jahrhundert* 124.
[183] Gieseke, *Vom Privileg zum Urheberrecht* 17, 33–34, 55, 70–71, 111; Kiesel & Münch, *Gesellschaft und Literatur im 18. Jahrhundert* 144 et seq.; Pohlmann, *Die Frühgeschichte des musikalischen Urheberrechts* 21 et seq.
[184] Schuster, *Das Urheberrecht der Tonkunst* 10–11; Gieseke, *Vom Privileg zum Urheberrecht* 110–11.
[185] *Cf.* Kiesel & Münch, *Gesellschaft und Literatur im 18. Jahrhundert* 124; Gieseke, *Vom Privileg zum Urheberrecht* 63, 69.
[186] On visual art see Luhmann, *Kunst der Gesellschaft* 262 et seq.; Becq, in Mattick Jr. (ed.) *Eighteenth-Century Aesthetics and the Reconstruction of Art* 240, 249. On literature see Kiesel & Münch, *Gesellschaft und Literatur im 18. Jahrhundert* 77 et seq.; Fontius, in Klotz et al. (eds.) *Literatur im Epochenumbruch* 409, 498 et seq.; Renouard, *Traité des droits d'auteur* 434; Thierse, 36 Weimarer Beiträge 240, 252 (1990). On the demise of dedications since the 1760ies Haferkorn, 5 Archiv für Geschichte des Buchwesens 523, 619, 634–35. On music see Pohlmann, *Die Frühgeschichte des musikalischen Urheberrechts* 136.
[187] Bosse, *Autorschaft als Werkherrschaft* 82 et seq.
[188] Kiesel & Münch, *Gesellschaft und Literatur im 18. Jahrhundert* 149 et seq.; Haferkorn, 5 Archiv für Geschichte des Buchwesens 523, 643 et seq.

good, which was embodied in all the copies sold, but which could nevertheless be distinguished from it.[189]

This change of perspective from the manuscript to the abstract work can even be dated quite precisely for the German book market. It went hand in hand with the change from a corporatist exchange to a paid 'net trade' initiated by Leipzig publishers after the end of the Seven Years' War in 1764.[190] Until then, the distribution of books in the numerous individual German states had been organised in such a way that publishers could exchange their books for others and thus offer a fairly comprehensive repertoire in their respective home territories. Under these circumstances, unauthorised reprints were rare. Furthermore, a sales fee was not an option, not least because the publisher contracting with the author did not generate any revenues from the sale of copies sold in exchange and did not know the final sales figures for these books. In 1764, however, Leipzig publishers suddenly began to sell their books to other publishers or booksellers only for a fee. The change in the business model of the leading publishers resulted in unauthorised reprints by publishers who could not or did not want to afford the Leipzig prices. On the other hand, this business basis made it possible for the first time to use fully remunerated sales to calculate author remuneration.

In the field of music, parallel commodification processes have been documented in particular by Lydia Goehr in her study *The Imaginary Museum of Musical Works*.[191] Here the decisive conceptual innovation did not take place until the beginning of the nineteenth century and thus somewhat later than in literature. It consisted in replacing the understanding of music as an ephemeral event, realised ad hoc by musicians and singers, with the idea of the abstract musical work, which is manifested only accidentally in performances and sheet music. This change of perspective was again triggered by improved reproduction technologies. Sheet music and musical instruments became mass products that the growing bourgeois class could afford.[192] They increasingly represented 'the music', which no longer took place in rare performances in the presence of the composer-interpreter, but permanently, everywhere and thus seemingly without time or space. At the same time, the composer mentioned on the sheet music replaced the musician or singer,

---

[189] Gaudrat, 221 RIDA 2, 18 (2009) (writers in seventeenth-century France). *See also* Scherer, *Quarter Notes and Banknotes* 197 et seq.; Bosse, *Autorschaft als Werkherrschaft* 61 et seq.; Pohlmann, *Die Frühgeschichte des musikalischen Urheberrechts* 136 et seq.; Schuster, *Das Urheberrecht der Tonkunst* 23; Haferkorn, 5 Archiv für Geschichte des Buchwesens 523, 631; Jaszi, 40 Duke L.J. 455, 478 (1991); Becker, *in* Gieseke, *Vom Privileg zum Urheberrecht* 174.

[190] Kiesel & Münch, *Gesellschaft und Literatur im 18. Jahrhundert* 124 et seq.; Haferkorn, 5 Archiv für Geschichte des Buchwesens 523, 633–34; Gieseke, *Vom Privileg zum Urheberrecht* 157–58.

[191] Goehr, *Imaginary Museum*, passim, in particular 87 et seq.; *also* Pohlmann, *Die Frühgeschichte des musikalischen Urheberrechts* 21 et seq. (Beethoven as the first representative of independent composers); Toynbee, 15 Music, Social & Legal Studies 77, 82 (2006).

[192] Schuster, *Das Urheberrecht der Tonkunst* 23–24; Toynbee, 15 Music, Social & Legal Studies 77, 80 (2006).

who was reduced to the role of an interchangeable interpreter of the given work. Composers like Beethoven behaved as geniuses and were perceived as such. Economically, they were increasingly dependent, as were writers, on sales fees from the sale of sheet music. The good that they brought to market was the abstract work, not the physical manuscript.[193]

The idea of literary and musical works, which are still at the top of the catalogue of copyrightable works today,[194] as abstract, immaterial objects spread from copyright to other areas. If books and sheet music embody immaterial goods, then the same applies to sculptures (artworks), machine models and patent documents (inventions),[195] fabric samples and other templates for the outer appearance of goods (designs) and ultimately to all reproducible artefacts.[196]

All these brute facts no longer stand for themselves, but count as embodiments of an abstract object – largely indeterminate in its boundaries – which exists in an immaterial World². Thus, as explained above, we are dealing with a Searlean status function: Under the conditions C of the industrialised market economy, book X counts as the embodiment of the work Y.[197] So the abstract work and other abstract IP objects are not timeless objects that only have to be recognised and regulated by law, but they have become social-institutional facts that only exist to the extent that for just over 200 years we have been speaking and thinking as if they existed.

As will be explained, this quite eccentric idea is now so self-evident that it is guiding activities – i.e. people act as if an abstract object exists – where such an object is not even consistently claimed. This irritating observation concerns the rights 'related' to copyright and plant variety rights, which each explicitly refer to brute artefacts – for example, to the first fixation of an audio recording, to a broadcasting signal or to propagating material of a plant. If these brute facts embody anything, then it is an investment that consists of countable and measurable economic transactions and that blocks itself against an idealisation analogous to the emphatic-romantic concept of the literary or musical 'work'.[198]

Commodification qua abstraction and objectification can finally be observed in real time in trademark law. Here, too, market processes have the effect of transforming a primarily unfair competition law type of regulation of the use of signs in business transactions into a fully fledged IP right in an abstract sign. The first step in this direction was the introduction of freedom of trade, which abolished all estate regulations governing the use of trademarks on the market and replaced them with

---

[193] Goehr, *Imaginary Museum* 205 et seq.
[194] Section 2(1) nos. 1 and 2 German Copyright Act (UrhG).
[195] Pottage & Sherman, *Figures of Invention*, passim.
[196] On the significance of reproduction technologies Section 3.2.1.1.
[197] Section 2.2.1.
[198] Section 5.1.1.2.

bourgeois laws guaranteeing fair and functioning competition.[199] The second wave of abstraction came from industrial mass production in the late nineteenth century, in the course of which house, company and factory marks were being replaced by fanciful trademarks such as 'Odol', which primarily communicate which product it is, but not who manufactured it or where.[200] The third and final impulse for the construction of a freely floating commercial sign – which refers to no origin, no commodity, but only to an image created by the sign itself – was the affluent society of the twentieth century, in which both producers and consumers develop a need for distinction through symbols.[201] At this stage, product marks ('brands') became a commodity in themselves and had to be commoditised in order to be produced and traded in accordance with the laws of the market.[202] European trademark law has responded to these developments by acknowledging a trademark ownership that protects at least well-known signs against unauthorised use, irrespective of the goods and services at stake and any likelihood of confusion.[203] The sign is allocated to the 'trademark sovereign'[204] for any use in the course of trade. The right holder alone may decide in which contexts the sign may be used commercially and which meaning may be attributed to it.[205] The abstract object of contemporary trademark law is thus the indefinite meaning of a sign – an empty signifier without a signified. Through trademark law, the creation of new symbols and new meanings of old symbols is delegated to market participants who are rewarded and stimulated.[206] Whether this logic also applies to geographical indications or whether the teleological and actual anchoring in local production sites (territoriality of geographical indications) stands in the way of GIs becoming abstract IP objects is also discussed.[207]

---

[199] Fezer, *Markenrecht* Einl A paras. 18 et seq.; In re Trade-Mark Cases, 100 US 82 et seq. (1879).
[200] LG Elberfeld GRUR 1924, 204–5; Isay, GRUR 1929, 23, 24 et seq.; Schechter, 40 Harvard L. Rev. 813, 819 (1927) with reference to LG Elberfeld; *cf.* Beebe, in Dreyfuss & Ginsburg (eds.) *Intellectual Property at the Edge* 59 et seq.
[201] Veblen, *Theorie der feinen Leute* 68–101; Galbraith, *The Affluent Society* 131–33; Hellmann, *Soziologie der Marke* 77 et seq., 377 et seq. with further references; Henning-Bodewig & Kur, *Marke und Verbraucher* I 14–18.
[202] Matal v. Tam, 137 S.Ct. 1744, 1752 (2017) ('The foundation of current federal trademark law is the Lanham Act, enacted in 1946. . . . By that time, trademark had expanded far beyond phrases that do no more than identify a good or service. Then, as now, trademarks often consisted of catchy phrases that convey a message. By that time, trademark had expanded far beyond phrases that do no more than identify a good or service. Then, as now, trademarks often consisted of catchy phrases that convey a message').
[203] Peukert, *Festschrift Fezer* 405, 410 et seq. with further references.
[204] Fezer, *Markenrecht* Section 14 German Trademark Act (MarkenG) paras. 74–75.
[205] On the communication function of trademarks see Fezer, *Markenrecht* Einl D paras. 10–11, 28; Schreiner, Die Dienstleistungsmarke 448 et seq.; Völker & Elskamp, 1 WRP 64, 69–70 (2010).
[206] Beebe, in Dinwoodie & Janis (eds.) *Trademark Law and Theory* 42, 51; McKenna, 82 Notre Dame L. Rev. 1839, 1843 (2007); Gangjee, in Howe & Griffiths (eds.) *Concepts of Property* 29, 57–58. ('intangible objects give rise to property description'); Peukert, *Festschrift Fezer* 405, 418 et seq. with further references.
[207] *Cf.* BGH 31 March 2016 Case no. I ZR 86/13, GRUR 741 paras. 11 et seq. with further references; Loschelder, in *Festschrift Fezer* 711 et seq.

3.2.2 *The Emergence of the Abstract IP Object*

Now that technologies, the fetish of the new, and the market have been explained as the three central enabling conditions for the emergence of the abstract IP object, it is time to trace how this new idea was articulated. This effort also serves to review Searle's social ontology. For if the abstract IP object is an 'institutional fact', then this social construct must not only have a history, but it must also be expressed in specific speech acts.[208] Whether and how this verbalisation took place will be explained in the following – first on the basis of the general history of terms such as 'work' and 'invention', which today are used to describe abstract IP objects (see Section 3.2.2.1), and then on the basis of legal texts from the time of the emergence of today's IP law (see Section 3.2.2.2).

3.2.2.1 A History of Terms: Work, Invention, Design

Nowadays, when a speaker wants to say which objects are allocated by IP rights to right holders according to the model of real property ownership, specific terms are available. The generic term in German is *Immaterialgut* (immaterial good), a neologism launched by Josef Kohler in the late nineteenth century with the purpose of firstly overcoming the limitations of traditional German property theory, which applied the term 'property' only to exclusive rights in movable and immovable tangibles, and secondly to provide a basis – a reality – for the emerging IP law.[209] In the English language, this function is taken over by the even more dazzling term 'intellectual property'.[210] In addition, each IP right has a specific term to designate its subject matter – the object of the right: the copyright work, the patented invention, the design etc.

Unlike in the case of *Immaterialgut*, however, the history of these words does not begin with today's IP law. The terms 'work' and 'invention' were in usage much earlier and especially during the privilege system – for which the idea of the abstract IP object was, as explained, still foreign. But this is not a contradiction in terms. For at that time the words mentioned had not yet assumed their present meaning. There was talk about 'works' and 'inventions' before the eighteenth century, but not in the sense of the abstract concept of 'work' or 'invention' that has applied since then.

As far as the conceptual history of the 'work' is concerned, this term is partly used as a synonym for 'book' in privileges from the sixteenth century. For example, a privilege written in poem form in 1512 orders that the respective 'artlich buch und künstlich wergk' [book and artificial work] may not be printed for the duration of ten

---

[208] Section 2.2.1.
[209] Pahlow, 6 ZGE 429 et seq. (2014).
[210] Peukert, in Basedow et al. (eds.) *Max Planck Encyclopaedia of European Private Law I* 926 et seq.; George, 7(1) W.I.P.O.J. 16, 18 (2015).

years.[211] The Basel printing regulation of 1531 states that no printer may reprint the works and books of others.[212] The Frankfurt printer regulation of 1598 allowed only honest and well-believed persons to operate the 'work and trade' (*Werck un Handel*) of the laudable art of printing (*löbliche[n] Kunst der Truckerey*), while it was to be avoided that two printers independently submit the same new 'work' to the censorship authority ('*unbewußt einerley neuwe Werck ... zur Censur lieffern*').[213] These formulations correspond to the predominant meaning of the word *Werk* (work), which has been common since the beginning of the written tradition as a general term for the most varied activities and work products of some significance.[214] Often the practical *Werk* – usually a craft or industrial product (see the German words *Bauwerk* (building), *Fachwerk* (master craft), *Handwerk* (craft)) – contrasted explicitly with intellectual efforts like rhetoric or teaching.[215] Where there was talk of literary and artistic 'works', then it was in the sense of a corporeal product such as an extensive or lavishly illustrated print ('book').[216] This non-specific concept of a 'work', which refers to brute facts, continues to form the basis of the law on contracts to produce a work in the German Civil Code (BGB), which under Section 631(2) concerns every production or alteration of a thing or another result to be achieved by work or by a service, including the drafting of a manuscript and every other production of a Master Artefact with physical existence.[217] This talk of works admittedly objectifies the human activity required to produce a tradable output.[218] Until the eighteenth century, however, that talk still lacked the specific meaning of a signifier for an abstract work that was only embodied in exemplary form in the original and its copies.

The history of the word 'invention' (*Erfindung, inventio, invention*) also goes back further than the eighteenth century. This way of speaking is documented for the sixteenth and seventeenth centuries, both within the privilege system and beyond.[219]

---

[211] Privileg für Arnolt Schlick (1512), in Bently & Kretschmer (eds.) *Primary Sources on Copyright* www.copyrighthistory.org.

[212] Baseler Druckerordnung (1531), in Bently & Kretschmer (eds.) *Primary Sources on Copyright* www.copyrighthistory.org ('hinfür kein drucker ... dem andren sine werck unnd biecher in dryen joren nochtrucken'); Gieseke, *Vom Privileg zum Urheberrecht* 72.

[213] Frankfurter Druckerordnung (1598), in Bently & Kretschmer (eds.) *Primary Sources on Copyright* www.copyrighthistory.org 3-4, 6.

[214] See Grimm & Grimm, *Deutsches Wörterbuch* IXXX 327 et seq. See also the entry 'Nachdruck derer Bücher', in Zedlers Universal-Lexicon (1740), in Bently & Kretschmer (eds.) *Primary Sources on Copyright* www.copyrighthistory.org.

[215] Grimm & Grimm, *Deutsches Wörterbuch* IXXX 329, columns 332 and 338; Pudelek, in Barck et al. (eds.) *Ästhetische Grundbegriffe* VI 521, 543; MacLeod, *Inventing the Industrial Revolution* 11 (with reference to an application for a privilege from 1537 for the protection of textiles as a 'kind of work'); May, 20 Prometheus 159, 165 (2002).

[216] See Grimm & Grimm, *Deutsches Wörterbuch* IXXX 341.

[217] See Birr, in Schmoeckel et al. (eds.) *Historisch-Kritischer Kommentar zum BGB Sections 631-51 German Civil Code (BGB)* para. 156.

[218] Gierke, *Deutsches Privatrecht* III 591-92; Erben, in *Festschrift Weisgerber* 221, 224 et seq.

[219] Grimm & Grimm, *Deutsches Wörterbuch* III 800; MacLeod, *Inventing the Industrial Revolution* 13; Kohler, 10 Archiv für Rechts- und Wirtschaftsphilosophie 235-36 (1917)

But apart from the reference of these privileges to specific machines and other artefacts, the concepts of invention and work before the *Sattelzeit* had a more general, unspecific meaning. Reference to an invention was a general expression of the fact that someone had *found* something – be it a rhetorical argument, a territory, a natural resource, a mechanism or a solution to a problem – or had introduced a machine or type of activity previously unknown at a location.[220] This understanding, still affected by the imitation episteme – according to which things can only be *found* but not *created*[221] – was so dominant that the early modern privilege or monopoly could be applied indiscriminately to discoverers, trading companies, importers and innovators.[222] The fact that in the age of the privilege the concept of novelty did not refer to an abstract state of knowledge, but to the question of whether the technology or action in question was new locally, proves that it was always a question of finding or producing certain brute facts at the place where the privilege was granted.[223] Only gradually and with the advance of modern enthusiasm for innovation in the eighteenth century was the word 'invention' reserved for the designation of objectively new technical teachings, while older meanings died out.[224]

The field of law, which is now predominantly called design law, was initially known in Germany as *Geschmacksmusterrecht* or *Musterrecht* – a right in a pattern.[225] The object of its protection, the design, underwent a change of meaning similar to that of works and inventions. There has also been talk of *Muster* (pattern/design) since early modern times. It is a loanword from the Romansh language that became customary in Germany in the course of the international trade of goods in the fifteenth century. The *Muster* designated a specimen or model of a fabric, a machine etc., which was shown, and after the model of which further specimens

---

(privilege for Juan de Lugo 1643: 'inventoribus alicuius machinae vel artificii reipublicae utilis'); Silberstein, *Erfindungsschutz und merkantilistische Gewerbeprivilegien* 215 (French privilege from the seventeenth century: 'ledict secret et machine soient de son invention').

[220] Kneale, *Proceedings of the British Academy* 85, 87–88 (Prometheus as the first inventor); Ong, *Orality and Literacy* 108–9; Silberstein, *Erfindungsschutz und merkantilistische Gewerbeprivilegien* 49, 162, 198, 210 et seq.; Damme, *Der Schutz technischer Erfindungen als Erscheinungsform moderner Volkswirtschaft* 58; MacLeod, *Inventing the Industrial Revolution* 13, 18, 203; Kurz, *Weltgeschichte des Erfindungsschutzes* 24.

[221] Luhmann, *Kunst der Gesellschaft* 423.

[222] *Edward Darcy Esquire v. Thomas Allin of London Haberdasher*, 74 E.R. 1131, 1140 (1599) ('... that where any man by his own charge and industry, or by his own wit or invention doth bring any new trade into the realm, or any engine tending to the furtherance of a trade that never was used before ... that in such cases the King may grant to him a monopoly patent for some reasonable time, until the subjects may learn the same, in consideration of the good that he doth bring by his invention to the commonwealth'); MacLeod, *Inventing the Industrial Revolution* 203.

[223] Biagioli, 73 *Social Research: An International Quarterly* 1129, 1146–47 (2006).

[224] Cf. e.g. Silberstein, *Erfindungsschutz und merkantilistische Gewerbeprivilegien* 254; Dölemeyer, in Otto & Klippel (eds.) *Geschichte des deutschen Patentrechts* 13, 30 (Saxon privilege 1723).

[225] See Breimesser, *Urheberrecht und Rechtsbegriff* 39 et seq.

could be produced if required.[226] The word 'design' has a very similar etymology. The root of the word also goes back to the act of showing (lat. *designare*, it. *disegnare*). From this the word *Disegno* is derived, which meant drawing or design.[227] All the signified mentioned are corporeal objects, i.e. things that can be touched and shown. Their peculiarity, which justifies calling them *Muster* to this day, is that they represent a newly produced artefact that can be reproduced. Such artefacts are called 'Master Artefacts' in this book. When industrialisation in the nineteenth century led to the fact that more and more products could not only be produced by machine, but also imitated on a massive scale and at relatively low cost, the 'art industry' demanded protection for the patterns, models, drawings and forms it generated.[228] At that time, the idea of the abstract IP object was already established and implemented in copyright and patent law. It was therefore no longer a particular conceptual difficulty to consider designs not as physical, two- or three-dimensional specimens to be protected against unauthorised imitation, but as embodiments of an immaterial design/model which forms the abstract object of a new, property-like IP right – the design right.[229]

The step from Abstraction[1] to Abstraction[2], from the common name of a multitude of brute artefacts (World[1]) to an idealised World[2] has now been repeated in all cases where new reproduction technologies or market changes have created a need for protection against unauthorised copies or imitations. Accordingly, topographies of semiconductor products and computer programs are today easily regarded as abstract objects capable of being owned and regulated accordingly.[230] The formerly 'wild' idea of abstract IP objects has become so self-evident that this semantics prevails even where the relevant legal regulations do not call for any immaterial object, but explicitly refer to brute artefacts such as sound recordings and plants.[231]

The 'sign', finally, as the object of trademark law, again occupies a special position. Also according to the prevailing view, it does not exist in the brute reality of physical things and actions, but in language in a broad sense, in written, visual and other communication. The sign denotes something that exists in the brute World[1] or an imagined abstract World[2]. Those who talk about signs and regulate them talk about language, apply a system of signs to signs. Consequently, it is impossible from the outset that the word history of the sign, as with the concepts of work, invention and design, can be traced back to a reproducible brute artefact such as a book, a machine, a pattern etc. At first glance, this semantics seems to predestine the 'sign' to be perceived as an abstract IP object and to be regulated

---

[226] Grimm & Grimm, *Deutsches Wörterbuch* XII 2761–64.
[227] Hirdina, in Barck et al (eds.) *Ästhetische Grundbegriffe II* 41; Luhmann, *Kunst der Gesellschaft* 426 with further references.
[228] Weigert, *Musterschutz* 10 et seq.; Breimesser, *Urheberrecht und Rechtsbegriff* 55.
[229] Meißner, *Vier Gesetze für das deutsche Gewerbewesen* 93 et seq.
[230] Section 1.1.
[231] Section 5.1.1.2.

accordingly. Yet the idea of the sign as an abstract property object is particularly demanding. For this, it is not sufficient for a sign to represent an immaterial object – as is the case, for example, with the signs (signifiers) of the copyrightable work, the patentable invention etc. Rather, the sign would have to be grasped as an immaterial object independent of the signified. This radical move, which cuts off all connections between a sign (the signifier) and designated products (the signified) and respective understandings of the public, stands in fundamental contradiction to the conventional meaning of the word 'sign', which always represents something. A signifier without a signified, an abstract IP object without meaning, is still such an eccentric idea in the twenty-first century that it has not (yet) gained an unrestricted foothold in trademark law.[232]

In sum, the change of the meaning of the terms 'work' (*Werk*), 'invention' (*Erfindung*) and 'design' (*Design*) is characterised by the fact that the signified is replaced. An abstract object takes the place of an indefinite number of sufficiently similar artefacts with a brute, measurable existence. This eliminates a mismatch between the signifier and the signified. While until the eighteenth century a single work title, a name of an invention etc. represented many artefacts, since then it has stood for one distinct object that like the signifier, however, can nowhere be seen or touched. This fundamental change in meaning was not controlled by anyone. It is a non-intentional development in the course of the *Sattelzeit*. Outsiders such as Young, Moritz and Koch may have pursued the intention of establishing a new paradigm of artistic creation.[233] The fact that their eccentric views became dominant was less due to conscious recognition by third parties than to the fact that their concepts fitted in with the new structures of the functionally differentiated society emerging in the eighteenth century, which left its more and more technological (and therefore capital-intensive) economy to the laws of the market. But the market presupposes ownership. And ownership requires an object. This is what the conceptual innovation discussed here delivered: an object that can be owned.

3.2.2.2 The Abstract IP Object in Legal Texts of the Eighteenth and Nineteenth Centuries

Against this background, it is not surprising that the development of the idea of the abstract IP object can also be traced in legal texts of the eighteenth and nineteenth centuries. Legal historians agree that the concepts of the abstract work and invention did not emerge until this time.[234] It is questionable, however, whether the law in this process merely followed social changes or – according to a view gaining ground – whether the legal discourse on the subject matter and justification of reprinting and

---

[232] *See* Section 5.1.1.1.
[233] *See* Section 3.2.1.2.
[234] *See* Chapter 3 note 54.

other imitation prohibitions made a decisive contribution to establishing the idea of the abstract IP object.[235] But even if one grants such an active influence to the law, it does not seem justified to regard the law as the sole or decisive determinant of the process of abstraction. For without novel facts, which cannot be mastered with the traditional concepts of property/ownership, lawyers would hardly have come up with the peculiar idea of 'intellectual property', and at any rate would not have done so in a momentous way.[236]

The influence of non-legal factors on the emergence of the abstract IP object is further demonstrated by the considerable inequalities in legal development that can be observed from a comparative legal perspective. In the fifteenth century, Venice was already familiar with a general regulation of privileges, which in many respects came closer to today's patent law than the Statute of Monopolies enacted in Britain 150 years later.[237] Yet Venice had long since sunk into meaninglessness when the technological, political and economic conditions for the formation of the abstract IP object were in place. At first, this was the case in the technologically and economically leading nations of the seventeenth and eighteenth centuries, namely France (see Section 3.2.2.2.1) and the United Kingdom (see Section 3.2.2.2.2). Here the current intellectual property paradigm can also be demonstrated first. Germany, which was territorially fragmented, politically conservative and technologically backward for a long time, did not implement the ultimately French innovation until the nineteenth century (see Section 3.2.2.2.3).

3.2.2.2.1 FRANCE The Statute of Monopolies from 1624 and the Statute of Anne from 1710 are often regarded as the oldest evidence of modern patent and copyright thinking.[238] But the idea of abstract IP objects and thus the concept of modern IP law is only incompletely realised in these English laws. Today's worldwide paradigm was codified for the first time in the French Revolutionary Laws on Patent and Copyright of 1791 and 1793, respectively.

The foundation for this legal innovation had already been laid in the ancien régime. In 1586, the Parlement de Paris nullified a royal privilege that had been obtained by a publisher not authorised by the heirs of the deceased author.[239] This decision focused on the perspective of authors and at the same time on the question of what is rightfully due to their heirs.[240] In the seventeenth century, the French *age*

---

[235] Plumpe, 23 Archiv für Begriffsgeschichte 175, 177 (1979); Otabe, 21 Aesthetics 141 et seq. (1996); Thierse, 36 Weimarer Beiträge 240, 253 (1990); Pudelek, in Barck et al (eds.) *Ästhetische Grundbegriffe* VI 545; Ortland, 52 DZPhil 773, 785 (2005); Barron, 15 Social & Legal Studies 101, 124 (2006); George, 7(1) W.I.P.O.J. 16, 19 (2015).
[236] Contra Plumpe, in Brackert & Stückrath (eds.) *Literaturwissenschaft* 179, 182; Pohlmann, *Die Frühgeschichte des musikalischen Urheberrechts* 123.
[237] *See* Section 3.2.1.3.1.
[238] Section 3.2.2.2.2.
[239] *See* Gaudrat, 221 RIDA 2, 12 et seq. (2009).
[240] *See* Gieseke, *Vom Privileg zum Urheberrecht* 80 et seq.

classique, this author- and work-centred discourse continued at the numerous founded academies.[241] It was therefore not unusual that the Paris publishers in the French counterpart to the English 'battle of the booksellers' already came up with the argument in 1725 that *'que la propriété d'une oeuvre littéraire est en tous points semblable à la propriété d'un meuble ou d'une terre'*. They accordingly demanded that the King grant them permanent privileges to print books, which the authors had permitted them to do, while the provincial publishers must refrain from reprinting.[242] In this argumentation, the phrase *oeuvre littéraire* is already used in today's abstract sense.

This becomes even clearer in the late-absolutist privilege orders from the 1770s and 1780s.[243] In separate regulations, they provided on the one hand for a temporary reprint protection for publishers and on the other hand for an permanent privilege for authors. The reprint protection related to books, the author's privilege to *son ouvrage*.[244] Privilege orders for *'ouvrage[s] des graveurs'*,[245] *'ouvrage[s] des musique, avec paroles ou sans paroles'*[246] and *'dessins'*[247] also operated with the abstract concept of the work and the design.

All of this prepared the ground for the revolutionary shift from the absolutist privilege system to property based on general laws. In the previous reprint debate, it had been clarified that the right of the author or inventor could not attach to the physical manuscript or the first model of a machine if it was to include reprints and even translations. Rather, the already established concepts of the abstract and relatively undefined work and invention offered themselves as suitable starting points for the regulatory purpose.[248] In an effort to avoid any appeal to absolutist

---

[241] See Chapter 3 note 134.
[242] See Louis d'Héricourt's memorandum (1725–26), in Bently & Kretschmer (eds.) *Primary Sources on Copyright* www.copyrighthistory.org; Hirsch, 36 UFITA 19, 27 (1962); Gaudrat, 221 RIDA 2, 18 (2009); van Dijk, *Grounds of the Immaterial* 14 et seq.
[243] Contra Teilmann-Lock, *The Object of Copyright* 21 et seq., 120 (distinguishing between oeuvre and ouvrage).
[244] French Decree on the duration of privileges (1777), in Bently & Kretschmer (eds.) *Primary Sources on Copyright* www.copyrighthistory.org (Art. 1: 'Aucuns Libraires & Imprimeurs ne pourront imprimer ou faire imprimer aucuns livres nouveaux, sans ... obtenu le Privilége'. Art. 5: 'Tout Auteur qui obtiendra en son nom le privilege de son ouvrage, aura le droit de le vendre ches lui ... à perpétuité ...'); Gaudrat, 221 RIDA 2, 20 et seq. (2009) with note 11.
[245] Déclaration en faveur de l'académie royale de peinture et de sculpture Royal declaration on sculpture and painting (1777), in Bently & Kretschmer (eds.) *Primary Sources on Copyright* www.copyrighthistory.org.
[246] Schuster, *Das Urheberrecht der Tonkunst* 35–36; French Decree on Musical Publications (1786), in Bently & Kretschmer (eds.) *Primary Sources on Copyright* www.copyrighthistory.org.
[247] Renouard, *Traité des brevets d'invention* 78. *Traité des brevets d'invention Traité des brevets d'invention*.
[248] Dölemeyer, in Otto & Klippel (eds.) *Geschichte des deutschen Patentrechts* 13, 28; Sieyès' report (1790) ('ouvrage imprimé'), Report of François Hell (1791) ('la propriété des productions scientifiques ou littéraires ... productions du genie sont ... les plus sacrées ... droits des auteurs ...'), Le Chapelier's report (1791) (*'La plus sacrée, la plus légitime, la plus inattaquable et, si je puis parler ainsi, la plus personnelle de toutes les propriétés, est l'ouvrage, fruit de la*

privileges, an emphatic rhetoric of property broke the ground, which pushed the realisation into the background that copyrights and patents represent '*une propriété d'un genre tout différent des autres propriétés*' after all.[249] The laws finally enacted declare that authors and inventors enjoy exclusive rights to their *ouvrages* or *idée nouvelle* and *découverte industrielle*.[250] They mark the conceptual point of no return that would already become a global paradigm in the nineteenth century.[251]

3.2.2.2.2 THE UNITED KINGDOM AND THE UNITED STATES OF AMERICA Developments in the Anglo-American legal system were less straightforward. The initial technological, political and economic conditions for the success of the idea of the abstract IP object were in some respects actually better than in France. In the Elizabethan era, a clever development and privilege policy had led to an economic and technological boom on the previously backward island.[252] In the seventeenth century, market economy structures continued to spread, and the Glorious Revolution preceded the French Revolution by a hundred years.

These conditions were reflected in the Statute of Monopolies of 1624, which granted royal privileges only in exceptional cases, e.g. for 'any manner of new manufacture' and 'the printing of books'. As ground-breaking as this regulation was at that time, it remained firmly anchored in the action- and artefact-based thinking of the privilege age. In the practice of English patent law, the term 'invention' was gradually used. However, it was not until the nineteenth century and the first actual codification of patent law in 1852 that the idea of an immaterial invention as an object of protection under patent law became established.[253]

---

pensée d'un écrivain'.), reprinted in Bently & Kretschmer (eds.) *Primary Sources on Copyright* www.copyrighthistory.org.

[249] Le Chapelier's report (1791), *in* Bently & Kretschmer (eds.) *Primary Sources on Copyright* www.copyrighthistory.org.

[250] See Art. 1 French Literary and Artistic Property Act (1793), *in* Bently & Kretschmer (eds.) *Primary Sources on Copyright* www.copyrighthistory.org ('*Les auteurs d'écrits en tout genre, les compositeurs de musique, les peintres et dessinateurs qui feront graver des tableaux et dessins, jouiront, durant leur vie entière du droit exclusif de vendre, faire vendre, distribuer leurs ouvrages dans le territoire de la République, et d'en céder la propriété en tout ou en partie*'.); French Patent Act 1791 Art. 1 and 3, reprinted in Kurz, Weltgeschichte des Erfindungsschutzes 243–45; *cf.* also Silberstein, Erfindungsschutz und merkantilistische Gewerbeprivilegien 250–51; Kurz, Weltgeschichte des Erfindungsschutzes 239; Galvez-Behar, La république des inventeurs 23.

[251] Bosse, Autorschaft als Werkherrschaft 100; Höffner, Geschichte und Wesen des Urheberrechts I 286 et seq.

[252] Damme, *Der Schutz technischer Erfindungen als Erscheinungsform moderner Volkswirtschaft* 51 et seq.; Edward Darcy Esquire v. Thomas Allin of London Haberdasher, 74 E.R. 1131, 1137 (1599).

[253] See MacLeod, Inventing the Industrial Revolution 68 et seq., 203; Bracha, Owning Ideas 530; Bracha, 38 Loyola of L.A. L. Rev. 177, 206–9 (2004); Lai, *in* Lai & Maget Dominicé (eds.) Intellectual Property and Access to Im/material Goods 94, 111 with further references; *also* Sherman & Bently, The Making of Modern Intellectual Property Law 101 et seq.

Until 1695, book printing – which was also exempted from the abolition of privileges – was subject to self-regulation by London publishers, partly supported by law (the Licensing Act), which laid out who was allowed to print which 'pamphlet or book'.[254] This dirigiste censorship regime was not continued after the revolution. It was replaced in 1710 by 'An Act for the Encouragement of Learning, by Vesting the Copies of Printed Books in the Authors or Purchasers of such Copies, During the Times therein mentioned' – the famous Statute of (Queen) Anne.[255] This law certainly has revolutionary elements. It changed the basic norm for information and knowledge from absolutist control to freedom of communication, and shifted decision-making power from London to authors and their publishers and thus ultimately to the decentralised anonymous market. To this end, the 'author' was granted exclusive rights as a 'proprietor' for an initial period of fourteen years. What remained unclear, however, was to what these rights attach.[256]

There was no mention of 'work' either in the Statute of Anne or in the numerous amending laws of the eighteenth and early nineteenth centuries.[257] According to the title of the Statute of Anne, 'Copies of Printed Books' were the subject of the rights of the authors or their contractual partners. Their sovereign right was to print a book written by them: '[T]he Author of any Book ... shall have the sole Right and Liberty of Printing such Book'. Thus, like the earlier privileges, the Statute of Anne granted an exclusive right to certain behaviour (printing) in relation to a thing (book). This understanding continues in the term 'copyright' to this day,[258] which implies an exclusive right to copy or to copies. The Statute of Anne is therefore not yet based on the concept of the abstract work. It breaks with the privilege system with regard to the source of rights (the law of parliament) and the original ownership of rights (the author), but not with regard to the subject matter of the rights.[259]

---

[254] Licensing Act (1662), *in* Bently & Kretschmer (eds.) *Primary Sources on Copyright* www.copyrighthistory.org.

[255] Statute of Anne (1710), *in* Bently & Kretschmer (eds.) *Primary Sources on Copyright* www.copyrighthistory.org; Patterson, *Copyright in historical perspective* 4.

[256] Barron, 15 Social & Legal Studies 101, 108 (2006); Cornish, 13 The Edinburgh L. Rev. 8, 10 (2009); Drassinower, *What's Wrong with Copying?* 159 et seq.

[257] *See* Kawohl & Kretschmer, 2 Intellectual Property Quarterly 209, 218 (2003) with further references.

[258] *Cf. also* Jaszi, 40 Duke L.J. 455, 471 (1991) ('Copyright began with "authorship"'.). The term 'copyright' was used for the first time in British law in the Copyright Act von 1801, 41 Geo.III, c.107, *in* Bently & Kretschmer (eds.) *Primary Sources on Copyright* www.copyrighthistory.org.

[259] Sherman & Bently, *The Making of Modern Intellectual Property Law* 17 et seq.; Kawohl & Kretschmer, 2 Intellectual Property Quarterly 209, 212–13 (2003) ('Eighteenth century copyright was practised as the sale of a manuscript from author to publisher against a one-off fee, and litigation between competing publishers'.); Deazley, *On the Origin of the Right to Copy* 221 et seq.; Barron, 15 Social & Legal Studies 101, 106 et seq. (2006); Barron, 52 New Formations, 58, 70 (2004) with further references; Hirsch, 36 UFITA 19, 24–25 (1962).

In this latter respect, there was agreement that the new rights were not classic property rights in tangible, printed matter. Their purpose was not to allocate certain tangibles, but to regulate the production and further use of a whole class of artefacts. These 'copies' and not the 'work' were at the heart of early British copyright law.[260] Decades of legal and political conflict in the eighteenth century revolved around the notion of the 'copy' and the 'book'. They were ignited by the question as to whether the authors and their legal successors were entitled to an eternal common law right to the 'copy of a book', so that they could take always action against unauthorised reprints, or whether the Statute of Anne represented an exhaustive regulation, so that after expiry of the statutory term of protection unauthorised reprints would be lawful.[261]

The contradictory and widely discussed decisions of the Court of the King's Bench in the 1769 case of *Millar v. Taylor* and of the House of Lords 1774 case of *Donaldson v. Beckett* show how difficult it was for the leading English lawyers of that time to put the subject matter of protection of the new law into words.[262] In the definition of 'copy' presented by Lord Mansfield in 1769, both a tangible-physical understanding and an idealistic-abstract concept are expressed:

> I use the word 'copy' in the technical sense in which that name or term has been used for ages, to signify an incorporeal right to the sole printing and publishing of somewhat intellectual, communicated by letters.[263]

According to this sentence, copyright is a right to print and publish that does not attach to corporeal documents, but to a 'somewhat intellectual' object that is

---

[260] Deazley, *On the Origin of the Right to Copy* 49.

[261] Donaldson v. Becket, Hansard, 1st ser., 17 953–1003 (1774), in Bently & Kretschmer (eds.) *Primary Sources on Copyright* www.copyrighthistory.org ('Whether, at common law, an author of any book or literary composition had the sole right of first printing and publishing the same for sale, and might bring an action against any person who printed, published, and sold the same without his consent?'); Sherman & Bently, *The Making of Modern Intellectual Property Law* 9 et seq.

[262] Sherman & Bently, The Making of Modern Intellectual Property Law 19 et seq.; Deazley, *On the Origin of the Right to Copy* 221 et seq.; Drassinower, *What's Wrong with Copying?* 164 et seq.; Jaszi, 40 Duke L.J. 455, 474 et seq. (1991); Pila, 71 Modern L. Rev. 535–36 (2008); van Dijk, *Grounds of the Immaterial* 12 et seq.

On the application of the Statute of Anne to musical scores see Bach v. Longman (1777), in Bently & Kretschmer (eds.) *Primary Sources on Copyright* www.copyrighthistory.org; Kawohl & Kretschmer, 2 Intellectual Property Quarterly 209, 214–15 (2003); contra Barron, 15 Social & Legal Studies 101, 119 (2006).

[263] *Millar v. Taylor*, 4 Burrow 2303, 2396 (1769); loc. cit., 2311, 2331, 2335 ('The name, "copy of a book", which has been used for ages, as a term to signify the sole right of printing publishing and selling, shews this species of property to have been long known, and to have existed in fact and usage, as long as the name. . . . From hence, it is clear, that there is a time, when without any positive statute, an author has a property in the copy of his own work, in the legal sense of the word. . . . He who engages in a laborious work, (such, for instance, as Johnson's Dictionary,) which may employ his whole life, will do it with more spirit, if, besides his own glory, he thinks it may be a provision for his family').

communicated in books that ultimately descend into an exchangeable carrier of information. Along the same lines, the 'original work' also becomes the focus of attention in Blackstone's influential *Commentaries on the Laws of England*, published in 1765/1769:

> When a man by the exertion of his rational powers has produced an original work, he has clearly a right to dispose of that identical work as he pleases, and any attempt to take it from him, or vary the disposition he has made of it, is an invasion of his right of property.[264]

Other lawyers could do little with these idealistic constructions. This displeasure is particularly clearly articulated by Judge Yates in his dissenting opinion in *Millar v. Taylor*. Yates works out in all desirable clarity that the subject matter of protection of the new law, the new 'property', only exists in our language and imagination:

> [T]he property here claimed is all ideal; a set of ideas which have no bounds or marks whatsoever, nothing that is capable of visible possession, nothing that can sustain any one of the qualities or incidents of property. Their whole existence is in the mind alone; incapable of any other modes of acquisition or enjoyment than by mental possession or apprehension; safe and invulnerable, from their own immateriality: no trespass can reach them; no tort affect them; no fraud or violence diminish or damage them. Yet these are the phantoms which the author would grasp and confine to himself: and these are what the defendant is charged with having robbed the plaintiff of.[265]

Yates considered the idea of such a property to be 'very difficult, or rather quite wild'.[266]

In early US IP law, the idea of abstract IP objects was also not fully implemented. After the United States declared independence in 1776, it was politically clear that the regulation of book printing and other technologies could no longer be based on privileges. At the same time, US law was in the tradition of English common law, and the French Revolutionary Laws on Patent and Copyright law did not yet exist. It is therefore not surprising that US law also describes the subject matter of protection of the new rights according to the British model in an ambivalent, predominantly physical manner. While the preamble of the first Copyright Act of an individual state already refers to 'work',[267] the Federal Constitution of 1787/1789 declares that

---

[264] Blackstone, *Commentaries on the Laws of England* II chapter 26 no. 8, 405–6; cf. Cornish, 13 The Edinburgh L. Rev. 8, 11 (2009).
[265] Millar v. Taylor, 4 Burrow 2303, 2361 (1769). See also Pottage & Sherman, *Figures of Invention* 45 note 2.
[266] Millar v. Taylor, 4 Burrow 2303, 2357 (1769).
[267] Connecticut Copyright Statute (1783), in Bently & Kretschmer (eds.) *Primary Sources on Copyright* www.copyrighthistory.org ('Whereas it is perfectly agreeable to the Principles of natural Equity and Justice, that every Author should be secured in receiving the Profits that may arise from the Sale of his Works …').

Congress is responsible for granting authors and inventors an exclusive right in their 'Writings and Discoveries'.[268] Neither the Patent Act nor the Copyright Act of 1790 place the concept of work or invention at their centre, but they refer to 'any useful art, manufacture, engine, machine, or device, or any improvement therein not before known or used'[269] and to 'any map, chart, book or books'.[270] While the concept of invention had already acquired greater codificatory significance in the course of a patent law reform in 1793,[271] in its first decision on copyright in 1834 the US Supreme Court still argued primarily on the basis of actions and artefacts: The 'literary man' could achieve the fair wage for his work by the transfer of the 'manuscript' and the sale of books.[272] In the United States American specialist literature of the early nineteenth century, one searches in vain for the term 'work'.[273]

The abstract work concept was only introduced into British law via the implementation of an international treaty with France in 1851 by which the contracting states intended to guarantee 'the enjoyment of copyright to works of literature and of the fine arts' for their nationals in the two territories.[274] Another sixty years passed before the Imperial Copyright Act of 1911 adopted the general concept of 'original works' in British law.[275] In the United States the term 'work' was first mentioned in the Copyright Act of 1870, in connection with the newly introduced right of authors

---

[268] US Const., Art. I, § 8, cl. 8 ('Congress shall have Power . . . To promote the Progress of Science and useful Arts, by securing for limited Times to Authors and Inventors the exclusive Right to their respective Writings and Discoveries').

[269] US Patent Act (1790), *in* Kurz, *Weltgeschichte des Erfindungsschutzes* 276 et seq.; *to that* Bracha, 38 Loyola of L.A. L. Rev. 177, 222 (2004) ('the framework of the 1790 Patent Act seems to be a hybrid between the particularistic privi-leges of the traditional English and state grants and the modern patent-rights model. The Act created a kind of a "universalised privilege" system'.); *contra* Pottage & Sherman, *Figures of Invention* 5 (first truly modern patent regime); Biagioli, 73 Social Research: An International Quarterly 1129, 1147 (2006) ('regime change').

[270] US Copyright Act (1790), *in* Bently & Kretschmer (eds.) *Primary Sources on Copyright* www.copyrighthistory.org; Bracha, *Owning Ideas* 529–30; Madison, 19 J. Intell. Prop. L. 325, 334 (2012).

[271] *See* Pottage & Sherman, *Figures of Invention* 65 (requirement 'to fully explain the principle, and the several modes in which he has contemplated the application of that principle or character, by which it may be distinguished from other inventions').

[272] Wheaton v. Peters, 33 US 591, 657 (1834) ('The argument that a literary man is as much entitled to the product of his labour as any other member of society, cannot be controverted. And the answer is, that he realises this product by the transfer of his manuscripts, or in the sale of his works, when first published'.).

[273] Curtis, *Law of Copyright* 83 et seq.; Madison, 19 J. Intell. Prop. L. 325, 334–35 (2012). On the subsumtion of music under 'writings' *see* Toynbee, 15 Music, Social & Legal Studies 77, 82–83 (2006). *But see* Drone, *A treatise on the law of property in intellectual productions in Great Britain and the United States* 97–98.

[274] Anglo-French Copyright Treaty (1851), *in* Bently & Kretschmer (eds.) *Primary Sources on Copyright* www.copyrighthistory.org.

[275] Cornish, 13 The Edinburgh L. Rev. 8, 17 (2009); Sherman & Bently, *The Making of Modern Intellectual Property Law* 129 et seq.

as 'proprietor[s] of copyright book' to 'reserve the right to dramatise or to translate their own works'.[276]

Both the context of the international copyright treaty and that of the adaptation right prove that these terminological changes are not superficial waste, but express a profound conceptual change of high normative relevance. Like German law, British law departed from the brute reality of reprinted books only under the impression of the internationally successful French paradigm. The latter was not ontologically more plausible than talking about copies and books, but it allowed to apply copyright to phenomena like translations of books and performances of musical compositions without the need to change the law in every single case. This normative functionality of the abstract IP object only gained real traction in the nineteenth century.[277]

3.2.2.2.3 GERMANY This observation is confirmed by the development of German law. As in France and England, the first approaches towards an abstract work as a legal object can be traced back to the first half of the eighteenth century.[278] However, even though attentive observers may have clearly seen at that time that the regulation of book printing can no longer be described in terms of manuscripts and (re-)printed books, it took a long time before the new conception – ownership of the abstract work – was clearly worked out and, above all, socially recognised.[279]

Thus, in the 1753 'General Encyclopaedia of Economics', the term 'book' was still defined as a physical good (*Waare*) and tool (*Werckzeug*) of the transmission of truth, in the production of which not only the writer but also the papermaker and

---

[276] 41st Congress, Second Session, chapter 240, Sections 85–111, An Act to revise, consolidate, and amend the statutes relating to patents and copyrights, Section 86. *See also* Section 4952 International Copyright Act (The Chace Act) (1891), *in* Bently & Kretschmer (eds.) Primary Sources on Copyright www.copyrighthistory.org ('and authors ... shall have exclusive right to dramatize and translate any of their works for which copyright shall have been obtained under the laws of the United States'); Copyright Act 1909, http://copyright.gov/history/1909act .pdf ('any person entitled thereto upon complying with the provisions of this Act, shall have the exclusive right (a) to print ... the copyrighted work'.); Barron, 52 New Formations 58, 70 (2004).

[277] Section 5.4.2; Kawohl & Kretschmer, 2 Intellectual Property Quarterly 209, 214 (2003) ('The main conceptual invention was an abstraction: the subject of protection was thought to be an identical work to which all acts of exploitation were related, be they publication, engraving, reprinting, recital, translation or arrangement. Previously, each of these activities were subject to their own separate regulation (or non-regulation) according to specific circumstances'.); Sherman, 12 Theoretical Inquiries in Law 99 et seq. (2011); Bracha, 118 Yale L.J. 186, 197–98, 248 (2008) ('The gradual embedding of authorship ideology in actual copyright doctrine took place only in the nineteenth century'.); Pudelek, *in* Barck et al. (eds.) *Ästhetische Grundbegriffe* VI 522.

[278] Gieseke, *Vom Privileg zum Urheberrecht* 123. On *Koch's* theory of the musical work *see* Section 3.2.1.2.

[279] Gieseke, *Vom Privileg zum Urheberrecht* 132.

many other persons were involved.[280] The debate that began in the 1770s over the unauthorised reprinting of books proved to be just as ambivalent as the dispute over the eternal common law copyright in the United Kingdom. On the one hand, it is clear from the historical record that those involved were aware that the new right of authors or publishers could not ultimately be justified with regard to the manuscript or other physical items.[281] If there was to be a proprietary right, then it had to have a different, somehow immaterial character. On the other hand, for a long time a corresponding terminology could not prevail against a way of speaking and thinking in terms of privileges to act (e.g. print) with regard to tangible things (e.g. books), which continued to dominate the codifications of the late-absolutist estates-based social order.[282] The primary point of contention was the legality and legitimacy of the unauthorised reprint of books, not an 'intellectual property' in abstract works. Only slowly, and above all from the 1780s onwards, did the discussion focus on the question of whether the author or the authorised publisher had an exclusive right to an abstract object, alternately called a *Buch* (book), *Schrift* (script), *Geistesprodukt* (intellectual product) and *Werk* (work).[283] As a book title, the diction of the copyrighted work prevailing today was used for the first time in 1789.[284] At the same time, reference to the technical *Erfindung* (invention) became more common.[285]

But unlike in France, England and the United States, there was no radical breakthrough. The ambivalence persisted – for example, in the late-absolutist provisions on the publishing contract in Prussian and Austrian law.[286] The idea of

[280] Zincke, *Allgemeines Oeconomisches Lexicon* 443. See also Woodmansee, *The Author, Art and the Market* 48–49.
[281] But see Klippel, in *Festschrift Wadle* 477, 481–82.
[282] Cf. *Preußische Cabinets-Ordre* (1766) and *Erstes Grundgesetz der neuerrichteten Buchhandlungsgesellschaft in Deutschland* (1765), both in Bently & Kretschmer (eds.) *Primary Sources on Copyright* www.copyrighthistory.org; Gieseke, *Vom Privileg zum Urheberrecht* 150 et seq. (Saxon regulation of book trade of 18.12.1773).
[283] See, in particular, Pütter, *Büchernachdruck* § 20, § 90; Cella, in Cella (ed.) *Freymüthige Aufsätze* 86; Reimarus, 1 *Deutsches Magazin* 383, 388 (1791) (literary works); v. Knigge, *Ueber den Bücher-Nachdruck* 34, 37–38 (content of a manuscript, content of a writing); Fichte (1793), in Bently & Kretschmer (eds.) *Primary Sources on Copyright* www .copyrighthistory.org 5 ('We can distinguish two aspects of a book: its physical aspect, the printed paper, and its ideal aspect . . . This ideal aspect is in turn divisible into a material aspect, the content of the book, the ideas it presents; and the form of these ideas, the way in which, the combination in which, the phrasing and wording in which they are presented'.); on Fichte see Kohler, 123 UFITA 99, 128 (1993) ('the most important achievement of the 18th century for the construction of intellectual property'); Klippel, 7 ZGE/IPJ 49, 60 (2015) with further references; Klippel, in *Festschrift Wadle* 477, 482, 491.
[284] Becker, *Das Eigenthumsrecht an Geisteswerken* (1789).
[285] Dölemeyer, in Otto & Klippel (eds.) *Geschichte des deutschen Patentrechts* 13, 19 (Austrian privilege 1801).
[286] See Sections 996, 997, 1034 General State Laws for the Prussian States 1794; Kawohl, Commentary on the reprinting provisions in the Prussian Statute Book (1794), in Bently & Kretschmer (eds.) *Primary Sources on Copyright* www.copyrighthistory.org; Gieseke, *Vom Privileg zum Urheberrecht* 191. See also General Civil Code of Austria of 1811, Section 1164. On the influence of the French concept of inventions on German law see Wadle, in *Festschrift Constantinesco* 871, 891; further Silberstein, *Erfindungsschutz und merkantilistische*

an abstract IP object experienced a temporary boom in the sphere of influence of French legal thought during the Napoleonic Wars, especially in Baden and Bavaria.[287] Beyond or after the end of French rule, however, the way of speaking and regulating that had been handed down from the privilege age, based on actions and artefacts, persisted. The debates continued to revolve around the legality of printing books.[288] Here, as in the case of technical innovations, an instrumental understanding dominated which made it possible to combine the regulation of printing with aspects of censorship and the patent system with dirigiste economic policies.[289] Still in the 1820s and 1830s, theorists like Hegel and Savigny did not succeed in bringing the idealistic conception of the legal object to a specific term that detached itself from the physicalistic modes of speech of the reprint debate.[290]

The turning point in the history of German copyright finally came in 1837, when a decree of the German Confederation (Deutscher Bund) on the protection of the 'Eigenthum[s] des literarischen oder artistischen Werkes' (ownership of literary or artistic works) and a Prussian law 'zum Schutze des Eigentums an Werken der Wissenschaft und der Kunst gegen Nachdruck und Nachbildung' (on the protection of the ownership of works of science and art against reprinting and reproduction) were enacted.[291] As the title of the Prussian law shows, this codification no longer proceeded from the prohibition of reprinting, but from the protection of the abstract work. The prohibition of certain conduct was replaced by an exclusive right in a protected object.[292] To base the law on the largely indefinite concept of the 'work' had the advantage that not only printed matter, but also speeches, musical performances and not least adaptations such as translations could be included in the scope of protection of the new law.[293] In general, the conviction had prevailed that the

---

Gewerbeprivilegien 267, 269. On the influence of the French design law 1806 see Werner, Die Geschichte des deutschen Geschmacksmusterschutzes 9 et seq.; Wadle, in Festschrift Constantinesco 871, 886–87.

[287] See Nachdruckverordnung Baden (1806), in Bently & Kretschmer (eds.) Primary Sources on Copyright www.copyrighthistory.org; art. 577 State law for the Grand-Duchy of Baden, 1810; art. 397 Strafgesetzbuch für das Königreich Bayern (1813), in Bently & Kretschmer (eds.) Primary Sources on Copyright www.copyrighthistory.org; Gräff, 137 UFITA, 111, 161–62 (1998); see also Bosse, Autorschaft als Werkherrschaft 103; Wadle, in Festschrift Constantinesco 871 et seq.; Plumpe, in Brackert & Stückrath (eds.) Literaturwissenschaft 179, 183.

[288] Art. 18d German Confederation Act 1815, reprinted in Eisenlohr, Sammlung der Gesetze 1; Section 1 Württembergisches Rescript v. 25.2.1815; Reprinting Act Anhalt-Cöthen 1828, reprinted in Eisenlohr, Sammlung der Gesetze 6.

[289] Dölemeyer, in Otto & Klippel (eds.) Geschichte des deutschen Patentrechts 13, 27–28.

[290] Hegel, Elements of the Philosophy of Right § 69; v. Savigny, in Wadle, Savignys Beitrag zum Urheberrecht 28 et seq. ('individuality of a book'); Hubmann, 106 UFITA 145 (1987) (the subject matter of protection remained obscure).

[291] Wadle, in Wadle (ed.) Geistiges Eigentum I 223 et seq.; Wadle, in Wadle (ed.) Beiträge zur Geschichte des Urheberrechts 73, 79; Gieseke, Vom Privileg zum Urheberrecht 237 et seq.; Kawohl & Kretschmer, 2 Intellectual Property Quarterly 209, 216 (2003).

[292] Wadle, in Wadle (ed.) Geistiges Eigentum I 167 et seq. with further references.

[293] On musical works see Kawohl, Urheberrecht der Musik in Preussen 109, 150.

book and art sector must also be organised according to the laws of the market, without however creating frictions with the monarchical form of government. From the middle of the nineteenth century onwards, it had finally become a matter of course among lawyers to assume the existence of immaterial works and inventions that were allocated to right holders by property-like exclusive rights.[294] The conceptual innovation rooted in the eighteenth century had found social recognition in Germany. It had become social reality and, starting from copyright and patent law, could spread to all areas of today's IP law.[295]

---

[294] *See* Bluntschli, *Deutsches Privatrecht* I 188; Stobbe, *Handbuch des deutschen Privatrechts* I 520; Schuster, *Das Urheberrecht der Tonkunst* 50; Planck, 1 UFITA 197, 203 (2012); on Klostermann and Kohler *see* Wadle, *in Festschrift Constantinesco* 871, 896 et seq.

[295] On design law *see* Section 25 Prussian Copyright Act 1837; Breimesser, *Urheberrecht und Rechtsbegriff*, passim; Damme, *Der Schutz technischer Erfindungen als Erscheinungsform moderner Volkswirtschaft* 12–13 with further references. On the property rights rhetoric in nineteenth-century British trademark law *see* Sherman & Bently, *The Making of Modern Intellectual Property Law* 167 et seq.; Bently, *in* Dinwoodie & Janis (eds.) *Trademark Law and Theory* 118 et seq.

4

Interim Summary: An Implausible Paradigm

Let us take stock. The reality of current IP rights cannot be made plausible in the way we depict and handle them – namely as immaterial objects embodied in, but not identical to, physical and mental tokens. Traditional metaphysical object ontology has failed to explain the existence of the abstract work and other abstract IP objects. Unlike conventional universals, these 'types' are indisputably neither timeless nor locationless, nor independent of material embodiments, nor acausal. They are created by humans as artefacts, have an effect on recipients, and can become lost. The evasion by some object ontologists that IP objects are to be understood as an abstract type *sui generis* is nothing other than an attempt to save the project of traditional metaphysics with its belief in a world of ideal objects.[1]

John Searle's social ontology, in contrast, provides a plausible explanation of abstract IP objects. According to this approach, works, inventions etc. are not objects that exist in brute, external reality, but language-based constructions that only exist because and to the extent that people speak and think as if there were immaterial works, inventions etc. Searle calls such facts 'institutional'. The construction in question here ties in with the brute, external reality, but then assigns to this brute reality a status which it (the brute reality) does not possess because of its given qualities, but which is attributed to it by a declarative speech act and its social recognition. The speech act states that a book, machine, or other tangible/corporeal artefact represents an independent abstract work, an abstract invention etc. The physically or mentally existing artefact is not considered and designated as such, but as a mere instantiation or manifestation of another, immaterial object. This eccentric concept is not really explicated, but is often unconsciously exercised in the dominant way of speaking of the abstract work etc.[2] The distinction between work exemplars and the copyrightable work, products and invention/design, product

---

[1] *See* Section 2.1.1.
[2] *Cf.* Tuomela, *Philosophy of Sociality* 186.

presentation and signs etc. has the logical form of a Searlean status function, which applies to all social-institutional facts. Thus, in context C, the artefact X counts as an exemplar of the immaterial object Y. While, for example, a book X exists measurably in brute reality, work Y exists only in our language practice and our collective imagination expressed in this way. In other words, it is not only the IP *right* that is a social construct, but also its subject matter.[3]

The subsequent diachronic analysis confirmed this finding. For the way of speaking and thinking abstracted from specific artefacts (such as books) and actions (such as reproduction, public performance, use) is the result of linguistic-social practices. A distinction was made between two levels of abstraction. A first, very old and permanently repeated language exercise aims at giving a multitude of brute artefacts a general name. This process can be divided into three logical steps. It starts with the change of external reality by man in the form of the creation of a new artefact – such as a new digital file, a manuscript, a drawing or a model. Some of these artefacts are stored or otherwise preserved and given a special designation by the creator or third parties (Master Artefact). Finally, identical and sufficiently similar copies, imitations and other Secondary Artefacts are designated by the name of the Master Artefact. Both the status of the Master Artefact and that of Secondary Artefacts are results of social negotiation processes that are often contentious. The corresponding designations refer to brute reality. Their signifier is always a single artefact or a plurality of artefacts with a concrete physical or mental existence.[4]

The legal counterpart to the first abstraction of many brute artefacts to the general term is the privilege.[5] Since early modern times, privileges have regulated who was allowed to produce and otherwise use books, machines and other products that were given a universal designation in general language practice and also in the context of privileges. The reality of privileges was therefore different from that of today's IP law. They did not assign abstract objects, but regulated the reprinting of books and other artefact-related actions.

The step from privilege to 'intellectual property' or *Immaterialgüterrecht* presupposed a legal object capable of being owned. Abstract IP objects assumed this function. From the point of view of linguistic analysis, this social-institutional construction is a new semantic. The long-established way of speaking of book, work, or invention 'X' took on a new meaning. It no longer referred to the Master Artefact and an indefinite number of Secondary Artefacts, but to the abstract work etc., which is manifested only accidentally in brute artefacts. The brute, measurable reality [Word$\downarrow\uparrow$World^1] was replaced by the idealistic idea of a world of abstract objects [Word$\downarrow\uparrow$World^2]. To repeat in the terms of the Searlean status function: the copy of a book no longer counted simply as a copy of a specifically named artefact, but as the embodiment of an imperceptible abstract object.

---

[3] *See* Section 2.2.2.
[4] ibid
[5] *See* Section 2.2.2, Section 3.2.1.3.1.

This semantic innovation took place in the course of the eighteenth century.[6] Its linguistic expression is the parlance of the literary and artistic 'work' and the technical 'invention'. These words articulate the novel notion of the object capable of ownership, which exists as a social-institutional fact in linguistic articulation alone. The emergence of the abstract concept of the copyrightable work, which is characteristic of abstract IP objects in general, was articulated by Romantic authors such as Edward Young and Karl Philipp Moritz. They declared that with a 'work' the author creates an ideal and, at the same time, a self-contained unity that is not exhausted in the specific manuscript. The surprising, seemingly superfluous duplication of reality fell on fertile ground. It provided the art, literary and technological markets that were formed during the *Sattelzeit* in the late eighteenth century with the necessary object of exchange. In the course of the maelstrom to modernism, it also contributed to the integration of intellectual (creative and innovative) activity into the capitalist mode of production.[7]

At the same time, this functionality constitutes the normativity of abstract IP objects, or more precisely of the status function, according to which a physical or mental artefact counts as the embodiment of an abstract-immaterial IP object.[8] The dominant paradigm objectifies activities that disappear behind the constructed object capable of being owned. Speaking and thinking in categories of abstract IP objects already constitutes and regulates power relations.

Before returning to this normativity of the abstract IP object,[9] the prevailing paradigm and the alternative ontology developed here – based on actions and artefacts – should again be subjected to a comparative examination, this time from a legal perspective. The purpose is to examine which of the competing understandings of reality is capable to better explain current IP law. By addressing the legal-theoretical explanatory power of the two ontologies, we return to the differences between real property and IP rights mentioned at the beginning.[10] The fact that these differences remain puzzling for the prevailing view makes it seem possible that a legal-realistic IP theory has greater explanatory power than an idealistic one. If this were the case, the function of the ontologically implausible construction of abstract IP objects would consist solely in inventing a property object in order to ultimately subject large parts of social communication and practice to the laws of the market.

---

[6] Section 3.2.
[7] Plumpe, 23 Archiv für Begriffsgeschichte 175, 176 et seq. (1979); Bourdieu, *Market of Symbolic Goods* 1 et seq.; Jaszi, 40 Duke L.J. 455, 479 (1991) ('The process of appropriation that began with the booksellers' unfurling the banner of "authorship" was completed through the legal objectification of the fruits of creative labor. Thus, the necessary conditions for a market in texts as commodities were in place'.); Toynbee, 15 Music, Social & Legal Studies 77, 79–80 (2006); Biagioli, 73 Social Research: An International Quarterly 1129, 1160 (2006) ('Intellectual property rights and right-bearing citizens were constructed at the same time, through the same process'.); van Dijk, *Grounds of the Immaterial* 23; on the etymology of the German term '*Werk*', see Erben, in *Festschrift Weisgerber* 221, 224 et seq.
[8] On the normativity of every status function, *see* Section 2.1.1.
[9] *See* Section 5.4, Chapter 6.
[10] Section 1.2.

5

The Legal Explanatory Power of the Two Ontologies

In order to get to the bottom of the legal-theoretical and normative significance of the idea of abstract IP objects, some core aspects of current IP law will be confronted with the two competing ontologies. It will be shown that an action- and artefact-based approach can make the structure and practice of current IP law (see Section 5.1), the differences between real property and IP rights (see Section 5.2) and the notorious difficulties in convincingly justifying IP rights (see Section 5.3) more comprehensible than a theory that presupposes works, inventions, designs, signs etc. as abstract legal objects. Not least, on the basis of the dominant paradigm, it is impossible to comprehend and criticise the normativity of the abstract IP object (see Section 5.4). It is the fiction that abstract IP objects, like tangible things, exist in external reality that has made possible the resilience and expansion of IP law for more than two centuries.

5.1 THE STRUCTURE AND PRACTICE OF CURRENT IP LAW

The first test for our two competing understandings of reality is to explain the structure and practice of current IP law. In this respect, the view that IP rights assign abstract objects such as the work, the invention and the design to a person – analogously to the real property of a person – undisputedly prevails and is in part expressly codified.[1]

5.1.1 *Scope of Application of the Prevailing Paradigm*

Surprisingly, however, this understanding is not implemented across the board in current law. At the edges of IP law, the idea of abstract IP objects is no longer being supported.

[1] Section 1.1.

5.1.1.1 Trademark Law

This observation relates first and foremost to trademark law. If this is to be an ownership right in an abstract sign, the signs of which a trademark may consist of pursuant to Section 3 of the German Trademark Act (MarkenG) and Article 4 of the EU Trademark Regulation must belong to the trademark proprietor *as such*. Such a legal regulation presupposes a sign that no longer represents a certain signified – a freely floating designation without a signified.[2] Only on the basis of this truly eccentric and paradoxical understanding can one speak of signs as abstract objects. If product signs are protected only in the context of their use for certain goods or services and the public's understandings as to their origin, there is a lack of an abstract IP object that is owned as such. The sign and its legal protection then remain embedded in competitive relationships that are regulated according to the model of unfair competition law.

Precisely this is the legal situation in the EU despite all legislative and commentatory rhetoric according to which trademark law has developed since the late twentieth century to a fully fledged IP law equivalent to copyright and patent law.[3] According to the settled case law of the Court of Justice of the European Union, trademark rights fulfil an 'essential role in the system of undistorted competition' in the internal market.[4] In order to achieve that purpose, the protected trademark must 'guarantee that all the goods or services bearing it have been manufactured or supplied under the control of a single undertaking which is responsible for their quality'.[5] The fact that that function continues to be the indispensable essential function of the protected trademark is demonstrated by the obligation to use, which is satisfied by the proprietor only if he uses the protected sign to create or preserve an outlet for the goods or services referred to in the registration but 'does not include token use for the sole purpose of preserving the rights conferred by the mark'.[6] The existence of trademark law is therefore linked to the use of the sign in a very specific product and sales context. Nor does the scope of protection of a trademark abstract from these competitive contexts. A trademark infringement requires that the contested designation is used 'like a trademark' or 'as a trademark', i.e. 'in the context of the sale of a product or service also serves to distinguish the goods or services of one undertaking from those of others'. On the other hand, it is not infringing to speak purely descriptively – e.g. in the news –

---

[2] Baudrillard, *The Consumer Society* 74–75, 78–80, 93.
[3] See Art. 1 para. 2 TRIPS as well as Section 1.5.
[4] CJEU Case C-63/97 BMW v. Ronald Karel Deenik, ECLI:EU:C:1999:82 para. 62; CJEU Case C-228/03 Gillette v. LA-Laboratories, ECLI:EU:C:2005:177 para. 29; CJEU Case C-500/14 Ford Motor Company v. Wheeltrims, ECLI:EU:C:2015:680 para 43.
[5] CJEU Case C-206/01 Arsenal Football Club v. Matthew Reed, ECLI:EU:C:2002:651 para. 48 with further references.
[6] CJEU Case C-689/15 W.F. Gözze v. Verein Bremer Baumwollbörse, ECLI:EU:C:2017:434 para. 37 with further references.

about a protected trademark.[7] Finally, the assessment of trademark use ('scope of trademark protection') is also based on considerations of unfair competition law that place the protected sign in a competitive context. This applies not only to collisions of similar signs or products, the assessment of which depends on a concrete likelihood of confusion, but also to cases of double identity and the protection of well-known trademarks.[8] The sign is therefore not protected as such, but only in a specific context – specifically as a product sign in the course of trade.

If one wanted to apply the idea of abstract IP objects to trademark law, one would consequently have to make an object other than the sign the object of protection. The designated goods or services cannot assume this role because they exist as brute artefacts in external reality. But perhaps the goodwill, the image, the good reputation which the brand communicates and which EU law calls 'distinctive character' and 'repute' with regard to well-known marks may be suitable objects.[9] To understand a trademark in this way can potentially provide the basis for an abstract IP object. Like the abstract work, it would take the place of the indefinite number of goods and services offered under the trademark. In order to assume this function, it is particularly helpful that nobody knows exactly what is meant by 'goodwill'.[10] However, the problem with this coherent theory of trademark law is that it only partly explains the law. The distinctive character and repute of a sign is only important in the case of well-known trademarks. Unknown trademarks do not enjoy a reputation, and they do not carry goodwill. Nevertheless, their position on the market is protected against the risk of confusion caused by identical or similar signs. Finally, the goodwill of well-known trademarks is not protected *in abstracto* either, but only under the premise that the challenged use of the sign has the object or effect of distorting competition.[11] Such a legal protection oriented towards the infringement does not have the characteristics of a property-like allocation of objects.

So far, it has not been possible to transform trademark law from a regulation of competitive behaviour into an IP right. The idea of a commercial sign, which has

---

[7] Translated from the original German. *Cf.* BGH 3 November 2016 Case no. I ZR 101/15, GRUR 2017, 520 para. 26 – MICRO COTTON; Drassinower, *What's Wrong with Copying?* 109.

[8] *Cf.* Section 14 German Trademark Act (MarkenG), Art. 9 EU Trademark Reg.; CJEU Case C-48/05 Adam Opel AG v. Autec AG, ECLI:EU:C:2007:55 paras. 24–25; BGH 14 January 2010 Case no. I ZR 88/08, GRUR 2010, 726 paras 17 et seq. – Opel Blitz II; CJEU Joined Cases C-236/08–238/08 Google France v. Louis Vuitton Malletier, Google France v. Viaticum and Luteciel, Google France v. Centre national de recherche en relations humains et al, ECLI:EU:C:2010:159 paras 95–98; CJEU Case C-323/09 Interflora v. Marks & Spencer, ECLI:EU:C:2011:604 paras. 61–62 (fair competition).

[9] *Cf.* Art. 10 (2) (c) EU Trademark Dir., Art. 9 (2) (c) EU Trademark Reg.

[10] Bone, 86 Boston University L. Rev. 571 (2006) ('No one might know exactly what goodwill was, but everyone could reason as if some thing actually existed, which the term goodwill named. And this made it possible to embrace the shift from mark to goodwill as the locus of property rights').

[11] See Chapter 5 note 8; *further* Peukert, *Festschrift Fezer* 405, 422 et seq. with further references.

neither a fixed external appearance nor a certain meaning, is (still) too eccentric to serve as the basis of a proprietary position.[12]

5.1.1.2 Rights in Innovation, in Particular Rights Related to Copyright and Plant Variety Rights

In the case of rights in innovation, the conceptual difficulties of the prevailing paradigm are of a different kind. In this respect, beyond copyright, patent and design law, it is often unclear what is meant by an innovation abstract from physical and mental artefacts.

Regarding the protection of layout-designs (topographies) of integrated circuits, the prevailing paradigm still seems viable. The abstract object here is the 'topography', or more precisely: the three-dimensional pattern of the layers of which a semiconductor product is composed.[13] This object of protection constitutes a special case of the area formerly known in German as *Geschmacksmusterrecht* (law of industrial models) and today as design law. An abstract object of protection in semiconductor and design law is the external appearance of products, which in individual cases only count as accidental embodiments of the abstract design.[14] Two- or three-dimensional appearances of products may also enjoy copyright protection as an artistic work pursuant to Section 2(1) no. 4 of the German Copyright Act (UrhG). The fact that Kant and Fichte, as outstanding representatives of German idealism at the turn of the nineteenth century, were still prepared to accept the abstract work concept for speeches and written literary works, but not for sculptures, paintings and other works of art, proves just how distant it is to stylise the replicable outer appearance of a tangible thing into an immaterial, 'intellectual' object.[15]

Regarding rights related to copyright, the prevailing paradigm is still implausible today. Their relatedness to copyright is not ontological. Rather, an ontological distinction is also expressed in the continental European separation of works eligible for copyright protection on the one hand (Part 1 of the German Copyright Act) and other achievements only 'related' to copyrightable creations (Part 2 of the German Copyright Act). Whereas literary works, musical works, the fine arts, choreographies and visual and cinematographic works are considered immaterial objects, artistic performances, simple photographs, sound and image carriers, press publications etc.

---

[12] On the resilience of trademark law against commodification processes *see* Bently, in Dinwoodie & Janis (eds.) Trademark Law and Theory 3, 7 et seq.

[13] *See* the definition of 'topography' in Art. 1(b) EU Topographies Dir. ('a series of related images, however fixed or encoded; (i) representing the three-dimensional pattern of the layers of which a semiconductor product is composed; and (ii) in which series, each image has the pattern or part of the pattern of a surface of the semiconductor product at any stage of its manufacture').

[14] Section 1.1.

[15] Kant (1785), *in* Bently & Kretschmer (eds.) *Primary Sources on Copyright* www.copyrighthistory .org 13; Fichte (1793), *in* Bently & Kretschmer (eds.) *Primary Sources on Copyright* www .copyrighthistory.org 21.

are regarded as actions and manufactured products with a brute, physical existence.[16] Anglo-American law renounces such metaphysical differentiations and, for example, subsumes 'phonorecords' and 'recordings' under the term 'work' capable of copyright protection without further ado – although according to the legal definition of the US Copyright Act sound carriers are 'material objects' such as CDs, DVDs or digital files.[17] The existence of different work concepts proves, firstly, that we are dealing with an historically contingent – and from country to country diverging – construction and not with a given fact of the outside world.[18] Secondly, the inappropriate application of the abstract work concept to material objects in British and US-American law confirms that exclusive rights always require a distinct object that is allocated to an owner.[19] If such an object does not exist in external reality, it must be asserted.

As far as rights related to copyright are concerned, however, it has remained unclear to this day what constitutes their subject matter. Their legal designation as merely 'related' or 'neighbouring' rights does not provide any information on this question. The concrete performances, photographs, sound carriers, databases and other 'products' (see Section 72(1) of the German Copyright Act (UrhG)) are precisely not immaterial objects. As in the case of single work exemplars (tokens), personality rights and real property rights may apply to these actions and things. The person entitled (e.g. the owner of a phonorecord) can, but does not have to, be identical with the owner of the right related to copyright – such as the producer of the recording.

If one applies the prevailing ontology of copyright *strictu sensu* and asks what could be 'embodied' in the brute artefacts referred to in the second part of the German Copyright Act, one encounters the personal or entrepreneurial-organisational 'investment' necessary to bring about a performance or the first fixation of an audio recording. The *sui generis* right of the database maker explicitly emphasises this, and the other related rights also serve to protect investments in

---

[16] On the related right of film producers *cf.* Government Draft UrhG 1965, BT-printed matter IV/270, 102 (the right relates to the film strip, i.e. the carrier medium on which the film has been recorded); Troller, 50 UFITA 385, 414 (1967) (pointing out the necessity to distinguish between related rights in physical work products and copyright in the abstract work).

[17] See 17 USC § 101 ('"Phonorecords" are material objects in which sounds, other than those accompanying a motion picture or other audiovisual work, are fixed by any method now known or later developed, and from which the sounds can be perceived, reproduced, or otherwise communicated, either directly or with the aid of a machine or device. The term phonorecords includes the material object in which the sounds are first fixed'.) and Section 102 (a)(7) as well as Section 1(1)(b) and (c) UK Copyright, Designs and Patents Act 1988 (sound recordings, films, broadcasts, the typographical arrangement of published editions); European Commission, Towards a modern, more European copyright framework, COM(2015) 626 final, note 5 ('"Works" is used in this document to mean both works protected by copyright and other subject matter protected by related rights, as relevant to the context'.).

[18] See Section 5.4.2.

[19] Section 1.1.

cultural production.[20] However, investments of money, time and other resources in the production of artistic performances and other cultural products are – unlike the concept of work, invention and design – not suitable as placeholders for an abstract object. They lack the intellectual element. They do not communicate information, but with their brute, physical existence they bring about a change in the outside world – the reproducible Master Artefacts to which the related rights attach (for example, the first fixation of a phonorecord). Advocates of the prevailing paradigm of abstract IP objects also admit that this ontology does not fit to rights related to copyright.[21]

In the case of plant variety rights, which like rights related to copyright were also not codified until the twentieth century, it already follows from the wording of the law that this IP law is not based on the concept of abstract IP objects.[22] Its reality is a plant variety, legally defined as 'a plant grouping',[23] whose distinct, uniform and stable characteristics are based on a particular genotype. If one wishes to trace the plant variety right back to an object, then to the latter, scientifically ascertainable, brute fact of a genotype which is replicated by natural propagation and manifests itself in a certain phenotype. Plant variety protection law is therefore based on a scientific view of World^1, not on an idealistic idea of an abstract World^2.[24]

The fact that, despite these exceptions, the paradigm of the abstract IP object continues to apply unquestioningly and could even radiate onto IP rights with a clearly physical subject matter proves its normative power. Since the late eighteenth century, we speak and think in categories of 'the' work, 'the' invention etc. Precisely because it remains unclear in such a way of speaking whether the term represents a multitude of brute artefacts [Word↓↑World^1] or an abstract IP object [Word↓↑World^2], the notion of a distinct property object functions even where such a notion is not asserted at all – as in plant variety law and in rights 'related' to copyright. Technological progress *and* language-based abstraction, being *and* consciousness, brute *and* institutional facts, bring about and implement the expansion of IP rights.[25]

---

[20] See Section 87a German Copyright Act (UrhG) as well as Rehbinder & Peukert, *Urheberrecht* para 760.

[21] See Troller, 50 UFITA 385, 414 (1967); Gaudrat, 221 RIDA 2, 30 (2009).

[22] See Chapter 3 note 41.

[23] Section 2 no. 1a German Plant Variety Act (SortSchG); Art. 5 (2) EU Plant Variety Reg.; Art. 1 (vi), 9 Convention for the Protection of New Varieties of Plants (UPOV).

[24] See also van Overwalle, in Sikorski & Zemła Pacud (eds.), Patents as an Incentive for Innovation; Seitz & Kock, 8/9 GRUR Int. 711, 712 (2012); Würtenberger et Al., EU Plant Variety Protection para. 3.14, 6.11; Leßmann & Würtenberger, *Sortenschutzrecht* Section 2 para. 73 (protection of a concrete plant variety in contrast to patent law); *contra* Sabelleck, in Metzger & Zech (eds.) *Sortenschutzrecht Section 2 German Plant Variety Act (SortSchG)* para. 11–13 with further references (the genome is 'physical stuff and immaterial information at the same time'). On patents in biological material, *cf*. Sections 9a, 9b German Patent Act (PatG) and Art. 3, 4 EU Biotechnology Dir.

[25] Section 5.4.1.

5.1.2 An Action- and Artefact-Based Reconstruction of IP Rights

If the applicable IP right is thus only partially based on the idea of the abstract IP object – namely in the historically oldest areas of 'intellectual property' – the question arises whether there is an alternative explanation of the reality and effect of IP rights that can claim validity across the board. Applying Ockham's razor and subjecting all IP rights to an analysis that renounces the abstract work, the abstract invention, the abstract design etc., the older and more realistic abstraction no. 1 reappears – according to which IP rights regulate the production and other use of reproducible, generally designated artefacts.[26] Current IP law can indeed be conclusively reconstructed from such an artefact- and activity-based perspective. The renunciation of the idea of immaterial objects even provides a better understanding of the law as it stands.[27] According to this ontology, IP rights attach to Master Artefacts that are claimed by the applicant or plaintiff in legal proceedings (see Section 5.1.2.1). In the case of an alleged infringement, the Master Artefact is compared with other artefacts. If these artefacts have sufficiently relevant similarities with the Master Artefact, they are considered Secondary Artefacts that are subsumed under the name of the Master Artefact and are thus identified as infringing (see Section 5.1.2.2). IP rights thus sanction the unauthorised production and other use of such Secondary Artefacts (see Section 5.1.2.3). They regulate behaviour in relation to certain artefacts.

5.1.2.1 The Master Artefact as the Reference Point of IP Rights

Although IP rights are directed towards regulating human behaviour – as ultimately any legal norm – their structure would be insufficiently explained if they were to be understood as a purely relational rule between the rightful proprietor and an indefinite number of third parties. It is theoretically consistently possible to split the exclusive right into innumerable claims constantly directed against everyone to not use the property object in question.[28] However, this view does not explain what makes the plurality of relational individual claims into a single property bundle, and why it makes sense to speak of *one* exclusive right. For this step, one cannot do without an object to which all rights and obligations refer. The one object forms the uniform point of departure and reference in which the unity of any exclusive right is founded.[29]

This also applies to IP rights. They too are exclusive rights between the proprietor and everyone in relation to an object. According to the prevailing view, the abstract

---

[26] Section 2.2.2, Section 3.2.1.3.1.
[27] Ross, 58 Tidsskrift for Rettsvitenskap 321, 345–49 (1945).
[28] Windscheid & Kipp, *Pandekten* I 184; critical Peukert, *Güterzuordnung* 866 with further references.
[29] Rognstad, *Property Aspects of Intellectual Property* 43–46, 124.

IP object functions as this point of reference. It is the whole purpose of this ontology to provide IP law with an unit capable of being owned. If this construct is banned from IP theory, the concept of exclusive rights seems to disintegrate at the same time. This is probably what Max Lange had in mind in 1858 when he summed up that a purely activity-related reconstruction of IP rights led from property theory 'into the field of obligations'.[30]

But there is a way out of this supposed conceptual impasse. The abstract IP object is not an indispensable basis for the legal concept of exclusive IP rights, which should therefore also be maintained for this area of property law.[31] The Master Artefact is available as an alternative. It can take over the function of the abstract IP object as a uniform point of reference for the subjective exclusive right. At the same time, it offers the advantage that it manages without idealising abstractions that lead away from regulated reality. The Master Artefact is the legally realistic alternative to the idealistic-abstract IP object.

What the Master Artefact is all about has already been explained in the context of the presentation of the first, historically very old abstraction, which runs from a multitude of similar artefacts to a general signifier.[32] The Master Artefact is a brute fact, such as the original artwork, the final manuscript, a patent specification, a photo or other image recorded in a register etc., which is named in a certain way and declared a Master Artefact. Both the nomenclature and the choice of a specific artefact as the Master Artefact are implemented in different ways in current IP law. Copyrighted works and rights to patents and other industrial property rights required to be registered are claimed by informal speech acts. In contrast, an entitlement to the grant of a patent and the right deriving from a registered patent or other industrial property right require specifically regulated applications or registrations which describe, depict and/or deposit the subject matter of protection.

Referring to the Master Artefact in the singular does not mean that there is always only one brute artefact X – such as a paper document, a digital file, a painting or a model – that can function as Master Artefact Y. The final version authorised by the author, inventor and/or patent attorney, for example, can be copied and modified. Moreover, it is often controversial and depends on legal formalities which copy or which version counts as the Master Artefact – for example, in the case of different language versions of a European patent.[33] In other words, the unity of the Master Artefact is not physical, but genealogical. It is based on the fact that any document,

---

[30] Lange, *Kritik der Grundbegriffe vom geistigen Eigentum* (1858), reprinted in 117 UFITA 169, 173–74, 179 (1991).
[31] See Section 6.1.2.
[32] Section 3.1; Scotchmer, *Innovation and Inventives* 32 ('What an intellectual property right protects is not the clock as an object, but rather the template for producing it. For information goods, the template is the information itself, for example music . . .').
[33] See Art. 70 (1) EPC ('The text of a European patent application or a European patent in the language of the proceedings shall be the authentic text in any proceedings before the European Patent Office and in any Contracting State'.); for a detailed case study on the construction of a

copy etc. accepted as a Master Artefact by patent offices, courts and other legal decision makers originates historically from a single template that exists or – as the case may be – existed as a reproducible artefact in external reality. This one authoritative prototype constitutes the objective starting and reference point of the exclusive IP right. The IP theory defended here, based on actions and artefacts, sets the unity of the exclusive right in a genealogy that leads back to an empirically verifiable origin – the first artefact[34] – which is claimed in the possibly altered form of the Master Artefact. The prevailing paradigm, on the other hand, establishes the unity of IP law through the fiction of the timelessly abstract IP object.

This idealistic approach firstly favours systematic ignorance of the genealogy of artefacts and thus of the reality that IP law regulates. Thus, the act of creating a new artefact, which in its original or modified version is later claimed as a Master Artefact, has no role to play in IP law. The creative, innovative and entrepreneurial activities that lead to the subject matter of IP rights and that constitute the primary justification of IP rights remain hidden. IP law begins with the marketable object.[35]

Secondly, the view that a copy of a work submitted in the course of infringement proceedings or a patent specification filed during the application process merely embodies the abstract work or invention, but is by no means identical to it, creates a permanent and profound uncertainty as to what the subject matter of the right in question is and how its limits are to be determined. The metaphysical object ontology only tells us that abstract types are characterised by considerable uncertainty.[36] From the point of view of Searlean social ontology, the replacement of the many similar genealogically linked artefacts by the one abstract IP object appears in a much more problematic light. Not only does it create legal uncertainty, it also delivers up reality to the claims of right holders and decision makers about a fictional IP object. The object of IP rights does not exist as a fact accessible to evidence in external reality, but as a social ('institutional') fact in our language and imagination. Such an institutional fact is produced by a declarative speech act. It is created by asserting that it is created.[37] This is exactly what applicants do before patent offices, claimants before courts and finally the competent decision makers: they declare that a certain artefact, such as a patent specification or the submitted copy of a literary work, *embodies* a protected invention or work. But because the artefacts concerned do not represent the object of protection exhaustively, there are infinite possibilities for modulation or manipulation qua deviating declaration. The practice of current IP rights confirms both this scope and the indispensable – ultimately central – role of the Master Artefact.

patented invention in the course of legal proceedings *see* van Dijk, Grounds of the Immaterial 77 et seq.
[34] Section 3.1.1.
[35] *See* Section 6.2.1.1.
[36] Section 2.1.3.
[37] Section 2.2.1.

First of all, Master Artefacts – in contrast to abstract IP objects – must be clearly identifiable as brute facts, perceptible (measurable) and thus accessible to evidence taking in order to serve as a starting point for legal protection. And indeed, a thought that has not yet been expressed, but which does exist as a mental artefact in the mind of the author, does not constitute a work that can be protected by copyright. Rather, an expression (sic!) is only copyrightable if it is accessible to human senses, be it as a verbal or instrumental performance (action), or be it as a physical object such as a printed publication or digital file.[38] The protection of living, self-reproducing and changing organisms such as newly bred plants faces a different problem – namely the identification of a distinguishable, homogeneous and stable object to which the exclusive right refers.[39] The indispensability of an explicit and subsequently ascertainable Master Artefact also proves itself in the protection of trade secrets. Its transformation from a tort into a property-like IP right repeatedly reaches the limit that only the holder of the secret has the Master Artefact at his disposal. Therefore, there is a lack of a sufficiently identifiable object to which an exclusive right can attach.[40]

Furthermore, the IP object must be specified in claims for injunctive relief (Section 253(2) no. 2 of the German Code of Civil Procedure, ZPO) and corresponding judgments (Section 313(1) no. 4 of the Code of Civil Procedure) in such a way that the opposing party and, if applicable, the enforcement authority can identify the artefacts to which the injunction relates – which in other words may no longer be produced or otherwise exploited.[41] When enforcing registered rights, it is sufficient to reproduce the patent claims or other register information in the claim for injunctive relief.[42] It is more difficult to specify the cause of action in the case of informal IP rights, such as copyright. Here, for example, it is not sufficient to list electronic files in the infringement claim without reproducing their contents. Rather, a copy of the data carrier on which the claimed computer program is stored must be attached to the claim for injunctive relief.[43] It is not surprising that the

---

[38] BGH 27 February 1962 Case No. I ZR 118/60, GRUR 1962, 470, 472 – AKI; Loewenheim/Leistner, in Schricker & Loewenheim (eds.) *Urheberrecht Section 2 German Copyright Act (UrhG)* para. 47 with further references.

[39] See CJEU Case C-625/15 P Schniga v. CPVO, ECLI:EU:C:2017:435 para. 54 ('the assessment of the characteristics of a plant variety necessarily contains a particular uncertainty due to the nature of the object itself to which the technical examination relates, namely a plant variety, as well as the length of time required to conduct such an examination'); for a historical perspective see Gaudillière & Kevles, in Gaudillière et al. (eds.) *Living Properties* 1, 3.

[40] Section 3.1.3.

[41] BGH 12 July 2001 Case no. I ZR 40/99, GRUR 2002, 86, 88 – Laubhefter with further references.

[42] See BGH 30 March 2005 Case no. X ZR 126/01, GRUR 2005, 569, 570 – Blasfolienherstellung. On the requirement to identify the infringing artefact see Section 5.1.2.2.

[43] Cf. BGH 9 May 1985 Case no. I ZR 52/83, GRUR 1985, 1041 – Inkasso-Programm; BGH 14 October 1999 Case no. I ZR 117/97, GRUR 2000, 228 – Musical-Gala; BGH 23 January 2003 Case no. I ZR 18/00, GRUR 2003, 786 – Innungsprogramm.

formulation of injunctive relief is a challenge from this point of view. It is obviously difficult to name in a few words the Master Artefact, the Secondary Artefact under attack and the behaviour to be omitted in this regard.

Similar difficulties arise when filing a patent or other right required to be registered with an IP office. At first sight, it would be expected that the formalisation of the application procedures, including the question of the format in which an image is to be filed,[44] would contribute to the precise specification of the subject matter of protection in a way that is more clearly defined than in the case of copyrights and the right to the patent which arise informally with the act of creation. But the opposite is true. By giving inventors, designers – and, above all, specialised patent attorneys – the opportunity to present and claim the Master Artefact not by submitting a concrete exemplar, they are given the chance to behave strategically. If they refer to a concrete specimen or if they choose a very precise description or representation (e.g. a chemical formula), they can clearly distinguish the claimed invention, design etc. from the state of the art. However, the scope of protection of an IP right claimed in this concrete way is relatively narrow parallel to the substantiation of the Master Artefact submitted. Conversely, if they opt for a general, namely functional, description of what was invented or designed, they expose the application to a greater probability of objections to novelty, but at the same time increase the potential scope of protection of the right.[45] Consequently, the way in which the object of protection is presented correlates with the scope of the IP right. Facts and the law are inseparably interwoven with each other.[46]

All these well-known practices that feed an entire service sector (namely patent attorneys) are understandable only on the basis of the view expressed here. If the objects of IP rights were given facts, their identity might be controversial, but not at the discretion of the applicants. If, on the other hand, the abstract invention or other IP object is understood as a constructed social fact, the central role of the claimant seems downright compelling. Who, if not the rights holder, should decide what is worthy of protection and for this purpose is fed into the process of social and legal recognition?[47]

---

[44] See e.g. German Patent and Trademark Office, Hinweise zur Wiedergabe Marke.
[45] Design law: PMS International Group Plc v. Magmatic Ltd, UKSC 12 (2016) paras. 30 et seq. – Trunki ('It is, of course, up to an applicant as to what features he includes in his design application. ... If he chooses too general a level, his design may be invalidated by prior art. If he chooses too specific a level he may not be protected against similar designs'.); patent law: BGH 11 September 2013 Case no. X ZB 8/12, GRUR 2013, 1210 para. 15 – Dipeptidyl-Peptidase-Inhibitoren; trademark law: Ingerl & Rohnke, *Markengesetz* Section 14 paras. 914 et seq.
[46] See Section 5.4.3.
[47] This thought can also be applied to the problematic case of self-plagiarism in copyright law (*see* Rehbinder & Peukert, *Urheberrecht* para. 529) (I would like to thank O. A. Rognstad for pointing out this issue). If the originator has the right to determine which utterance is considered a Master Artefact at all, then *a maiore ad minus* he also has the right to further develop the Master Artefact and claim the results of this work for himself. Conflicts with users

In this respect, plant variety and patent law with regard to microorganisms give the least scope for subject matter declaration. Here, the applicants must submit actual specimens of the claimed plant or microorganism. These scientifically analysable Master Artefacts can be used for evidence purposes in infringement proceedings.[48] Rights arising informally must also be asserted in the course of infringement proceedings in the form of actual exemplars. In design and trademark law, the subject matter and scope of protection are still relatively clearly based on illustrations and other representations of the appearance or the sign in the register.[49]

On the other hand, patent law beyond deposited microorganisms is regarded as notoriously susceptible to manipulation and legal uncertainty. This peculiarity can also be explained by the concept of the Master Artefact. In patent law, it is already unclear which artefact can be considered the Master Artefact. The reason for this is a deep genealogical gap between the act of creating the first technical artefact and the assertion of the Master Artefact in the application procedure. The technical product or process is not claimed as an example – as a three-dimensional model or at least as a two-dimensional representation – but primarily in verbal form. The scope of protection of German and European patents and patent applications is determined by the patent claims; the description and the drawings are only ('however') to be used for the interpretation of the patent claims.[50] The legal requirement that the new artefact be translated into human language and primarily claimed (sic!) in this form allows the actors involved to model the verbalised facts almost at will.

Firstly, the patent specification has its own language. It can describe the new artefact with newly created words, or give a new meaning to old words.[51] Therefore, according to settled case law, the interpretation of patent claims is always necessary and must not be omitted even if the wording of the claim appears to be clear.[52]

---

of previous versions are to be resolved solely on the basis of contract and unfair competition law.
[48] On plant variety protection see BGH 30 April 2004 Case No. Xa ZR 156/04, GRUR 2009, 750 para. 13 – Lemon Symphony; on the deposition of microorganisms for patenting purposes see Kraßer & Ann, Patentrecht 253, 737.
[49] See Chapter 2 notes 19–20.
[50] Section 14 German Patent Act (PatG), Art. 69 EPC, 35 USC § 112 ('The specification shall contain a written description of the invention, and of the manner and process of making and using it, in such full, clear, concise, and exact terms as to enable any person skilled in the art to which it pertains, or with which it is most nearly connected, to make and use the same, and shall set forth the best mode contemplated by the inventor or joint inventor of carrying out the invention. ... The specification shall conclude with one or more claims particularly pointing out and distinctly claiming the subject matter which the inventor or a joint inventor regards as the invention'.).
[51] BGH 12 March 2002 Case no. X ZR 43/01, GRUR 2002, 511, 512 – Kunststoffrohrteil; BGH 12 May 2015 Case no. X ZR 43/13, GRUR 2015, 875 para. 16 – Rotorelemente.
[52] BGH 29 April 1986 Case no. X ZR 28/85, GRUR 1986, 803 – Formstein; BGH 12 March 2003 Case no. X ZR 168/00, GRUR 2002, 515 – Schneidmesser I; BGH 17 April 2004 Case no. X ZB 9/06, GRUR 2007, 859 – Informationsübermittlungsverfahren I; BGH 17 July 2012 Case no. X ZR 117/11, GRUR 2012, 1124 – Polymerschaum I; BGH 12 March 2002 Case no. X ZR 43/01,

Secondly, this 'interpretation' is characterised by continuous uncertainties. For example, it is disputed on a comparative legal basis whether patent claims are to be interpreted like declarations of intent, like contracts, like statutory provisions or according to a separate method of patent claim construction;[53] how claims, descriptions and drawings relate to each other and whether the latter may give rise to an understanding of the invention which openly contradicts the wording of the claims;[54] and whether, by way of exception, earlier versions of the patent application and thus the genesis of the Master Artefact may also be used for interpretation purposes.[55] Thirdly, offices and courts repeatedly refer to the 'inventive idea' or the 'essence of the invention' if they find that these are only incompletely expressed in the patent specification.[56] In such cases, the relevant Master Artefact is practically exchanged. The verbalised version in the patent specification is replaced by the technical artefact explained by the claimant in the nullification or infringement proceeding. It is, in other words, unclear whether patent law protects what was invented, or only what was claimed in the patent specification and granted by the patent office.[57]

Patent law therefore does not have any facts that would be accessible to evidence taking. Its facts are texts prepared by lawyers and legal technicians (patent attorneys, examiners) in accordance with legal requirements. The verbalisation of the technical artefact initially contributed to the idea that the subject matter of the patent was something intellectual, an immaterial invention, which is only accidentally

---

GRUR 2002, 511, 512 – Kunststoffrohrteil; BGH 12 May 2015 Case no. X ZR 43/13, GRUR 2015, 875 para. 16 – Rotorelemente.

[53] Cf. BGH 13 October 2015 Case no. X ZR 74/14, GRUR 2016, 169 – Luftkappensystem with further references (the interpretation of patent claims has to aim at the 'technological meaning' of words); Austrian Supreme Court 21 October 2003 Case no. 4 Ob 178/03k, ÖBl. 2004, 83 – Amlodipin (patents are not to be interpreted like contracts but according to patent law's own rules); Teva Pharm. USA, Inc. v. Sandoz, Inc., 135 S. Ct. 831 (2015) (patent claim construction compared to statutory interpretation and the construction of other written instruments such as deeds and contracts).

[54] Cf. BGH 14 October 2014 Case no. X ZR 35/11, GRUR 2015, 159 para. 26 – Zugriffsrechte.

[55] BGH 10 May 2011 Case no. X ZR 16/09, GRUR 2011, 701 – Okklusionsvorrichtung; BGH 17 July 2012 Case no. X ZR 117/11, GRUR 2012, 1124 – Polymerschaum I; BGH 12 May 2015 Case no. X ZR 43/13, GRUR 2015, 875 para. 17 with further references – Rotorelemente (in exceptional cases, the examination history may be considered in patent claim construction).

[56] On the German legal development: Winkler, 79 GRUR 394, 396 (1977); UK law: Kirin-Amgen Inc. & Ors v. Hoechst Marion Roussel Ltd. & Ors., UKHL 46 (2014), paras. 21–22, 109 ('essence of the invention', 'inventive concept'); US law: Liivak, 42 Seton Hall L. Rev. 1 (2012).

[57] On this distinction see Austrian Supreme Court 17 December 1968 Case no. 4 Ob 325/68, GRUR Int. 1970, 284 – Unten-Entnahmefräsen; Austrian Supreme Court 26 July 1973 Case no. 4 Ob 324/73, GRUR Int. 1974, 281 – Gleitgerät; Austrian Supreme Court 3 April 1984 Case no. 4 Ob 321/84, GRUR Int. 1985, 766 – Befestigungsvorrichtung für Fassadenelemente; Austrian Supreme Court 15 January 2013 Case no. 4 Ob 214/12t, ZTR 2013, 151 – Schischaufel mit Materialaussparung. Further Winkler, 79 GRUR 394, 396 (1977) (engineers are used to focus on concrete contrivances 'whereas the invention really is a human thought').

embodied in an exemplar or model.[58] In the meantime, the interpretation of the claims no longer has the aim of coming close to the brute reality of technical artefacts. Rather, it should 'combine a fair protection for the patent proprietor with a reasonable degree of legal certainty for third parties'.[59] The reality of patent law is inherently normative; 'is' and 'should' are no longer separable. The reason for this normativity of the subject matter of patent law is its abstract verbalisation. According to Searle, language is the basic institutional fact that structures power relations.[60] A legal object consisting only of language shares this ontological character. It exists as a social-institutional fact and as such generates intentionality-independent reasons for action among the actors involved.[61]

5.1.2.2 Secondary Artefacts

The Master Artefact forms the singular reference point of exclusive IP rights. With regard to it, it is first decided whether the protection requirements of the IP right in question are met: Is the script, the sound or image sequence etc. original and creative? Is the technology described in the application new, does it involve an inventive step, and is it commercially applicable? Is the appearance of a product new and does it have individual character? Is the sign distinctive? To answer these questions, the Master Artefact will be compared with other artefacts which, according to the opponent's submission, represent purely routine creation (copyright), the state of the art, previously known forms or older seniority trademarks.[62]

Of course, the purpose of IP rights is not to guarantee the owner that he can deal with the Master Artefact at will and exclude all third parties from the use of this tangible or corporeal object.[63] The purpose of IP rights is rather to regulate the reproduction of this prototype. Copies, imitations and other reproductions, however, have their own brute existence, temporally and spatially separate from the Master

---

[58] See Chapter 3 note 27.
[59] Protocol on the Interpretation of Art. 69 EPC; on the admissibility of functionally defined component features of an invention see EPO [BoA] 27 January 1988 Case no. T 292/85 para. 3.1.5 – Polypeptide Expression/GENENTECH I; BGH 11 September 2013 Case no. X ZB 8/12, GRUR 2013, 1210 para. 20 – Dipeptidyl-Peptidase-Inhibitoren; Collins, 41 Connecticut L. Rev. 493, 500 (2008) ('courts inevitably both construct things and define the meaning of meaning whenever they talk about the reach of literal claim scope').
[60] Section 2.2.1.
[61] Section 5.4.1, Chapter 6.
[62] George, 7(1) W.I.P.O.J. 16, 22 (2015) ('When assessing the scope of an alleged intellectual property object, the boundaries around the object, in a particular instance, can only be assessed by reference to other similar objects').
[63] Cf. Section 903 German Civil Code (BGB) and Biron, 93 The Monist 382, 391–92 (2010); Zech, Information als Schutzgegenstand 131.

Artefact.[64] Their proprietor and rightful owner is not the IP rights holder, but a third party who infringes IP rights in the exercise of his rights.[65]

If IP rights therefore do neither assign Master Artefacts nor their unauthorised reproductions to the IP rights holder for exclusive possession and use on the model of real property ownership, the question arises as to what the subject matter of IP rights should then be. Since IP rights are exclusive rights, such an object is conceptually indispensable.[66] Is there therefore no way around abstract IP objects after all?

This conclusion appears inevitable only if, based on the model of property law, exclusive rights are deemed possible only for individually existing static objects. In order to extend on this basis the formula: one thing – one property to the field of interest here, the countless, independently existing artefacts of innovative entrepreneurial and repetitive action must be merged into the fictitious unity of the abstract IP object and disappear behind it.[67]

A different – both ontologically and legally more convincing – understanding of the subject matter of IP rights results if one understands its objective unity as a *similarity relation* between independently existing brute artefacts. This relation is established by a *comparison* between artefacts and sealed by a declarative speech act.[68] A judge or other decision-maker checks whether the artefacts challenged as infringing (copies, performances, products etc.) have a sufficient relationship to the Master Artefact, because they refer to or are connected to the Master Artefact historically and/or display relevant similarities. If this is the case, the allegedly infringing artefact is subsumed under the name of the Master Artefact and also

---

[64] Jefferson, in Kurland & Lerner (eds.) 3 *The Founders' Constitution*; White-Smith Music Pub. Co. v. Apollo Co., 209 US 1, 19 (1908, Holmes, J., concurring) ('The notion of property starts, I suppose, from confirmed possession of a tangible object, and consists in the right to exclude others from interference with the more or less free doing with it as one wills. But in copyright property has reached a more abstract expression. The right to exclude is not directed to an object in possession or owned, but is in vacuo, so to speak. It restrains the spontaneity of men where, but for it, there would be nothing of any kind to hinder their doing as they saw fit. It is a prohibition of conduct remote from the persons or tangibles of the party having the right. It may be infringed a thousand miles from the owner and without his ever becoming aware of the wrong. It is a right which could not be recognized or endured for more than a limited time and therefore, I may remark, in passing, it is one which hardly can be conceived except as a product of statute, as the authorities now agree'.); Epstein, 62 Stanford L. Rev. 455, 457 (2009) ('one huge difference that no form of intellectual property can be reduced to possession'); *also* Schmidt, 52 DZPhil 755, 759 (2004) (substantial difference).

[65] Art. 10 Enforcement Dir. and *e.g.* Section 98 (1) sentence 2, (2) German Copyright Act (UrhG); *further* BGH 10 July 2015 Case No. V ZR 206/14, NJW 2016, 317 para. 20 – Helmut Kohl with further references; Impression Prod., Inc. v. Lexmark Int'l, Inc., 137 S. Ct. 1523, 1531 et seq. (2017).

[66] Rognstad, *Property Aspects of Intellectual Property* 43–46, 124.

[67] Rognstad, *Property Aspects of Intellectual Property* 124 (the concept of IPRs as related to legal objects 'should not be abandoned – and nor could it be').

[68] Rognstad, *Property Aspects of Intellectual Property* 42–67, 123–25; van Dijk, *Grounds of the Immaterial* 246 ('the matter of dispute is not a corporeal object, nor an immaterial entity, but a gathering in conflict of a complex web of relations').

under the IP right concerned. It is then considered a Secondary Artefact, the production or use of which would have required the prior consent of the rights holder. Otherwise, the claim will be dismissed and the challenged artefact may be freely used and further reproduced under a different or generic name.[69]

As unusual as this reconstruction may be, it faithfully reflects the effect of IP rights and daily IP practice. The claimant must not only identify the Master Artefact (Section 5.1.2.1), but also the concrete infringement, namely the allegedly infringing product etc., in the pleading.[70] This also fixes the cause of action of infringement proceedings, which are 'normally determined essentially by the *actual design of a particular product*, usually referred to as the challenged form of execution, with regard to the features of the asserted patent claim'.[71] The comparison itself is in turn carried out quite concretely by inspection of objects, comparative expert opinions and other suitable evidence up to a comparative cultivation of plant varieties.[72]

The substantive-law standards of this comparison follow – and this is decisive from a normative-legal point of view – not from an abstract concept of 'a' work, 'an' invention, 'a' design or sign, but from the legal prerequisites for an infringement. In this respect, there are considerable differences between IP rights. Copyrights, related rights and the unregistered Community Design right only extend to copies and imitations that trace their historical origin back to the Master Artefact. Independently created works, achievements and designs are not covered by the aforementioned rights, even if their external characteristics are completely identical to those of the Master Artefact (double creations).[73]

Regarding other industrial property rights, on the other hand, it is not important whether the artefacts in dispute were produced deliberately or without knowledge of

---

[69] On the lawful use of titles of public domain works see BGH 5 December 2002 Case no. I ZB 19/00, GRUR 2003, 342, 342–43 – Winnetou.

[70] On industrial property see BGH 30 March 2005 Case no. X ZR 126/01, GRUR 2005, 569, 570 – Blasfolienherstellung; BGH 30 April 2004 Case No. Xa ZR 156/04, GRUR 2009, 750 para. 17 – Lemon Symphony; on copyright see Wimmers, in Schricker & Loewenheim (eds.) Urheberrecht Section 97 German Copyright Act (UrhG) para. 340 with further references.

[71] Translated from the original German. BGH 21 February 2012 Case no. X ZR 111/09, NJW-RR 2012, 872 para. 19 – Rohrreinigungsdüse II (my emphasis).

[72] Plant variety protection: OLG Düsseldorf 3 July 2015 Case No. I-15 U 75/14, GRUR-RS 2015, 11859 para. 57 – Summerdaisys Maxima; von Gierke & Trauernicht, in Metzger & Zech (eds.) Sortenschutzrecht Section 37 German Plant Variety Act (SortSchG) para. 11. Copyright: Rotstein, 68 Chicago-Kent L. Rev. 725, 776 et seq. (1993); Balganesh, 62 Duke L.J. 203 (2012); Balganesh (et al.), 100 Iowa L. Rev. 267 (2014); Bellido, 10 Law Culture and the Humanities 66 et seq. (2014). For a case study on the comparison of technologies in a patent infringement proceeding see van Dijk, *Grounds of the Immaterial* 111 et seq. On trademark law see ibid., 175.

[73] Rehbinder & Peukert, *Urheberrecht* paras 173, 233; Art. 19 para. 2 EU Design Reg. (an unregistered Community design only protects against 'copying' the protected design, not against an 'independent work of creation by a designer who may be reasonably thought not to be familiar with the design made available to the public by the holder'); Hick, 51 British Journal of Aesthetics 185, 192–93 (2011).

the Master Artefact. Inventions made completely independently by third parties may also only be used with the consent of the patent holder.[74] It suffices that the artefacts in question have certain objective similarities with a protectable Master Artefact. Which features are relevant depends on the respective IP law. Patent law deals with the technical teaching implemented, design law with the external appearance of products, trademark law with the origin of goods and services. Also with regard to the minimum degree of similarity required between Master Artefacts and Secondary Artefacts, there are requirements specific to each field of IP law, some of which are expressly regulated by law. The tendency, of course, is to bring such artefacts as Secondary Artefacts within the scope of the asserted Master Artefact, in addition to identical copies ('pirated copies', 'piracy'), which in some cases differ considerably from the Master Artefact asserted.[75]

All these legal operations do not presuppose an abstract IP object. It is true that it is easier to accept adaptations and other modifications of the Master Artefact as unlawful if one introduces an abstract IP object within whose indefinite 'scope of protection' the attacked artefact is to fall.[76] But this way of speaking and looking at things is by no means compelling. Current IP law itself expressly stipulates that the exclusive right covers not only identical copies of a Master Artefact, but also artefacts similar to it.[77] In practice, the abstract IP object does not function as *tertium comparationis* in any other way either.[78] How could it, since it cannot be perceived and is inherently indeterminate as a type? What is compared are specific artefacts accessible to inspection and evidence taking. Whether an infringement is present depends solely on whether the comparison of physical artefacts produces so many similarities that the relevant legal requirements are met.[79] The decisive factor here is not the proprietor's point of view, but an objective point of view of a fictitious third party – namely the public 'reasonably familiar with and open to' art and music,[80] the average person skilled in the art,[81] the informed user of a design[82] and the public addressed by a trademark – that is to say, in the case of mass products, the reasonably

---

[74] See Kraßer & Ann, *Patentrecht* 364 et seq.
[75] See Sections 23 German Copyright Act (UrhG), 14(2) no. 2 German Trademark Act (MarkenG) (likelihood of confusion), 38(2) sentence 1 German Design Act (DesignG) ('The protection conferred by a registered design shall include any design which does not produce on the informed user a different overall impression'.), 10(3) German Plant Variety Act (SortSchG) (definition of varieties which are 'essentially derived from' the protected variety).
[76] Sections 5.4.2 and 6.2.2.
[77] See Chapter 5 note 75.
[78] Contra Fromer, 76 Chicago L. Rev. 719, 748–49 (2009) ('... the copyrighted work itself is used as the prototype against which all allegedly infringing works are compared to see if they share sufficient salient characteristics to fall within the scope of the copyright holder's rights'.).
[79] Peukert, Gemeinfreiheit 183 et seq. with further references.
[80] BGH 19 March 2008 Case no. I ZR 166/05, GRUR 2008, 984 para. 20 – St. Gottfried; BGH 16 April 2015 Case no. I ZR 225/12, GRUR 2015, 1189 para. 63 – Goldrapper.
[81] Section 4(1) German Patent Act (PatG) and Kraßer & Ann, *Patentrecht* 325 et seq., 756 et seq.
[82] Section 38(2) German Design Act (DesignG).

well-informed, circumspect consumer.[83] These fictitious persons ultimately represent the participants of the social practices from which both the Master Artefact and the Secondary Artefacts emerge as institutional facts.

Those who, on the other hand, derive the decision of an IP dispute from the concept of the abstract work, the invention etc., attract the classic legal realist accusation of *Begriffsjurisprudenz* (jurisprudence of concepts).[84] The IP theory developed here excludes such rhetorical tricks and self-empowerment from the outset. It forces decision makers to disclose the reasons for sanctioning Secondary Artefacts. The fewer historical references and similarities with the Master Artefact are given, the more demanding the justification becomes. This is convincing not least from a normative point of view, because every sanction under IP law represents an encroachment on the opponent's civil liberties that requires justification.[85] The constitutionally required development of normative hurdles to justification presupposes the dismantling of metaphysical constructs, which have so far spared decision makers the need for transparent justification.

5.1.2.3 Regulation of Behaviour in Relation to Secondary Artefacts

In any case, abstract objects are not suitable as the subject matter of legal regulations. For law can legitimately only order or prohibit actions or omissions that are possible for human beings.[86] But it is impossible to behave as a subject of law towards immaterial objects, and it is also impossible to control objects that exist only in a shared social language practice and imaginary world². Neither abstract types nor social-institutional facts can be controlled by an individual, whether he is the right holder or a third party, in such a way that a legitimate liability could attach. In contrast, individuals are able to keep a check on brute artefacts existing in the physical world – such as digital files, machines, products etc. – as well as their

---

[83] BGH 2 March 2017 Case no. I ZR 30/16, GRUR 2017, 914 para. 22 – Medicon-Apotheke/MediCo Apotheke.

[84] Chin, 74 University of Pittsburgh L. Rev. 263, 268–70 (2012) with further references; In re Nuijten, 500 F.3d 1346, 1367 (Fed. Cir. 2007) (en banc) (Linn, J., concurring-in-part and dissenting-in-part) ('[T]he outer limits of statutory subject matter should not depend on metaphysical distinctions such as those between hardware and software or matter and energy, but rather with the requirements of the patent statute. . . .'); Kalamazoo Loose Leaf Binder Co. v. Wilson Jones Loose Leaf Co., 286 F. 715, 720 (S.D.N.Y. 1920) (Hand, J.) (against 'the metaphysical question whether [a binder and rack] form a "combination" or an "aggregation"'.); Earle v. Sawyer, 8 F. Cas. 254 (C.C. Mass. 1825) (Story, J.) ('It did not appear to me at the trial, and does not appear to me now, that this mode of reasoning upon the metaphysical nature, or the abstract definition of an invention, can justly be applied to cases under the patent act. That act proceeds upon the language of common sense and common life, and has nothing mysterious or equivocal in it'.).

[85] Peukert, *Gemeinfreiheit* 66 et seq. with further references. On the normative critique of the abstract IP object, *see* Chapter 6.

[86] On copyright *see* Ulmer, *Urheber- und Verlagsrecht* 13; Spoor, 105 Weekblad voor Privaatrecht 165, 165–66 (1974).

behaviour relating to these artefacts. And it is precisely such behaviour that is covered by exclusive IP rights. They grant their holder the exclusive right to produce and use Secondary Artefacts or to carry out otherwise infringing acts, such as public live performances.[87]

It is widely recognised that IP rights should be thought of as relational rights between legal subjects. Exclusive IP rights give their holders the power, in relation to all third parties, to 'authorise' or 'prohibit' behaviour – some of which is only generally specified, some of which is enumerated.[88] Statutory remuneration rights are also linked to acts such as reproduction and public reproduction.[89]

But what is the object of these actions? According to the prevailing paradigm, IP rights and their legal basis should refer to the abstract work, the invention, the design, the sign etc. For that is the object which is exclusively assigned to the rights holder. And indeed, under the German Copyright Act, copyright law means protecting the author 'in respect of the use of the work', the exploitation of which is reserved to him in 'material' and 'non-material' form (Section 11 sentence 1, Section 15(1) and (2) of the Copyright Act, UrhG), in order ultimately to monetise the private enjoyment of the work.[90] The patent, design and trademark law provisions on infringing acts also refer to the invention, design and sign which – according to prevailing opinion – is immaterial and which may only be 'used' by the rights holder.[91]

But this fiction of an immaterial object cannot be sustained, neither in the orthodox version of an abstract IP object nor – as advocated by Kant, Wiener and post-structuralist theorists – in the sense of dynamic-communicating objects ('speech') – an understanding that remains halfway along the path of the conception advocated here.[92] For law can only refer to possible human behaviour in the 'World'

---

[87] Breakey, in Howe & Griffiths (eds.) *Concepts of Property* 137, 152–53 ('ownership of the activity'); Balganesh, in Howe & Griffiths (eds.) *Concepts of Property* 161, 177 ('exclusivity relates to the performance of certain specified actions in relation to the expression'); Scotchmer, *Innovation and Inventives* 32 ('What an intellectual property right protects is not the clock as an object, but rather the template for producing it'.), 34; Burk, in Lai & Maget Dominicé (eds.) *Intellectual Property and Access to Im/material Goods* 44, 47.

[88] See e.g. Art. 11, 16, 26(1), 28 TRIPS agreement; Art. 9 Berne Convention; Art. 8 WCT.

[89] Cf. Sections 52, 54 German Copyright Act (UrhG).

[90] Cf. Rehbinder & Peukert, *Urheberrecht* paras 413 et seq.; *further* Troller, 50 UFITA 385, 417 (1967).

[91] Sections 9 sentence 1 German Patent Act (PatG), 38(1) German Design Act (DesignG), 14(1) and (2) German Trademark Act (MarkenG).

[92] Cf. Kant (1785), in Bently & Kretschmer (eds.) *Primary Sources on Copyright* www.copyrighthistory.org 2 et seq. (the work is a speech (opera) of the author and not an object (opus); similar Drassinower, *What's Wrong with Copying?* 64–65, 111, 169–70 (with reference to Judge Mansfield's observation in Miller v. Taylor that the subject matter of copyright is 'somewhat intellectual, communicated by letters'); Wiener, *The Human Use of Human Beings* 134 (information more a 'matter of process than a matter of storage'); Rotstein, 68 Chicago-Kent L. Rev. 725, 739 et seq. (1993) (from work to text). On trademarks as communication *see* Peukert, *Festschrift Fezer* 405, 419–20 with further references; Matal v. Tam, 137

of tangible or at least corporeal, brute facts. One can philosophise about idealised conceptual worlds, but one cannot establish any legitimate commands or prohibitions in this respect. Consequently, at a certain point, codifications that are carefully oriented to the dominant paradigm are forced to bid farewell to the abstract IP object and turn to reality, to the brute facts of physical objects, and to human actions.

In copyright law, these are the original or copies of the original which are reproduced, distributed or exhibited;[93] further personal recitations and performances;[94] and public performances which take place using technical means such as radio, screens etc. as physical, measurable facts.[95] The codified cases of use of a design concern 'the making, offering, putting on the market, importing, exporting, using of a product in which the registered design is *incorporated* or to which it is applied, or *stocking such a product* for those purposes'.[96] Section 9 (1) sentence 2 no. 1 of the German Patent Act (PatG) even declares such inorganic 'products' as well as biological material (Section 9a (1) of the Patent Act) to be the 'subject matter of the patent', which only the patent holder may produce, offer, market, use or either import or possess for the aforementioned purposes. Such products do not have to be tangible like things within the meaning of Section 90 of the Civil Code (BGB). However, they must be corporeal in some way – i.e. physically existent, such as in the form of perceptible video data coded in a certain technical manner.[97] The same applies to technical-mechanical working and manufacturing processes which are the subject of a process patent and which may be used, in particular for the direct production of again tangible or corporeal products only with the consent of the patent holder.[98] This physicalist approach ultimately follows from the concept of invention under patent law. On the one hand, the concept is particularly suitable for idealistic abstractions, because it is about the protection of ideas, of technical teachings. On the other hand, these must be *technical* ideas, defined by German courts as the 'use of controllable forces of nature to achieve a

---

S.Ct. 1744, 1752 (2017) ('trademarks often consist[ed] of catchy phrases that convey a message'), 1760 ('Trademarks are private ... speech'.).

[93] Exploitation in 'material form': Sections 15(1), 16–19 German Copyright Act (UrhG).
[94] Section 19 German Copyright Act (UrhG).
[95] Communication of a work in 'non-material form', Sections 15(2), 19a-22 German Copyright Act (UrhG) and Zech, Information als Schutzgegenstand 352 et seq. (allocation of 'syntactic information' that is always embodied on physical carriers).
[96] Section 38(1) sentence 2 German Design Act (DesignG), Art. 12 EU Design Protection Dir., Art. 19 EU Design Reg.
[97] BGH 21 August 2012 Case No. X ZR 33/10, GRUR 2012, 1230 paras. 20, 23; BGH 27 September 2016 Case No. X ZR 124/15, GRUR 2017, 261 para. 21.
[98] Sections 9(1) sentence 2 no. 2 and 3, 9a(2) German Patent Act (PatG); BGH 17 February 2004 Case No. X ZB 9/03, GRUR 2004, 495, 497; Scharen, *in* Benkard, *Patentgesetz Section 9 German Patent Act (PatG)* para. 49; *see also* Hetmank, 7 ZGE 460 et seq. (2015) with further references.

causally overseeable result', for production 'with the means of the forces of nature'.[99] And forces of nature are the prime examples of brute, scientifically measurable reality. Also belonging to this brute reality is the course of trade in which traders use signs *for* goods or services by affixing them *to* goods.[100] With regard to the protection of trade secrets, the actual location of replicable artefacts even forms the starting point and connecting point of legal protection, and their unlawful acquisition, use or disclosure also takes place in a spatial and temporal manner.[101] Finally, the generally realistic concept of plant variety protection has 'the effect that only the holder of the plant variety protection is entitled to produce propagating material of the protected variety'.[102]

While no exception to this structure, a slightly different regulatory approach can be found in the law concerning customs enforcement of IPRs. In contrast to substantive IP law, the primary point of reference for these provisions is not conduct that is illegal because it relates to a protected Master Artefact, but, conversely, a 'good suspected of infringing an intellectual property right'.[103] By referring to an object and its abstract status as a prohibited imitation or copy, the question of what the declarant or owner of the goods wants to do with them, and whether it is therefore justified to address prohibitions and commands to him, is pushed into the background. This change of perspective becomes of practical relevance when considering whether the mere transit of infringing goods should also be regarded as an infringement of IP rights. This problematic outcome can be more easily justified by focusing on the status of the Secondary Artefact rather than its manufacture or other use.[104] Ultimately, however, the rules on the border seizure of infringing goods are also based on the concept explained here. They regulate the handling of artefacts (i.e. infringing goods) whose status as Secondary Artefacts is based on a comparison with the Master Artefact.[105]

The fact that all these statutory provisions have a structure based on behaviour and artefacts that permeates and characterises all IP law is furthermore confirmed by private international law. In this respect, too, parallels between the rules applicable to property and IP rights are initially apparent. Both property regimes are subject to a

---

[99] BGH 27 March 1969 Case No. X ZB 15/67, GRUR 1969, 672, 673; BGH 30 June 2015 Case no. X ZB 1/15, GRUR 2015, 983 para. 27 – Flugzeugstand.

[100] *Cf.* Section 14(1)–(3) German Trademark Act (MarkenG), Art. 10(2) and (3) EU Trademark Dir., Art. 9(2) and (3) EU Trademark Reg.; Beebe, *in* Dinwoodie & Janis (eds.) *Trademark Law and Theory* 42, 47.

[101] *See* Art. 2 no. 1, Art. 4 EU Trade Secrets Dir.

[102] Section 10(1) German Plant Variety Act (SortSchG).

[103] *See* Art. 1, Art. 2 no. 5–7 EU Customs Enforcement Reg. and Art. 51 TRIPS agreement.

[104] *Cf.* Art. 10(4) EU Trademark Dir., 9(4) EU Trademark Reg.; Hesse, EU-Grenzbeschlagnahmeverfahren.

[105] *See* Art. 2 no. 5(a) and (c) EU Customs Enforcement Reg. (definition of 'counterfeit goods'); Hesse, EU-Grenzbeschlagnahmeverfahren.

strict territoriality principle. German property and IP law applies only to the territory of the Federal Republic of Germany, French IP law only in France etc. However, this result is achieved through different connecting factors. International real property law refers to the location of the property (*lex rei sitae*).[106] This connecting factor, however, cannot be made fruitful for IP rights even according to the prevailing view, since intangible IP is considered 'ubiquitous', i.e. it is everywhere and nowhere.[107] Instead, the decisive factor is the territory for which the claimant seeks protection,[108] or the territory 'in which an act of infringement has been committed or threatens to be committed'.[109] In both versions, international jurisdiction and applicable law depend on the place where the infringing act occurred or threatens to occur.[110] Again, the fiction of the unified legal object splits into countless, independent actions whose commonality is based solely on the fact that they refer to a prototype – the Master Artefact.

This decentralised structure also explains why IP rights that extend or prolong the legal protection of works and other IP subject matter (= Master Artefacts) created in the past do not have a genuine retroactive effect, which is generally considered unconstitutional.[111] IP rights regulate neither the creation of the first artefact[112] nor the status of this or any other particular object, but the production and use of Secondary Artefacts and the exercise of cognitive-emotional abilities (personal performances). As far as such behaviours do not lie as closed facts in the past, laws that extend IP protection for existing Master Artefacts generate no retroactive effect.[113]

---

[106] Art. 43 Introductory Law to the German Civil Code (EGBGB).

[107] *Cf.* Dreier, in Dreier & Schulze (eds.), *Urheberrechtsgesetz Introduction* para. 14.

[108] CJEU Case C-523/10 Wintersteiger AG v. Products 4U Sondermaschinenbau GmbH, ECLI: EU:C:2012:220 paras. 19 et seq. (international jurisdiction) and Art. 8(1) as well as recital 26 EU Rome II Reg. (applicable law); *further* Rehbinder & Peukert, *Urheberrecht* 1324 et seq. with further references.

[109] Art. 82(5) EU Design Reg.; on the infringement of an EU trademark CJEU Case C-360/12 Coty Germany GmbH v. First Note Perfumes NV, ECLI:EU:C:2014:1318 paras 24 et seq.

[110] *Cf.* Troller, *Internationale Zwangsverwertung* 105 (immaterial goods as objects of human activity). In contrast, mere financial damage, which materialises directly in a bank account, is an insufficient connecting factor in international IP law *cf.* CJEU Case C-12/15 Universal Music International Holding BV v. Schilling (and others), ECLI:EU:C:2016:449 para. 31; contra Google Inc. v. Equustek Solutions Inc., SCC 34 (2017) para. 41 ('The problem in this case is occurring online and globally. The Internet has no borders – its natural habitat is global. The only way to ensure that the interlocutory injunction attained its objective was to have it apply where Google operates – globally. As Fenlon J. found, the majority of Datalink's sales take place outside Canada. If the injunction were restricted to Canada alone or to google.ca, as Google suggests it should have been, the remedy would be deprived of its intended ability to prevent irreparable harm'.).

[111] *But see* Swiss Federal Supreme Court 13 January 1998 Case no. 124 III 266, 272 – Felix Bloch Erben.

[112] Section 6.2.1.1.

[113] Küppers, *Challenging the public domain*.

5.2 STRUCTURAL DIFFERENCES BETWEEN REAL PROPERTY AND IP RIGHTS

In summary, an action- and artefact-based theory can better explain the structure and practice of current IP law than the prevailing paradigm of the abstract IP object. On the basis of this realist ontology, the structural similarities and differences between real property and IP rights also appear in a new light.

What both types of exclusive rights have in common is that they establish relational rights and obligations with regard to an object.[114] Against this background, the fact that the circle of behaviour reserved for the owner of a tangible thing is regulated more undefined and more comprehensively than in the case of some IP rights, which list the infringing acts enumeratively, is merely a gradual and somewhat technical legal difference, but not a qualitative-structural difference.[115] Furthermore, real and intellectual property rights trigger conflicts between the fundamental right to property on the one hand and the freedom of action of third parties limited by private property rights on the other.[116]

However, the object to which the indefinite number of legal relations between the rights holder and the excluded third parties refer is of a very different nature in real and in intellectual property law. The object of real property ownership is the movable or immovable thing which exists on its own, spatially limited, and which can be touched and thus effectively controlled.[117] IP rights, on the other hand, do not allocate such tangible nor otherwise corporeal objects (data, DNA etc.). Rather, they concern a similarity relation between a Master Artefact and a Secondary Artefact. If tangible or otherwise corporeal objects or actions are sufficiently similar to a Master Artefact, they are considered infringing copies, forms of infringement, performances etc. Such Secondary Artefacts may no longer be used or exercised, although they exist or occur spatially separate from the rights holder, and the infringer exercises his own rights protected by fundamental rights – namely his freedom of action and, if applicable, his right to real property.

These fundamentally different subject matter cause the differences between real and intellectual property rights. On the basis of the ontology explained in Section 2.2.2, it is easy to see why only real property ownership guarantees certainty of expectation with regard to peaceful possession, whereas the purpose of IP rights is not to guarantee the rights holder undisturbed handling of a physical object – such

---

[114] Ross, On Law and Justice 184; Häberle, 109 AöR 36, 75 (1984); Gray, 50 Cambridge L.J. 252, 299 (1991); Waldron, 68 Chicago-Kent L. Rev. 841, 842 (1993) ('... the most important thing about any property right is what it prohibits people from doing ... This applies to intellectual property as much as to property in material resources'.); Breakey, in Howe & Griffiths (eds.) *Concepts of Property* 137, 148–49.

[115] Contra Biron, in Goldhammer et al. (eds.) *Geistiges Eigentum im Verfassungsstaat* 127, 137 with reference to Penner, *Idea of Property* 119–20.

[116] *Cf.* BVerfG 31 May 2016 Case no. 1 BvR 1585/13, GRUR 2016, 690 para. 90 – Metall auf Metall.

[117] Peukert, *Güterzuordnung* 213 et seq. with further references; Jänich, *Geistiges Eigentum* 229.

as the original of a work or the unpublished manuscript.[118] IP rights do not protect what the rights holder has in his possession and wants to use undisturbed, but they determine whether third parties require his prior consent for their actions.[119] With this 'public' object of regulation, IP rights also differ from the protection of factual secrets by personality rights and unfair competition law.[120]

The indefinite duration of real property rights can also be traced back to the idea of securing possession. This is because the expectation of being able to proceed with one's movable or immovable property undisturbed at will claims legitimate consideration as long as the property exists. IP rights, on the other hand, do not refer to a specific tangible or corporeal matter whose unimpaired continued existence is to be ensured. The restrictions on the freedom of action of third parties inevitably and systemically associated with IP rights can rather only be justified for a limited period of time and/or in connection with a working requirement on the part of the beneficiary.[121] The decentralised, action-based structure of IP rights also makes it necessary to define the infringing acts in detail – or at least in a sufficiently predictable way – while the limits of the scope of protection of real property rights already derive from the necessary connection to the protected thing. Accordingly, a legally relevant 'influence' on the tangible object presupposes that the actual domination of the property by the owner is impaired by using the object in a rival way, i.e. by reducing the utility value for the owner.[122]

Furthermore, because ownership in real property relates to a particular physical object the use of which is rivalrous, overlapping rights that exist in a certain thing with which its rights holders block each other must be prevented. This is the purpose of the *numerus clausus* of dispositions *in rem*, which in turn does not apply in IP law.[123] Because here there is no legal object whose use is rivalrous. Even millions of derived, identical or varying licences do not create any danger of a mutual blockade of the licensees. On the contrary: the more Secondary Artefacts circulate and are used in an authorised manner, the more needs are satisfied and the more income the rights owner can generate.[124]

In the absence of a required authorisation of the rights holder for the use of Secondary Artefacts, it is questionable how damages are to be assessed. In real

---

[118] Bluntschli, *Deutsches Privatrecht I* 189; Schefczyk, 52 DZPhil 739, 746–47 (2004); Balganesh, in Howe & Griffiths (eds.) *Concepts of Property* 161, 177; O'Connor, 27 George Mason Law Review 205, 210 (2019).

[119] *Contra* Hauptmann, *Festgabe der Juristischen Fakultät der Universität Freiburg (Schweiz)* 50, 64 (the purpose of author's rights is to allow the author to reproduce his work).

[120] Klippel, 6 ZGE 443, 455 (2014); regarding the protection of trade secrets *see* Druey, *Information als Gegenstand des Rechts* 104–5.

[121] Section 1.2 and Section 5.3.1.

[122] *See* Peukert, *Güterzuordnung* 219 et seq. with further references; *further* Biron, *in* Goldhammer et al. (eds.) *Geistiges Eigentum im Verfassungsstaat* 127, 137. On the non-rivalrousness of the subject matter of IP rights Section 5.3.2.

[123] *See* Chapter 1 note 17.

[124] Peukert, *in* Grundmann & Möslein (eds.) *Vertragsrecht und Innovation*, 69 et seq.

property law as well as in the case of an impairment of other corporeal objects,[125] the damage calculation codified as the normal case pursuant to Section 249(1) of the German Civil Code (BGB) dominates in this respect – which in turn leads a complete shadowy existence in IP law.[126] The practical irrelevance of the traditional form of damage calculation in IP law is not only (and not even primarily) due to the fact that the market value of works, inventions etc. would be systematically more difficult to determine than in the case of movables, real estate or corporeal data. Because there are tangible things for which there is no market – and therefore no established market price – as well as everyday IP such as photographs, product designs etc., which are remunerated according to widespread tariffs. The true reason for the irrelevance of traditional ways of damage calculation in IP law is that an IP infringement does not affect the tangible and otherwise corporeal assets in the rights holder's balance sheet, and the Secondary Artefacts challenged as infringing are not recorded in the rights holder's balance sheet. The similarity relationship between Master Artefact and Secondary Artefact is not an asset that can be accounted for abstractly. From the point of view of accounting, an 'intangible asset' does not follow from the static ownership of an embodied technical solution, a manuscript or a design, but from the expected future economic benefit.[127] However, it is not known in advance how many Secondary Artefacts will be produced and how they will be used.[128] This depends on the demand, which even IP rights can neither create nor guarantee. Therefore, the damage in IP law cannot be calculated other than on the basis of probabilities (Section 252 of the Civil Code, BGB), normative fictions (licence analogy) or the infringer's profit, which is frowned upon in the Civil Code as a basis for calculating damage.[129]

5.3 PARTICULARITIES OF THE JUSTIFICATION OF IP RIGHTS

On the basis of an action- and artefact-based theory, the difficulties and peculiarities of the justification of IP rights can also be satisfactorily explained. In this respect, as outlined at the beginning, a whole series of unsolved puzzles arise.[130]

---

[125] See Art. 2(9) EU Digital Content Dir. ('"digital environment" means hardware, software and any network connection used by the consumer to access or make use of digital content or a digital service'); Peukert, in *Festschrift Schricker* 149 et seq.
[126] See Chapter 1 note 18.
[127] International Accounting Standard 38, Intangible Assets, Section 21.
[128] See Section 5(2) German Income Tax Act (EStG) ('immaterial economic goods' such as IP may be capitalised for taxation purposes only if they were acquired against payment). *See also* International Accounting Standard 38, Intangible Assets, Section 10 (an intangible asset is defined by identifiability, control over a resource and existence of future economic benefit), Section 13 ('The capacity of an entity to control the future economic benefits from an intangible asset would normally stem from legal rights that are enforceable in a court of law'.), Section 51 ('It is sometimes difficult to assess whether an internally generated intangible asset qualifies for recognition').
[129] Wimmers, in Schricker & Loewenheim (eds.) *Urheberrecht Section 97 German Copyright Act (UrhG)* paras. 265 et seq.; Raue, *Dreifache Schadensberechnung* passim.
[130] Section 1.2.

5.3.1 Effect and Justification of IP Rights

That IP rights, unlike real property ownership, cannot be based on the acquisition of ownership of the first artefact (such as a manuscript) has been widely agreed since the great reprint debates of the eighteenth century. For the function of IP rights only unfolds in the moment in which this first possession is abandoned and the innovation or trademark reaches the public.[131] While this publicity of IP rights is only considered in German and European fundamental rights law as a gradual circumstance in the context of the examination of the social limits of property, US constitutional law provides for special competence norms for patents and copyrights on the one hand and trademark rights on the other.[132] Real property and IP law are, furthermore, subject to diametrically opposed basic norms – namely ownership and the public domain, respectively.[133] In addition, ownership of a tangible object retains its good sense as a guarantor of security of expectation with regard to peaceful possession, even if no third party is about to engage in a rivalrous use of the thing. In contrast, conflicts with the freedom of action of third parties are systemic in IP law, and there is even a tense relationship to real property ownership, which is primarily cushioned by the exhaustion principle.[134] Finally, it is noticeable that real property ownership and IP rights are recognised or disputed to varying degrees. While hardly anyone in the industrialised countries is calling for the abolition of land ownership, let alone of movable property, demands to abolish IP rights are even being debated at the German Lawyers' Conference (Deutscher Juristentag).[135]

These observations can also be explained if one no longer understands IP rights as allocations of distinct immaterial objects in analogy to real property, but as exclusive rights to produce and use certain physical artefacts or to exercise cognitive-emotional abilities. On the basis of this alternative ontology, it becomes evident that the regulatory effects of IP rights are not properly described by the terms *gehören* (to belong) and *zu Eigen sein* (to be owned). Neither Secondary physical Artefacts nor actions such as personal performances 'belong' to the IP rights holder. As a rule, the owner of infringing copies or machines is the infringer or an uninvolved third party, not the IP rights holder. A person and their actions are not capable of ownership from the outset.

As Max Lange already pointed out in 1858, the effects of IP rights correspond structurally to obligations.[136] For obligations also relate solely to the behaviour of the

---

[131] Plumpe, in Brackert & Stückrath (eds.) *Literaturwissenschaft* 179, 184; *but see* Drassinower, *What's Wrong with Copying?* 115.
[132] *See* Chapter 1 note 19.
[133] *See* Chapter 1 notes 22–23.
[134] Schefczyk, 52 DZPhil 739, 751 (2004); Schmidt, 52 DZPhil 755, 767 (2004); Tushnet, 114 Yale L.J. 535 (2004). On conflicts between IP rights and real property ownership *cf.* Ulmer, *Urheber- und Verlagsrecht* 13; Bell, in Thierer & Crews (eds.), *Copy Fights* 1, 4; Chapdelaine, 23 Intellectual Property Journal 23, 83 et seq (2010).
[135] *See* Waldron, 68 Chicago-Kent L. Rev. 841, 848 (1993); Lemley, 90 N.Y.U. L. Rev. 460 (2015).
[136] Lange, 117 UFITA 169, 173–79 (1991) [1858].

debtor, who may be obliged to do or refrain from an act regarding a certain object. Obligations do not, however, create any rights *in rem*.[137]

In contrast to relative obligations, IP rights are not only effective against certain debtors, but against all third parties. They are not based on individual consent, but on a law whose generality represents the generality of the prohibitions to act. In principle, this holds also true for real property ownership.[138] IP laws and rights are nevertheless more unstable and conflict-laden than real property ownership. Firstly, their whole purpose is to displace the freedom of ownership and action of all unauthorised persons, which causes irritation ('I *may not do* this with *my* computer?'). Secondly, IP rights enjoy less reciprocal recognition. While practically everyone owns some real property and in this position needs and advocates property protection, only a small minority of private law subjects are active and entitled as authors, inventors, designers or brand entrepreneurs.[139] These justification problems become more acute the more IP rights need to be respected and the wider their scope of protection. If an ensuing conflict is not taken into account in the scope and limits of IP rights, courts change from a hard-core property-like approach to a balancing exercise, as it is known from tortious wrongdoing.[140] In such cases, the façade of the exclusively allocated immaterial object cannot be maintained. The reason for these dissolution phenomena is that IP rights cause interruptions of social practices and communications with/about art, literature, science, technology, commerce etc., and are thus latently contrary to what constitutes society, namely communication and collective action in a 'we' mode.[141] When the going gets tough, courts are more willing to subject IP rights to unwritten limitations than to watch IP rights undermine their own conditions through ever more communications interruptions and, in extreme cases, a total blockade of technical and other transactions.[142]

IP protection is subject to even greater resistance when it comes to bred or biotechnologically generated organisms that reproduce naturally. In principle, the idea of the abstract IP object can be applied to this field just as in the case of inorganic artefacts produced and reproduced by humans. However, the example of plant variety protection shows that abstractions do not go beyond DNA and thus a

---

[137] Peukert, *Güterzuordnung* 51. Therefore, German sales contract law applies to the sale of real property, to the sale of rights, and to the sale of 'other objects', *cf.* Sections 433, 453(1) German Civil Code (BGB).
[138] Peukert, *Güterzuordnung* 884 et seq.
[139] Peukert, in Christophe Geiger (ed.) *Criminal Enforcement of Intellectual Property* 151, 162 et seq.
[140] Critical Peukert, in Geiger (ed.) *Handbook on Human Rights and IP* 132 et seq. with further references.
[141] Luhmann, *Gesellschaft der Gesellschaft* 80; Baecker, in Barck et al. (eds.) *Ästhetische Grundbegriffe* III 384, 388. On collective intentionality and the we-mode *see* Tuomela, *Philosophy of Sociality* 182 et seq.
[142] *See also* Schmidt, 52 DZPhil 755, 771 (2004).

physical, but replicable, entity.[143] To think of plant varieties or 'biological material'[144] as immaterial is apparently too eccentric even for IP lawyers. In the case of humans and animals, there is also the fact that they are not capable of ownership at all or only to a limited extent.[145] It would be contrary to these value decisions to accept patents on cloned or genetically modified humans and animals. That meant nothing other than a right of the patent holder to decide on the life and death of such organisms.[146] This is (so far) only accepted for plants.[147]

5.3.2 Economic Analysis of IP Rights

The now widely dominant model for justifying IP rights is provided by economic analysis. According to this model, IP rights should provide an incentive and a legally secure environment to innovate or invest.[148] The classical version of economic analysis assumes, in accordance with the prevailing ontology of IP rights, that works, inventions, designs and trademarks are goods that can be owned. At the same time, it is generally accepted among economists that these immaterial objects differ fundamentally from tangibles in that they are non-rivalrous and non-exclusive. For example, if a work is publicly available, 'it' is no longer be scarce, since 'it' can be copied at will. However, in the absence of incentives to create new works, IP rights create an artificial scarcity, which right holders can remedy by granting licences, thus encouraging further innovation and investment. However, given the ubiquitous availability of production and distribution technologies, Lemley has recently raised the serious question of whether we are not at the beginning of an age of widespread non-scarcity, also as regards innovation.[149]

Only those who build their economic models on the fiction of the abstract IP object can arrive at such obviously utopian assumptions. Since the abstract IP object exists only as a linguistic construct, the same applies to its supposedly artificial, given or lack of scarcity – it, too, is fictitious. The talk of the scarcity of immaterial objects refers to no brute reality. Like the abstract IP object, the alleged scarcity of IP exists and functions merely as a conceptual abstraction, this time within the framework of economic models.

---

[143] Section 5.1.1.2.
[144] *Cf.* Section 9a German Patent Act (PatG).
[145] Concerning animals *see* Section 90a of the German Civil Code (BGB): 'Animals are not things. They are protected by special statutes. They are governed by the provisions that apply to things, with the necessary modifications, except insofar as otherwise provided'.
[146] *Cf.* Sections 1a, 2, 2a(1) German Patent Act (PatG); CJEU Case C-34/10 Oliver Brüstle v. Greenpeace e.V., ECLI:EU:C:2011:669.
[147] *Cf.* Section 37a SortSchG (claim to destruction of infringing propagating material subject to the principle of proportionality).
[148] Nazari-Khanachayi, *Rechtfertigungsnarrative des Urheberrechts* 67 et seq. with further references.
[149] Lemley, 90 N.Y.U. L. Rev. 460, 466 et seq. (2015).

Those who, instead, base their economic analysis on the realist ontology proposed here, arrive at empirically ascertainable scarcities and demands. Undoubtedly, the iron laws of earthly scarcity govern human capacity to innovate and to do business, as well as the material resources necessary to produce new artefacts, but also to reproduce or imitate them. An economic theory that wants to make verifiable statements about the reality of technical and other innovations must be concerned with the efficient allocation of these mental and physical resources.[150] While general economic studies of innovation satisfy this requirement, the vast majority of economic analyses of IP rights are under the spell of the fictional ontology on which the rights are also based.[151] They therefore arrive at correspondingly fictional, and ultimately unverifiable, results.[152]

5.4 THE NORMATIVITY OF THE ABSTRACT IP OBJECT

If the prevailing notion of the subject matter of IP law is not based on a coherent ontology, cannot satisfactorily explain current IP law and cannot convincingly justify it, then the question arises as to why the fiction of the abstract IP object has been able to advance to become a matter of course that is largely unquestioned. The reason for the triumph of this concept is its normativity. The abstract IP object may represent an ontologically contradictory and otherwise eccentric construction distant from observable reality. However, it fits perfectly into the modern form of marketable commodities, which became widespread in the late eighteenth century.

5.4.1 *The Raison d'Être of the Abstract IP Object Is Its Normativity*

That the raison d'être of talking and thinking in categories of immaterial-abstract goods is not a descriptive but a normative one cannot be understood on the basis of the dominant opinion. For, according to this view, works, inventions, designs, signs etc. constitute the objects of IP rights, just as the tangible thing is the legal object of real property. However, according to the conventional view, such 'is' does not have any normativity inherent in it. Normative are only the commands and prohibitions of the law, which refer to immaterial goods as the objects of IP law.[153]

---

[150] *But see* Boldrin & Levine, 2 Review of Economic Research on Copyright Issues 45, 47 (2005) ('The fundamental point we make is that classical competitive theory applies to ideas, and their copies, the same way it applies to wheat, and its copies'.).

[151] Boldrin & Levine, 2 Review of Economic Research on Copyright Issues 45, 49, 66 (2005); Scotchmer, *Innovation and Inventives* 32 et seq.; Sherman, 12 Theoretical Inquiries in Law 99, 104 (2011); Gruner, 13 Colum. Sci. & Tech. L. Rev. 1, 8–9 (2012) (allocations of invention inputs such as the scarce time of key inventors and the scarce innovation resources of corporations).

[152] *Cf.* Lemley, 62 UCLA L. Rev. 1328, 1331–32 (2015).

[153] Wilson, 93 The Monist 450, 455 et seq. (2010); Penner, *Idea of Property* 119 ('in general it does no harm to speak of rights in ideas, or in manuscripts, or in marks, any more than it does to

This still descriptive insight is so important that it justifies repetition: The paradigm of the abstract IP object cannot comprehend its normativity because it sees itself as a description of reality.

The tendency in philosophy and social theory to dismiss ontological questions or even analyses as obsolete per se[154] has contributed to the fact that the simple notion of the immaterial good as an object capable of ownership has become a practically unchallenged way of thinking. Critical questions about the construction and inherent normativity of the reality of IP law – as formulated in the last twenty years by authors such as Jaszi, Bently, Sherman, Pottage, Tamura, Biagioli and most recently van Dijk – have not yet seriously irritated mainstream IP theory and doctrine. Authors such as Kohler, Elster and Troller, who did not yet wear ontological blinkers, drew frank and free normative conclusions from the supposed intellectuality or immateriality of works, inventions etc. For Kohler, for example, the numerous limitations of IP law were due to the 'nature of the legal object itself'.[155] In 1932, on the basis of an idealistic object ontology, Alexander Elster pleaded for a copyright law in which not the creative person but the work was at the centre.[156] As late as 1967, Alois Troller wrote: 'The nature of intellectual property exerts an ontological constraint that restricts legislative freedom. ... The being of intellectual property is prescribed to the legislature. This cannot be changed'.[157] With a slightly different direction, Abraham Drassinower recently argued, following Kant's text on the unlawfulness of the reprinting of books, that the copyrightable work should be regarded as the author's speech to the public and, accordingly, that only those uses should be considered relevant to copyright in which the work is used 'as a work' in this sense, i.e. as public communication.[158] Here, too, legal conclusions are derived from the essence (*Wesen*) of a somehow dynamic, but still immaterial-object-like subject matter of protection.[159]

As outdated as such essentialist analyses may seem to postmodern observers, they transparently and honestly set out their normative starting points. And indeed, the history of IP law proves the normative function of the abstract IP object. Its construction was an indispensable prerequisite for the extension of the idea of property from physical things to the reproduction and further use of artefacts: without an object capable of being owned, there would be no property; without the abstract IP object, there would be no IP law.[160]

---

refer to one's rights in one's labour'); contra Rognstad, *Property Aspects of Intellectual Property* 123–24 (stressing the normative significant of 'object talk').

[154] Section 2.1.2; Zech, *Information als Schutzgegenstand* 36, 109 (it suffices to adopt a layman's understanding of information as an object that one can own).

[155] Kohler, *Forschungen aus dem Patentrecht* 116–17.

[156] Elster, 6 RabelsZ 903, 917 (1932).

[157] Troller, 50 UFITA 385, 394, 396 (1967); on Troller *see also* van Dijk, *Grounds of the Immaterial* 29–30; Zahrádka, 65 Filosofický časopis 739, 760 (2017).

[158] Drassinower, *What's Wrong with Copying?* 103.

[159] Section 1.5.

[160] Sections 1.1 and 3.2. Further Rognstad, *Property Aspects of Intellectual Property* 42–67, 94–126; Peukert, in Drahos et al. (eds.) *Kritika* 1 114, 116 et seq.

If one regards the work or the invention with the usual IP theory and practice unquestioningly as a segment of reality, one only confirms and reinforces a commoditisation that its historical proponents and later epigones pursued with decidedly normative objectives.[161] Once one operates in the mode of ownership, all powerful justifications and rhetorical figures on which property is based are also at hand.[162] Once the idea of the existence of abstract objects has become established, any reproducible artefact – no matter how physical it may be, such as a sound carrier or a personal performance – can be declared the mere embodiment of an abstract type and thereby be pushed into the background.[163] By focusing on the allocation of a supposedly immaterial object, the double property analogy – namely the object related and the legal – conceals that the effect of IP rights is to regulate the behaviour of third parties in dealing with their own artefacts and abilities.[164]

It follows from all this that the 'communicative reality' of the abstract IP object alone already generates reasons for action that are independent of brute reality and thus *deo*ntological.[165] Because we talk and think as if there were immaterial works etc., we act accordingly. We respect the exclusivity of the IP rights holder just as that of the owner of a tangible thing, although the effects of IP and real property rights differ fundamentally. The omission of IP infringements is therefore not only the consequence of social or legal norms, but an expression of speaking and thinking in categories of immaterial objects. The idea of the abstract IP object itself is normative. It regulates power relations.[166]

It should be noted that this finding does not just restate the well-known normative force of the factual. For the abstract IP object is not a brute, scientifically ascertainable fact, but a socially constructed one. That such 'institutional' facts have an inherent normativity is one of the central findings of John Searle's social ontology. For Searle, 'the whole point of the creation of institutional reality is [...] to create

---

[161] See Section 3.2.1.2 as well as Madison, 56 Case Western Reserve L. Rev. 381, 404 et seq. (2005) ('Thing-by-Nature'); Biagioli, *in* Gaudillière et al. (ed.) *Living Properties* 241 et seq.; Tamura, Nordic Journal of Commercial Law 1, 2 (2012) ('strong metaphor'); Rognstad, *Property Aspects of Intellectual Property* 123–24 (warning against problematic analogies following from 'object talk').

[162] Rotstein, 68 Chicago-Kent L. Rev. 725, 804 (1993) ('If the text can be treated as akin to a tangible object, then the terms "theft", "appropriation", "pirate", "harvest", and "sown" can easily flow from a judge's pen'.).

[163] See Section 5.1.1.2 as well as Wreen, 93 The Monist 433, 439–40 (2010); Gangjee, *in* Howe & Griffiths (eds.) *Concepts of Property* 29, 57–58 ('intangible objects give rise to property description'); Biagioli, 73 Social Research: An International Quarterly 1129, 1153 (2006); Griffiths, 33(4) Oxford Journal of Legal Studies 767, 785 (2013); Kölbel, 10 Text. Kritische Beiträge 27.

[164] *Cf*. Balganesh, *in* Howe & Griffiths (eds.) *Concepts of Property* 161, 178, 179; Rognstad, *Property Aspects of Intellectual Property* 123–24; Peukert, *in* Drahos et al. (eds.) *Kritika* 1 114, 116 et seq.

[165] Thierse, 6 Zeitschrift für Germanistik 441–42 (1985); Tamura, Nordic Journal of Commercial Law 1, 2 (2012); Rognstad, *Property Aspects of Intellectual Property* 123–24; *see also* Möllers, *Möglichkeit von Normen* 246 et seq. (on the normativity of artworks).

[166] Drahos, *Philosophy of IP* 153.

and regulate power relationships between people'.[167] The normativity of institutional facts is anchored in the status function, with which the members of a language community ascribe to the brute reality a function and meaning that this reality does not inherently possess. In the case of the abstract IP object, the status function is that a brute artefact X counts as a mere embodiment of an abstract IP object Y in a given context C. This institutional fact Y ('the' work, 'the' invention etc.) therefore does not represent an observer-independent reality, but its purpose is to constitute an object to which the legal form of property rights can be applied. The construction of the abstract IP object is constitutive for the form of ownership, which, in turn, institutionalises the market economy for reproducible artefacts.[168] It forms an extremely powerful 'background'[169] upon which further institutional facts can be built: IP *rights*, organisations such as collecting societies and patent offices, their regulation etc. This is a 'structure of rules'[170] that individuals cannot disregard.[171] For the abstract IP object – and with it IP laws and rights – are based as institutional facts on a collective recognition of certain ideas, which in turn can only be changed through collective intentionality.[172]

Ultimately, the normativity of the abstract IP object already follows from the fact that it consists of speech acts embedded in a practiced language. Both the first, unilateral declaration – an X is henceforth considered a Y – and its social recognition take place in and through language. But language as the most basic human institution structures power relations. A socially constructed legal object such as the immaterial invention or the immaterial work that exists only in linguistic communication participates in this normativity.[173] The more deeply rooted the concept of immaterial objects is in our language and mind-set, the more powerful it is and the easier it is to use the 'infinite generative capacity of natural languages'[174] to provide social recognition for newly declared immaterial assets (such as entrepreneurial achievements or topographies of integrated circuits).

5.4.2 Proof: The Reach of Physical and Idealistic IP Regimes

The normativity of the abstract IP object cannot only be proven by historical and linguistic analyses, it also becomes apparent in the law. For idealistic IP jurisdictions

---

[167] See Section 2.2.1 as well as Searle, *Making the Social World* 106.
[168] On the difference between constitutive and regulative institutional facts see Searle, *in* Gephart & Suntrup (eds.), *Normative Structure of Human Civilization* 21, 24, 25.
[169] Searle, *The Construction of Social Reality* 129.
[170] Searle, *The Construction of Social Reality* 146.
[171] Berger & Luckmann, *The Social Construction of Reality* 59.
[172] Tuomela, *Philosophy of Sociality* 209; Luhmann, *Kunst der Gesellschaft* 16 (anything is impossible); Esposito, *in* John et al. (eds.), *Ontologien der Moderne* 137, 141 et seq. (a world in which nothing is determined but little can be changed).
[173] On the significance of normativity in *Searle's* social ontology see Section 2.2.1.
[174] Searle, *Making the Social World* 64–65, 68.

with a fully developed concept of the abstract IP object tend to provide more comprehensive legal protection than physicalist IP legal systems, which are in part still based on the action- and artefact-based concept of the privilege age.

The best-known manifestations of this difference are continental European authors rights (*droit d'auteur/Urheberrecht*) on the one hand and Anglo-American copyright on the other. As explained, the abstract-emphatic concept of 'the' work was first implemented in French law, while British and US law imported this conceptual innovation only in the middle of the nineteenth century.[175] Despite the internationalisation of the abstract work concept, the copyright system has not yet shed all artefact- and action-based regulatory concepts.

The very term 'copyright' indicates that the material object of the 'copy' still plays an essential, if not central, role.[176] An expression of this fact is the fixation requirement, according to which copyright protection and thus also the legal concept of a work, presuppose that an ephemeral utterance or performance needs to be fixed in a 'tangible medium of expression' to be copyrightable.[177] This requirement of protection is alien to French and German copyright law, 'because the subject of copyright is not a tangible object, but the work as a spiritual, immaterial good'.[178] While under German law this immaterial good is strictly separated from material results of cultural labour, which are the subject of related rights (*verwandte Schutzrechte*),[179] in the copyright system it does not cause insurmountable difficulties to extend the not fully idealised concept of 'the' work to sound carriers and other physical

---

[175] Section 3.2.2.2.2.

[176] *See* 17 USC § 101 ('"Copies" are material objects, other than phonorecords, in which a work is fixed by any method now known or later developed, and from which the work can be perceived, reproduced, or otherwise communicated, either directly or with the aid of a machine or device'.). *But see* Section 44(1) German Copyright Act (UrhG) ('If the author sells the original of a work he shall, in cases of doubt, not be deemed to have granted a right of use to the buyer'.); Art. L-111-1 CPI ('L'auteur d'une oeuvre de l'esprit jouit sur cette oeuvre, du seul fait de sa création, d'un droit de propriété incorporelle exclusif et opposable à tous'.), Art. 111-3 CPI ('La propriété incorporelle définie par l'article L. 111-1 est indépendante de la propriété de l'objet matériel'.).

[177] *Cf.* Art. 2(2) Berne Convention ('It shall, however, be a matter for legislation in the countries of the Union to prescribe that works in general or any specified categories of works shall not be protected unless they have been fixed in some material form'.); 17 USC § 101 ('A work is "created" when it is fixed in a copy or phonorecord for the first time'), Section 102(a) ('original works of authorship fixed in any tangible medium of expression'); White-Smith Music Pub. Co. v. Apollo Co., 209 US 1, 17 (1908) ('The statute has not provided for the protection of the intellectual conception apart from the thing produced, however meritorious such conception may be, but has provided for the making and filing of a tangible thing, against the publication and duplication of which it is the purpose of the statute to protect the composer'.); critical Mann, 34 Colum. J.L. & Arts 201 (2011). Ambivalent Section 3(2) UK CDPA 1988 ('Copyright does not subsist in a literary, dramatic or musical work unless and until it is recorded, in writing or otherwise'); Pila, 71 Modern L. Rev. 535, 540 (2008).

[178] BGH 27 February 1962 Case No. I ZR 118/60, GRUR 1962, 470, 472 – AKI; Art. L111-1, L111-2, L112-1 and L112-2 CPI.

[179] Section 5.1.1.2.

artefacts.[180] The higher degree of concretisation is also reflected in exhaustive lists of copyrightable work categories and exclusive rights, while the abstract work concept in continental European law has precisely the normative function of closing gaps in legal protection.[181] US-American law additionally counteracts still effective, expansive tendencies of the abstract work concept with the idea/expression dichotomy and the fair use exception.[182] The physicalist and concretistic concept of copyright corresponds to its primarily instrumental teleology. Limited exclusive rights to copy are granted in order to promote learning and progress in the public interest. This approach is closer to reality than continental European authors rights law, which places the fiction of the abstract work at its centre and is less consequentialist in purpose.[183] To the extent that the notion of the property object abstracts from brute reality, the telos of the respective property rights can also disregard their measurable consequences.

In patent law, international harmonisation has now progressed so far that the connection between the idealisation of the legal object on the one hand and the scope and self-referentiality of legal protection on the other can only be examined in retrospect. If one undertakes such a diachronic comparison, however, abstraction and parallel expansion tendencies can also be observed.[184] It began with the development of the concept of the immaterial invention, to which the replacement of three-dimensional models by their verbalisation in patent specifications made an essential contribution.[185] Today, patentability only requires that the invention can be carried out by a person skilled in the art; it does not have to be realised or fully understood.[186] After the patent has been granted, there is also no legal obligation to work the invention.[187] Patents for inventions which the person entitled neither practices nor licences himself and which he may not even have realised can at best be justified indirectly with their effects. If the patent specification is the only manifestation of the otherwise abstract invention, patent law's subject matter and

---

[180] Cf. Section 1, 5A (sound recordings), 5B(1) ('"film" means a recording on any medium ...'), 6 ('"broadcast" means an electronic transmission ...'), 8 ('typographical arrangement of a published edition') UK CDPA 1988; Barron, 67 (2) Modern L. Rev. 177, 193 et seq. (2004); 17 USC § 101 ('"Sound recordings" are works that result from the fixation of a series of musical, spoken, or other sounds, but not including the sounds accompanying a motion picture or other audiovisual work, regardless of the nature of the material objects, such as disks, tapes, or other phonorecords, in which they are embodied'.).

[181] Cf. Section 1 et seq., 16 CDPA 1988; 17 USC § 102 and Griffiths, 33(4) Oxford Journal of Legal Studies 767, 776 (2013), with Sections 2, 15 German Copyright Act (UrhG), Art. L112–1 f. CPI.

[182] Bracha, 118 Yale L.J. 186, 224 et seq. (2008) with further references, 238.

[183] Griffiths, 33(4) Oxford Journal of Legal Studies 767, 768 (2013).

[184] Cotropia, 69 Vand. L. Rev. 1543 et seq. (2016).

[185] See Chapter 3 note 27.

[186] Kraßer & Ann, Patentrecht 200 et seq. with further references; Schäfers, in Benkard (ed.), Patentgesetz Section 34 German Patent Act (PatG) para. 15d (speculative yet plausible commercial uses suffice).

[187] Art. 5A (2) and (4) Paris Convention as well as Kuntz-Hallstein, 6 GRUR Int. 347 et seq. (1981).

purpose have completely disconnected from the real circumstances in research, development and production.[188] Patent law has become a purpose in itself.

The connection between the abstractness of the subject matter of protection and the scope of legal protection is, finally, particularly evident in the extension of the scope of IP rights beyond copies in the strict sense. Privileges for reprinting books or for the manufacture or use of certain machines initially referred only to reproductions that largely coincided with the Master Artefact.[189] When the privilege system was replaced in the late eighteenth and early nineteenth centuries by a property-like protection of works and inventions, the restriction to identical Secondary Artefacts continued for a long time. Even in France, the forerunner of idealistic abstraction, the inclusion of translations and musical arrangements of original works in the scope of protection of authors' rights caused considerable argumentative difficulties.[190] In Anglo-American jurisdictions, even the advocates of property rights in works considered translations and other adaptations to be perfectly legal.[191] The same applies to the German reprint debate at the end of the eighteenth century.[192] Still the Prussian Copyright Act of 1837, which marks the turning point in the historical emergence of the abstract work concept in Germany, generally does not consider translations as prohibited reprints.[193] Only when the abstract work concept had been established as the central topos of authors rights and copyright were the conceptual obstacles removed. It is therefore no coincidence that the term 'work' found its way into the legal language of US copyright at the very moment when authors were granted the right to 'to dramatize or to translate their own works' in 1870.[194] The

---

[188] Cotropia, 69 Vand. L. Rev. 1543, 1545, 1546 (2016) ('The patent document became the ultimate required 'product' of the system'.).

[189] Section 3.2.1.3.1.

[190] See Cour d'appel de Rouen (1845), in Bently & Kretschmer (eds.) *Primary Sources on Copyright* www.copyrighthistory.org; Teilmann-Lock, *The Object of Copyright* 24.

[191] *Cf.* Blackstone, Commentaries on the Laws of England II chapter 26 no. 8, 405–6 (property right in 'identical works'); Millar v. Taylor, 4 Burrow 2303, 2348 (1769) ('He may improve upon it, imitate it, translate it; oppose its sentiments: but he buys no right to publish the identical work. ... The imitated machine, therefore, is a new and a different work: the literary composition, printed on another man's paper, is still the same'.); Cornish, 13 The Edinburgh L. Rev. 8, 11 (2009). On US law *see* Stowe v. Thomas, 23 F. Cas. 201 (Grier, Circuit Justice, C.C.E.D. Pa. 1853) and Bracha, 118 Yale L.J. 186, 224 et seq. (2008).

[192] *See* Cella, Vom Büchernachdruck 1784, as quoted by Klippel, in Festschrift Wadle 477, 494–95; Section 1027 General State Laws for the Prussian States (prALR) (translations are to be considered as new, original writings). On musical works *cf.* Wadle, in Wadle (ed.) *Geistiges Eigentum II* 185, 190; Kawohl, *Urheberrecht der Musik in Preussen* 33 et seq., 151–52.

[193] *See* Section 4 Prussian Copyright Act 1837 (prUrhG 1837) (translation not considered a reprint that requires authorisation); Hitzig, *Das Preußische Gesetz 1837* 57 et seq.

[194] 41st Congress, Second Session, chapter 240, Sections 85–111, An Act to revise, consolidate, and amend the statutes relating to patents and copyrights, Section 86. *See also* Section 4952 International Copyright Act (1891), in Bently & Kretschmer (eds.) *Primary Sources on Copyright* www.copyrighthistory.org ('and authors ... shall have exclusive right to dramatize and translate any of their works for which copyright shall have been obtained under the laws of the United States'); *see further* Barron, 52 New Formations 58, 70 (2004). The current statutory

abstractness and vagueness of the concept of a copyrightable work allows deviations from the Master Artefact to be regarded as infringements without any major justification effort.[195] As Kohler said, it should only depend on whether the 'individual core' (*individuelle[n] Kern*) or the 'inner character' (*innere[r] Charakter*) of the work was preserved.[196] What characterises this 'core' could and should remain open. For it was, and still is, precisely this abstraction and flexibility that makes Kohler's concept of the immaterial good so tempting – and which prompted Alf Ross' legal realist critique of 1945.

Today, the scope of protection of all IP rights extends beyond perfect, identical copies. It does not come as a surprise that the production and use of adaptations of works, of equivalent technical solutions, of designs without a different overall impression, of similar signs etc. may require authorisation. Works, inventions, designs and signs are thought of as abstract types whose existence and parallel legal scope of protection are not exhausted in their perceptible embodiments. They represent an undefined field in which only the rights holder may operate. The limits of exclusivity are marked by a requirement of sufficient similarity between Master Artefacts and Secondary Artefacts.[197] What is important in the comparison and what standards are to be applied can only be deduced from the concept of the copyrightable work and other abstract IP objects if these aspects have previously been inserted into the per se indefinite – even empty – definition of the term in question. At this point, too, the normativity of the dominant paradigm proves itself. The raison d'être of the abstract IP object is to make understandable commands and prohibitions that would otherwise have to be explained and justified more closely. This too is reflected in current IP law. Highly idealised IP laws simply designate 'adaptations and other modifications' ('*Bearbeitungen und andere Umgestaltungen*': Section 23 of the German Copyright Act, UrhG) and elements which are 'equivalent to an element specified in the claims' (Art. 2 Protocol on the interpretation of Art. 69 EPC) as infringing. It is up to courts to define these very general provisions and apply them to a concrete case. In areas of IP law in which the dominant paradigm is weaker or not at all pronounced, the scope of protection is, in contrast, already explained in more detail in the statutes.[198]

---

definition of 'derivative work' in 17 USC § 101 does not use the traditionally central concept of the 'copy': 'A "derivative work" is a work based upon one or more preexisting works, such as a translation, musical arrangement, dramatization, fictionalization, motion picture version, sound recording, art reproduction, abridgment, condensation, or any other form in which a work may be recast, transformed, or adapted'.).

[195] *See* Kawohl & Kretschmer, 2 Intellectual Property Quarterly 209, 215–16 (2003); Sherman & Bently, *The Making of Modern Intellectual Property Law* 32, 51 et seq.; Barron, 15 Social & Legal Studies 101, 120–22 (2006); Barron, 67(2) Modern L. Rev. 67 177, 203 (2004); Bracha, *Owning Ideas* 530; Madison, 19 J. Intell. Prop. L. 1, 10 (2012); Griffiths, 33(4) Oxford Journal of Legal Studies 767, 769, 770 (2013); Teilmann-Lock, *The Object of Copyright* 6.

[196] Kohler, 123 UFITA 99, 108 (1993).

[197] Section 5.1.2.2.

[198] *See* Section 38(2) German Design Act (DesignG) (no different overall impression), Section 14 (2) no. 2 German Trademark Act (MarkenG) (likelihood of confusion), Section 10(2) German

5.4.3 The Instability of the Distinction between Law and Reality

To recognise the inherent normativity of the idealised reality of IP law is thus helpful to improve our understanding of the peculiarities of this field of law. One of these peculiarities is the difficulty – already mentioned several times – of distinguishing between 'is' and 'ought', between legal object and subjective right. This problem already occurs with informal rights such as copyright. For example, it is questionable whether a urinal that is declared a work of art, exhibited in a museum and discussed in aesthetic discourses is to be regarded as a copyrightable work on the basis of these circumstances alone.[199]

The differentiation between 'is' and 'ought' is particularly precarious in the case of registered rights, the object of protection of which (Master Artefact) is laid down in an administrative act. According to settled case law, patent claims have the character of legal norms, which is why it is the original task of the courts to interpret the patent claims – possibly using descriptions and drawings as a secondary means of interpretation – while technical experts only have the accessory task of explaining to the court 'the technical contexts necessary for understanding the protected teaching and to provide the necessary insight into the knowledge, skills and experience of the typical, average representatives of the relevant professional circles, including their methodological approach'.[200] This at first glance clear division of tasks between lawyers and non-legal experts only leads, however, to the next aporia, because 'even the answer to questions as to which technical circumstances are relevant and which expert view is to be taken as a basis can only be found on the basis of a valuation'.[201] The average person skilled in the art is, eventually, just another legal fiction.[202] And the aim of

---

Plant Variety Act (SortSchG) (plant variety protection extends to varieties that are 'essentially derived from' the protected variety).

[199] *Cf.* Schack, *Kunst und Recht* 9 et seq.

[200] BGH 22 December 2009 Case no. X ZR 56/08, GRUR 2010, 314 paras. 25–26 – Kettenradanordnung II with further references. On US law Markman v. Westview Instruments, Inc., 517 US 370, 388–89 (1996) ('when an issue "falls somewhere between a pristine legal standard and a simple historical fact, the fact/law distinction at times has turned on a determination that, as a matter of the sound administration of justice, one judicial actor is better positioned than another to decide the issue in question". So it turns out here, for judges, not juries, are the better suited to find the acquired meaning of patent terms'); Teva Pharm. USA, Inc. v. Sandoz, Inc., 135 S. Ct. 831, 833–34 (2015) ('subsidiary factual matters' may be submitted to a jury).

[201] Translated from the original German. BGH 22 December 2009 Case no. X ZR 56/08, GRUR 2010, 314 para. 29 – Kettenradanordnung II.

[202] Teva Pharm. USA, Inc. v. Sandoz, Inc., 135 S. Ct. 831, 849 (2015) (Thomas, J., dissenting) ('the "fact" of how a skilled artisan would understand a given term or phrase at a particular point in history is a legal fiction; it has no existence independent of the claim construction process. There is no actual "skilled artisan" who, at the moment the application was filed, formed an understanding of the terms of the claim – an understanding that an omniscient factfinder could ascertain. Neither is the skilled artisan's understanding a proxy for some external fact that, could the court know it, would supply the meaning of a patent claim'.).

the whole exercise is not to come close to the brute reality of technical artefacts, but to combine, through patent interpretation, 'fair protection for the patent proprietor with a reasonable degree of legal certainty for third parties'.[203] That, however, is nothing but a genuinely normative exercise.

The collapse of the is/ought dichotomy does not cause the mainstream view any particular headache.[204] In the 'most metaphysical branch of modern law'[205] one is dealing with abstract types, the limits of which are only defined in a legal procedure.

Such fatalism is theoretically unsatisfactory and insufficient, because no attempt is even made to explain a phenomenon that is at odds with the is/ought-foundation of modern law. The Searlean understanding of the abstract IP object as an inherently normative, institutional fact instead offers a viable explanation. According to this social ontology, works, inventions and other IP objects are based on a declarative, socially accepted speech act according to which brute artefacts count as the embodiment of an abstract type. The attribution of this function unfolds normativity because it is based solely on language-based, social recognition. Because and insofar as we accept the idea that there is an abstract invention, we can and will act as if, for example, an invention were an object like a tangible thing that is capable of being owned. That is the whole point of this fiction. It provides intentionality-independent reasons to respect the 'intellectual property' of the rights holder, i.e. to act differently than one might. For example, only the fiction of the abstract IP object allows one to imagine the following: 'Because A has filed a patent application for an invention with the content pronounced by the court before me, it belongs to him. That is why I am not allowed to use the technical solution in question'.

Of course, this norm – which is deeply rooted in speech and thought and therefore very effective – has its price. By the fact that the law accepts a fact that is already inherently normative, the effectively regulated reality moves into the background. In current IP law, this happens because the statutes do not link to concrete artefacts and actions, but to an abstract IP object that, according to prevailing jargon, has an objective scope of protection that is violated by 'encroachments'. This conceptual abstraction constitutes and reinforces the property norm, but conceals the fact that IP rights have a very different effect from real property ownership – namely a regulation of artefacts and actions which are in a spatial distance from the rights holder and only come under the spell of his rights because there is a certain

---

[203] Protocol on the Interpretation of Art. 69 EPC.
[204] An exception is George, Constructing Intellectual Property 90–134, who, however, discusses the abstract ('ideational') IP object as a mere function of IP laws; *see id.* at 15 ('How is "intellectual property" constructed within the legal system?').
[205] *Hogg v. Emerson*, 47 US 437, 485–86 (1848).

similarity between the Master Artefact in question and the challenged Secondary Artefacts, which need not even be genealogical.[206]

The not inconsiderable challenge of justifying such effects must be tackled offensively by the law. From the point of view of legal realism, it is not enough to refer to fictitious objects whose purpose is to make the explication of this justification superfluous. Law must face up to reality and its effects on reality.

---

[206] Balganesh, *in* Howe & Griffiths (eds.) *Concepts of Property* 161, 177.

6

Normative Critique of the Abstract IP Object

This legal realist credo also guides the following normative critique of the prevailing paradigm. Such a critique only makes sense against the background that the abstract IP object does not form part of brute reality, but rather represents an inherently normative, institutional-social fact. In other words: If the subject matter of IP law is normative in kind, it can be challenged from a normative perspective. In this respect, the question is: Should lawyers speak and think of the existence of immaterial objects that can be owned?

6.1 RADICAL CRITIQUE WITHOUT EXTREME CONSEQUENCES

It has already been indicated that I prefer a negative answer. However, I am not in favour of dismissing the idea of exclusive rights. The following criticism is therefore radical, but not extreme.

6.1.1 *In Support of a New Understanding of Reality*

My critique is radical in the sense that it advocates rethinking the ontology of IP law. It questions the abstract IP object and thus the root of the property analogy, and it does not settle for permanently balancing the systemic conflicts between IP rights and conflicting freedoms of third parties, as well as for the economic and social dysfunctionalities and overshooting tendencies of IP rights.[1] For as long as fictitious commodity thinking takes its place, there are distortions in the perception of regulated reality, legal structures and their justification. With regard to an accurate description of IP rights and their effects, the dominant paradigm creates the problem that the imagined reality of immaterial goods must first be traced back to its real

---

[1] *But see* Scotchmer, *Innovation and Inventives* 97; Madison, 19 J. Intell. Prop. L. 1, 29 (2012) ('The work both can and should be flexible'.)

foundations (artefacts and actions) before the actual effects of IP rights can be reconstructed and criticised.[2] The misleading rather than helpful analogies the economic analysis of IP rights draws to the regulation of lighthouses and other public goods bear witness to this problem.[3] Furthermore, the prevailing discourse and thinking in terms of immaterial goods that can be owned cannot explain the legal structures of IP law conclusively. An IP theory based on this ontology gives the wrong impression that IP rights are just a variant of real property ownership. This legal classification of IP rights in turn favours a 'property logic' (*Eigentumslogik*),[4] flanked and fuelled by the high legitimacy of the idea of property in general, which is capable of concealing negative effects of IP rights on individual freedoms and the general welfare.[5]

In order to eliminate these factual, juridic and justificatory misconceptions and to ensure a more realistic legal description and legitimisation of IP rights, a different understanding of the subject matter (reality) of IP rights is called for, which makes the descriptive findings of this book normatively fruitful. According to this approach, the fictional abstract IP object should be replaced by an action- and artefact-based mode of speaking and thinking about IP. Such an IP theory would draw the attention of lawyers to the resources and actions to which IP rights actually relate and have an impact: innovative, investing and imitative activities and the scarce resources used in them. This change in perspective would, in itself, contribute to a more realistic assessment of the positive and negative effects of IP rights. In addition, this approach would move Master Artefacts and Secondary Artefacts to their rightful place at the centre of attention, whereas the prevailing theory considers them only as accidentals.[6]

An action- and artefact-based understanding of IP rights furthermore seems advantageous because of its legitimatory implications. It expresses the fact that at its core we are dealing with exclusive rights to act.[7] Such privileges were one of the central tenets of the modern revolutions. They were attacked and eventually abolished as a regulatory instrument of the ancien régime. In this historical situation, the construct of the immaterial work (object) capable of being owned had the normative function of bringing exclusive rights to act into a form that was acceptable under the

---

[2] On the widespread lack of understanding why unauthorised peer-to-peer file sharing for non-commercial purposes is copyright infringement Peukert, *in* Geiger (ed.) *Criminal Enforcement of Intellectual Property* 151 et seq.
[3] Section 5.3.2.
[4] Tamura, Nordic Journal of Commercial Law 1, 3 (2012). Dreier, *in* Schricker et al. (eds.) *Geistiges Eigentum* 51, 70 et seq., 76 et seq. (describing instances of 'property logic'); *see also* Luhmann, *in* Krawietz et al. (eds.) *Technischer Imperativ* 43, 49, 50.
[5] Peukert, *Güterzuordnung* 899 et seq.; Peukert, *Gemeinfreiheit* 1 et seq.
[6] Section 5.1.2.
[7] Tamura, Nordic Journal of Commercial Law 1, 2 (2012) ('a right restricting a certain pattern of human action'), id. at 5 ('Intellectual property rights do not constitute protection over an "intangible thing" – an intellectual work – but they are rights that restrict the freedom of persons who are not right-holders').

new circumstances of modern society as a whole. Royal privileges were replaced by 'intellectual property', which was based on a general law adopted by parliament.[8] If one now looks again at the fact that IP rights de facto do nothing other than make the use of cognitive abilities and one's own physical resources dependent on the prior consent of an IP right holder, this highlights the privilege-like effects of IP rights, which thus certainly deserve a certain mistrust.[9]

Against this background, it is another advantage of an action- and artefact-based IP theory that the justification requirements for IP rights become more stringent. This justificatory pressure can be demonstrated by the adaptation right under copyright law. If one argues on the basis of an abstract-undefined work and the requirement (which is also motivated by moral rights concerns) that in principle every adaptation or other transformation of 'the work' requires prior authorisation, then independently written sequels of a novel can also be regarded as copyright infringements.[10] If one asks, instead, on the basis of the view held here, whether only the author of a novel should be entitled to write sequels, a respective claim for protection presents itself differently and clearly more problematically. Why should it be at the sole discretion of the first author whether sequels written independently by third parties see the light of day, as long as they do not go along with violations of personality rights, misleading commercial practices or infringements of the right to the title of the original? The IP theory developed here favours such unprejudiced questions and thus generally a more instrumental understanding of IP rights, their purposes and effects.[11] The fact that this approach tends to be more strongly represented in the Anglo-American legal system than in continental Europe is no coincidence, given the reduced Anglo-Saxon propensity for idealistic dreaming.[12]

6.1.2 *In Support of the Form of Exclusive Rights*

However, such a change of perspective – in contrast to what Max Lange apparently thought[13] – does not necessarily have to go hand in hand with the abandonment of the legal concept of the exclusive right. It is conceptually demanding – but, as explained, possible – to break down the fiction of the abstract IP object into real actions and artefacts without abandoning the form of the exclusive right. The object

---

[8] Section 3.2.2.2.
[9] For a legal-doctrinal critique *see* Peukert, *Güterzuordnung* 895 *et seq.*
[10] BGH 29 April 1999 Case No. I ZR 65/96, GRUR 1999, 1984.
[11] Drahos, *Philosophy of IP* 213 et seq. (instrumentalism); sceptical Drassinower, What's Wrong with Copying? 147.
[12] *Cf.* Hargreaves, *Digital Opportunity* 8, 20, 98 ('Government should ensure that development of the IP System is driven as far as possible by objective evidence'.); de Beer, 19(5–6) J World IP 150 et seq. (2016), with further references.
[13] Lange, *Kritik der Grundbegriffe vom geistigen Eigentum* (1858), *reprinted in* 117 UFITA 169, 173–74, 179 (1991) (decomposing the abstract IP object supports an understanding of IP rights as obligations).

required for this, which bundles the relational rights and obligations, is the Master Artefact, which is compared with other artefacts according to the requirements set out in IP laws.[14] It is, moreover, not desirable to dismiss the form of the exclusive right only because the idea of the abstract IP object has proven to be a misleading, normative, institutional fact. The fiction of the romantic-abstract work and its offspring in other areas of IP law should be abandoned, as it does not correspond to what is actually regulated. Regarding the property form, which is also a socially constructed institutional fact, a much more conservative attitude is called for.[15]

As the public domain of countless basic information and formerly IP-protected works and inventions proves, the use of reproducible artefacts can proceed in an orderly manner on the basis of real property and contract law.[16] Indeed, the basic norm of IP law is that anyone may copy and otherwise imitate Master Artefacts by employing their own material resources and cognitive abilities, so long as no IP rights and other private rights of third parties (in particular rights in real property and in trade secrets and personality rights) stand in the way. Such an exercise of the general freedom of action is not illegitimate, but an expression of equal negative freedom. It is also sustainable because there is no good that would be destroyed by excessive use.[17] What exists and what is scarce are human and other resources needed to produce Master Artefacts and Secondary Artefacts. These resources are fully protected by real property ownership and personality rights.

Nevertheless, it would be unrealistic to believe that medicines, film productions and many other complex, labour-intensive but relatively easily reproducible artefacts would continue to be produced in the same quantity as today if the innovators and investors involved could not rely on IP rights to recoup their sunk investments in time, money and other resources.[18] History and experience have shown that in the absence of IP rights, actors seek and find other ways to internalise innovation rents. They keep their innovations secret, set up cartels or otherwise attempt to prevent unauthorised copying on a contractual basis.[19] Whether these alternatives are more efficient than IP rights seems very doubtful.[20]

---

[14] Section 5.1.2.1.
[15] Searle, *Mind, Language and Society: Philosophy in the Real World* 161.
[16] Peukert, *Gemeinfreiheit* 49 et seq. with further references.
[17] Peukert, *Gemeinfreiheit* 66 et seq.
[18] Lemley, 90 N.Y.U. L. Rev. 460 et seq. (2015); Gross, Harvard Business School Working Paper 16–109, 1 ('competition unambiguously motivates creativity, but . . . heavy competition discourages further investment').
[19] On the formation of publisher's syndicates in nineteenth-century Germany *see* Bosse, *Autorschaft als Werkherrschaft* 23 et seq.; Höffner, *Geschichte und Wesen des Urheberrechts II* 299 et seq. On the reaction of Dutch and Swiss enterprises on the abolition of patent law in the nineteenth century *see* Moser, 95 The American Economic Review 1214 et seq. (2005). On strategies of plant and animal breeders *see* Kevles, in Biagioli et al. (eds.) *Making and Unmaking IP* 253 et seq.
[20] Moser, 95 The American Economic Review 1214, 1223 (2005) (patents channel innovative activity into certain branches of industry but do not boost the general level of innovation).

The efficiency of IP rights is, however, not the decisive point. The reasons for adhering to the form of the exclusive right go deeper. They are related to a preference for the market as the regulatory principle of economic activity. According to this view, the market economy has a higher input and output legitimacy than alternative economic systems, in particular those based on central state planning. It combines freedom with responsibility, leaves it to market participants whether and how they innovate and invest, allocates profits and losses to those who are responsible for them, and forces no one to offer and demand products.[21] Those who consider these effects desirable cannot do without the form of property/ownership because it is constitutive for market transactions and price formation.[22] The market price and the income of all market participants depend on the market success of their offer, not on the joy and preference of private patrons or state agencies.[23] If authors, inventors, designers, brand manufacturers and other innovators and investors are subject to the laws of the market, it would be inconsistent and ultimately unjust to deny them the legal instruments by means of which they can monetise their output, i.e. reproducible Master Artefacts.[24] And this exactly is the function of IP rights. They enable entrepreneurs to live an economically independent life in the market economy.[25]

6.1.3 *Alternative Terminology*

However, it is proving difficult to establish a suitable terminology that on the one hand dismisses the fiction of the abstract IP object, but at the same time retains the form of the exclusive right. For lack of alternatives, it will not be possible to do without talking about the work, the invention, the design etc. To continue naming the objects of protection of IP rights in this way appears to be acceptable, as long as one is only aware that this terminology signifies – depending on the context – either all protectable Master Artefacts (statutory, general concept of 'the' work and 'the'

---

[21] *See* Scotchmer, *Innovation and Inventives* 97.
[22] Epstein, 62 Stanford L. Rev. 455, 520–21 (2010); Merges, *Justifying Intellectual Property* 5 ('For me, it is this powerful logic of individual control that makes property appropriate and appealing; it has little to do with the nature of the assets in question'.).
[23] Renouard, *Traité des droits d'auteur* 462.
[24] Renouard, *Traité des droits d'auteur* 434 et seq.; Peukert, in *Festschrift 50 Jahre UrhG* 305, 313. In contrast, publicly financed innovative activity is and should be subject to different, less stringent exploitation rights; *cf.* Section 38(4) German Copyright Act (UrhG) ('The author of a scientific contribution which results from research activities at least half of which were financed by public funds and which was reprinted in a collection which is published periodically at least twice per year also has the right, if he has granted the publisher or editor an exclusive right of use, to make the contribution available to the public upon expiry of 12 months after first publication in the accepted manuscript version, unless this serves a commercial purpose. The source of the first publication must be cited. Any deviating agreement to the detriment of the author shall be ineffective'.).
[25] Peukert, *Güterzuordnung* 665 et seq.

invention) or a particular Master Artefact and the Secondary Artefacts sufficiently similar to it (e.g. Goethe's *Faust*).[26] That such a terminology can achieve social recognition is demonstrated by the linguistic practice before the emergence of the abstract IP object, and nowadays by the rights related to copyright and plant variety rights, which manage without the fiction of the abstract IP object and merely refer in a generalising way to phono records, plant propagation material and other reproducible artefacts.[27]

No other generic term to describe all these artefacts is currently available. Kohler's *Immaterialgut* (immaterial good) is far too much an expression of the current paradigm to be used any longer. The same applies to the even more dazzling talk of 'intellectual property'. In the absence of better alternatives, I refer to 'IP' rights in this book, but with this internationally accepted abbreviation I do not mean more than the sum of those provisions that grant private rights to use reproducible artefacts.

The term 'intellectual property' should be avoided. More precise and thus preferable is the well-established jargon of copyrights and industrial property rights. If one aspires to bring all these rights under a generic term, which brings their effects to the fore, then there are two albeit problematic candidates. One is the term 'monopoly right', which appears unsuitable, as it has always functioned as a discursive weapon, and is also factually misleading, since IP rights only protect a monopoly in the economic sense, i.e. a position as the only supplier of a particular commodity, in very exceptional cases.[28]

Instead, the effect of IP rights is nicely summed up by the term 'privilege'. Because this is what IP rights grant: a privileged legal position according to which only the rights holder may copy, imitate and use the Master Artefact, while all others require prior consent for these actions.[29] The privileges of the early modern period

---

[26] On this abstraction no. 1 see Sections 2.2.2, 3.1 and 3.2.1.3.1.
[27] Section 5.1.1.2.
[28] But see *Edward Darcy Esquire v. Thomas Allin of London Haberdasher*, 74 E.R. 1131, 1133 (1599); *Impression Prod., Inc. v. Lexmark Int'l, Inc.*, 137 S. Ct. 1523, 1531, 1532 (2017) ('The Patent Act "promote[s] the progress of science and the useful arts by granting to [inventors] a limited monopoly" that allows them to "secure the financial rewards" for their inventions'.); Smith, Wealth of Nations 256 ('When a company of merchants undertake, at their own risk and expense, to establish a new trade with some remote and barbarous nation, it may not be unreasonable to ... to grant them ... a monopoly of the trade for a certain number of years. It is the easiest and most natural way in which the state can recompense them for hazarding a dangerous and expensive experiment, of which the public is afterwards to reap the benefit. A temporary monopoly of this kind may be vindicated, upon the same principles upon which a like monopoly of a new machine is granted to its inventor, and that of a new book to its author. But upon the expiration of the term, the monopoly ought certainly to determine ... By a perpetual monopoly, all the other subjects of the state are taxed very absurdly in two different ways'); Penner, *Idea of Property* 109, 119–20; Biron, 93 The Monist 382 (2010); Abbott, *in* Drahos et al. (eds.) *Kritika* 1 1, 15–6; Gaudrat, 221 RIDA 2, 8 (2009). On the history of the monopoly rhetoric *see* Rose, 66 Law & Contemp. Probs. 75, 84 (2003); Mossoff, 92 Cornell L. Rev. 953, 984 (2007).
[29] *Cf.* Renouard, *Traité des droits d'auteur* 464; Bell, 58 Syracuse L. Rev. 58 523, 524 (2008); Balganesh, *in* Howe & Griffiths (eds.) *Concepts of Property* 161, 177, 178; Drahos, *Philosophy of IP* 213 (liberty-inhibiting privileges); Schmidt, 52 DZPhil 755, 760–61 (2004) (allocation of the

had exactly this structure. They granted the privileged person the exclusive right to print a certain book, to use a machine etc.[30]

There is no doubt that the privilege is a historically compromised concept. The modern bourgeois revolutions in England, the United States and France, in the course of which the first modern IP codifications were enacted, were decidedly directed against the absolutist-mercantilist privilege system.[31] They wanted to put an end to the often arbitrary granting of individual preferential rights to favourites of the rulers and replace them with marketable rights available without discrimination on a general statutory basis. Above all, the French revolutionary legislation was very careful to avoid any appeal to the privileges of the ancien régime. The means to this end was the 'intellectual property' in the abstract work and the abstract invention. Anglo-American legal history, on the other hand, proves that a market-based organisation of cultural and technological production directed against censorship and state control can also be codified and practised on the basis of pre-modern terminology. Even today, British and US-American law, especially copyright law, shows clear traces of a realist, action- and artefact-based way of thinking. Accordingly, its character is more instrumental and consequentialist.[32]

In any case, it goes without saying that in a liberal, democratic society under the rule of law there can be no return to absolutist privileges granted in individual cases at the discretion of the ruler.[33] Private exclusive rights require a formal statutory basis that determines their content and limits.[34] But there is no apparent reason why such rights should not be called privilege rights in the twenty-first century. Their character is thus aptly described: They privilege a person to do something that third parties are not allowed to do, even though the non-owners factually could do it without violating the law. The problem of such a right and the requirements for its exceptional justification are emphasised by its designation as a privilege, which in turn favours a realistic and purposeful IP regulation. Unlike at the time of the early modern revolutions, the market is so firmly established as the principle of economic activity that there is currently no serious danger of a relapse into feudal or mercantilist, central-planning structures. On the contrary: Precisely where such rigidities are evident today, they are also based on the strategic use of 'intellectual property'

---

exclusive, transferable right to exhibit a certain activity); Deazley, *Rethinking Copyright* 161 (suggesting 'the language of Intellectual Property Freedoms (IPFs) and Intellectual Property Privileges (IPPs), and in that order'); Ross, *On Law and Justice* 176; sceptical Drassinower, *What's Wrong with Copying?* 174–75.

[30] Section 3.2.1.3.1.
[31] *See* Section 3.2.2.2 and Bracha, 38 Loyola of L.A. L. Rev. 177, 218–19 (2004) ('A century earlier this would have been unthinkable'.); Pottage & Shermann, *Figures of Invention* 5 (first truly modern patent regime).
[32] Section 5.4.2.
[33] *Cf.* Pahlow, in Cordes et al. (eds.) *Handwörterbuch zur deutschen Rechtsgeschichte* 2010 et seq.; Renouard, *Traité des droits d'auteur* 5.
[34] Art. 14(1) sentence 2 German Basic Law (GG) and Peukert, *Güterzuordnung*, passim.

rights.[35] Moreover, a twenty-first-century talk of privileges would not tie in with the late-absolutist privilege system, but with the middle of the nineteenth century, when the prohibitive and possibly excessive effects of IP rights were so conspicuous that even the French legislature was prepared to replace the revolutionary construct of 'intellectual property' in immaterial objects with the exclusive right to exploit a technology.[36]

Although lawyers in particular should strive to be precise in their speech, I am aware that the chances of a renaissance of the concept of the privilege are extremely slim. Firstly, the prevailing paradigm of the abstract IP object is too deeply anchored in codifications at all levels as well as in everyday legal and colloquial language to be seriously disrupted. Due to a lack of better alternatives, I also speak of 'IP rights'. Secondly, the normative criticism formulated in Section 6.1.1 only concerns the way the law conceives of its subject matter, while the legal side – the form of the private exclusive right – is to be retained. Such a kind of half U-turn is too weak to induce a shift in language and reasoning. But at least IP theory can be expected to adopt a precise and realistic language and understanding. Because private rights legalise the natural,[37] the 'is' must be signified as precisely as possible.

6.2 CHANGE OF PERSPECTIVE: FROM IMMATERIAL OBJECTS TO ACTORS, ACTIONS AND ARTEFACTS

Achieving this goal requires a new perspective on the subject matter and function of IP rights. Instead of assuming an abstract, indeterminate IP object, the theory and practice of IP law should focus on the actors involved, their actions and the artefacts they use.[38] For these are the persons affected by the commandments and prohibitions of IP law and the scarce physical resources whose use is regulated. The justification of IP rights must be focused on these two aspects if the desired extent of innovative and investment activity is to be achieved.[39]

---

[35] Braithwaite & Drahos, *Information Feudalism* passim.
[36] See in particular Art. 1 French Patent Act 1844 (*'Toute nouvelle découverte ou invention dans tous les genres d'industries confère à son auteur, sous les conditions et pour le temps ci-après déterminés, le droit exclusif d'exploiter à son profit ladite découverte ou invention'.*); Hirsch, 36 UFITA 19, 42–43 (1962); Galvez-Behar, *La république des inventeurs* 29 et seq. On copyright Renouard, *Traité des droits d'auteur* 456. On US patent law Bloomer v. McQuewan, 55 US 539, 549–50 (1852) ('The franchise which the patent grants, consists altogether in the right to exclude every one from making, using, or vending the thing patented, without the permission of the patentee'); see also Merges, in Rochelle C. Dreyfuss & Justine Pila (eds.), *The Oxford Handbook of Intellectual Property Law*, forthcoming.
[37] Menke, *Kritik der Rechte* 15 et seq.
[38] Madison, 19 J. Intell. Prop. L. 1, 29 (2012).
[39] Boldrin & Levine, 2 Review of Economic Research on Copyright Issues 45, 50 (2005) ('socially optimal amount of creative (and in the case of trade marks of marketing) *activity* to take place'); George, 7(1) W.I.P.O.J. 16 (2015) ('thinking clearly about the nature of the imaginary objects

6.2.1 Actors and Actions

With regard to the persons affected by IP rights, a further distinction must be made between the behaviour of right holders and that of third parties who must respect the rights.

6.2.1.1 Innovators and Investors

Regarding innovators and investors, the approach advocated here counteracts an uncritical and inherent commoditisation. The fiction of immaterial commodities is replaced by the regulated activity, whether it is carried out as an entrepreneur or as an employee.

Again, this train of thought refers back to thinking in the privilege age, which was much more concerned than today with the amount of work or effort required to produce the book, machine or other product for which a privilege was sought.[40] However, after romantic outsiders like Karl Philipp Moritz had proclaimed the idea of the self-contained work and this eccentric concept had found broad social recognition due to its suitability as a property object for the emerging markets for books and other reproducible artefacts, the abstract IP object pushed the activity required for its creation further into the background. This objectification was helped by the fact that from the early twentieth century onwards courts declared themselves incapable of making aesthetic or otherwise qualitative assessments of works and other achievements in order to determine whether they were worthy of protection. What remained as the yardstick was economic success, which in case of doubt was sufficient to justify the grant of legal protection.[41] Apart from patent and plant variety protection law, where an official examination of the substantive requirements for protection is carried out, courts assume in case of doubt that a Master Artefact claimed to be worthy of protection – which the parties apparently consider to be so valuable and therefore marketable that they litigate about it – fulfils the

---

created by intellectual property laws might help to improve chances that these laws produce the outcomes that law-makers intend'.).

[40] Sherman & Bently, *The Making of Modern Intellectual Property Law* 173 ('It is not too far from the truth to suggest that mental labour was the most influential organising principle of pre-modern intellectual property law'.). On the primacy of concrete activities and situations in oral societies *see* Ong, *Orality and Literacy*, 42–43, 49.

[41] *See* Bleistein v. Donaldson Lithographing Co., 188 US 239, 252 (1903) ('Yet if they command the interest of any public, they have a commercial value, – it would be bold to say that they have not an aesthetic and educational value, – and the taste of any public is not to be treated with contempt. It is an ultimate fact for the moment, whatever may be our hopes for a change. That these pictures had their worth and their success is sufficiently shown by the desire to reproduce them without regard to the plaintiffs' rights'.); Beebe, 117 Colum. L. Rev. 319 et seq. (2017); *further* Bourdieu, *Market of Symbolic Goods* 1 et seq.; Sherman & Bently, *The Making of Modern Intellectual Property Law* 176 ('growing fear of judgment'); Rehbinder & Peukert, *Urheberrecht* paras 230–32.

requirements for protection.[42] In the end, there is often a circular reasoning from market value to exclusive right of high value.[43]

The labour undertaken or investment spent by the claimant, on the other hand, does not constitute a relevant legal yardstick. Interestingly, this fact is emphasised by observers arguing ontologically – such as Alois Troller, who wrote: 'the achievement, the process of creation is not taken into account at all'.[44] Or Stig Strömholm in his summary of the Scandinavian discussion about Alf Ross' legal realist critique of the 'fiction' of the work: 'The lawyer should leave the process of creation alone'.[45] The situation is only different with regard to the *sui generis* right in databases, for which the claimant must prove a 'substantial investment'.[46] This right is aptly described as a *sui generis* right, since it is not linked to an object, but to an activity – namely an entrepreneurial investment.

The otherwise prevailing ignorance of innovative or entrepreneurial achievements reflects the fact that the exchange value of a good or service in a market economy does not depend on the labour that went into the product but on the demand for it. As explained in Section 6.1.2, this measure of price formation and thus the concept of commoditisation are not criticised here – in contrast to Marxist writings.[47] Moreover, in legal practice it hardly seems possible to make the worthiness of protection of artefacts dependent on the circumstances in which they originated, which are often difficult to ascertain.

And yet at least the justification of IP rights and their teleological assessment in borderline cases should focus on the question which entrepreneurial and other activities are required to bring about a Master Artefact worthy of protection and whether IP rights actually foster this desired behaviour.[48] In principle, this approach is shared by the prevailing view. According to mainstream IP theory, IP rights are legitimate because activities that lead to desired innovations or products should be

---

[42] BGH 20 September 2012 Case no. I ZR 90/09, ZUM-RD 2013, 371 – UniBasic-IDOS; Peukert, Gemeinfreiheit 176 et seq.

[43] Critical Peukert, *Güterzuordnung* 739 et seq. Thus, the decidedly anti-market romantic work concept (*see* in particular Moritz, Werke 1, 255, 274) laid the ground for the total commodification of artistic creativity; on this irony/dialectic *see* Thierse, 36 Weimarer Beiträge 240, 258 (1990).

[44] Troller, 50 UFITA 385, 398 (1967). *See also* Elster, 6 RabelsZ 903, 913–14 (1932); Göpel, *Über Begriff und Wesen des Urheberrechts* 16–17; BGH 2 May 1985 Case no. I ZB 8/84, NJW-RR 1986, 219, 220 (copyright in computer programs protects a work product, not the production process itself); Star Athletica, L.L.C. v. Varsity Brands, Inc., 137 S.Ct. 1002, 1015 (2017) ('The statute's text makes clear, however, that our inquiry is limited to how the article and feature are perceived, not how or why they were designed'.).

[45] Strömholm, GRUR Int. 481, 489 (1963).

[46] *Cf.* Section 87a(1) sentence 1 German Copyright Act (UrhG); recitals 38 et seq. and Art. 7 et seq. Database Dir.

[47] *Cf.* Drahos, Philosophy of IP 95 et seq.; *see also* Pottage & Shermann, *Figures of Invention* 28 et seq.

[48] Heymann, 34 J. Corp. L. 1009, 1012 (2009); Fisher III, 101 Harvard L. Rev. 1659, 1773, 1774 (1988).

rewarded (ex post consideration) or promoted (ex ante consideration). In the practical application of the law, however, this activity – apart from the *sui generis* database law – is not taken into account. All that counts is the finished object: the work, the invention, the design, the sound carrier etc. Whether an author is a civil servant, a scientist or a freelance artist, whether an inventive improvement was achieved by chance in the course of an official activity or after billions of euros in investment, is not even of secondary relevance with regard to the worthiness of the protection of the works and inventions.[49]

This ignorance is problematic.[50] The strict separation of the activity from its result should not be abolished but made more permeable by an action- and artefact-based IP theory. For economic analysis, this means that IP rights should not only be discussed in the context of current law as a solution to a property problem, but should always be focused on the scarcity of innovative entrepreneurial skills, sunk opportunity costs and alternative possibilities for appropriating innovation and investment rents.[51] Legal protection is only necessary if desired innovations and investments are not made under competitive conditions.[52] A realistic and instrumental approach to IP rights does not even have difficulty in recognising that far-reaching legal protection creates misdirected incentives in such a way that too many resources are channelled into certain fields of activity, while other areas that are just as important for society as a whole are neglected. It is sufficient to refer to the oversupply of journalists and artists and the undersupply in many areas of traditional

---

[49] *But see* Section 38(4) German Copyright Act (UrhG) ('The author of a scientific contribution which results from research activities at least half of which were financed by public funds and which was reprinted in a collection which is published periodically at least twice per year also has the right, if he has granted the publisher or editor an exclusive right of use, to make the contribution available to the public upon expiry of 12 months after first publication in the accepted manuscript version, unless this serves a commercial purpose. The source of the first publication must be cited. Any deviating agreement to the detriment of the author shall be ineffective'.); Sections 40–42 German Employee Inventions Act (ArbnErfG) (special provisions for inventions made by civil servants and university employees).

[50] van Eechoud, The Work of Authorship 7 ('One might be forgiven to think that, being concerned with (the study of) regulating creative practices, legal scholars of copyright as well as policymakers are deeply interested in how works get made, how authors operate. But there is remarkably little in the way of academic publications and policy documents to show that this is in fact so'.).

[51] Boldrin & Levine, 2 Review of Economic Research on Copyright Issues 45, 50 (2005) ('The issue here is not what makes creators richer or as rich as possible, but how to allocate to them enough of the sur- plus from creative activity so that they have the incentive to carry it out efficiently, from a social view point'.); Scotchmer, *Innovation and Inventives* 39, 58, 59; Benkler, Networks 39 et seq.; Nazari-Khanachayi, *Rechtfertigungsnarrative des Urheberrechts* 107 et seq. (copyright should not focus on the homo oeconomicus but on the 'homo creativus'); Rachum-Twaig, 27 Fordham Intell. Prop. Media & Ent. L.J. 287 et seq. (2017); Fromer, 104 Nw. U. L. Rev. 1441. 1443 (2010); Gross, Harvard Business School Working Paper 16–109 1 ('competition unambiguously motivates creativity, but ... heavy competition discourages further investment').

[52] BGH 19 November 2015 Case no. I ZR 149/14, GRUR 2016, 725 para. 28 – Pippi Langstrumpf II; Peukert, *Güterzuordnung* 812 et seq.; Scotchmer, *Innovation and Inventives* 283.

trades, or the phenomenon of neglected diseases.[53] A neutral perspective on these phenomena is precisely the advantage of the approach suggested here. It shifts the normative assessments of external reality to where they belong, namely to law, while the subject matter of law is again perceived as what it *should* be from the legal perspective: an external, brute fact.

6.2.1.2 Manufacture and Use of Secondary Artefacts by Third Parties

The de-commoditisation and de-normativisation of the subject matter of IP rights also opens up a different view on those who have to observe IP rights. Their behaviour is no longer considered only in terms of whether they have interfered in the scope of protection of copyrights etc. without authorisation by the right holder. Rather, they finally emerge on the scene as actors who make use of their own cognitive abilities and their own resources to produce or otherwise use artefacts. Conscious copying may be considered unjustified in many – but by no means all – constellations, as the public domain status of formerly protected innovations proves. In the case of independently generated innovations or investments without knowledge of the Master Artefact, additional grounds for a verdict of illegality are already required.[54] The same applies to follow-on innovations and other changes to the Master Artefact. Why should an IP rights holder be able to control the creation and further use of artefacts that were produced by the alleged infringer and that differ from the Master Artefact?[55] In trademark law, the corresponding question is whether the prohibition of the allegedly infringing use of a sign contributes to ensuring undistorted but intense competition.[56] An action- and artefact-based IP theory does not imply a specific answer to such questions. However, it prevents a tendency towards self-referential reasoning, which perceives the objects of protection in isolation rather than embedded in a context of social practices. Such a holistic perspective favours an informed and appropriate decision.

The change of perspective advocated here is not only restating the general and ultimately trivial requirement that a legal assessment should, as far as possible, take into account all relevant circumstances. The plea to not consider reproductive and

---

[53] Lunney, Jr., 49 Vand. L. Rev. 483 (1996); J. Cohen, 94 Texas L. Rev. 1, 33 (2015).
[54] On the disclosure requirement in patent law Schneider, MittdtschPatAnw 49 et seq. (2016).
[55] *See* Kant (1785), *in* Bently & Kretschmer (eds.) *Primary Sources on Copyright* www.copyrighthistory.org 13 et seq.; Ortland, 52 DZPhil 773, 791 (2005); Laskowska & Mania, 132 Prace z prawa własności intelektualnej 91, 102 (2016); J. Cohen, 94 Texas L. Rev. 1, 32 et seq. (2015); Balganesh, 122 Harv. L. Rev. 1569, 1571 (2009) ('this Article proposes a test of "foreseeable copying" to limit copyright's grant of exclusivity to situations where a copier's use was reasonably foreseeable at the time of creation – the point when the incentive is meant to operate'.); Balganesh, 117 Colum. L. Rev. 1 (2017); Beebe, 117 Colum. L. Rev. 319, 385 (2017) ('that aesthetic labor in itself is its own reward and that the facilitation of more such labor represents progress').
[56] *See* Section 5.1.1.1.

imitative activities solely under the rubric of a possible encroachment with a sphere of ownership rather reflects a peculiarity of the subject matter of IP rights, which can be well described on the basis of the view represented here. According to this view, neither the creation of new Master Artefacts leading to legal protection nor the production and use of identical or similar Secondary Artefacts take place in a vacuum. Innovations, investments and reproductions always form part of a network of communicative or entrepreneurial activities that must be regulated as such if the intended effects are to be achieved and undesirable side effects avoided. Consumptive and transformative uses of Master Artefacts should therefore be conceived of as integral parts of the social reality regulated by IP rights.

In this respect, too, IP rights and their subject matter differ from real property ownership. True, tangible objects are also allocated not for their own sake, but because of their significance for the individual and society as a whole. In the case of real property, it nevertheless seems justified to regulate the behaviour of non-owners primarily from the perspective of the prohibited influence on the tangible property. For this perspective pays tribute to the fact that the safeguarding of the owner's expectation of being able to proceed with their property at will, and without disruption, has a legitimate status of its own. Beyond any social purpose, real property ownership has the important (if not ultimate) aim of enabling the owner to lead an isolated life by the lonely consumption of things.[57] This way of enjoying ownership does not apply to IP rights. Their purpose is to regulate uses in relation to a *publicly known* Master Artefact. The interest of an author, inventor or designer to practise their creativity and innovative capacity separately from the world only for themself is not protected by IP rights. The legal bases for this are real property, personality rights and the protection of secrecy. IP rights, in contrast, only take effect after a right holder has knowingly and deliberately published the Master Artefact, and has thus entered into a social context that must not be ignored in the subsequent legal assessment.

This social context is communicative and/or competitive. Works, inventions and trademarks communicate something. Works linguistically, visually or otherwise aesthetically express meaning (the copyright-free 'idea', the Kantian 'speech'),[58]

---

[57] Menke, *Kritik der Rechte* 381 et seq.
[58] Kant (1785), in Bently & Kretschmer (eds.) *Primary Sources on Copyright* www.copyrighthistory .org 13 ('The writing of someone else, however, is the speech of that person (opera) ...'); Drassinower, *What's Wrong with Copying?* 8 with reference to Kant (1785), in Bently & Kretschmer (eds.) *Primary Sources on Copyright* www.copyrighthistory.org 1 et seq.; Peukert, *Festschrift 50 Jahre UrhG* 305, 314, 315 with further references; Stallberg, *Urheberrecht und moralische Rechtfertigung* 308 et seq. (works as complex speech acts); Star Athletica, LLC v. Varsity Brands, Inc., 137 S.Ct. 1002, 1013 with note 2 (2017) ('A drawing of a shovel could, of course, be copyrighted. And, if the shovel included any artistic features that could be perceived as art apart from the shovel, and which would qualify as protectable pictorial, graphic, or sculpturalworks on their own or in another medium, they too could be copyrighted. But a shovel as a shovel cannot'.).

inventions teach technical solutions,[59] and trademarks inform about the origin of products and convey an image.[60] Through the initially one-sided act of publication, the artistic, technical and commercial Master Artefacts enter into a social, communicative context.[61] The one-sided message of rights holders or their contractual partners is, however, only the first step in at least a two-act, communicative process. The message must be perceived and understood by a recipient. Only then is the communication complete.[62] Accordingly, the purely private consumption of works, inventions and trademarks already constitutes a conduct which has an intrinsic value and deserves consideration – not only as a connecting factor for determining the asset value of the use, but also as a second, indispensable part of a communication process initiated by the rights holder. Consequently, IP rights leave otherwise lawful private consumption unaffected.[63]

Further feedback and follow-up communications then presuppose that the recipients of the Master Artefact actively feed their Secondary Artefacts into the social dialogue in unchanged or changed form as well as possibly in new communication contexts. It is only through these reactions that a socially accepted idea of what characterises a work of art or a well-known brand is constituted.[64] Because there is a public interest in this enrichment of communication, IP rights are subject to numerous exceptions and limitations – for example, with regard to quotations and artistic collages, experiments and trademark parodies.[65]

---

[59] BGH 27 March 1969 Case No. X ZB 15/67, GRUR 1969, 672, 673; BGH 30 June 2015 Case no. X ZB 1/15, GRUR 2015, 983 para. 27 – Flugzeugstand; BGH 27 September 2016 Case no. X ZR 124/15, GRUR 2017, 261 para. 21. contra Drassinower, *What's Wrong with Copying?* 64–65 (the invention as a 'relation between a person and an object').

[60] Matal v. Tam, 137 S.Ct. 1744, 1752 (2017) ('trademarks often consist[ed] of catchy phrases that convey a message'); Peukert, *Festschrift Fezer* 405, 419–20 with further references; Fezer, Markenrecht Einl D paras. 29–30 ('The trademark ... communicates a message'.); Hellmann, Soziologie der Marke 431–32; Drassinower, *What's Wrong with Copying?* 80 et seq.

[61] On copyrighted works *see* BVerfG 31 May 2016 Case no. 1 BvR 1585/13, GRUR 2016, 690 para. 87 – Metall auf Metall with further references ('... once a work is published it is no longer its owner's sole disposal, but enters the social sphere, just as it was intended to do, and can thereby become an independent factor that helps define the cultural and intellectual scene of its era. As over time, the work is no longer only subject to disposal under private law and becomes common intellectual and cultural property, the author must accept that it will increasingly serve as a link to an artistic dialogue'.); CJEU Case C-476/17 Pelham and others, ECLI:EU:C:2019:624, para 71 (by quoting a work, one enters 'into "dialogue" with that work').

[62] Luhmann, *Gesellschaft der Gesellschaft* 80 et seq.

[63] Rehbinder & Peukert, *Urheberrecht* paras 420 et seq., 690 et seq.; on the freedom of acts done privately and for non-commercial purposes regarding patented inventions and other subject matter of industrial property rights *see e.g.* Sections 11 no. 1 German Patent Act (PatG), 40 no. 1 German Design Act (DesignG); *see also* Biagioli, 86 Notre Dame L. Rev. 1847, 1860 (2011); Tushnet, 114 Yale L.J. 535 (2004).

[64] Peukert, *Festschrift Fezer* 405, 420 (trademark rights as exclusive rights in the outcome of a social process); on artworks in this sense *see* Fisher III, 101 Harvard L. Rev. 1659, 1768 et seq. (1988).

[65] *See* Sections 24 (free uses), 51 (quotations) German Copyright Act (UrhG); BVerfG 31 May 2016 Case no. 1 NvR 1585/13, GRUR 2016, 690, paras. 81 et seq. – Metall auf Metall; Porter, 49 British Journal of Aesthetics 1 et seq. (2009); Young, 55 British Journal of Aesthetics 1 (2015);

At the same time, these uses of Secondary Artefacts have economic value, are often commercial in kind, and, in any case, subject to the law of scarcity. Works, inventions and trademarks enter not only into a scientific, artistic and commercial communicative context, but also into a network of interrelated competitive practices which, taken as a whole, make up the market. Only this network of economic practices is at issue when phonograms, plant varieties and designs, which communicate no meaning, are reproduced and otherwise used. Since this employment of resources of non-owners satisfies economic and other needs, it has some legitimacy.[66] Even taking into account that innovators and investors must be in a position to appropriate their innovation and investment benefits in line with market conditions, IP rights should always be designed in such a way that they do not restrict but promote intensive, undistorted and otherwise legal competition between providers of substitute artefacts.[67] In trademark law, this aspect is still an inherent aspect of the law. Otherwise, these concerns are largely outsourced to competition law.[68]

The dominant paradigm of the abstract IP object capable of being owned also pushes these social contexts into the background. Instead of considering a similarity relationship between a Master Artefact and Secondary Artefacts created by third parties with their own resources, the prevailing opinion assumes an object with largely indefinite boundaries, which is allocated exclusively to a rights holder. This way of looking at things is fixated on the object of property and does not place the allegedly infringing activities in a communicative-competitive context.[69] This increases the danger that IP rights interrupt networked communication and competitive processes so often or so profoundly that social and business exchange comes to a complete standstill – a scenario that is unfortunately by no means unrealistic.[70]

Barron, 15 Social & Legal Studies 25, 32 et seq. (2006). For an aesthetic critique on the abstract work concept *see* Thierse, 36 Weimarer Beiträge 240, 259 (1990); Pudelek, *in* Barck et al (eds.) *Ästhetische Grundbegriffe* VI 523 et seq. with further references. On lawful experimental uses *see* Sections 11 no. 2 German Patent Act (PatG), 40 no. 2 German Design Act (DesignG). On trademark parodies *see* Art. 14(1)(c) EU Trademark Dir.; BGH 2 April 2015 Case no. I ZR 59/13, GRUR 2015, 1114 paras. 44 et seq. – Springender Pudel with further references.

[66] Boldrin & Levine, 2 Review of Economic Research on Copyright Issues 45, 48 et seq. (2005).
[67] Tamura, Nordic Journal of Commercial Law 1, 7 (2012).
[68] *See* Section 5.1.1.1 as well as Sections 44a no. 1, 55, 56, 58 German Copyright Act (UrhG) and Section 24 German Patent Act (PatG).
[69] *Cf.* BVerfG 29 June 2000 Case no. 1 BvR 825/98, MMR 2000, 686, 687 – Germania 3; BVerfG 31 May 2016 Case no. 1 BvR 1585/13, GRUR 2016, 690 para. 81 et seq. – Metall auf Metall; BGH 3 February 2005 Case no. I ZR 159/02, NJW 2005, 2856, 2857 – Lila Postkarte.
[70] On hyperlinking *see* CJEU Case C-160/15 GS Media BV v. Sanoma (and others), ECLI:EU:C:2016:644 para. 31; generally Peukert, 1 GRUR-Beilage 77, 92–93 (2014) with further references. On the refusal to license standard essential patents *see* CJEU Case C-170/13 Huawei Technologies v. ZTE, ECLI:EU:C:2015:477 paras. 477 et seq., LG Mannheim 17 November 2016 Case no. 7 O 19/16, BeckRS 2016, 108197. On the lawfulness of using protected trademarks in comparative advertising *see* CJEU Joined Cases C-236/08–238/08 Google France v. Louis Vuitton Malletier, Google France v. Viaticum and Luteciel, Google France v. Centre national de recherche en relations humains et al, ECLI:EU:C:2010:159 paras 95–98; CJEU Case C-323/09 Interflora v. Marks & Spencer, ECLI:EU:C:2011:604 para. 64.

6.2.2 Master Artefacts, Secondary Artefacts and Similarity

The view taken here, in addition to the actors and their behaviour, also focuses on the artefacts of IP law. The prevailing view is that both the Master Artefact – such as the original of a work of art, the patent specification and other entries in IP registers – and Secondary Artefacts such as copies and other reproductions are merely accidental embodiments of the abstract IP object, the boundaries of which are not definitively fixed by all these manifestations. An artefact-based IP theory, in which the Master Artefact forms the central anchor and point of reference, and in which a comparison with concretely challenged Secondary Artefacts according to statutory criteria decides about an infringement, eliminates such abstractions and thus limits possibilities for legal manipulations of the subject matter and scope of IP protection. The reality of IP law consists solely of brute facts, of physical and corporeal objects, and of human behaviour. These artefacts – which are ontologically clearly defined and accessible to evidence taking – offer a more stable basis for legal decisions than fictions based on declarative speech acts and their social recognition. A realistic IP theory is therefore conducive to legal certainty.

Firstly, this concerns the definition of the subject matter of protection, which should be strictly oriented towards a Master Artefact and its external features. In the case of rights that arise informally, it is thus decisive, which prototype (the original or a faithful copy of it) the rights holder submits in an infringement proceeding.[71] If several different exemplars of a work, design or trademark are submitted, the judge may not abstract from these tokens and consider a merely declared but unproven tertium to be the object of protection. Rather, each Master Artefact must be assessed separately regarding its protectability.

Even more practically relevant is the concept of the Master Artefact with regard to registered rights. Here there are at least two potential connecting factors for determining the subject matter and scope of legal protection – namely the product or process actually invented or designed or the sign used in the course of trade etc. on the one hand, and the patent claim or other entry in the register on the other. However, if IP rights make legal protection dependent on formal registration, then only this act can form the authoritative basis of the Master Artefact. The actually invented, designed or used artefact can, instead, only become legally relevant in another legal context – in particular in unfair competition law.[72]

In patent law even this specification of the subject matter of protection does not suffice. This is because the invented product or process is not registered in the form of two- or three-dimensional drawings or models plus descriptions, but primarily in

---

[71] Section 5.1.2.1.
[72] Contra Hetmank, 7 ZGE 460, 472 (2015); Liivak, 42 Seton Hall L. Rev. 1, 5 (2012); Cotropia, 53 Wm. & Mary L. Rev. 1855, 1856 (2012).

the form of written patent claims.[73] The translation of brute technical artefacts into human language (claims and descriptions) leads to a permanent and fundamental uncertainty as to how the subject matter of protection is to be defined.[74] This situation – which negatively impacts both the rightful owner and the general public – should be improved by replacing written patent claims by two- or three-dimensional (possibly also video-animated) representations of the invented product or process, which are to be explained by mathematical-scientific signs (numbers, formulae etc.) and only additionally by linguistic descriptions.[75] This is because models, numbers and measures help to 'define the objective success to be achieved according to the invention more precisely and, if necessary, more narrowly than would be the case with mere verbal paraphrasing'.[76] The same applies to all other registered rights. These considerations imply that it is generally time to bring apparently subordinate, practical procedural regulations on the use and presentation of registered Master Artefacts to the centre of legal attention.[77]

The sensitivity towards the brute facts of IP law demanded here also applies to the artefacts produced or used by those who have to respect IP rights. Whether these third parties infringe an IP right depends, as explained, on a comparison between the Master Artefact and Secondary Artefacts, which comparison ultimately defines the scope of protection of the IP right at stake. If there is sufficient similarity, the use of a Secondary Artefact is infringing. If this is not the case, a legally independent artefact of the opposing party is in dispute, whose use is not subject to an authorisation of the rights holder, because his privilege does not extend so far.[78] Both results do not follow from an abstract, inherently normative concept of a work, invention or sign. The purpose of the action- and artefact-based IP theory advocated here is to remind legal practice of this legal realist credo.

---

[73] Cf. Art. 78(1) lit. d EPC, Section 34(3) no. 5 German Patent Act (PatG), Art. 7 PCT ('(1) Subject to the provisions of paragraph (2)(ii), drawings shall be required when they are necessary for the understanding of the invention. (2) Where, without being necessary for the understanding of the invention, the nature of the invention admits of illustration by drawings: (i) the applicant may include such drawings in the international application when filed, (ii) any designated Office may require that the applicant file such drawings with it within the prescribed time limit'; Kraßer & Ann, *Patentrecht* 514, 752.

[74] Section 5.4.3.

[75] Pottage & Sherman, in Howe & Griffiths (eds.) *Concepts of Property* 11, 27, 28. *But see* Art. 27(1) PCT ('No national law shall require compliance with requirements relating to the form or contents of the international application different from or additional to those which are provided for in this Treaty and the Regulations'.)

[76] BGH 12 March 2002 Case no. X ZR 43/01, GRUR 2002, 511, 512 – Kunststoffrohrteil with further references.

[77] Fromer, 76 Chicago L. Rev. 719 et seq. (2009).

[78] Sections 5.1.2.2 and 5.1.2.3.

Summary in Theses

1. 'Intellectual property' (IP) law is based on a specific understanding of non-legal reality. According to this ontology, immaterial goods such as works, inventions and designs exist as abstract types which are to be strictly distinguished from their embodiments in books, products etc.[1]
2. These abstract IP objects are allocated to the rights holder according to the model of real property ownership. The legal structures of real property ownership and IP rights are therefore the same. Both types of property rights are transferable exclusive rights with a statutorily defined scope, the infringement of which triggers secondary remedies. The constitutional and philosophical justifications of real and intellectual property also run largely in parallel.[2]
3. At the same time, IP rights differ from real property rights in many respects. In particular, they are of limited duration (rights in innovation) or are subject to a use requirement (trademark law). Even the *Grundnorm* of the two fields of law differs: all tangible things are owned by someone or can be (re)appropriated, while IP rights are an exception to the principle of the public domain.[3]
4. Furthermore, unlike real property ownership, IP rights cannot be justified by the protection of legitimately acquired possession. Economic analysis also stresses the special characteristics of works, inventions etc. as non-rivalrous and non-exclusive public goods. Even the concept of scarcity is different from that regarding tangible things. Scarcity does not exist with regard to the availability of already existing works, inventions etc., but with regard to not yet created, future innovations or signs.[4]

---

[1] *See* Section 1.1.
[2] Ibid.
[3] *See* Section 1.2.
[4] Ibid.

5. These legal and justificatory differences cannot themselves be explained by legal and philosophical considerations. Rather, they are an expression of a categorically different mode of existence of immaterial objects compared to tangible and other physical, corporeal objects ('things' and 'other objects' within the meaning of the German Civil Code, BGB). Since the peculiar character of IP rights cannot be made understandable on the basis of the prevailing paradigm of the abstract IP object, this ontology must be subjected to a critical examination.[5]
6. Overall, efforts in this direction have remained rare. The fictional character of the abstract work and other immaterial objects has been pointed out on various occasions. An alternative ontology and corresponding legal theory that claims validity for the entire area of IP law has not been presented so far.[6]
7. There is an extensive philosophical literature that deals in particular with the ontological status of works of art. Its exponents assume that the common talk of immaterial works of art represents an actually existing entity. This object is explained as an abstract type, which is manifested accidentally in tokens such as books or machines, but exists independently of them.[7]
8. An examination of this classical-metaphysical object ontology, however, shows that it cannot hold out its thesis of a copyrightable work as an abstract type without contradiction. For even in the opinion of its advocates, copyrightable works and other subject matter of IP rights do not exhibit the characteristics of abstract types or universals according to general metaphysics. Firstly, the objects of protection of IP law are the result of certain human actions, and they have an effect, they are therefore not acausal. Secondly, works and other immaterial objects are dependent in their temporal existence on the existence of at least one physical or mental token (embodiment, instantiation). But then, for reasons of internal theoretical consistency, they cannot be considered abstract objects/types. On the one hand we speak, think and regulate as if there were an abstract IP object, on the other hand the existence of such an object cannot be made plausible.[8]
9. This apparent contradiction dissolves when, in contrast to metaphysical object ontology, one assumes that humans can create a social reality – such as the reality of the idea of the abstract immaterial good – that is to some extent decoupled from brute, physical reality. The US philosopher

---

[5] See Section 1.3.
[6] See Sections 1.4 and 1.5.
[7] See Section 2.1.1.
[8] See Section 2.1.3.

John R. Searle provides an elaborate theory for such an understanding: He distinguishes between an observer-*independent*, 'brute' reality of scientifically measurable facts on the one hand and an observer-*dependent*, language-based and socially constructed reality of 'institutional' facts on the other.[9]

10. An application of Searle's social ontology to the subject of this study shows that immaterial objects as the subject matter of IP laws and rights belong to the latter category of institutional facts. Works, inventions etc. are not objects that exist in brute, external reality, but language-based constructs that only exist – and this reality is not denied here – because and as far as people speak and think as if there were immaterial works, inventions etc. The starting point of this social construction is a declarative speech act: According to this assertion, a tangible or otherwise physical artefact such as a book, a machine or a digital file does not stand for itself, but embodies/represents an abstract work, an abstract invention etc., which exists independently of the exemplar. If this declaration is acknowledged by third parties, it, and with it the abstract IP object, becomes social reality.[10]

11. If it is true that not only IP *law* is a language-based, social construct, but already its perceived subject matter – the immaterial good ('intellectual property') – then this latter institutional fact should also have a history that can be reconstructed in its logic and historically proven. And indeed, a diachronic analysis confirms that the thinking in categories of abstract IP objects has a history.[11]

12. In that regard, a distinction must be made between two levels of abstraction. A first, very old and permanently repeated language practice is to signify a multitude of brute artefacts with a general signifier. This naming process can be divided into three logical steps. At the beginning there is the change of external reality by man in the form of the creation of a new artefact, such as a new digital file, a three-dimensional model etc. Some of these artefacts are preserved and specifically named by the creator or a third party (Master Artefact). Finally, identical and sufficiently similar artefacts (copies and imitations) are designated by the name of the Master Artefact (Secondary Artefacts). Both the status of the Master Artefact and that of the Secondary Artefacts are results of often-contentious social-negotiation processes. All corresponding signifiers refer to brute reality. The signified is always a single artefact or a plurality of artefacts with a brute

---

[9] See Section 2.2.1.
[10] See Section 2.2.2.
[11] See Chapter 3.

physical or mental existence. The legal counterpart of this first level abstraction is the early modern privilege.[12]

13. The abstract IP object and its legal counterpart, IP laws/rights, are the result of a second process of abstraction that began in the late Middle Ages and, according to generally accepted legal-historical knowledge, was only completed in the course of the eighteenth century. Its conditions were, firstly, reproductive technologies such as book printing, which generated a need for regulation; secondly, the replacement of the mimesis idea by a generally positive connotation of the new, ideally created by geniuses; and thirdly, the emergence of anonymous markets where any input and output must be tradable, including the achievements of those who bring about reproducible Master Artefacts.[13]

14. The formation of today's concepts of the copyrightable work and the patentable invention can firstly be observed etymologically. The words 'work', 'invention' and *disegno/Muster* (design) were already familiar before the eighteenth century. At that time, however, they did not designate an abstract, immaterial object capable of being owned, but physical achievements worth mentioning whose production and use were regulated via privileges. The idea of a self-contained, and at the same time immaterial, abstract work of art was first formulated by Romantic authors (Edward Young, Karl Philipp Moritz). This new semantics then influenced the idea that technical inventions, designs and other subject matter of today's IP law also exist as abstract types. This object ontology quickly gained social recognition because it provided the art, literature, and technology markets that formed in the *Sattelzeit* with the necessary commodity.[14]

15. The new object of ownership was first incorporated into law in France. The conceptual ground for the legal innovation had already been laid during the ancien régime. The paradigm that now prevails worldwide was codified for the first time in the French Revolutionary Laws on patents and authors' rights of 1791 and 1793 respectively.[15]

16. The formation of the idea of abstract IP objects was less straightforward in common law jurisdictions. Both the Statute of Monopolies (1624) and the Statute of Anne 'for the Encouragement of Learning' (1710) still operated with the understanding of reality of the former privilege system. The acts regulated the production of 'new manufacture' or granted authors 'the sole Right and Liberty of Printing [a] Book'. The

---

[12] See Section 3.1.
[13] See Section 3.2.1.
[14] See Section 3.2.2.1.
[15] See Section 3.2.2.2.1.

ontological status of the subject matter of these regulations remained unclear for a long time and was a central issue in the battle of the booksellers in the eighteenth century. The abstract concepts of work and invention only found their way into British and US law in the nineteenth century as legal transplants from France.[16]

17. Regarding German law, the intense debate about the (il)legality of the reprinting of books [sic] proves that the new concept – ownership of the abstract work – had not yet been brought to the fore in the late eighteenth century, let alone that it was socially recognised. The turning point in this regard was marked only by the Prussian Copyright Act of 1837.[17]

18. The ontological and historical analyses result in two competing understandings of reality: the dominant paradigm of the abstract IP object on the one hand and on the other an approach based on actions and artefacts, as it was predominant in the early modern period. These ontologies can be examined from a legal-theoretical point of view. The question is which ontology has the better legal explanatory power?[18]

19. Copyright law in particular, but also patent and design law and related areas such as utility model and semiconductor chip protection laws, explicitly refer to immaterial works, inventions and designs as objects of protection. These abstract-immaterial goods form the admittedly imaginary legal objects that are exclusively allocated to a rights holder.[19]

20. But already in trademark law this concept is not (yet) fully implemented. Irrespective of all legislative and scholarly rhetoric according to which trademark law constitutes a genuine 'intellectual property right', signs are still not protected as such, but only in a specific context: as product signs in the course of trade. The idea of a commercial sign that has neither a defined external appearance nor a certain meaning is (still) too eccentric to serve as the object of an exclusive property right.[20]

21. In the case of rights protecting innovations, the conceptual difficulties of the prevailing paradigm are of a different kind. In this respect, beyond copyright, patent and design law, it is often unclear what one should imagine as an innovation abstract from physical and mental artefacts.[21]

---

[16] See Section 3.2.2.2.2.
[17] See Section 3.2.2.2.3.
[18] See Chapter 5.
[19] See Section 5.1.
[20] See Section 5.1.1.1.
[21] See Section 5.1.1.2.

22. This problem firstly manifests itself in the case of rights related to copyright. Even according to the dominant paradigm, their proximity to copyrights in works is not ontological. Rather, the continental European separation of authors' rights in works and related/neighbouring rights expresses the fact that artistic performances and various cultural products are perceived and regulated as simple acts and products with a brute, physical existence.[22]

23. The investment that goes into these actions and artefacts is not a suitable starting point for the construction of an abstract IP object. This is because investments of money, time and other resources lack the 'intellectual'. With their measurable, physical existence, they bring about a change in the outside world – the reproducible artefacts to which rights related to copyright attach.[23]

24. Plant variety protection law is also not based on the idea of the abstract IP object. Its reality is a variety, defined as 'a set of plants or parts of plants' whose distinct, homogeneous and stable characteristics are based on a particular genotype that can be scientifically determined.[24]

25. A legal realist, actions- and artefact-based IP theory has better explanatory power than the prevailing paradigm of the abstract IP object. According to this alternative ontology, IP rights are exclusive rights for the production and other use of certain, reproducible artefacts.[25]

26. The conceptually indispensable, uniform object of exclusive IP rights – and thus at the same time the legal realist alternative to the abstract IP object – is the 'Master Artefact'. The term 'Master Artefact' signifies the work exemplars, application documents and register entries that are considered by judges and examiners in order to decide whether the requirements for IP protection are met.[26]

27. Current IP law places different requirements on the way the Master Artefact is presented and claimed [sic]. In some cases, IP rights must be claimed by presenting the original or a faithful copy (informal IP rights, in particular copyright); in others, the application or registration documents (registered rights) are decisive.[27]

28. The uncertainty prevailing in patent law as to the subject matter of a patent is due to the fact that it is already unclear which artefact qualifies for the Master Artefact: what was invented in the form of a drawing or a prototype or what was claimed and granted in the form of a patent

---

[22] Ibid.
[23] Ibid.
[24] Ibid.
[25] See Section 5.1.2.
[26] See Section 5.1.2.1.
[27] Ibid.

specification? In addition, the legal requirement to translate the technical artefact into human language and primarily claim it in this form allows the actors involved to mould the relevant facts almost at will.[28]

29. In order to assess its protectability, the Master Artefact is compared with other artefacts which, according to the findings of the patent office or the opponent's submission, represent purely routine achievements (copyright), earlier priority trademarks, or form part of the state of the art.[29]

30. If this examination reveals that the Master Artefact meets the requirements for IP protection, it is compared in a second step with the allegedly infringing artefact. The subject matter of IP rights is therefore not an imaginary-abstract object, but a similarity relation between independently existing brute artefacts. If a sufficient similarity is found, the challenged artefact is subsumed under the name of the Master Artefact and at the same time under the IP right concerned.[30]

31. However, an infringement of an IP right is only given if the conduct of the alleged infringer is also covered by the codified exclusive or remuneration rights. The relevant provisions even in copyright, patent and design statutes no longer refer to the abstract IP object, but to originals, copies, products and processes realised in machines or organisms which may not be reproduced, performed in public or otherwise used. Private international law confirms this structure based on artefacts and behaviour. It focusses on the place where the infringing act occurred or threatens to occur.[31]

32. If the subject matter of IP rights is understood as a legally established similarity relationship between a Master Artefact and independently existing Secondary Artefacts, the differences between real and 'intellectual' property rights become understandable. The *numerus clausus* of legally admissible dispositions about real property rights does not apply to IP rights because there is no object whose rival use could be blocked by overlapping rights. The classical method of calculating damages according to a measurable difference in asset values does not play a role in IP law because an IP infringement does not affect assets recorded in the rights holder's balance sheet – whereas the Secondary Artefacts, which are challenged as infringing, are owned by the infringer or other third parties.[32]

---

[28] Ibid.
[29] Ibid.
[30] *See* Section 5.1.2.2.
[31] *See* Section 5.1.2.3.
[32] *See* Section 5.2.

33. On the basis of an action- and artefact-based theory, the particularities of the justification of IP rights in comparison to real property ownership can also be made understandable. Unlike property rights in tangible things, IP rights do not protect what the rights holder has in his possession and wants to use undisturbed, but they determine whether third parties require the prior authorisation of the IP rights holder for certain actions, including the use of things such as personal computers belonging to them. The associated restrictions on the freedom of action and ownership can only be justified for a limited period of time and/or in connection with an obligation for the entitled person to exercise the right.[33]

34. Economic analyses that consider the abstract IP object as a resource forming part of external reality are concerned with fictitious problems. The widespread talk of public goods being artificially scarce does not correspond to economic reality. If economics strives to make testable statements about the reality of technical and other innovations, it has to address and study (1) the efficient allocation of human abilities to innovate and to act entrepreneurially, as well as (2) the scarce physical resources needed to produce new artefacts, but also to reproduce and imitate these.[34]

35. The paradigm of the abstract IP object is understood as a representation of reality ('is'), which is regulated by law. With this understanding, the prevailing ontology cannot comprehend that the *raison d'être* of the ontologically and legal-doctrinally implausible immaterial good is its normativity.[35]

36. The normativity of the abstract IP object enables the expansion of the idea of property: without immaterial ('intellectual') objects, no 'intellectual property' law. Because we talk and think as if there were immaterial works etc., we act accordingly. We respect the exclusivity of the rights holder just as that of the owner of movable and immovable things, although the effects of IP and real property rights differ fundamentally. With talking and thinking in terms of immaterial objects that can be owned, all justifications and rhetorical concepts on which real property ownership is based also come into play. The idea of the abstract IP object constitutes and regulates power relations.[36]

37. The normativity of the abstract IP object is not only be proven by historical and linguistic analysis; it is also reflected in the law. For

---

[33] See Section 5.3.1.
[34] See Section 5.3.2.
[35] See Section 5.4.
[36] See Section 5.4.1.

idealistic IP jurisdictions with a fully developed concept of the abstract IP object tend to provide more comprehensive legal protection than physicalist jurisdictions, which in part are still based on the action- and artefact-based concept of the privilege age.[37]

38. To recognise the inherent normativity of the abstract IP object helps to explain further peculiarities of this field of law. One of these peculiarities is the notorious difficulty of distinguishing between is and ought, between legal object and subjective right. The reason for this difficulty is that the perceived reality of IP law is itself already an inherently normative, social construct.[38]

39. If the fictitious reality of IP law is inherently normative, it can be challenged from a normative perspective. In this respect, the question is: Should the law be phrased and practiced as if immaterial objects/types existed?[39]

40. This question must be answered in the negative because otherwise normatively significant distortions of the perception of the regulated reality, of legal structures and their justification will occur. The dominant thinking in terms of goods and ownership favours a 'property logic' that is capable of concealing negative effects of IP rights for individual freedoms and the public interest. An action- and artefact-based IP theory avoids such tendencies and is therefore also normatively preferable.[40]

41. The radical rejection of the dominant ontology, however, must and should not lead to the extreme consequence of dismissing the legal form of the exclusive right. For this form is constitutive for the market economy, which merits preference over centralised planning systems.[41]

42. There is no terminology that avoids the fiction of the abstract IP object, but at the same time adheres to the form of the exclusive right. For lack of alternatives, this book also speaks of 'the' work, 'the' invention, 'the' design etc. To continue naming the objects of protection of IP rights in this way appears justifiable as long as one is only aware that this terminology refers – depending on the context – to all protectable Master Artefacts (general concept of the copyrightable work or the patentable invention) or to a certain Master Artefact and similar Secondary Artefacts with brute physical or mental existence, which are designated by a common general denominator ('Goethe's *Faust*'). A general term that signifies all respective exclusive rights is also not

---

[37] See Section 5.4.2.
[38] See Section 5.4.3.
[39] See Chapter 6.
[40] See Section 6.1.1.
[41] See Section 6.1.2.

available. In the absence of better alternatives, this study speaks of 'IP' rights. What is meant by this internationally accepted abbreviation, however, is nothing more than the sum of the laws granting private exclusive rights in the use of reproducible artefacts.[42]

43. Otherwise, the enigmatic term 'intellectual property' should be avoided. Preferable is the more precise terminology of copyright and industrial property rights, which has prevailed for a long time. If one wants to bring all these rights under a dogmatic umbrella term at all, a renaissance of the concept of the privilege would offer itself, albeit in the context of a democratic society governed by the rule of law.[43]

44. In order to improve the coherence between IP law and its reality, a new understanding and perspective on the subject matter of IP rights is needed. A legal realist IP theory provides the tools for this. Instead of assuming the existence of an abstract and indeterminate IP object, IP theory and practice should focus on the *actors* involved, their *actions* and the *artefacts* they use.[44]

45. The philosophical justification of IP rights and their teleological assessment in borderline cases should focus on the question of which *innovation* or *investment* is needed to bring about a Master Artefact worthy of protection, and to what extent IP rights favour this desired behaviour.[45]

46. Furthermore, non-owners who have to respect IP rights should no longer merely appear as potential infringers but also as *actors* using their own cognitive skills and other resources to *produce* or otherwise *use artefacts*. This approach also reveals the social contexts in which already the creation of the Master Artefact is embedded.[46]

47. Finally, a legal realist IP theory puts brute *artefacts* in the forefront. This includes both the Master Artefact – such as the original of a work of art, the patent specification and other register entries – and Secondary Artefacts such as copies and other imitations of originals. These artefacts are suitable for evidence-taking and thus provide a more stable basis for legal practice than purely language-based fictions. A realistic IP theory therefore also contributes to legal certainty.[47]

---

[42] See Section 6.1.3.
[43] Ibid.
[44] See Section 6.2.
[45] See Section 6.2.1.1.
[46] See Section 6.2.1.2.
[47] See Section 6.2.2.

Bibliography

Abbott, Frederick M., 'Rethinking Patents: From "Intellectual Property" to "Private Taxation Scheme"', in Peter Drahos, Gustavo Ghidini & Hanns Ullrich (eds.), *Kritika: Essays on Intellectual Property* (Cheltenham: Edward Elgar Publishing, 2015), pp. 1–16.

Albers, Irene & Bernd Busch, 'Fotografie/fotografisch', in Karlheinz Barck et al. (eds.), *Ästhetische Grundbegriffe* (ÄGB), Vol. 2 (Berlin: Akademie-Verlag, 2001), pp. 494–550.

Alexander, Isabella & H. Tomás Gómez-Arostegui, *Research Handbook on the History of Copyright Law* (Cheltenham: Edward Elgar Publishing, 2016).

Alexander-Katz, Richard, 'Die zeitliche Begrenzung der Immaterial-Güterrechte. Ein Beitrag zur Theorie dieser Rechte', in *Festgabe der Rechtsanwaltschaft des Kammergerichts für den Geheimen Justizrath Dr. Richard Wilke* (Berlin: Vahlen, 1900), pp. 1–45.

Aoki, Keith, 'Adrift in the Intertext: Authorship and Audience "Recoding Rights" - Comment on the Robert H. Rotstein, "Beyond Metaphor: Copyright Infringement and the Fiction of the Work"' (1993), 68 *Chicago-Kent Law Review*, 805–39.

Aristotle, *Poetics*, reprint (Harmondsworth: Penguin Books, 1996).

Baecker, Dirk, 'Kommunikation', in Karlheinz Barck et al. (eds.), *Ästhetische Grundbegriffe* (ÄGB), Vol. 3 (Berlin: Akademie-Verlag, 2001), pp. 384–426.

Bahr, Amrei, 'Was heißt "ein Artefakt illegitim kopieren"? Grundlagen einer artefaktbezogenen Ethik des Kopierens' (2013), 61 *Deutsche Zeitschrift für Philosophie*, 283–99.

Balganesh, Shyamkrishna, 'Foreseeability and Copyright Incentives' (2009), 122 *Harvard Law Review*, 1569–1633.

'The Normativity of Copying in Copyright Law' (2012), 62 *Duke Law Journal*, 203–84.

'Alienability and Copyright Law', in Helena R. Howe & Jonathan Griffiths (eds.), *Concepts of Property in Intellectual Property Law* (West Nyack: Cambridge University Press, 2013), pp. 161–81.

'Causing Copyright' (2017), 117 *Columbia Law Review*, 1–77.

Barron, Anne, 'Commodification and Cultural Form: Film Copyright Revisited' (2004), 52 *New Formations*, 58–81.

'The Legal Properties of Film' (2004), 67 *Modern Law Review*, 177–208.

'Copyright Law's Musical Work' (2006), 15 *Social and Legal Studies*, 101–27.

'Introduction: Harmony or Dissonance? Copyright Concepts and Musical Practice' (2006), 15 *Social and Legal Studies*, 25–51.

'Copyright Infringement, "Free-Riding" and the Lifeworld', in Lionel Bently, Jennifer Davis & Jane C. Ginsburg (eds), *Copyright and Piracy: An Interdisciplinary Critique* (Cambridge: Cambridge University Press, 2010), pp. 93–127.

'Kant, Copyright and Communicative Freedom' (2012), 31 *Law and Philosophy*, 1–48.

Barthes, Roland, 'From Work to Text', in Roland Barthes (ed.), *Image, Music, Text* (New York: Hill and Wang, 1988), pp. 155–64.

Bartsch, Michael, 'Software als Rechtsgut. Zur Wahrnehmung von Software aus Sicht des Rechts, zur Begriffsbildung im Recht und zu den praktischen Konsequenzen' (2010), 9 CR, 553–59.

Baudrillard, Jean, *The Consumer Society: Myths and Structures* (London: Sage, 1998).

Becker, Rudolf Zacharias, *Das Eigenthumsrecht an Geisteswerken mit einer dreyfachen Beschwerde über das Bischöflich-Augsburgische Vikariat wegen Nachdruck, Verstümmelung und Verfälschung des Noth- und Hilfsbüchleins* (Frankfurt, 1789).

Becq, Annie, 'Creation, Aesthetics, Market: Origins of the Modern Concept of Art', in Paul Mattick Jr (ed.), *Eighteenth-Century Aesthetics and the Reconstruction of Art* (Cambridge: Cambridge University Press, 1993), pp. 240–54.

Beebe, Barton, 'The Semiotic Analysis of Trademark Law' (2004), 51 *UCLA Law Review*, 621–704.

'The Semiotic Account of Trademark Doctrine and Trademark Culture', in Graeme B. Dinwoodie & Mark D. Janis (eds.), *Trademark Law and Theory. A Handbook of Contemporary Research* (Cheltenham: Edward Elgar Publishing, 2008), pp. 42–64.

'Bleistein, the Problem of Aesthetic Progress, and the Making of American Copyright Law' (2017), 117 *Columbia Law Review*, 319–97.

de Beer, Jeremy, 'Evidence-Based Intellectual Property Policymaking: An Integrated Review of Methods and Conclusions' (2016), 19 *The Journal of World Intellectual Property*, 150–77.

Bell, Tom W., 'Indelicate Imbalancing in Copyright and Patent Law', in Adam Thierer & Clyde Wayne Crews Jr (eds.), *Copy Fights: The Future of Intellectual Property in the Information Age* (Washington, DC: Cato Institute, 2002), pp. 1–16.

'Copyright as Intellectual Property Privilege' (2008), 58 *Syracuse Law Review*, 523–46.

Bellido, Jose, 'Looking Right: The Art of Visual Literacy in British Copyright Litigation' (2014), 10 *Law, Culture and the Humanities*, 66–87.

Bendel-Larcher, Sylvia, 'Vom Unkraut zum Epistem – Wie Sprache Wirklichkeit schafft', in René John, Jana Rückert-John & Elena Esposito (eds.), *Ontologien der Moderne* (Wiesbaden: Springer VS, 2013), pp. 55–74.

Benkard, Georg, *Patentgesetz* (Munich: C. H. Beck, 2015).

Benkler, Yochai, *The Wealth of Networks* (New Haven, CT: Yale University Press, 2006).

Bently, Lionel, 'From Communication to Thing: Historical Aspects of the Conceptualisation of Trademarks as Property', in Graeme B. Dinwoodie & Mark D. Janis (eds.), *Trademark and Unfair Competition Law*, Vol. 1 (Cheltenham: Edward Elgar Publishing, 2014), pp. 118–56.

Berger, Peter L. & Thomas Luckmann, *The Social Construction of Reality* (New York: Doubleday, 1966).

Bergström, Svante, 'Die neue schwedische Gesetzgebung über das Urheberrecht' (1962), 7–8 *Gewerblicher Rechtsschutz und Urheberrecht Auslands- und Internationaler Teil*, 364–81.

Bertolini, Simona, 'Beings in the World: Elements for a Comparison between Nicolai Hartmann and Roman Ingarden', in Keith Peterson & Roberto Poli (eds.), *New Research on the Philosophy of Nicolai Hartmann* (Boston: De Gruyter, 2016), pp. 171–90.

Biagioli, Mario, 'Patent Republic: Representing Inventions, Constructing Rights and Authors' (2006), 73 *Social Research: An International Quarterly*, 1129–72.

'Nature and the Commons: The Vegetable Roots of Intellectual Property', in Jean-Paul Gaudillière, Daniel J. Kevles & Hans-Jörg Rheinberger, *Living Properties: Making Knowledge and Controlling Ownership in the History of Biology* (Berlin: Max Planck Institute for the History of Science Preprint 382, 2009), pp. 241–50.

'Genius against Copyright: Revisiting Fichte's Proof of the Illegality of Reprinting' (2011), 86 *Notre Dame Law Review*, 1847–67.

'Between Knowledge and Technology: Patenting Methods, Rethinking Materiality' (2012), 22 *Anthropological Forum*, 285–99.

Biron, Laura, 'The Elusive "Objects" of Intellectual Property', in Michael Goldhammer, Michael Grünberger & Diethelm Klippel (eds.), *Geistiges Eigentum im Verfassungsstaat* (Tübingen: Mohr Siebeck, 2016), pp. 127–41.

'Two Challenges to the Idea of Intellectual Property' (2019), 93 *The Monist*, 382–94.

Blackstone, William, *Commentaries on the Laws of England*, Vol. 2 (Oxford: Clarendon Press, 1765).

Blumenberg, Hans, 'Nachahmung der Natur. Zur Vorgeschichte der Idee des schöpferischen Menschen [1957]' in Hans Blumenberg (ed.), *Ästhetische und metaphorologische Schriften* (Frankfurt: Suhrkamp, 2003), pp. 9–46.

'Paradigmen zu einer Metaphorologie' (1960), 6 *Archiv für Begriffsgeschichte*, 7–142.

Theorie der Unbegrifflichkeit (Frankfurt: Suhrkamp, 2007).

Bluntschli, Johann Caspar, *Deutsches Privatrecht I* (Munich: Literarisch-artistische Anstalt, 1853).

Boldrin, Michele & David K. Levine, 'Intellectual Property and the Efficient Allocation of Social Surplus from Creation' (2005), 2 *Review of Economic Research on Copyright Issues*, 45–67.

Against Intellectual Monopoly (New York: Cambridge University Press, 2008).

Bone, Robert G., 'Hunting Goodwill: A History of the Concept of Goodwill in Trademark Law' (2006), 86 *Boston University Law Review*, 547–622.

Bosse, Heinrich, *Autorschaft ist Werkherrschaft. Über die Entstehung des Urheberrechts aus dem Geist der Goethezeit* (Paderborn: Fink, 2014).

Bourdieu, Pierre, 'The Market of Symbolic Goods', in *The Field of Cultural Production: Essays on Art and Literature* (New York: Columbia University Press, 1993), pp. 112–41.

Bracha, Oren, 'The Commodification of Patents 1600–1836: How Patents Became Rights and Why We Should Care' (2004), 38 *Loyola of LA Law Review*, 177–244.

Owning Ideas: A History of Anglo-American Intellectual Property (2005), https://law.utexas.edu/faculty/obracha/dissertation/.

'The Ideology of Authorship Revisited: Authors, Markets, and Liberal Values in Early American Copyright' (2008), 118 *Yale Law Journal*, 187–271.

Braithwaite, John & Peter Drahos, *Information Feudalism* (London: Earthscan Publications Ltd, 2002).

Breakey, Hugh, 'Properties of Copyright. Exclusion, Exclusivity, Non-Interference and Authority', in Helena R. Howe & Jonathan Griffiths, *Concepts of Property in Intellectual Property Law* (West Nyack: Cambridge University Press 2013), pp. 137–60.

Breimesser, Florian Christof, *Urheberrecht und Rechtsbegriff: eine Untersuchung am Beispiel des Designrechts* (Baden-Baden: Nomos, 2016).

Burk, Dan L., 'Copyright and the New Materialism', in Jessica Lai & Antoinette Maget Dominicé, *Intellectual Property and Access to Im/material Goods* (Cheltenham: Edward Elgar Publishing, 2016), pp. 44–62.

'Patent Silences' (2016), 69 *Vanderbilt Law Review*, 1603–30.

Carnap, Rudolf, *The Logical Structure of the World* (London: Routledge and Kegal Paul, 1968).

Carrara, Massimiliano & Marzia Soavi, 'Copies, Replicas, and Counterfeits of Artworks and Artefacts' (2010), 93 *The Monist*, 414–32.

Carrier, Michael A., 'Cabining Intellectual Property through a Property Paradigm' (2004), 54 *Duke Law Journal*, 1–145.

Carvalko, Joseph R., Jr, 'Introduction to an Ontology of Intellectual Property' (2005), 2 *ABA SciTech Lawyer*, 7–9.

Cella, Johann Jacob, 'Vom Büchernachdruck" in *Freymüthige Aufsätze* (Anspach: Haueisen, 1784), pp. 76–168.

Chapdelaine, Pascale, 'Living in the Shadow of the Intangible: The Nature of the Copy of a Copyrighted Work (Part One)' (2010), 23 *Intellectual Property Journal*, 83–103.

Chin, Andrew, 'The Ontological Function of the Patent Document' (2012), 74 *University of Pittsburgh Law Review*, 263–332.

Coase, Ronald, 'The Lighthouse in Economics' (1974), 17 *Journal of Law and Economics*, 375–76.

Cohen, Felix S., 'Transcendental Nonsense and the Functional Approach' (1935), 35 *Columbia Law Review*, 809–49.

Cohen, Julie E., 'What Kind of Property Is Intellectual Property?' (2014), 52 *Houston Law Review*, 691–707.

'Property as Institutions for Resources: Lessons from and for IP' (2015), 94 *Texas Law Review*, 1–57.

Collins, Kevin Emerson, 'The Reach of Literal Claim Scope into After-Arising Technology: On Thing Construction and the Meaning of Meaning' (2008), 41 *Connecticut Law Review*, 493–559.

Cornish, William, 'Conserving Culture and Copyright: A Partial History' (2009), 13 *Edinburgh Law Review*, 8–26.

Cotropia, Christopher A., 'What Is the "Invention"?' (2012), 53 *William & Mary Law Review*, 1855–1914.

'Physicalism and Patent Theory' (2016), 69 *Vanderbilt Law Review*, 1543–71.

Curtis, George Tickner, *Treatise on the Law of Copyright. In Books, Dramatic and Musical Compositions, Letters and other Manuscripts, Engravings and Sculpture, as Enacted and*

Administered in England and America with some Notices of the History of Literary Property (Boston: Freeman and Bolles, 1847).

Damme, Felix, *Der Schutz technischer Erfindungen als Erscheinungsform moderner Volkswirtschaft* (Berlin: Liebmann, 1910).

Danto, Arthur, 'The Artworld' (1964), 61 *The Journal of Philosophy*, 571–84.

Deazley, Ronan, *On the Origin of the Right to Copy* (London: Hart Publishing, 2004).

Rethinking Copyright (Cheltenham: Edward Elgar Publishing, 2006).

Decock, Lieven & Igor Douven, 'Similarity after Goodman' (2011), 2 *Review of Philosophy and Psychology*, 61–75.

Demsetz, Harold, 'Information and Efficiency: Another Viewpoint' (1969), 12 *Journal of Law and Economics*, 1–22.

Di Palma, Salvatore, *The History of Marks from Antiquity to the Middle Ages* (Paris: Société des écrivains, 2015).

Dilworth, John, 'The Abstractness of Artworks and Its Implications' (2008), 66 *The Journal of Aesthetics and Arts Criticism*, 341–53.

Dölemeyer, Barbara, 'Erfinderprivilegien und frühe Patentgesetze', in Martin Otto & Diethelm Klippel (eds.), *Geschichte des deutschen Patentrechts* (Tübingen: Mohr Siebeck, 2015), pp. 13–36.

Dogan, Stacey L. & Mark A. Lemley, 'A Search-Costs Theory of Limiting Doctrines in Trademark Law' (2007), 97 *The Trademark Reporter*, 1223–51.

Drahos, Peter, *A Philosophy of Intellectual Property* (London: Taylor and Francis, 1996).

Drassinower, Abraham, *What's Wrong with Copying?* (Cambridge, MA: Harvard University Press, 2015).

Dreier, Thomas, 'Primär- und Folgemärkte', in Gerhard Schricker, Thomas Dreier & Annette Kur (eds.), *Geistiges Eigentum im Dienst der Innovation* (Baden-Baden: Nomos, 2001), pp. 51–81.

Drone, Eaton Sylvester, *A Treatise on the Law of Property in Intellectual Productions in Great Britain and the United States. Embracing Copyright in Works of Literature and Art, and Playright in Dramatic and Musical Compositions* (Boston: Little, Brown and Company, 1879).

Druey, Jean-Nicolas, *Information als Gegenstand des Rechts. Entwurf einer Grundlegung* (Zürich: Schulthess, 1995).

Edelman, Bernard, *Ownership of the Image: Elements for a Marxist Theory of Law* (London: Routledge and Kegan Paul, 1979).

'Une exposition peut être une œvre de l'esprit', in Bernard Edelman & Nathalie Heinich (eds.), *L'art en conflits* (Paris: La Découverte, 2002), pp. 43–53.

Eisenlohr, Christian Friedrich, *Sammlung der Gesetze und internationalen Verträge zum Schutze des literarisch-artistischen Eigenthums in Deutschland, Frankreich und England* (Heidelberg: Bangel u. Schmitt, 1857).

Eisenstein, Elizabeth L., *The Printing Revolution in Early Modern Europe*, 2nd ed. (Cambridge: Cambridge University Press, 2012).

Eller, Klaas Hendrik, 'Rechtskritik durch Vertrag. Zu den Semantiken des transnationalen Rechts' (2014), 97 *Kritische Vierteljahresschrift für Gesetzgebung und Rechtsprechung*, 191–216.

Elster, Alexander, 'Zur Ontologie des Urheberpersönlichkeits- und Urhebervermögensrechts. Ein rechtsvergleichender Beitrag zum § 12 des deutschen Urheberrechts-Gesetzentwurfs' (1932), 6 *RabelsZ*, 903–25.

Epstein, Richard A., 'The Disintegration of Intellectual Property – A Classical Liberal Response to a Premature Obituary' (2010), 62 *Stanford Law Review*, 455–524.

Erben, Johannes, 'Zur Geschichte der Deutschen Kollektiva', in Helmut Gipper (ed.), *Sprache – Schlüssel zur Welt, Festschrift für Leo Weisgerber* (Düsseldorf: Schwann, 1959), pp. 221–28.

Esposito, Elena, 'Die Ontologie des Finanzwesens', in René John, Jana Rückert-John & Elena Esposito (eds.), *Ontologien der Moderne* (Wiesbaden: Springer, 2013), pp. 137–52.

Feather, John, 'From Rights in Copies to Copyright: The Recognition of Authors' Rights in English Law and Practice in the Sixteenth and Seventeenth Centuries', in Martha Woodmansee & Peter Jaszi (eds.), *The Construction of Authorship: Textual Appropriation in Law and Literature* (Durham: Duke University Press, 1994), pp. 191–210.

Fezer, Karl-Heinz, *Markenrecht*, 4th ed. (Munich: C. H. Beck, 2009).

Fichte, Johann Gottlieb, 'Proof of the Unlawfulness of Reprinting (1793)', reprint, Lionel Bently & Martin Kretschmer (eds.), *Primary Sources on Copyright (1450–1900)*, www.copyrighthistory.org.

Fisher, William W., 'Reconstructing the Fair Use Doctrine' (1988), 101 *Harvard Law Review*, 1659–1795.

Fontius, Martin, 'Produktivkraftentfaltung und Autonomie der Kunst', in Günther Klotz, Winfried Schröder & Peter Weber (eds.), *Literatur im Epochenumbruch* (Berlin: Aufbau-Verlag, 1977), pp. 409–529.

Foucault, Michel, *The Order of Things* (New York: Pantheon Books, 1970).

'What Is an Author?', in Paul Rabinow & Nikolas Rose (eds.), *The Essential Foucault: Selections from Essential Works of Foucault, 1954–1984* (New York: New Press, 2003), pp. 377–91.

Frege, Gottlob, 'Thoughts', in Gottlob Frege (ed.), *Logical Investigations* (Oxford: Blackwell, 1977), pp. 7–30.

Fromer, Jeanne C., 'Claiming Intellectual Property' (2009), 76 *Chicago Law Review*, 719–96.

'A Psychology of Intellectual Property' (2010), 104 *Northwestern University Law Review*, 1441–1509.

Gärtner, Janina-Maria, *Ist das Sollen ableitbar aus einem Sein – Eine Ontologie von Regeln und institutionellen Tatsachen unter besonderer Berücksichtigung der Philosophie von John R. Searle und der evolutionären Erkenntnistheorie* (Berlin: Duncker & Humblot, 2010).

Galbraith, John Kenneth, *The Affluent Society* (Harmondsworth: Penguin Books, 1967).

Galvez-Behar, Gabriel, *La république des inventeurs. Propriété et organisation de l'innovation en France (1791–1922)* (Rennes: Presses Univ. de Rennes, 2008).

Gangjee, Dev, 'Property in Brands. The Commodification of Conversation', in Helena R. Howe & Jonathan Griffiths (eds.), *Concepts of Property in Intellectual Property Law* (Cambridge: Cambridge University Press, 2013), pp. 29–59.

Gaudillière, Jean-Paul & Daniel J. Kevles, 'Introduction', in Jean-Paul Gaudillière, Daniel J. Kevles & Hans-Jörg Rheinberger (eds.), *Living Properties: Making Knowledge and Controlling Ownership in the History of Biology* (Berlin: Max-Planck-Institute for the History of Science, 2009), pp. 1–9.

Gaudillière, Jean Paul, Daniel J. Kevles & Hans-Jörg Rheinberger (eds.), *Living Properties: Making Knowledge and Controlling Ownership in the History of Biology* (Berlin: Max-Planck-Institut für Wissenschaftsgeschichte, 2009).

George, Alexandra, *Constructing Intellectual Property* (Cambridge: Cambridge University Press, 2012).

'The Metaphysics of Intellectual Property' (2015), 7(1) *The WIPO Journal*, 16–28.

Gephart, Werner & Jan Christoph Suntrup, *The Normative Structure of Human Civilization* (Frankfurt: Vittorio Klostermann, 2017).

Gergen, Thomas, *Die Nachdruckprivilegienpraxis Württembergs im 19. Jahrhundert und ihre Bedeutung für das Urheberrecht im Deutschen Bund* (Berlin: Duncker & Humblot, 2007).

Geulen, Eva, 'Law and Literature: Who Owns It?', in Werner Gephart (ed.), *Rechtsanalyse als Kulturforschung* (Frankfurt: Klostermann, 2012), pp. 309–22.

Giddens, Anthony, 'Action, Subjectivity, and the Constitution of Meaning' (1986), 53 *Social Research*, 529–45.

Gierke, Otto, *Deutsches Privatrecht III: Schuldrecht* (Leipzig: Duncker & Humblot, 1917).

Gieseke, Ludwig, *Vom Privileg zum Urheberrecht. Die Entwicklung des Urheberrechts in Deutschland bis 1845* (Baden-Baden: Nomos, 1995).

Ginsburg, Jane C., 'Proto-property in Literary and Artistic Works: Sixteenth Century Papal Printing Privileges', in Isabella Alexander & H. Tomás Gómez-Arostegui (eds.), *Research Handbook on the History of Copyright Law* (Cheltenham: Edward Elgar Publishing, 2016), pp. 237–67.

Godenhielm, Berndt, 'Ist die Erfindung etwas Immaterielles?' (1996), 45 *Gewerblicher Rechtsschutz und Urheberrecht International* 327–30.

Goehr, Lydia, *The Imaginary Museum of Musical Works: An Essay in the Philosophy of Music* (Oxford: Clarendon Press, 1992).

Göpel, Ernst, *Über Begriff und Wesen des Urheberrechts* (Altenburg: Schnuphase in Comm., 1881).

Gräff, Ernst Martin, 'Versuch einer einleuchtenden Darstellung des Eigentums und der Eigentumsrechte des Schriftstellers und Verlegers und ihrer gegenseitigen Rechte und Verbindlichkeiten (1794)', reprint, (1998), 137 *UFITA*, 111–227.

Gray, Kevin, 'Property in Thin Air' (1991), 50 *Cambridge Law Journal*, 252–307.

Grewendorf, Günther & Georg Meggle, *Speech Acts, Mind, and Social Reality. Discussions with John R. Searle* (Dordrecht: Kluwer, 2002).

Griffiths, Jonathan, 'Dematerialization, Pragmatism and the European Copyright Revolution' (2013), 33(4) *Oxford Journal of Legal Studies*, 767–90.

Grimm, Jacob & Wilhelm Grimm, *Deutsches Wörterbuch III* (Leipzig: Verlag von S. Hirzel, 1860), 799–800.

Gross, Daniel, 'Creativity under Fire: The Effects of Competition on Creative Production' (2016), *Harvard Business School Strategy Paper No. 16–109*, 1–27, https://ssrn.com/abstract=2520123.

Gross, Neil, 'Comment on Searle' (2006), 6 *Anthropological Theory*, 45–56.

Gruner, Richard S., 'Dispelling the Myth of Patents as Non-Rivalrous Property: Patents as Tools for Allocating Scarce Labor and Resources' (2012), 13 *Columbia Science & Technology Law Review*, 1–70.

Habermas, Jürgen, *The Structural Transformation of the Public Sphere* (Cambridge: Polity Press, 1989).

Häberle, Peter, 'Vielfalt der Property Rights und der verfassungsrechtliche Eigentumsbegriff' (1984), 109 *Archiv des öffentlichen Rechts*, 36–76.

Häseler, Jens, 'Original/Originalität', in Karlheinz Barck et al. (eds.), *Ästhetische Grundbegriffe (ÄGB)*, Vol. 7 (Stuttgart: J. B. Metzler Verlag, 2005), pp. 638–55.

Haferkorn, Hans-Jürgen, 'Der freie Schriftsteller' (1964), 5 *Archiv für Geschichte des Buchwesens*, 523–712.

Hargreaves, Ian, 'Digital Opportunity: A Review of Intellectual Property and Growth', UK Government (London, 2011), http://gov.uk/government/uploads/system/uploads/attachment_data/file/32563/ipreview-finalreport.pdf.

Hartmann, Nicolai, *Das Problem des geistigen Seins. Untersuchungen zur Grundlegung der Geschichtsphilosophie und der Geisteswissenschaften* (Berlin: De Gruyter, 1949).

Hauptmann, Felix, 'Wesen und Begriff der sogenannten Immateriellen Güter. Dogmatische Untersuchung', in Schweizerischer Juristenverein, *Festgabe der Juristischen Fakultät der Universität Freiburg (Schweiz) zur 59. Jahresversammlung des Schweizerischen Juristenvereins* (Freiburg: Librairie de L'Université, 1924), pp. 50–69.

Hay, Colin, 'Good in a Crisis: The Ontological Institutionalism of Social Constructivism' (2016), 21 *New Political Economy*, 520–35.

Hediger, Vinzenz, 'The Original Is Always Lost', in Marijke de Valck & Malte Hagener (eds.), *Cinephilia: Movies, Love and Memory* (Amsterdam: University Press, 2005), pp. 133–47.

Hegel, Georg Wilhelm Friedrich, 'Elements of the Philosophy of Right' (1821), reprint, Allen Wood (ed.), *Hegel. Elements of the Philosophy of Right* (Cambridge: Cambridge University Press, 2011), § 69.

Hellmann, Kai-Uwe, *Soziologie der Marke* (Frankfurt: Suhrkamp, 2003).

Henning-Bodewig, Frauke & Anette Kur, *Marke und Verbraucher, Volume 1: Grundlagen* (Munich: C. H. Beck, 2000).

Hesse, Carla, 'The Rise of Intellectual Property, 700 B.C.-A.D. 2000: An Idea in the Balance' (2002), 131 *Daedalus*, 26–45.

Hesse, Nora, *Die Vereinbarkeit des EU-Grenzbeschlagnahmeverfahrens mit dem TRIPS-Abkommen* (Tuebingen: Mohr Siebeck, 2018).

Hetmank, Sven, 'Was ist Prüfungs- und Schutzgegenstand des Patentrechts? – Die Ambiguität des Erfindungsbegriffs' (2015), 7 *Zeitschrift für Geistiges Eigentum*, 460–72.

Heymann, Laura A., 'A Tale of (at Least) Two Authors: Focusing Copyright Law on Process over Product' (2009), 34 *Journal of Corporation Law*, 1009–32.

Hick, Darren Hudson, 'Toward an Ontology of Authored Works' (2011), 51 *British Journal of Aesthetics*, 185–99.

'Ontology and the Challenge of Literary Appropriation' (2013), 71 *The Journal of Aesthetics and Art Criticism*, 155–65.

Hilpinen, Risto, 'Authors and Artifacts' (1993), 93 *Proceedings of the Aristotelian Society*, 155–78.

Hirdina, Heinz, 'Design', in Karlheinz Barck et al. (eds.), *Ästhetische Grundbegriffe (ÄGB)*, Vol. 2 (Stuttgart: J. B. Metzler Verlag, 2001), pp. 41–63.

Hirsch, Ernst E., 'Die Werkherrschaft. Ein Beitrag zur Lehre von der Natur der Rechte an Geisteswerken' (1962), 36 *UFITA*, 19–54.

Hitzig, Julius Eduard, *Das Königl. Preußische Gesetz vom 11. Juni 1837 zum Schutze des Eigenthums an Werken der Wissenschaft und Kunst gegen Nachdruck und Nachbildung* (Berlin: Dümmler, 1838).

HKK, *Historisch-Kritischer Kommentar zum BGB*, Mathias Schmoeckel, Joachim Rückert & Reinhard Zimmermann (eds.), Vol. 3 (Part 1) (Tuebingen: Mohr Siebeck, 2013).

Höffner, Eckhard, *Geschichte und Wesen des Urheberrechts*, Vols. 1 and 2 (Munich: Verlag Europäische Wirtschaft, 2010).

Houston, Robert Allan, *Literacy in Early Modern Europe: Culture and Education, 1500–1800*, 2nd ed. (London: Routledge, 2014).

Hubmann, Heinrich, *Das Recht des schöpferischen Geistes. Eine philosophisch-juristische Betrachtung zur Urheberrechtsreform* (Berlin: De Gruyter, 1954).

'Immanuel Kants Urheberrechtstheorie' (1987), 106 *UFITA*, 145–54.

Hughes, Justin, 'Created Facts and the Flawed Ontology of Copyright Law' (2007), 83 *Notre Dame Law Review*, 43–108.

Ingerl, Reinhard & Christian Rohnke, *Markengesetz. Kommentar*, 3rd ed. (Munich: C. H. Beck, 2010).

Irvin, Sherri, 'The Artist's Sanction in Contemporary Art' (2005), 63 *The Journal of Aesthetics and Art Criticism*, 315–26.

Isay, Hermann, 'Die Selbstständigkeit des Rechts an der Marke' (1929), *Gewerblicher Rechtsschutz und Urheberrecht*, 23–42.

Jacob, Jan, *Ausschließlichkeitsrechte an immateriellen Gütern – eine kantische Rechtfertigung des Urheberrechts* (Tuebingen: Mohr Siebeck, 2010).

Jänich, Volker, *Geistiges Eigentum – eine Komplementärerscheinung zum Sacheigentum?* (Tuebingen: Mohr Siebeck 2002).

Jansen, Ludger, *Gruppen und Institutionen: Eine Ontologie des Sozialen* (Wiesbaden: Springer, 2017).

Jaszi, Peter, 'Toward a Theory of Copyright. The Metamorphoses of "Authorship"' (1991), 40 *Duke Law Journal*, 455–502.

Jefferson, Thomas, 'Letter to Isaac McPherson, 13.8.1813', in Philip B. Kurland & Ralph Lerner (eds.), *The Founders' Constitution*, Vol. 3 (Chicago: University of Chicago Press, 2000), Article 1, Section 8, Clause 8, Document 12, http://press-pubs.uchicago.edu/founders/documents/a1_8_8s12.html.

Jhering, Rudolf von, *Scherz und Ernst in der Jurisprudenz* (Leipzig: Breitkopf & Härtel, 1884).

John, René, Jana Rückert-John & Elena Esposito (eds.), *Ontologien der Moderne* (Wiesbaden: Springer, 2013).

Johns, Adrian, *The Nature of the Book: Print and Knowledge in the Making* (Chicago: University of Chicago Press, 2000).

Kant, Immanuel, 'On the Unlawfulness of Reprinting (1785)', reprint, Lionel Bently & Martin Kretschmer (eds.), *Primary Sources on Copyright (1450–1900)*, www.copyrighthistory.org.

Kawohl, Friedemann, 'Wie der Wein in die Flaschen kam. Oder: Die Entstehung des musikalischen Formbegriffs aus dem Geist des Urheberrechts', in Sabine Sanio & Christian Scheib (eds.), *Form – Luxus, Kalkül und Abstinenz: Fragen, Thesen und Beiträge zu Erscheinungsweisen aktueller Musik* (Saarbrücken: Pfau, 1999), pp. 136–47.

Urheberrecht der Musik in Preußen (1820–1840) (Tutzing: Schneider, 2002).

Kawohl, Friedemann & Martin Kretschmer, 'Abstraction and Registration: Conceptual Innovations and Supply Effects in Prussian and British copyright (1820–50)' (2003), 2 *Intellectual Property Quarterly*, 209–28.

Kevles, Daniel J., 'Inventions, Yes; Nature, No: The Products-of-Nature Doctrine From the American Colonies to the US Courts' (2015), 23 *Perspectives on Science*, 13–34.

'New Blood, New Fruits: Protections for Breeders and Originators, 1789–1930', in Mario Biagioli, Peter Jaszi & Martha Woodmansee (eds.), *Making and Unmaking Intellectual Property* (Chicago: University of Chicago Press, 2011), pp. 253–76.

Kiesel, Helmut & Paul Münch, *Gesellschaft und Literatur im 18. Jahrhundert – Voraussetzungen und Entstehung des literarischen Markts in Deutschland* (Munich: C. H. Beck, 1977).

Kitch, Edmund W., 'The Nature and Function of the Patent System' (1977), 20 *Journal of Law and Economics*, 265–90.

Klippel, Diethelm, 'Ueber die Unzulässigkeit des Büchernachdrucks nach dem natürlichen Zwangsrecht. Der Diskurs über den Büchernachdruck im Jahre 1784', in Tiziana J. Chiusi, Thomas Gergen & Heike Jung (eds.), *Das Recht und seine historischen Grundlagen, Festschrift für Elmar Wadle zum 70. Geburtstag* (Berlin: Duncker & Humblot, 2008), pp. 477–98.

'Persönlichkeitsrecht und Persönlichkeitsrechte bei Josef Kohler' (2014), 6 *Zeitschrift für Geistiges Eigentum*, 443–69.

'Geistiges Eigentum, Privileg und Naturrecht in rechtshistorischer Perspektive' (2015), 7 *Zeitschrift für Geistiges Eigentum*, 49–76.

Kneale, W. C., 'The Idea of Invention' (1955), 41 *Proceedings of the British Academy*, 86–108.

v. Knigge, Adolph, 'Ueber den Bücher-Nachdruck. An den Herrn Johann Gottwerth Müller, Doctor der Weltweisheit in Itzehoe' (1792), reprint, Albrecht Götz v. Olenhusen (ed.), 1974, pp. 1–56.

Kober, Michael & Jan G. Michel, *John Searle* (Paderborn: Mentis, 2011).

Köbler, Gerhard, 'Vom Urheber und Patent zum Urheberrecht und Patentrecht', in Tiziana J. Chiusi, Thomas Gergen & Heike Jung, *Das Recht und seine historischen Grundlagen, Festschrift für Elmar Wadle zum 70. Geburtstag*, (Berlin: Duncker & Humblot, 2008), pp. 499–523.

Kölbel, Martin, 'Das literarische Werk. Zur Geschichte eines Grundbegriffs der Literaturtheorie' (2005), 10 *Text. Kritische Beiträge*, 27–44.

König, Michael, 'Software (Computerprogramme) als Sache und deren Erwerb als Sachkauf' (1993), 48 *NJW*, 3121–24.

Kohler, Josef, *Das Autorrecht: eine zivilistische Abhandlung; zugleich ein Beitrag zur Lehre vom Eigenthum, vom Miteigenthum, vom Rechtsgeschäft und vom Individualrecht* (Jena: Fischer, 1880).

Das Recht des Markenschutzes (Würzburg: Stahel, 1884).

'Die Immaterialgüterrechtsidee im Jahre 1875', in *Forschungen aus dem Patentrecht* (Mannheim: Bensheimer, 1888), pp. 116–24.

Handbuch des deutschen Patentrechts in rechtsvergleichender Darstellung (1900), reprint, (Aalen: Scientia-Verlag, 1980).

Urheberrecht an Schriftwerken und Verlagsrecht (Stuttgart: Enke, 1907).

Musterrecht: Geschmacks- und Gebrauchsmusterrecht (Stuttgart: Enke, 1909).

'Die Idee des geistigen Eigentums' (1993), 123 *UFITA*, 99–167.

'Die spanischen Naturrechtslehrer des 16. und 17. Jahrhunderts' (1917), 10 *Archiv für Rechts- und Wirtschaftsphilosophie*, 235–63.

Kostylo, Joanna, 'Commentary on the Venetian Statute on Industrial Brevets (1474)', in Lionel Bently & Martin Kretschmer (eds.), *Primary Sources on Copyright (1450–1900)*, www.copyrighthistory.org.

Kristeller, Paul Oskar, 'The Modern System of the Arts: A Study in the Historics of Aesthetics, Part I' (1951), 12 *Journal of the History of Ideas*, 496–527.

'The Modern System of the Arts: A Study in the Historics of Aesthetics, Part II' (1952), 13 *Journal of the History of Ideas*, 17–46.

Kruse, Frederik Vinding, *Das Eigentumsrecht*, Vol. 1 (Berlin: de Gruyter, 1931).

Künne, Wolfgang, *Abstrakte Gegenstände: Semantik und Ontologie* (Frankfurt: Klostermann, 2007).

Küppers, Monika, *Challenging the Public Domain – Protection of Traditional Cultural Expression in the Light of Retroactive Copyright Protection* (Köln: Carl Heymanns Verlag, 2018).

Kulenkampff, Jens, 'Gibt es ein ontologisches Problem des Kunstwerks?', in Reinold Schmücker (ed.), *Identität und Existenz. Studien zur Ontologie der Kunst* (Paderborn: Mentis, 2003), pp. 121–40.

Kunz-Hallstein, Hans Peter, 'Verschärfter Ausübungszwang für Patente? – Überlegungen zur geplanten Revision des Art. 5 A PVÜ' (1981), 6 *Gewerblicher Rechtsschutz und Urheberrecht International*, pp. 347–57.

Kurz, Peter, *Weltgeschichte des Erfindungsschutzes. Erfinder und Patente im Spiegel der Zeiten* (Köln: Heymann, 2000).

Lai, Jessica C., 'A Tale of Two Histories: The "Invention" and Its Incentive Theory', in Jessica C. Lai & Antoinette Maget Dominicé (eds.), *Intellectual Property and Access to Im/material Goods* (Cheltenham: Edward Elgar Publishing, 2016), pp. 94–120.

Landes, William M. & Richard A. Posner, *The Economic Structure of Intellectual Property Law* (Cambridge, MA: Belknap Press, 2003).

Lange, Max, 'Kritik der Grundbegriffe vom geistigen Eigentum (1837)', reprint, (1991), 117 *UFITA*, 169–248.

Laskowska, Ewa & Grzegorz Mania, 'Copyright as a Service: How Does the Development of the Music Business Determine the Shape of Copyright?' (2016), 132 *Prace z Prawa Wlasnosci Intellektualnej*, 91–103.

Lee, Nari, 'Patent Eligible Subject Matter Reconfiguration and the Emergence of Proprietarian Norms – The Patent Eligibility of Business Methods' (2005), 45 *IDEA: The Journal of Law and Technology*, 321–59.

Lemley, Mark A., 'Property, Intellectual Property, and Free Riding' (2005), 83 *Texas Law Review*, 1031–75.

'Taking the Regulatory Nature of IP Seriously' (2014), 92 *Texas Law Review*, 107–19.

'Faith-Based Intellectual Property' (2015), 62 *UCLA Law Review*, 1328–46.

'IP in a World Without Scarcity' (2015), 90 *New York University Law Review*, 460–515.

Levinson, Jerrold, 'What a Musical Work Is' (1980), 77 *The Journal of Philosophy*, 5–28.

Liivak, Oskar, 'Rescuing the Invention from the Cult of the Claim' (2012), 42 *Seton Hall Law Review*, 1–54.

Livingston, Paisley, 'History of the Ontology of Art', in Edward N. Zalta (ed.), *The Stanford Encyclopedia of Philosophy*, Summer 2016 ed., http://plato.stanford.edu/archives/sum2016/entries/art-ontology-history/.

Long, Pamela O., 'Invention, Authorship, "Intellectual Property", and the Origin of Patents: Notes toward a Conceptual History' (1991), 32 *Technology and Culture*, 846–84.

Loschelder, Michael, 'Die Rechtsnatur der geographischen Herkunftsangaben', in Wolfgang Büscher et al. (eds.), *Marktkommunikation zwischen Geistigem Eigentum und Verbraucherschutz. Festschrift für Karl-Heinz Fezer zum 70. Geburtstag* (Munich: C. H. Beck, 2016), pp. 711–24.

Luhmann, Niklas, 'Das Kunstwerk und die Selbstreproduktion der Kunst', in Hans Ulrich Gumbrecht & K. Ludwig Pfeiffer (eds.), *Stil. Geschichten und Funktionen eines kulturwissenschaftlichen Diskurselements* (Frankfurt: Suhrkamp, 1986), pp. 620–72.

'Der Ursprung des Eigentums und seine Legitimation', in Werner Krawietz, Antonio A. Martino & Kenneth I. Winston (eds.), *Technischer Imperativ und Legitimationskrise des Rechts* (Berlin: Duncker & Humblot, 1991), pp. 43–57.

Die Wirtschaft der Gesellschaft (Frankfurt: Suhrkamp, 1994).

Die Kunst der Gesellschaft (Frankfurt: Suhrkamp, 1997).

Die Gesellschaft der Gesellschaft, Vols. 1 and 2 (Frankfurt: Suhrkamp, 1998).

Lunney, Glynn S., Jr, 'Reexamining Copyright's Incentives-Access Paradigm' (1996), 49 *Vanderbilt Law Review*, 483–656.

MacLeod, Christine, *Inventing the Industrial Revolution: The English Patent System 1660–1800* (Cambridge: Cambridge University Press, 1988).

Madison, Michael J., 'Law as Design: Objects, Concepts, and Digital Things' (2005), 56 *Case Western Reserve Law Review*, 381–478.

'The End of the Work as We Know It' (2012), 19 *Journal of Intellectual Property Law*, 325–55.

Mann, Larisa, 'If it Ain't Broke ... Copyright's Fixation Requirement and Cultural Citizenship' (2011), 34 *The Columbia Journal of Law & the Arts*, 201–29.

Margolis, Joseph, 'The Ontological Peculiarity of Works of Art' (1977), 36 *The Journal of Aesthetics and Art Criticism*, 45–50.

Marinkovic, Daniel F., *Sprache – Geltung – Recht* (Saarbrücken: VDM Müller, 2007).

May, Christopher, 'The Venetian Moment: New Technologies, Legal Innovation and the Institutional Origins of Intellectual Property' (2002), 20 *Prometheus*, 159–79.

McKenna, Mark P., 'The Normative Foundations of Trademark Law' (2007), 82 *Notre Dame Law Review*, 1839–1916.

McLuhan, Marshall, *The Gutenberg Galaxy* (Toronto: University of Toronto Press, 1962).

Meixner, Uwe, *Einführung in die Ontologie* (Darmstadt: Wissenschaftliche Buchgesellschaft, 2004).

Menke, Christoph, *Recht und Gewalt* (Berlin: Augst Verlag, 2012).

Kritik der Rechte (Frankfurt: Suhrkamp, 2015).

Merges, Robert P., *Justifying Intellectual Property* (Cambridge, MA: Harvard University Press, 2011).

'What Kind of Rights Are Intellectual Property Rights?', in Rochelle Cooper Dreyfuss & Justine Pila (eds.), *The Oxford Handbook of Intellectual Property Law* (Oxford: Oxford University Press, 2018), pp. 57–94.

Merkl, Joachim, *Der Begriff des Immaterialgüterrechts* (Erlangen: Erlangen-Nürnberg Jur. F., 1961).

Miller, Seumas, 'Social Institutions', in Edward N. Zalta (ed.), *The Stanford Encyclopedia of Philosophy*, Winter 2014 ed., https://plato.stanford.edu/archives/win2014/entries/social-institutions/.

Milton, John, 'Areopagitica: A Speech of Mr. John Milton for the Liberty of Unlicenc'd Printing, to the Parliament of England' (1644), www.dartmouth.edu/~milton/reading_room/areopagitica/text.shtml.

Möllers, Christoph, *Die Möglichkeit der Normen. Über eine Möglichkeit jenseits von Moralität und Kausalität* (Frankfurt: Suhrkamp, 2015).

Moritz, Karl Philipp, 'Über den Begriff des in sich selbst Vollendeten (1785)', reprint, Jürgen Jahn (ed.), *Karl Philipp Moritz: Werke in zwei Bänden*, Vol. 1 (Berlin: Verlag Neues Leben, 1973), pp. 203–11.

Moser, Petra, 'How Do Patent Laws Influence Innovation? Evidence from Nineteenth-Century World's Fairs' (2005), 99 *The American Economic Review*, 1214–36.

Mossoff, Adam, 'Who Cares What Thomas Jefferson Thought about Patents? Reevaluating the Patent "Privilege" in Historical Context' (2007), 92 *Cornell Law Review*, 953–1012.

Nazari-Khanachayi, Arian, *Rechtfertigungsnarrative des Urheberrechts im Praxistest* (Tuebingen: Mohr Siebeck, 2016).

Niebel, Rembert, 'Das Know-how auf dem Weg zum Immaterialgüterrecht', in Wolfgang Büscher et al. (eds.), *Marktkommunikation zwischen Geistigem Eigentum und Verbraucherschutz. Festschrift für Karl-Heinz Fezer zum 70. Geburtstag* (Munich: C. H. Beck, 2016), pp. 799–814.

Oberndörfer, Pascal, *Die philosophische Grundlage des Urheberrechts* (Baden-Baden: Nomos, 2005).

O'Connor, Sean M., 'Distinguishing Different Kinds of Property in Patents and Copyrights' (2019), 27(1) *George Mason Law Review*, 205–61.

Ohly, Ansgar, 'Geistiges Eigentum?' (2003), 58 *Juristenzeitung*, 545–54.

Ong, Walter J., *Orality and Literacy*, 3rd ed. (London: Routledge, 2012).

Opderbeck, David W., 'Deconstructing Jefferson's Candle: Towards a Critical Realistic Approach to Cultural Environmentalism and Information Policy' (2009), 49 *Jurimetrics Journal*, 203–44.

Ortland, Eberhard,'Zur Konstitution des musikalischen Gegenstandes', in Michael Polth, Oliver Schwab-Felisch & Christian Thorau (eds.), *Klang – Struktur – Metapher: Musikalische Analyse zwischen Phänomen und Begriff* (Stuttgart: J. B. Metzler, 2000), pp. 3–27.

'Genie', in Karlheinz Barck et al. (eds.), *Ästhetische Grundbegriffe (ÄGB)*, Vol. 2 (Stuttgart: J. B. Metzler, 2001), pp. 661–709.

'Urheberrecht und ästhetische Autonomie' (2004), 52 *Deutsche Zeitschrift für Philosophie*, 773–92.

Ortland, Eberhard & Reinold Schmücker 'Copyright & Art' (2005), 6 *German Law Journal*, 1762–76.

Osterrieth, Albert, 'Die Geschichte des Urheberrechts in England mit einer Darstellung des geltenden englischen Urheberrechts (1895) – 1. Teil' (1996), 131 *UFITA*, 171–274.

'Die Geschichte des Urheberrechts in England mit einer Darstellung des geltenden englischen Urheberrechts (1895) – 2. Teil' (1996), 132 *UFITA*, 101–231.

Otabe, Tanehisa, 'Die moderne Eigentumslehre und der Begriff der Kunst. Zur Politik der modernen Ästhetik' (1996), 21 *Journal of the Faculty of Letters, the University of Tokyo, Aesthetics*, 141–52.

Pahlow, Louis, 'Geistiges Eigentum', in Albrecht Cordes et al. (eds.), *Handwörterbuch zur deutschen Rechtsgeschichte (HRG)*, Vol. 1 (Berlin: Erich Schmidt Verlag, 2008).

'Josef Kohler und der Begriff des Immaterialgüterrechts' (2014), 6 *ZGE*, 429–42.

Parry, Bronwyn, 'Material Cultures of "Type Specimen" Generation and Their Role in Practices of Biological Regulation', in Jean-Paul Gaudillière, Daniel J. Kevles & Hans-

Jörg Rheinberger (eds.), *Living Properties: Making Knowledge and Controlling Ownership in the History of Biology* (Berlin: Max Planck Institute for the History of Science, 2009), pp. 21–29.

Patterson, Lyman Ray, *Copyright in Historical Perspective* (Tennessee: Vanderbilt University Press, 1968).

Patzig, Günther, 'Über den ontologischen Status von Kunstwerken', in Reinold Schmücker (ed.), *Identität und Existenz: Studien zur Ontologie der Kunst*, 2nd ed. (Paderborn: Mentis, 2005).

Penner, James, *The Idea of Property in Law* (Oxford: Oxford University Press, 1997).

Pettersson, Anders, *The Idea of a Text and the Nature of Textual Meaning* (Amsterdam: John Benjamins Publishing Company, 2017).

Peukert, Alexander, 'Das Sacheigentum in der Informationsgesellschaft', in Ansgar Ohly et al. (eds.), *Perspektiven des Geistigen Eigentums und Wettbewerbsrechts, Festschrift für Gerhard Schricker zum 70. Geburtstag* (Munich: C. H. Beck, 2005), pp. 149–63.

Güterzuordnung als Rechtsprinzip (Tuebingen: Mohr Siebeck 2008).

'"Sonstige Gegenstände" im Rechtsverkehr', in Stefan Leible, Matthias Lehmann & Herbert Zech (eds.), *Unkörperliche Güter im Zivilrecht* (Tuebingen: Mohr Siebeck, 2011), pp. 95–122.

Die Gemeinfreiheit (Tuebingen: Mohr Siebeck, 2012).

'Intellectual Property', in Jürgen Basedow, Klaus J. Hopt & Reinhard Zimmermann (eds.), *The Max Planck Encyclopedia of European Private Law*, Vol. 1 (Oxford: Oxford University Press, 2012), pp. 926–30.

'Why Do "Good People" Disregard Copyright on the Internet?', in Christophe Geiger (ed.), *Criminal Enforcement of Intellectual Property: A Handbook of Contemporary Research* (Cheltenham: Edward Elgar Publishing, 2012), pp. 151–67.

'Die Expansion des Urheberrechts – eine polanyische Perspektive', in Thomas Dreier & Reto M. Hilty (eds.), *Vom Magnettonband zu Social Media – Festschrift 50 Jahre Urheberrechtsgesetz (UrhG)* (Munich: C. H. Beck, 2015), pp. 305–17.

'Intellectual Property: The Global Spread of a Legal Concept', in Peter Drahos, Gustavo Ghidini & Hanns Ullrich (eds.), *Kritika: Essays on Intellectual Property*, Vol. 1 (Cheltenham: Edward Elgar Publishing, 2015), pp. 114–33.

'The Fundamental Right to (Intellectual) Property and the Discretion of the Legislature', in Christophe Geiger (ed.), *Research Handbook on Human Rights and Intellectual Property* (Cheltenham: Edward Elgar Publishing, 2015), pp. 132–48.

'Vom Warenzeichen zum Markeneigentum. Ein polanyischer Erklärungsversuch', in Wolfgang Büscher et al. (eds.), *Marktkommunikation zwischen Geistigem Eigentum und Verbraucherschutz: Festschrift für Karl-Heinz Fezer zum 70. Geburtstag* (Munich: C. H. Beck, 2016), pp. 405–26.

'Vereinheitlichung des Immaterialgüterrechts: Strukturen, Akteure, Zwecke' (2017) 81 *RabelsZ*, 158–93.

'Fictitious Commodities: A Theory of Intellectual Property Inspired by Karl Polanyi's "Great Transformation"' (2019), 29 *Fordham Intellectual Property Media and Entertainment Law Journal*, 1151–1200.

'Immaterialgüterrecht, Privatautonomie und Innovation', in Stefan Grundmann & Florian Möslein (eds.), *Innovation und Vertragsrecht* (Tuebingen: Mohr Siebeck, 2020), pp. 69–98.

Pfister, Bernhard, *Das technische Geheimnis 'Know How' als Vermögensrecht* (Munich: C. H. Beck, 1974).

Pfister, Laurent, 'La propriété intellectuelle est-elle une propriété?' (2005), 205 *Revue internationale du droit d'auteur*, 117–209.

Phillips, Jeremy, 'The English Patent as a Reward for Invention: The Importation of an Idea' (1982), 3 *Journal of Legal History*, 71–79.

Pila, Justine, 'An Intentional View of the Copyright Work' (2008), 71 *The Modern Law Review*, 535–58.

Planck, Gottlieb, 'Vorlesung Immaterialgüterrecht (1902)', reprint, (2012), 1 *UFITA*, 197–251.

Plumpe, Gerhard, 'Eigentum – Eigentümlichkeit. Über den Zusammenhang ästhetischer und juristischer Begriffe im 18. Jahrhundert' (1979) 23 *Archiv für Begriffsgeschichte*, 175–96.

'Der Autor als Rechtssubjekt', in Helmut Brackert & Jörn Stückrath (eds.), *Literaturwissenschaft. Grundkurs 2* (Reinbek: Rowohlt, 1981), pp. 179–93.

Pohlmann, Hansjörg, *Die Frühgeschichte des musikalischen Urheberrechts* (Kassel: Bärenreiter-Verlag, 1962).

Polanyi, Karl, *The Great Transformation: The Political and Economic Origins of Our Time* (Boston: Beacon Press, 2001).

Porter, James I., 'Is Art Modern? Kristeller's "Modern System of the Arts" Reconsidered' (2009), 49 *British Journal of Aesthetics*, 1–24.

Pottage, Alain & Brad Sherman, *Figures of Invention: A History of Modern Patent Law* (Oxford: Oxford University Press, 2010).

'On the Prehistory of Intellectual Property', in Helena R. Howe & Jonathan Griffiths, *Concepts of Property in Intellectual Property Law* (Cambridge: Cambridge University Press, 2013), pp. 11–28.

Prager, Frank D., 'History of Intellectual Property from 1545 to 1787' (1944) 26 *Journal of the Patent Office Society*, 711–60.

Pudelek, Jan-Peter, 'Werk', in Karlheinz Barck et al. (eds.), *Ästhetische Grundbegriffe (ÄGB)*, Vol. 6 (Stuttgart: J. B. Metzler, 2010), pp. 520–88.

Pütter, Johann Stephan, *Der Büchernachdruck nach ächten Grundsätzen des Rechts geprüft* (1774), reprint, (München: Kraus International, 1981).

Rachum-Twaig, Omri, 'Recreating Copyright: The Cognitive Process of Creation and Copyright Law' (2017), 27 *Fordham Intellectual Property, Media & Entertainment Law Journal*, 287–348.

Raue, Benjamin, *Die dreifache Schadensberechnung. Eine Untersuchung zum deutschen und europäischen Immaterialgüter-, Lauterkeits- und Bürgerlichen Recht* (Baden-Baden: Nomos, 2017).

Redeker, Helmut, 'Information als eigenständiges Rechtsgut. Zur Rechtsnatur der Information und dem daraus resultierenden Schutz' (2011), 27 *Computer und Recht*, 634–39.

Rehbinder, Manfred & Alexander Peukert, *Urheberrecht*, 18th ed. (Munich: C. H. Beck, 2018).

Reich, Philipp Erasmus, *Der Bücher-Verlag in allen Absichten genauer bestimmt* (Leipzig, 1773).

Reicher, Maria Elisabeth, 'Eine Typenontologie der Kunst', in Reinold Schmücker (ed.), *Identität und Existenz: Studien zur Ontologie der Kunst* (Paderborn: Mentis, 2003), pp. 180–99.

'Materielle und abstrakte Artefakt-Fragmente', in Kay Malcher et al. (eds.), *Fragmentarität als Problem der Kultur und Textwissenschaften* (Paderborn: Fink, 2013), pp. 211–32.

'Wie aus Gedanken Dinge werden. Eine Philosophie der Artefakte' (2013), 61 *Deutsche Zeitschrift für Philosophie*, 219–32.

'Ontologie fiktiver Gegenstände', in Tobias Klauk & Tilmann Köppe (eds.), *Fiktionalität: Ein interdisziplinäres Handbuch* (Berlin: De Gruyter, 2014), pp. 159–89.

'Kommunikative Absichten und die Ontologie des Literarischen Werkes', in Jan Borkowski et al. (eds.), *Literatur interpretieren* (Muenster: Mentis, 2015), pp. 191–217.

Reimarus, Johann Albert, 'Der Bücherverlag, in Betrachtung der Schriftsteller, der Buchhändler und des Publikums abermals erwogen' (1791), 1 *Deutsches Magazin*, 383–414.

Renouard, Augustin-Charles, *Traité des droits d'auteur, dans la littérature, les sciences et les beaux-arts*, Vol. 1 (Paris: J. Renouard, 1838).

Traité des brevets d'invention (Paris, 1844).

Ricolfi, Marco, 'The New Paradigm of Creativity and Innovation and Its Corollaries for the Law of Obligations', in Peter Drahos, Gustavo Ghidini & Hanns Ullrich (eds.), *Kritika: Essays on Intellectual Property*, Vol. 1 (Cheltenham: Edward Elgar Publishing, 2015), pp. 134–205.

Rognstad, Ole-Andreas, *Property Aspects of Intellectual Property* (Cambridge: Cambridge University Press, 2018).

Rose, Mark, *Authors and Owners: The Invention of Copyright* (Cambridge, MA: Harvard University Press, 1993).

'Nine-Tenths of the Law: The English Copyright Debates and the Rhetoric of the Public Domain' (2003), 66 *Law & Contemporary Problems*, 75–87.

Ross, Alf, 'Ophavsrettens grundbegreber' (1945), 58 *Tidsskrift for Rettsvitenskap*, 321–53.

On Law and Justice (Berkeley: University of California Press, 1959).

Rothe, Arnold, *Der literarische Titel: Funktionen, Formen, Geschichte* (Frankfurt: Klostermann, 1986).

Rotstein, Robert H., 'Beyond Metaphor: Copyright Infringement and the Fiction of the Work' (1993), 68 *Chicago-Kent Law Review*, 725–804.

Rudner, Richard, 'The Ontological Status of the Esthetic Object' (1950), 10 *Philosophy and Phenomenological Research*, 380–88.

Savigny, Friedrich Carl von, 'Savignys Notizen zum Gesetz über den Nachdruck', reprint, Elmar Wadle (ed.), *Friedrich Carl von Savignys Beitrag zum Urheberrecht* (Cologne: Heymann, 1992), pp. 28–46.

Schack, Haimo, *Kunst und Recht* (Tuebingen: Mohr Siebeck, 2017).

Schechter, Frank I., 'The Rational Basis of Trademark Protection' (1927), 40 *Harvard Law Review*, 813–33.

Schefczyk, Michael, 'Rechte an Immaterialgütern – eine kantische Perspektive' (2004), 52 *Deutsche Zeitschrift für Philosophie*, 739–53.

Scherer, Frederic M., *Quarter Notes and Banknotes. The Economics of Music Composition in the Eighteenth and Nineteenth Centuries* (Princeton: Princeton University Press, 2004).

Schmidt, Christian, 'Die zwei Paradoxien des geistigen Eigentums' (2004), 52 *Deutsche Zeitschrift für Philosophie*, 755–72.

Schmücker, Reinold, *Was ist Kunst? Eine Grundlegung* (Frankfurt: Klostermann, 2014).

Schneider, Dieter, 'Die Klarheit von Patentansprüchen – Anmerkungen zum deutschen und europäischen Recht' (2016), *Mitteilungen der deutschen Patentanwälte*, 49–54.

Schreiner, Rupert, *Die Dienstleistungsmarke* (Cologne: Heymann, 1983).

Schricker, Gerhard & Ulrich Loewenheim, *Urheberrecht. Kommentar*, 6th ed. (Munich: C. H. Beck, 2020).

Schützeichel, Rainer, 'Searle und die Soziologie' (2015), 38 *Soziologische Revue*, 503–14.

Schuster, Heinrich M., *Das Urheberrecht der Tonkunst. In Oesterreich, Deutschland und andern europäischen Staaten: Mit Einschluss der allgemeinen Urheberrechtslehren. Historisch und dogmatisch dargestellt* (Munich: C. H. Beck, 1891).

Scotchmer, Suzanne, *Innovation and Incentives* (Cambridge, MA: The MIT Press, 2004).

Searle, John R., 'Minds, Brains and Programs' (1980), 3 *The Behavioral and Brain Sciences*, 417–57.

The Construction of Social Reality (New York: Free Press, 1995).

Speech Acts: An Essay in the Philosophy of Language (Cambridge: Cambridge University Press, 1997).

Mind, Language and Society (London: Weidenfeld & Nicolson, 1999).

'Social Ontology and the Philosophy of Society', in Eric Margolis & Stephen Laurence (eds.), *Creations of the Mind* (Oxford: Oxford University Press, 2007), pp. 3–18.

Making the Social World: The Structure of Human Civilization (Oxford: Oxford University Press, 2010).

'The Normative Structure of Human Civilization', in Werner Gephart & Jan Christoph Suntrup (eds.), *The Normative Structure of Human Civilization: Readings in John Searle's Social Ontology* (Frankfurt: Vittorio Klostermann, 2017), pp. 21–32.

Seitz, Claudia & Michael A. Kock, 'Wettbewerbsrechtliche Aspekte von Sortenschutz- und Patentlizenzen im Saatgutbereich – Schutzrechtslizenzen zwischen sortenschutzrechtlichen, patentrechtlichen und kartellrechtlichen Vorgaben' (2012), *Gewerblicher Rechtsschutz und Urheberrecht International* 711–20.

Shavell, Steven, *Foundations of Economic Analysis of Law* (Cambridge, MA: Belknap Press of Harvard University Press, 2004).

Sherman, Brad, 'What Is a Copyright Work?' (2011), 12 *Theoretical Inquiries in Law Forum*, 99–121.

Sherman, Brad & Lionel Bently, *The Making of Modern Intellectual Property Law: The British Experience, 1760–1911* (Cambridge: Cambridge University Press, 1999).

Sherman, Brad & Leanne Wiseman, *Copyright and the Challenge of the New* (Alphen: Wolters Kluwer Law & Business, 2012).

Shiffrin, Seana, 'Lockean Arguments for Private Intellectual Property', in Stephen Munzer, *New Essays in the Legal and Political Theory of Property* (Cambridge: Cambridge University Press, 2001), pp. 138–67.

― 'Intellectual Property', in Robert Goodin, Philip Pettit & Thomas Pogge (eds.), *A Companion to Contemporary Political Philosophy* (Malden, MA: Blackwell, 2007), pp. 653–69.

Silberstein, Marcel, *Erfindungsschutz und merkantilistische Gewerbeprivilegien* (Zurich: Polygraphischer Verlag, 1961).

Smith, Adam, *The Wealth of Nations* (Hamburg: Management Laboratory Press, 2008).

Spindler, Gerald, 'Roboter, Automation, künstliche Intelligenz, selbst-steuernde Kfz – Braucht das Recht neue Haftungskategorien? Eine kritische Analyse möglicher Haftungsgrundlagen für autonome Steuerungen' (2015), 12 *CR*, 766–76.

Spoor, Jacob Hendrik, 'De twee Betekenissen van het Woord ‚Verveelvoudigen' in de Auteurswet 1912' (1974), 105 *Weekblad voor Privaatrecht*, 165–70.

Stallberg, Christian G., *Urheberrecht und moralische Rechtfertigung* (Berlin: Duncker und Humblot, 2006).

Star, Susan Leigh, 'Boundary Object: Reflections on the Origin of a Concept' (2010), 35 *Science, Technology, & Human Values*, 601–17.

Star, Susan Leigh & James R. Griesemer, 'Institutional Ecology, "Translations" and Boundary Objects: Amateurs and Professionals in Berkeleys Museum of Vertebrate Zoology' (1989), 19 *Social Studies of Science*, 387–420.

Steinvorth, Ulrich, 'Natürliche Eigentumsrechte, Gemeineigentum und geistiges Eigentum' (2004), 52 *Deutsche Zeitschrift für Philosophie*, 717–38.

Sterne, Jonathan, *The Audible Past: Cultural Origins of Sound Reproduction* (Durham: Duke University Press, 2003).

Stobbe, Otto, *Handbuch des deutschen Privatrechts*, Vol. 1 (Berlin: Hertz, 1882).

Strömholm, Stig, 'Der urheberrechtliche Werkbegriff in der neueren nordischen Rechtslehre – 1. Teil' (1963), *Gewerblicher Rechtsschutz und Urheberrecht International*, 433–43.

― 'Der urheberrechtliche Werkbegriff in der neueren nordischen Rechtslehre – 2. Teil' (1963), *Gewerblicher Rechtsschutz und Urheberrecht International*, 481–89.

Tamura, Yoshiyuki, 'Conceptual Fallacies behind the Idea of Unprotected Intellectual Works' (2012), *Nordic Journal of Commercial Law*, 1–10.

Teilmann-Lock, Stina, *The Object of Copyright: A Conceptual History of Originals and Copies in Literature, Art and Design* (London: Routledge, 2015).

Thierse, Wolfgang, 'Thesen zur Problemgeschichte des Werk-Begriffs' (1985), 6 *Zeitschrift für Germanistik*, 441–49.

'Das Ganze aber ist das, was Anfang, Mitte und Ende hat. Problemgeschichtliche Beobachtungen zur Geschichte des Werkbegriffs' (1990), 36 *Weimarer Beiträge*, 240–64.

Thomasson, Amie L., 'Ontological Innovation in Art' (2010), 68 *The Journal of Aesthetics and Art Criticism*, 119–30.

Toynbee, Jason, 'Copyright, the Work and Phonographic Orality' (2006), 15 *Music, Social and Legal Studies*, 77–99.

Troller, Alois, *Internationale Zwangsverwertung und Expropriation von Immaterialgütern* (Basel: Verlag für Recht und Gesellschaft, 1955).

'Urheberrecht und Ontologie' (1967), 50 *UFITA*, 385–418.

Immaterialgüterrecht, Vol. 1 (Basel: Helbing und Lichtenhahn, 1983).

Tsohatzidis, Savas L., *Intentional Acts and Institutional Facts: Essays on John Searle's Social Ontology* (Dordrecht: Springer, 2007).

Tuomela, Raimo, *The Philosophy of Sociality: The Shared Point of View* (Oxford: Oxford University Press, 2007).

Tushnet, Rebecca, 'Copy This Essay: How Fair Use Doctrine Harms Free Speech and How Copying Serves It' (2004), 114 *Yale Law Journal*, 535–90.

Ulmer, Eugen, *Urheber- und Verlagsrecht* (Berlin: Springer, 1980).

van Dijk, Niels, *Grounds of the Immaterial: A Conflict-Based Approach to Intellectual Rights* (Cheltenham: Edward Elgar Publishing, 2017).

van Eechoud, Mireille, 'Voices Near and Far', in Mireille van Eechoud (ed.), *The Work of Authorship* (Amsterdam: Amsterdam University Press, 2014), pp. 7–17.

van Overwalle, Geertrui, 'Rethinking IP Protection for Plants? Revisiting the Exclusivity-Access Balance through the Type-Token Ontology', in Rafał Sikorski & Żaneta Zemła Pacud (eds.), *Patents as an Incentive for Innovation* (Alphen: Kluwer Law International, forthcoming).

Veblen, Thorstein, *The Theory of the Leisure Class* (Oxford: Oxford University Press, 2007).

Völker, Stefan & Gregor Elskamp, 'Die neuen Markenfunktionen des EuGH' (2010), 1 *WRP*, 64–72.

Vogt, Tobias, *Untitled. Zur Karriere unbetitelter Kunst in der jüngsten Moderne* (Paderborn: Fink, 2006).

Wadle, Elmar, 'Der Einfluß Frankreichs auf die Entwicklung gewerblicher Schutzrechte in Deutschland: Eine Skizze zur Rechtsgeschichte des 19. Jahrhunderts', in Gerhard Lüke et al. (eds.), *Rechtsvergleichung, Europarecht und Staatenintegration: Gedächtnisschrift für Léontin-Jean Constantinesco* (Cologne: Heymann, 1983), pp. 871–98.

Geistiges Eigentum: Bausteine zur Rechtsgeschichte, Vol. 1 (Munich: C. H. Beck, 1996).

Geistiges Eigentum: Bausteine zur Rechtsgeschichte, Vol. 2 (Munich, C. H. Beck, 2003).

'Urheberrecht zwischen Gestern und Morgen. Anmerkungen eines Rechtshistorikers', in Elmar Wadle (ed.), *Beiträge zur Geschichte des Urheberrechts* (Berlin: Duncker & Humblot, 2012), pp. 11–28.

'Urheberrecht im Horizont historischer Disziplinen', in Elmar Wadle (ed.), *Beiträge zur Geschichte des Urheberrechts* (Berlin: Duncker & Humblot, 2012), pp. 29–38.

Wächter, Oscar von, *Das Urheberrecht an Werken der bildenden Künste, Photographien und gewerblichen Mustern* (Stuttgart: Enke, 1877).

Waldron, Jeremy, 'From Authors to Copiers: Individual Rights and Social Values in Intellectual Property' (1993), 68 *Chicago-Kent Law Review*, 841–87.

Werner, Hans, *Die Geschichte des deutschen Geschmacksmusterrechts unter Berücksichtigung der Entwürfe und Vorschläge zur Änderung des Gesetzes vom 11. Januar 1876* (Erlangen, 1954).

Wetzel, Michael, 'Autor/Künstler', in Karlheinz Barck et al. (eds.), *Ästhetische Grundbegriffe (ÄGB)*, Vol. 1 (Stuttgart: Metzler, 2000), pp. 480–544.

Wiener, Norbert, *The Human Use of Human Beings* (Boston: Houghton Mifflin, 1950).

Wilson, James, 'Ontology and the Regulation of Intellectual Property' (2010), 93 *The Monist*, 450–63.

Windscheid, Bernhard & Theodor Kipp, *Lehrbuch des Pandektenrechts unter vergleichender Darstellung des deutschen bürgerlichen Rechts*, Vol. 1, reprint, (Frankfurt, 1906).

Winkler, Heinz, 'Der Schutzumfang der Patente in Vergangenheit, Gegenwart und Zukunft' (1977), 79 *Gewerblicher Rechtsschutz und Urheberrecht*, 394–404.

Wittgenstein, Ludwig, *Philosophical Investigations* (Oxford: Blackwell, 1958).

Woodmannsee, Martha, *The Author, Art and the Market: Rereading the History of Aesthetics* (New York: Columbia University Press, 1994).

Wreen, Michael, 'The Ontology of Intellectual Property' (2010), 93 *The Monist*, 433–49.

Würtenberger, Gert & Martin Ekvad, Paul van der Kooij and Bart Kiewiet, *European Union Plant Variety Protection* (Oxford: Oxford University Press, 2015).

Young, Edward, 'On Lyric Poetry, 1728', in *Conjectures on Original Composition* (Manchester: Manchester University Press, 1918), pp. 56–62.

Young, James O., 'The Ancient and Modern System of the Arts' (2015), 55 *British Journal of Aesthetics*, 1–17.

Zahrádka, Pavel, 'Ontologie díla v autorském zákoně České republiky' [The Ontology of the Work in the Copyright Act of the Czech Republic] (2017), 65 *Filosofický časopis*, 739–61.

Zech, Herbert, *Information als Schutzgegenstand* (Tuebingen: Mohr Siebeck, 2012).

'Die Dematerialisierung des Patentrechts und ihre Grenzen: Zugleich Besprechung von BGH "Rezeptortyrosinkinase II"' (2017), 119 *Gewerblicher Rechtsschutz und Urheberrecht*, 475–78.

MATERIALS

Anglo-French Copyright Treaty (1851) in Lionel Bently & Martin Kretschmer (eds.), *Primary Sources on Copyright (1450–1900)*, www.copyrighthistory.org.

Bach v. Longman (1777) in Lionel Bently & Martin Kretschmer (eds.), *Primary Sources on Copyright (1450–1900)*, www.copyrighthistory.org

Baseler Druckerordnung (1531), Basel Printers' Statute, Basel (1531) in Lionel Bently & Martin Kretschmer (eds.), *Primary Sources on Copyright (1450–1900)*, www.copyrighthistory.org

Berne Convention, Berne Convention for the Protection of Literary and Artistic Works

Government Draft UrhG 1965, Draft of an Act on Copyright and Related Rights, BT-printed matter IV/270

Connecticut Copyright Statute (1783), in Lionel Bently & Martin Kretschmer (eds.), *Primary Sources on Copyright (1450–1900)*, www.copyrighthistory.org

Copyright Act, London (1801), in Lionel Bently & Martin Kretschmer (eds.), *Primary Sources on Copyright (1450–1900)*, www.copyrighthistory.org

Cour d'appel de Rouen (1845), Court of Appeal on translations, Paris (1845), in Lionel Bently & Martin Kretschmer (eds.), *Primary Sources on Copyright (1450–1900)*, www.copyrighthistory.org

CPI, Code de la propriété intellectuelle (French Intellectual property code)

Déclaration en faveur de l'académie royale de peinture et de sculpture Royal declaration on sculpture and painting (1777), Royal declaration on sculpture and painting, Paris (1777), in Lionel Bently & Martin Kretschmer (eds.), *Primary Sources on Copyright (1450–1900)*, www.copyrighthistory.org

Der Bücherdieb. Gewarnet und ermahnet, Hamburg (1658), Schupp: The Book Thief, N.N. [Hamburg] (1658), in Lionel Bently & Martin Kretschmer (eds.), *Primary Sources on Copyright (1450–1900)*, www.copyrighthistory.org

Donaldson v Becket (1774), in Lionel Bently & Martin Kretschmer (eds.), *Primary Sources on Copyright (1450–1900)*, www.copyrighthistory.org

EPC, Convention on the Grant of European Patents (European Patent Convention), www.epo.org/law-practice/legal-texts/html/epc/2016/e/EPC_conv_20180401_en_20181012.pdf

EPO, European Patent Office

Erstes Grundgesetz der neuerrichteten Buchhandlungsgesellschaft in Deutschland (1765), Philipp Erasmus Reich and the Leipzig publishers' cartel, N.N. [Leipzig] (1765), in Lionel Bently & Martin Kretschmer (eds.), *Primary Sources on Copyright (1450–1900)*, www.copyrighthistory.org

EU Biotechnology Dir., Directive 98/44/EG of the European Parliament and of the Council of 6 July 1998 on the legal protection of biotechnological inventions, OJ L 213/134

EU Customs Enforcement Regulation, Regulation (EU) No 608/2013 of the European Parliament and of the Council of 12 June 2013 concerning customs enforcement of intellectual property rights and repealing Council Regulation (EC) No 1383/2003

EU Database Dir., Directive 96/9/EC of the European Parliament and of the Council of 11 March 1996 on the legal protection of databases, OJ L 77/20

EU Design Protection Dir. 98/71/EC of the European Parliament and of the Council of 13 October 1998 on the legal protection of designs, Council Regulation (EC) No 6/2002 of 12 December 2001 on Community designs

EU Digital Content Dir., Directive (EU) 2019/770 of the European Parliamentand of the Council of 20 May 2019 on certain aspects concerning contracts for the supply of digital content and digital services, OJ L 136/1

EU Enforcement Dir., Directive 2004/48/EC of the European Parliament and of the Council of 29 April 2004 on the enforcement of intellectual property rights, OJ L 157/45

EU Plant Variety Reg, Council Regulation (EC) No 2100/94 of 27 July 1994 on Community plant variety rights, OJ L 227/1

EU Rome II Reg., Regulation (EC) No 864/2007 of the European Parliament and of the Countil of 11 July 2007 on the law applicable to non-contractual obligations (Rome II), OJ L 199/40

EU Topograophies Dir. Council Directive of 16 December 1986 on the legal protection of topographies of semiconductor products (87/54/EEC), OJ L 24/36

EU Trade Secrets Dir Directive 2016/943/EC of the European Parliament and of the Council of 8 June 2016 on the protection of undisclosed know-how and business information (trade secrets) against their unlawful acquisition, use and disclosure

EU Trademark Dir., Directive (EU) 2015/2436 of the European Parliament and of the Council of 16 December 2015 to approximate the laws of the Member States relating to trade marks, OJ L 336/1

EU Trademark Reg., Regulation (EU) 2017/1001 of the European Parliament and of the Council of 14 June 2017 on the European Union trade mark, OJ L 154/1

European Commission, Statement by the Commission of 13 April 2005 concerning Article 2 of Directive 2004/48/EC of the European Parliament and of the Council on the enforcement of intellechtual property rights (2005/295/EC), OJ L 94/37

European Commission, Towards a modern, more European copyright framework, COM (2015) 626 final

Frankfurt Printers' Ordinance (1598), in: Lionel Bently & Martin Kretschmer (eds.), Primary Sources on Copyright (1450–1900), www.copyrighthistory.org

French Decree on Musical Publications (1786), in Lionel Bently & Martin Kretschmer (eds.), Primary Sources on Copyright (1450–1900), www.copyrighthistory.org

French Decree on the duration of privileges (1777), in Lionel Bently & Martin Kretschmer (eds.), Primary Sources on Copyright (1450–1900), www.copyrighthistory.org

French Literary and Artistic Property Act (1793), in Lionel Bently & Martin Kretschmer (eds.), Primary Sources on Copyright (1450–1900), www.copyrighthistory.org

French Royal letters patent (1701), in Lionel Bently & Martin Kretschmer (eds.), *Primary Sources on Copyright (1450–1900)*, www.copyrighthistory.org

German Patent and Trademark Office, Wie reichen Sie die Wiedergabe einer Marke ein?, www.dpma.de/docs/marken/wiedergabe_marken.pdf

International Accounting Standard 38, Intangible assets, Commission Regulation (EC) No 1126/2008 of 3 November 2008 adopting certain international accounting standards in accordance with Regulation (EC) No 1606/2002 of the European Parliament and of the Council Annex, IAS 38, OJ L 320/1

International Copyright Act (1891), in Lionel Bently & Martin Kretschmer (eds.), *Primary Sources on Copyright (1450–1900)*, www.copyrighthistory.org

Le Chapelier's report (1791), in Lionel Bently & Martin Kretschmer (eds.), *Primary Sources on Copyright (1450–1900)*, www.copyrighthistory.org

Licensing Act (1662), in Lionel Bently & Martin Kretschmer (eds.), *Primary Sources on Copyright (1450–1900)*, www.copyrighthistory.org

Louis d'Héricourt's memorandum (1725–1726), in Lionel Bently & Martin Kretschmer (eds.), *Primary Sources on Copyright (1450–1900)*, www.copyrighthistory.org

Luther, Warnung an die Drucker (1545), Luther's ‚Warning to the Printers' (1545), in Lionel Bently & Martin Kretschmer (eds.), *Primary Sources on Copyright (1450–1900)*, www.copyrighthistory.org

Nachdruckverordnung Baden (1806), Reprinting Regulation for the Grand Duchy of Baden, Karlsruhe (1806), in Lionel Bently & Martin Kretschmer (eds.), *Primary Sources on Copyright (1450–1900)*, www.copyrighthistory.org

Nürnberger Druckerordnung (1673), Nuremberg Printers' Ordinance, Nürnberg (1673), in Lionel Bently & Martin Kretschmer (eds.), *Primary Sources on Copyright (1450–1900)*, www.copyrighthistory.org

öOGH, Oberster Gerichtshof, Österreich (Supreme Court, Austria)

PCT, Patent Cooperation Treaty

prALR, Allgemeines Landrecht für die Preußischen Staaten, 1794 (General State Laws for the Prussian States 1794)

Preußische Cabinets-Ordre (1766), Prussian Cabinet Order, Potsdam or Berlin (1766), in Lionel Bently & Martin Kretschmer (eds.), *Primary Sources on Copyright (1450–1900)*, www.copyrighthistory.org

Privileg des Erzbischoffs von Würzburg (1479), Privilege of the Prince-Bishop of Würzburg, Würzburg (1479), in Lionel Bently & Martin Kretschmer (eds.), *Primary Sources on Copyright (1450–1900)*, www.copyrighthistory.org

Privileg für Arnolt Schlick (1512), Imperial Privilege for Arnolt Schlick, Speyer (1512), in Lionel Bently & Martin Kretschmer (eds.), *Primary Sources on Copyright (1450–1900)*, www.copyrighthistory.org

prUrhG 1837, Gesetz zum Schutz des Eigentums an Werken der Wissenschaft und Kunst gegen Nachdruck und Nachbildung, Preußen, 1837 (Prussian Copyright Act 1837)

Report of François Hell (1791), in: Lionel Bently & Martin Kretschmer (eds.), *Primary Sources on Copyright (1450–1900)*, www.copyrighthistory.org

Privilege of the Elector of Saxony, Wittenberg (1534), in Lionel Bently & Martin Kretschmer (eds.), *Primary Sources on Copyright (1450–1900)*, www.copyrighthistory.org

Sieyès' report (1790), in Lionel Bently & Martin Kretschmer (eds.), *Primary Sources on Copyright (1450–1900)*, www.copyrighthistory.org

Statute of Anne (1710), in Lionel Bently & Martin Kretschmer (eds.), *Primary Sources on Copyright (1450–1900)*, www.copyrighthistory.org

Statute of Monopolies, Westminster (1624), in Lionel Bently & Martin Kretschmer (eds.), *Primary Sources on Copyright (1450–1900)*, www.copyrighthistory.org

TRIPS, Agreement on Trade-Related Aspects of Intellectual Property Rights, of 15 April 1994

Strafgesetzbuch für das Königreich Bayern (1813), Bavarian Penal Law Book, München (1813), in Lionel Bently & Martin Kretschmer (eds.), *Primary Sources on Copyright (1450–1900)*, www.copyrighthistory.org

UK CDPA 1988, United Kingdom Copyright, Designs and Patents Act 1988

UPOV, International Union for the Protection of New Varieties of Plants

US Copyright Act (1790), in Lionel Bently & Martin Kretschmer (eds.), *Primary Sources on Copyright (1450–1900)*, www.copyrighthistory.org

USC, United States Code

WCT, World Intellectual Property Organization Copyright Treaty

Index

abstract IP object 1-4, 24-34, 61-100, 104-42
abstraction 50-100
acausality 28
actant 11
adaptation 120, 138-39, 145
administrative act 140
affluent society 69, 84
ancien régime 90, 144, 149, 164
animal 37, 57, 131
antiquity 65, 70
application 55, 112-17
Aristotle 47, 65, 70
art 67, 70
artefact 51-61, 110-26, 150-59
artefact, mental 113
artefact, physical 13, 31, 49, 56, 77
artwork 32-34, 47, 69-74
author 7-15, 71-74, 81-82, 90-92

Biagioli, Mario 62, 77, 133
Boldrin, Michele 14-15, 31
book 44-45, 73, 97
book publisher 74-78, 86
border measures 124-25
boundary objects 11
brands 69, 84
brute fact 36-37, 39-41, 51-52, 154

calculation of damages 127-28, 167
carrier medium 67-68, 107-8
claim 59, 112, 119
Cohen, Felix 8
commodification 79-85, 134, 151-52
computer program *See* software
concrete damage 4
construct 35, 163

copy 44-45, 57, 94, 117-26
copyright 9-10, 93-95
corporatist 75, 82
creation 54
creativity 47, 70, 155
critical theory 22-23

data 1, 123, 126, 128
data carrier 2, 10, 113
database 54, 68, 108, 152-53
declaratory speech act 38-41, 45, 101, 112, 158, 163
design 20, 47-48, 87-89, 107, 119, 123
design law 17, 59, 87, 107
digitisation 57, 68
Donaldson v. Beckett 94
drawing 54-56, 88, 115-16, 158
droit d'auteur 136
Dürer, Albrecht 71, 79

economic analysis 3, 26, 131-32, 153
efficiency 147
Elster, Alexander 8, 133
embodiment 10, 30, 39-40, 46, 83
equitable licence fee 80-82
equivalent 39, 139
EU Customs Enforcement Reg. 124
EU Trademark Regulation 105
European Patent Convention 111
exclusive right 2, 145-50
exemplar 26, 67, 102

factory mark 84
Fichte, Johann Gottlieb 67, 107
fiction 12-14, 131-32, 140-42

201

file 1, 53, 58, 113, 163
fixation 108, 136
Foucault, Michel 27
France 90–92
Frege, Gottlob 29
fundamental right 5, 126–29

genius 47, 70–73
genotype 59, 109, 166
German Basic Law (GG) 2
German Civil Code (BGB) 128
German Civil Code (BGB) 4, 86, 128
German Copyright Act (UrhG) 67, 107, 122, 139
German Patent Act (PatG) 123
German Plant Variety Act (SortSchG) 55, 59, 109
German Trademark Act (MarkenG) 105
German Utility Model Act (GebrMG) 29
Germany 97–100
Goehr, Lydia 63, 82
goodwill 21, 106
guild 78–79

happening 32
human being 22, 35–41, 52, 71, 130

imitation 64, 69–74, 88
immovable 2
industrial property law 68, 119, 148
informed user 120
infringement 60, 105, 110, 120, 125, 134
innovation 14–15, 107–10
innovator 154
institutional fact 36–37, 39–42, 109, 135
intellectual property 4–7, 20–21, 85, 90, 133, 148–50
international jurisdiction 125
invention 56, 87, 96, 123
investment 83, 108, 150–54
investor 151–54
IP law 20–21, 29, 112, 140

Jefferson, Thomas 3, 10

Kant, Immanuel 3, 5–6, 10, 107, 122, 133
Koch, Heinrich Christoph 73, 89
Kohler, Josef 6, 9, 12–13, 133, 139

Lange, Max 12–13, 145
language 24–25, 37–42, 115–17, 135
legal realism 8, 42, 121, 142
Lemley, Mark 3, 6, 131
Levine, David 14–15, 31
literary works 13, 67, 107
Locke, John 5
Luhmann, Niklas 27–28

manufacture 77
manuscript 12, 81–83
market economy 74, 147, 169
marriage 35–42
Master Artefact 16, 52–57, 110–17, 158–59
metaphysics 24, 26–28, 101, 162–63
microorganism 55, 115
Middle Age 65, 70–71, 75
Millar v. Taylor 94–95
mimesis 71, 164
model 30, 54–56, 87–88, 163
money 36–38
monopoly 53, 76–78, 148
Moritz, Karl Philipp 73, 103
musica poetica 71

new manufacture 76–77, 92, 164
nominalists 24, 26–27
normativity 18, 103, 132–42, 168–69
numerus clausus 4, 127, 167

ontology 24–49, 104
organic 35–37, 55–57
original 13–15, 52–54, 67
originality 47
ownership 2, 4–8

patent 54–57, 76–77, 111–17, 164–67
patent claim 115–16, 140, 158–59
patent specification 111–13, 137–38, 158, 167, 170
pattern 87–89
performance 16, 25, 46, 73, 81–82
phenotype 109
photograph 68, 107
piracy 120
plant variety protection 59–60, 124
Plant variety protection 166
possession 5, 126–27, 161, 168
power 41–42, 45, 103, 134–35, 168
printing ordinance 78
private international law 124, 167
privilege 16, 20, 44, 74–79, 85–87, 90–94, 102, 148
process 54–55
product 13, 108, 123
propagation material 148
property right 3, 7, 137, 161
prototype 52–55, 112, 125, 158
public domain 5, 29, 129, 146, 161
public good 11, 144, 161, 168

real property law 18, 46, 125, 128
register 55, 111
registration 17, 68, 105, 158

Index

related right 17, 49, 68, 107–10, 136, 166
replicable 107, 124, 131
rights holder 1, 114, 139
Ross, Alf 8, 13–14, 17, 42, 139

sample 79, 83
scarcity 6–7, 131–32, 157, 161
Searle, John R. 35–49, 101–3, 134
Secondary Artefact 57–61, 117–28, 154–59
secret 60–61, 113, 124
semiconductor topographies 68–69, 88, 107
sign 21, 84, 88–89, 105–6
social ontology 34–49, 163
software 1, 10
sound recording 55, 88
speech act 38–46, 111, 135
state of the art 35, 59, 114, 117
Stationers Company 78
status function 39–49, 83, 101–3, 135
Statute of Anne 90, 93–94, 164
Statute of Monopolies 77, 90, 92, 164

tangible 2, 4–7, 126–28
technology 64–69

territoriality 125
thing 1, 12–13, 43, 126–28
token 25–26, 162
trademark law 21–22, 105–7, 165
TRIPS Agreement 20
Troller, Alois 8–9, 133, 152
type 26, 101

United Kingdom 92–97
universalists 24–27
USA 92–97
utility model 20

Venice 76, 90

work 8–11, 25–26, 70–74, 99–100
work concept 61–63, 96–97, 135–39
working requirement 127
writing 44–45, 65–67

Young, Edward 47, 72, 74, 103

CAMBRIDGE INTELLECTUAL PROPERTY AND INFORMATION LAW

Titles in the Series (formerly known as Cambridge Studies in Intellectual Property Rights)

Graeme W. Austin, Andrew F. Christie, Andrew T. Kenyon and Megan Richardson *Across Intellectual Property: Essays in Honour of Sam Ricketson*

Brad Sherman and Lionel Bently *The Making of Modern Intellectual Property Law*

Irini A. Stamatoudi *Copyright and Multimedia Products: A Comparative Analysis*

Pascal Kamina *Film Copyright in the European Union*

Huw Beverley-Smith *The Commercial Appropriation of Personality*

Mark J. Davison *The Legal Protection of Databases*

Robert Burrell and Allison Coleman *Copyright Exceptions: The Digital Impact*

Huw Beverley-Smith, Ansgar Ohly and Agnès Lucas-Schloetter *Privacy, Property and Personality: Civil Law Perspectives on Commercial Appropriation*

Catherine Seville *The Internationalisation of Copyright Law: Books, Buccaneers and the Black Flag in the Nineteenth Century*

Philip Leith *Software and Patents in Europe*

Geertrui van Overwalle *Gene Patents and Clearing Models: Patent Pools, Clearinghouses, Open Source Models and Liability Regimes*

Lionel Bently, Jennifer Davis and Jane C. Ginsburg *Trade Marks and Brands: An Interdisciplinary Critique*

Jonathan Curci *The Protection of Biodiversity and Traditional Knowledge in International Law of Intellectual Property*

Lionel Bently, Jennifer Davis and Jane C. Ginsburg *Copyright and Piracy: An Interdisciplinary Critique*

Megan Richardson and Julian Thomas *Fashioning Intellectual Property: Exhibition, Advertising and the Press, 1789–1918*

Dev Gangjee *Relocating the Law of Geographical Indications*

Andrew Kenyon, Megan Richardson and Ng-Loy Wee-Loon *The Law of Reputation and Brands in the Asia Pacific*

Edson Beas Rodrigues, Jr *The General Exception Clauses of the TRIPS Agreement: Promoting Sustainable Development*

Annabelle Lever *New Frontiers in the Philosophy of Intellectual Property*

Sigrid Sterckx and Julian Cockbain *Exclusions from Patentability: How Far Has the European Patent Office Eroded Boundaries?*

Sebastian Haunss *Conflicts in the Knowledge Society: The Contentious Politics of Intellectual Property*

Helena R. Howe and Jonathan Griffiths *Concepts of Property in Intellectual Property Law*

Rochelle Cooper Dreyfuss and Jane C. Ginsburg *Intellectual Property at the Edge: The Contested Contours of IP*

Normann Witzleb, David Lindsay, Moira Paterson and Sharon Rodrick *Emerging Challenges in Privacy Law: Comparative Perspectives*

Paul Bernal *Internet Privacy Rights: Rights to Protect Autonomy*

Peter Drahos *Intellectual Property, Indigenous People and their Knowledge*

Susy Frankel and Daniel Gervais *The Evolution and Equilibrium of Copyright in the Digital Age*

Edited by Kathy Bowrey and Michael Handler *Law and Creativity in the Age of the Entertainment Franchise*

Sean Bottomley *The British Patent System during the Industrial Revolution 1700–1852: From Privilege to Property*
Susy Frankel *Test Tubes for Global Intellectual Property Issues: Small Market Economies*
Jan Oster *Media Freedom As a Fundamental Right*
Sara Bannerman *International Copyright and Access to Knowledge*
Editd by Andrew T. Kenyon *Comparative Defamation and Privacy Law*
Pascal Kamina *Film Copyright in the European Union* (second edition)
Tim W. Dornis *Trademark and Unfair Competition Conflicts: Historical-Comparative, Doctrinal, and Economic Perspectives*
Ge Chen *Copyright and International Negotiations: An Engine of Free Expression in China?*
David Tan *The Commercial Appropriation of Fame: A Cultural Analysis of the Right of Publicity and Passing Off*
Jay Sanderson *Plants, People and Practices: The Nature and History of the UPOV Convention*
Daniel Benoliel *Patent Intensity and Economic Growth*
Jeffrey A. Maine and Xuan-Thao Nguyen *The Intellectual Property Holding Company: Tax Use and Abuse from Victoria's Secret to Apple*
Megan Richardson *The Right to Privacy: Origins and Influence of a Nineteenth-Century Idea*
Martin Husovec *Injunctions against Intermediaries in the European Union: Accountable but Not Liable?*
Estelle Derclaye *The Copyright/Design Interface: Past, Present and Future*
Magdalena Kolasa *Trade Secrets and Employee Mobility: In Search of an Equilibrium*
Péter Mezei *Copyright Exhaustion: Law and Policy in the United States and the European Union*
Graham Greenleaf and David Lindsay *Public Rights: Copyright's Public Domains*
Ole-Andreas Rognstad *Property Aspects of Intellectual Property*
Elena Cooper *Art and Modern Copyright: The Contested Image*
Paul Bernal *The Internet, Warts and All: Free Speech, Privacy and Truth*
Sebastian Felix Schwemer *Licensing and Access to Content in the European Union: Regulation between Copyright and Competition Law*
Daniela Simone *Copyright and Collective Authorship: Locating the Authors of Collaborative Work*
Emily Hudson *Drafting Copyright Exceptions: From the Law in Books to the Law in Action*
Graeme Gooday and Steven Wilf *Patent Cultures: Diversity and Harmonization in Historical Perspective*
Mark Burdon *Digital Data Collection and Information Privacy Law*
Edited by Niklas Bruun, Graeme B. Dinwoodie, Marianne Levin and Ansgar Ohly *Transition and Coherence in Intellectual Property Law: Essays in Honour of Annette Kur*
Tanya Aplin and Lionel Bently *Global Mandatory Fair Use: The Nature and Scope of the Right to Quote Copyright Works*

CPSIA information can be obtained
at www.ICGtesting.com
Printed in the USA
LVHW080919030821
694401LV00004B/278